CW01206690

THE DIVINE SENSE

In the first book-length treatment of this subject, A. N. Williams examines the conception of the intellect in patristic theology from its beginnings in the work of the Apostolic Fathers to Augustine and Cassian in the early fifth century. The patristic notion of intellect emerges from its systematic relations to other components of theology: the relation of human mind to the body and the will; the relation of the human to the divine intellect; of human reason to divine revelation and secular philosophy; and from the use of the intellect in both theological reflection and spiritual contemplation. The patristic conception of the intellect is therefore important for the way it signals the character of early Christian theology as both systematic and contemplative and as such, distinctive in its approach from secular philosophies of its time and modern Christian theology.

Dr ANNA N. WILLIAMS is Lecturer in Patristic and Medieval Theology at the University of Cambridge. She is author of *The Ground of Union: Deification in Aquinas and Palamas* (1999).

THE DIVINE SENSE

The Intellect in Patristic Theology

A. N. WILLIAMS

CAMBRIDGE UNIVERSITY PRESS

CAMBRIDGE UNIVERSITY PRESS
Cambridge, New York, Melbourne, Madrid, Cape Town, Singapore, São Paulo

Cambridge University Press
The Edinburgh Building, Cambridge CB2 2RU, UK

Published in the United States of America by Cambridge University Press, New York

www.cambridge.org
Information on this title: www.cambridge.org/9780521793179

© A. N. Williams 2007

This publication is in copyright. Subject to statutory exception
and to the provisions of relevant collective licensing agreements,
no reproduction of any part may take place without
the written permission of Cambridge University Press.

First published 2007

Printed in the United Kingdom at the University Press, Cambridge

A catalogue record for this publication is available from the British Library

ISBN-13 978-0-521-79317-9 hardback

Cambridge University Press has no responsibility for the persistence or accuracy of URLs for external or third-party internet websites referred to in this publication, and does not guarantee that any content on such websites is, or will remain, accurate or appropriate.

To the memory of Rut Britta Viola Williams née Karlsson

18.vii.31–26.ii.04

*Det sköna är evigt; med fiken håg
vi fiska dess guldsand ur tidens våg.*
                                    Tegnér

Contents

Acknowledgements — page viii
List of abbreviations — ix

Introduction — 1

1. The dawn of Christian theology — 21
2. Early Alexandrians: Clement and Origen — 44
3. Cappadocian theology: Nazianzen and Nyssen — 86
4. Augustine — 143
5. Monastic writings — 190

Epilogue — 232

Bibliography — 240
Index — 250

Acknowledgements

I would like to thank several people who contributed in different ways to the writing of this book. My former colleague, Denys Turner, was supportive from the time he saw the proposal (which was before he and I became colleagues or even knew each other), through the years of the book's writing. His thoughts on the philosophical background to the issues were of particular help, but most of all, I am grateful for his distinctive brand of wiry encouragement. For bibliographic assistance, my thanks go to my former students Christopher Wells and Ben Fulford, supported by funds from Yale Divinity School and the Cambridge Faculty of Divinity respectively. A one-term research leave grant from the Arts and Humanities Research Council allowed me to recoup some forfeited sabbatical time and complete the manuscript. The genesis of the book owes its inspiration to a moment of insight during a seminar at Yale Divinity School; my students in the years 1997–2000, through their questions, lively debate and personal commitment to contemplation taught me more than I could ever express. Most of all, my long-suffering husband, Dale Gingrich, patiently sorted out computer problems, located books left behind in the office and listened uncomplainingly to the daily litany of frustrations and minor triumphs. And because writing anything would be much more dreary without feline companionship, I record my appreciation of Pushkin and Persika, who often gave me paws for thought.

ANW
Feast of Clement of Alexandria, 2005

Abbreviations

Abl	Nyssen, *Against Ablabius*
ACW	Ancient Christian Writers
AD1 and 2	Basil of Caesarea, *Ascetical Discourses* 1 and 2
ANF	Ante-Nicene Fathers
Anim	Tertullian, *On the Soul*
1/2 Apol	Justin Martyr, *First* and *Second Apologies* or Tertullian, *Apology*
Barn	Epistle of Barnabas
Beat	Nyssen, *On the Beatitudes*
CallC	Nyssen, *What It Means to Call Oneself a Christian*
CC	Corpus christianorum
CCels	Origen, *Contra Celsum*
CD	Augustine, *The City of God*
CEun	Nyssen, *Contra Eunomium*
2CEun	Nyssen, Response to Eunomius' Second Book
CFth	Basil of Caesarea, *Concerning Faith*
ChrM	Nyssen, *On the Christian Mode of Life*
Clem	Clement of Rome, Letter to the Corinthians
Cnfr	Cassian, *Conferences*
Conf	Augustine, *Confessions*
Cred	Augustine, *On the Usefulness of Believing*
CRud	Augustine, *On the Catechizing of the Uninstructed*
CSEL	Corpus Scriptorum Ecclesiasticorum Latinorum
CtOr	Nyssen, *Great Catechetical Oration*
CWS	Classics of Western Spirituality
Dial	Justin Martyr, *Dialogue with Trypho*
Did	*Didache*
Diog	Letter to Diognetus
Disc	Justin Martyr, *Discourse against the Greeks*
Doct	Augustine, *On Christian Teaching*

EE	*Exhortation to Endurance* (*To the Newly Baptised*)
Ench	Augustine, *Enchiridion*
Eph	Ignatius, Epistle to the Ephesians
Eust	Nyssen, *Against Eustathius*
Exhort	Justin, *Exhortation to the Greeks*
Fast	Tertullian, *On Fasting*
FC	Fathers of the Church
FSym	Augustine, *On Faith and the Creed*
GChr	Augustine, *On the Grace of Christ*
GCS	*Die griechischen christlichen Schriftsteller*
Gnos	Evagrius, *Gnostikos*
Govt	Justin Martyr, *On Government*
Haer	Irenaeus of Lyons, *Adversus haereses*
Herm	Tertullian, *Against Hermogenes*
HSp	Nyssen, *On the Holy Spirit*
HumP	Nyssen, *On the Making of the Human Person*
Inf	Nyssen, *On Infants' Early Deaths*
Inst	Cassian, *Institutes*
Judg	Basil of Caesarea, *Concerning Judgement*
LA	Athanasius, *Life of Antony*
LArb	Augustine, *On the Freedom of the Will*
LCC	Library of Christian Classics
LM	Nyssen, *Life of Moses*
LP	Nyssen, *On the Lord's Prayer*
LR	Basil of Caesarea, *Long Rules*
Mag	Augustine, *The Teacher*
Magn	Ignatius, Epistle to the Magnesians
Marc	Tertullian, *Against Marcion*
MarP	Martyrdom of Polycarp
MEcc	Augustine, *On the Morals of the Catholic Church*
Monc	Evagrius, *Ad Monachos*
Mor	Basil of Caesarea, *Morals*
Mort	*On the Care to Be Had of the Dead*
NBon	Augustine, *On the Nature of the Good*
NPNF	Nicene and Post-Nicene Fathers
Or	*Oration*
PArch	Origen, *Peri Archōn* (*On First Principles*)
Pat	Augustine, *On Patience*
Paed	Clement of Alexandria, *Paedagōgos* (*The Teacher*)
Perf	Nyssen, *On Perfection*

List of abbreviations

PG	Migne, Patrologia Graeca
Phil	Ignatius, Letter to the Philadelphians
Phlp	Polycarp, Letter to the Philippians
PL	Patrologia Latina
PMer	Augustine, *On Sin and Merit*
Pol	Ignatius, Letter to Polycarp
Prae	Augustine, *On Predestination*
Prak	Evagrius, *Praktikos*
Prax	Tertullian, *Against Praxeas*
Pray	Evagrius, *Chapters on Prayer*
Pros	Tertullian, *Proscription against the Heretics*
Prot	Clement of Alexandria, *Protreptikos*
Rich	Clement of Alexandria, *What Rich Person Can Be Saved?*
Rom	Ignatius of Antioch, Epistle to the Romans
Resr	Justin Martyr or Tertullian, *On the Resurrection*
SC	Sources chrétiennes
Smyr	Ignatius of Antioch, Epistle to the Smyrneans
SpLt	Augustine, *On the Spirit and the Letter*
Sol	Augustine, *Soliloquies*
Soul	Nyssen, *On the Soul and Resurrection*
Str	Clement of Alexandria, *Stromateis* (*Carpets*)
Tral	Ignatius of Antioch, Epistle to the Trallians
Trin	Augustine, *De Trinitate*
VRel	Augustine, *On True Religion*
Virg	Nyssen, *On Virginity*

Introduction

Anyone accustomed to reading early Christian theological texts would notice, on turning to those of modern Christian writers, a large and far-reaching difference. This difference concerns, not a single locus, or a culturally conditioned ideational supposition, or even a means or form of argumentation, but the broad temper of this theology, characterised by the ease with which early Christian writings move between discussion of technical theological matters and spiritual or ascetical ones. Even to describe this linkage as a movement perhaps overstates the matter, for these concerns weave in and out of each other with a seamlessness suggesting their authors did not regard them as distinct. Patristic writers reason from forms of prayer or liturgical practice to theological positions, and from theological data to principles of ascetical life, with a smoothness betokening the unstated presumption that these areas, far from being remote from each other – or indeed, even quite distinct – belong to the same sphere of discourse and concern.[1]

Modern theology makes no such assumption. Although one may find some appeal to liturgical or sacramental practice,[2] academic theology rarely mentions prayer or worship, much less ascetical disciplines such as fasting or control of anger. Conversely, contemporary works on

---

[1] Cf Wilken (2003), whose survey of early Christian thought opens with the claim that the Christian religion is inescapably ritualistic, uncompromisingly moral and unapologetically intellectual (xiii), a characterisation undoubtedly true of the period with which his book is concerned, but rather less true of some later ones. Louth characterises the patristic period as both Wilken and I do, but acknowledges a later separation of dogmatic and mystical concerns. He however sees signs of rapprochement between the two areas in the thought of Barth and Balthasar (1981, xi–xiii). The way I am describing patristic theology corresponds closely to Leclerq's characterisation of monastic theology, although the latter is largely concerned with medieval authors, and is at pains to distinguish monastic from scholastic theology (1961, passim, but esp. 5).

[2] There is, for example, a systematic theology based around liturgy, that of Wainwright (1980), but his methodological approach seems to have had little impact on the field as a whole. The sheer fact that its liturgical approach constitutes an 'approach', one which makes it stand out from other contemporary theologies, suffices to indicate it comes from an era whose theological temper differs markedly from that of the early Christian centuries.

spirituality are as bare of theological insight as theological ones are uninterested in spirituality: they float free of explicit theological grounding, some even actively discouraging intellectual engagement (though admittedly, few evince interest in ascetical disciplines, either). Indeed, a good deal of contemporary spirituality overtly suggests that thinking damages prayer, that modern people think too much in general, and that they need to unlearn the latter bad habit if they are to become prayerful or holy persons.[3]

The suspicion of cognition in modern spirituality points towards the factor underlying the difference in spirit of patristic and modern theological writing: a shift in the role of the intellect. The function of the intellect in patristic theology, especially in articulating the resemblance of humanity to God and a means by which we are able to grow towards God, allows for the exploration of key themes in dogmatic and speculative theology, while also inviting discussion of ascetical issues, such as the mind's regulation of the appetites. The emphasis on intellect as a divine attribute, a definitive human faculty, and a basis for human sanctification allows the theologians of the early church to write theology in a way scarcely envisageable today, in which both strictly academic or technical questions can be pursued alongside spiritual ones. One of the central contentions of this study is that the lack of tension, or even proper distinction, between these areas in patristic theologies is attributable to the systematic role of the mind within the theoretical framework as a whole. That role stipulates that the proper telos of the human person is intelligent adoration of God and that the proper function of Christian theology is to instantiate an act of such adoration. The theologies of the patristic period are therefore on this account quintessentially contemplative.

Part of the purpose of this study is to uncover the contemplative and spiritual dimension of works that might be read as sheerly dogmatic, indeed polemical, and part to make explicit the theological lineaments of texts that might seem solely ascetical. The fact that both kinds of texts emerge from this examination looking very similar in the complex of issues with which they are concerned suggests such genre distinctions mean little in this period, a fact that in itself attests eloquently to its theological temper. Tracing the role of the intellect in these texts requires that the reader attend to systematic connections within them: how the

---

[3] A typical example is De Mello's enormously popular (an in many respects, highly valuable) *Sadhana: a Way to God* (1984).

intellect is portrayed in relation to other constituents of human nature, such as the will and the body, and how the intellect grounds human growth in likeness to God. Tracing these themes, in turn, necessitates attending to their authors' conceptions of the spiritual life.

At this point, we might well pause to question the application of the term 'systematic' to patristic theology in the first place.[4] Is patristic theology not presystematic? are the first Christian systematic theologies not the *summae* of the medieval schools? The answer to the first question is no, even though the answer to the second is arguably yes – though no more than arguably, given a case can be made for Origen's *De principiis*, Damascene's *De fide orthodoxa* and, as a miniature, Nyssen's *Catechetical Oration*. Even if we discount these, though, we would have shown no more than that *a* systematic theology is hard to identify in the patristic period, and that is quite a different matter from the systematic nature of its theology. The first term (*a* systematic theology) designates a single work presenting a comprehensive set of loci in orderly fashion; the second idea concerns the forms of reasoning exhibited in a text (movement from a point established in one locus to another, for example, from the doctrine of God to anthropology), as well as in concerns for coherence, both internally and externally (with Biblical or liturgical data, for instance). In this second sense, patristic theology is highly systematic, showing its authors' relentless awareness of their reflecting a whole – a picture of the cosmos and of human life *coram Deo* – whose origin lies in the divine mind and which therefore must be orderly and intelligent, even if human beings are only imperfectly able to grasp its content or design. The systematic awareness of patristic theologians reflects the role of the intellect in their theology: they expect in what they write to reflect the divinely ordained order of the cosmos. The *ratio* of theology, subsistent in its systematisation, reflects the divine *ratio* and the divinely given human *ratio* which is able to grasp both, and so to adore.

The systematic quality of this theology is thus intrinsically linked to the role of the intellect within it. The assumption that all that exists is either identified with divine wisdom (that is, is God), or is created by this

---

[4] That patristic theology is systematic is denied both generally and on the occasion of specific authors and works. In regard to the latter, see Crouzel's judgement of Origen's *On First Principles*, cited in ch. 3. In regard to the former, cp. Young: 'During the early Christian period there was no such thing as systematic or scholastic theology' (1997, 681); note the linking of 'systematic' and 'scholastic'. She later acknowledges that one of the leading features of patristic theology is 'intellectual comprehensiveness', which she glosses as 'the disciplined drive to account for all reality . . . in relation to its divine creator' (688–89), which is in significant part what systematic theology is, assuming that its comprehensiveness is taken to include cohesion, or at least non-contradiction.

wisdom, stipulates a *ratio* underlying every possible object of contemplation. If the rational harmony of creation has been disrupted by the Fall, no human action could overthrow the divine design completely: the cosmos and all that is in it still reflects the divine creative and sustaining intelligence. The insistence on human reasonableness, even in its post-lapsarian state, follows from the assertion of its origin in divine wisdom; to impugn the former would, in the Fathers' view, necessarily impugn the latter. Their relatively sanguine estimation of human intellect thus differs fundamentally from any Enlightenment exaltation of Reason: not human dignity and autonomy is celebrated, but the beauty of divine Mind, reflected in creation. Equally, however, because rightly glorifying God entails acknowledging the human capacity for rational reflection, the Fathers cannot slide into a pessimistic apophaticism holding that the order of the universe, or indeed divine nature itself, lies entirely beyond human ken. Again, to impugn our capacity to know God, at least dimly, would amount to claiming God had deliberately left us bereft of the only means to good, happy and purposeful lives, and would deny, therefore, any conceivable telos to creation. Inasmuch as theology purports to state what is the case about God, the cosmos and the relation of the two, it must reflect both divine *ratio* and the divinely-given human capacity to grasp this *ratio*, and must, therefore, be in itself systematic, that is, logical, orderly and coherent.

The order and coherence of patristic texts are of a specifically theological kind, and as such, the very nature of the texts rules out some of the approaches that might have been taken to the general complex of questions which are the matter of this study. This is not an investigation of patristic epistemology per se, although it necessarily touches on a variety of epistemological questions. Whether in the view of the Fathers we know by remembering what was once imprinted on our minds but which we have for some reason forgotten, or by manipulating the residue of sensory experience left in our minds (phantasms), or by some other means altogether, is not the question this study seeks to explore. It would in any case be difficult to determine the answer, since the Fathers rarely address such issues directly; for all that they operate with philosophical presuppositions, some of which are made explicit, they are finally not philosophers but theologians, and the questions they pursue are thoroughly theological, explored using theologians' tools. Their interest in the mind focuses not on how it acquires and processes information generally, but in its role in ordering the relation of God and humanity.

No more does this study set out to give an account of the Fathers' lexical usage as it pertains to word fields, such as 'mind' or 'knowledge'. The latter enterprise would be doomed by the almost total absence of definitions in patristic treatments of mind or intellect (the two terms will be used in this book interchangeably). The fact that the writers examined here do not define *mens* or *nous* or that the Greek writers do not specify how the latter is to be distinguished clearly from *gnōmē*, for example, constitutes only part of the problem. Another part of it lies in the fact that much of what is relevant to determining the patristic conception of the intellect does not spring from the usages of individual words: if one claims we know God in such-and-such a way, what one says has significance for one's account of how our mind apprehends God, even if the word 'mind', or some analogous term, is not being used. Likewise, to maintain that we can envisage God with the aid of scripture but not through logic alone is implicitly to make a claim about the limitations of human deductive reasoning, even if there is no talk of mind as such. I have from time to time noted parenthetically the Greek or Latin word or phrase lying behind texts to which I refer, when the particular term used seemed significant; but for the most part, the subtle variegation of shades of meaning among closely-related terms has little bearing on a study of this kind, which is concerned with the systematic interactions of theological loci and themes.[5]

Because of the absence of definitions of key terms pertaining to the intellect in patristic texts, and because even if these existed, they would still not render the fullness of the relevant concepts, we are seeking the way in which several broad areas of concern in this thought intersect. The most important of these connections we are pursuing is that between the divine and the human intellect. This nexus is important for Christian theology for two quite different reasons. The first is that, although the Fathers more often assume mind in God than take pains to stipulate it specifically, they are concerned to associate the imago Dei in humanity with mind or the rational faculty in degrees varying from virtual identification to the simple assumption that the capacity for thought is an

---

[5] The basic attitude towards terminology which I take here thus differs from that of Louth, who insists on the untranslatability and non-correspondence of the key terms in English and Greek (1981, xv). I would not incline, to the extent he does, to separate *nous* from the activities of discursive reasoning (though it is of course by no means confined to such activity) and although the essential thrust of this study is to underline the much broader meaning that it has in patristic literature than 'mind' has in contemporary English, I do not share his qualms about translating it as 'mind' or 'intellect'. The reader is invited to stretch her view of mind, rather than to subscribe to a belief in the untranslatability of certain words.

essential part of what it means to be made in the image of God. This move is necessarily relational; one of the definitive features of Christian anthropology is that it declines to define humanity in solely human terms. On the Christian account, one can only understand what it means to be human by looking to the non-human, to the divine creator and source of life, a procedure which entails not only making certain assumptions about our relation to the persons of the Trinity, but also certain assumptions about divine nature itself, for humanity's imaging of the latter entails at least some form of similarity. All talk of the imago Dei is therefore at once talk of humanity, talk of the divine nature reflected in the image, and talk of humanity's relation to the divine. Or, to put the matter another way, any doctrine of the imago Dei is a systematic theology in miniature.

The relationality of the human intellect pertains not only *ad extra*, towards the divine, but *ad intra*, to the other constituents of human nature, notably, the will and the body. For although the Fathers, following Genesis, took our similarity to God as the cornerstone of their anthropology, they also followed Genesis in taking our divinely-given bodies to be constitutive of our nature. No anthropology that would qualify as Christian can omit the body or regard it as a temporary nuisance or ill, an obstacle to salvation or the knowledge of God, a point on which the supposedly Platonising Christian tradition parts company with most varieties of Platonism. However much a Christian theology stresses the mind and its apprehension of the divine, it must simultaneously state this mind's relation to the body in a way which neither does violence to either element, nor impugns the creative intention behind their being yoked together.

The mind's relation to the body portends its broader role as the head of the 'household' that is the human person, and is an indicator of the will's significance to the schema, for without the latter, what the mind envisages could not translate into action, body or no body. Equally, however, actions in which there is no element of deliberate intent are not properly speaking willed, so the will moves at the mind's behest and is therefore in some sense always secondary to it. This necessary and systematic relation of mind and will indicates a further relationship: that of contemplation to ethics, of theology to ascesis.

To put the matter in this last way is to indicate the mind's role in two areas of central concern to the Fathers: theology and prayer. One of the chief signifiers that these are related in patristic theology in a very different way from that of some later periods is that in patristic texts, either sort of activity may be what is designated as *theōria* or *contemplatio*, contemplation. While the rigorous pursuit of intellectual questions and difficulties often leads the Fathers into a controversial mode which seems remote from the adoration that is prayer, the questions they pursue – the nature of trinitarian relations, for example – are in essence contemplative, inasmuch as they lead orator and listener, writer and reader, to ponder and gaze upon divine nature and divine things. The sheer fact that a complex theological discussion holds the mind's attention on the things of God indicates the possible functioning of this discussion as at least the preliminary to prayer, if not as prayer itself. Patristic texts not only display their authors' awareness of this fact, but enact it, holding the reader's gaze upon God even as they expose the theological conditions of the possibility of such gazing.

The act of contemplation is nevertheless always ripe for disruption. The monastic texts we shall consider especially reveal a powerful awareness of this fact, and if in them we find a particularly strong emphasis on the struggle against the passions, then this is not only because the monastic is supposed to be virtuous in a general sort of way, but equally because the passions particularly assail the mind at prayer. The monastic and ascetical texts do not, therefore, display their authors' interest in ascesis because ascesis is a worthy or superior substitute for intellectual activity, but because the latter is infeasible without control of the emotions and bodily desires. Significantly, however, the difference between monastic texts and others lies not in the presence of an interest in ascesis in one versus its absence in others, but simply in the strength of focus on matters of spiritual discipline. In one sense, ascetical theology cannot be said to exist in this period, not because such concerns do not figure in its thought, but because they are never cordoned off and separated from other theological issues, and consequently never become the exclusive province of certain kinds of writers.

Following what the Fathers have to say of the mind, therefore, necessarily leads the reader to see various kinds of unity in their writings. The inseparability of what we now call theology from spirituality (in both theory and practice) is one such unity. Another is the psychosomatic unity of the human person, and another, the unity in knowledge and love of the human person and God. The likeness to God we are given in virtue of the imago is the dynamic basis of that evolving likeness of holiness which comes from ascesis and contemplation. We might put the matter in a slightly different way: the personal union of the Trinity with human persons is reflected in two methodological unities, one at the level of systematic theology (the unity of the doctrine of God and theological anthropology) and the other at the subdisciplinary level (of theology proper to ascetical theology or spirituality, as well as to ethics). The treatment of the intellect is not the only means by which the Fathers hold all these together coherently, but it is one of the most powerful and important ones. Because the themes under consideration converge on such questions, the study is as much an investigation of the nature of Christian theology, as illuminated by the mind of the early church, as it is in inquiry into particular theological loci. Evagrius wrote: 'The spiritual knowledge [gnōsis] of God is the breast of the Lord; the one resting upon it will be a theologian',[6] and in a way, this study represents nothing more than a detailed exposition of what he means.

Grasping these unities is vital if we are to understand the complex relation of this theology to the philosophical systems which preceded it, or, as in the case of neo-Platonism, developed alongside it. Studies of patristic theology, church history and the cultural history of the ancient world often assume an immediate connection between ancient philosophy of one variety or another and early Christian theology. Any talk of ascent is taken to be neo-Platonic, for example, and appeals to reason as the ruling principle frequently traced to the Stoic notion of the *hēgemonikon*.[7] The difficulty with such assumptions lies both in their unverifiability and their too-easy assumption of causality; one can certainly show similarities between one assertion and another, but with much greater difficulty does one establish that the reason for the similarity lies in influence. In part, the problem lies in our having little firm evidence about what particular patristic writers had and had not read (though of course some absorption of philosophical views may have come from *ouï-dire*). Even more importantly, however, the simple fact that writer X read writer Y does not in itself establish that X adopted view Z because it was found in Y's work. If Platonists assert the soul's ascent, so do the psalms frequently speak of going up to find God; if the Stoics think in terms of a *hēgemonikon*, the Old Testament also extols guidance by wisdom and right understanding. To point to a similarity between the

---

[6] Monc 120.
[7] As a particularly stark example, we might take the claim of Festugière: 'Quand les pères "pensent" leur mystique, ils platonisent. Tout n'est pas original dans l'édifice'(1936, 5). The response of this study is that it is precisely the 'tout' which is original. Stead maintains with equal economy that the patristic concept of mind derived from Platonism (1982, 40), even though he had previously just acknowledged that it is Aristotle who described God as Mind (39), and later maintains that many of the Fathers were untouched by Platonism (52) – these, it would seem, must therefore have been operating without any concept of Mind.

two bodies of thought does not in itself establish a causal connection, if only because the content of the thought may be equally, indeed perhaps more plausibly, attributable to another source. Even in cases where an idea expressed in a patristic text seems distinctively that of a particular philosopher or school, it must still be remembered that the Christian writer was under no obligation to adopt any of these. The ancient world offered a smörgåsbord of philosophical options, making any one of them rather less than inevitable, and Christians always maintained a certain critical distance from philosophy, mingled as it frequently was with views in one sense or another religious. Given the range of options available, the adoption of any philosophical datum represents a choice on the theologian's part, a choice that at least precludes the ascription of any mechanical notion of influence.[8]

Perhaps the most widespread claims of influence pertain to the supposedly pervasive shaping power of the various Platonisms, and there are some undoubted parallels between the latter and patristic theology in its many varieties. The image from the *Phaedrus*, for example, of the charioteer struggling to control his horses, one of which is virtuous and obeys its master, the other of which is unruly and disobedient,[9] is echoed by many early Christian theologians as they describe the struggle in the human person between the forces of rationality and irrationality, the mind's attempt to guide the soul with its passions. That the echoing is a deliberate borrowing from Plato seems clear enough from the closeness of the parallel; whether it demonstrates influence is another matter. One need know no Plato to be aware of the tug-of-war between reason and irrational desire – any well-fed person considering a second helping at dinner knows it. Plato's image vividly evokes a perennial fact of the human condition, but it would be absurd to suppose it commended itself because of Plato's authority or because his philosophy was widely taught in the ancient world: it commends itself because it points to a truth any human being has experienced in daily life. What is being taken from Plato is not this insight, depressingly mundane as it is, but a vivid image that memorably encapsulates the perennial situation.

---

[8] A case in point is Armstrong, who points to the verbal parallel between passages in Plotinus, Basil and Nyssen, which indicate the last two must have borrowed from the first in rejecting the existence of *hylē* (1979, 8.428). Armstrong however offers no explanation of why they should have borrowed the idea, even though he admits that in doing so, they stand apart from the patristic tradition (8.429). We are left with the simple fact of a parallel, which raises questions of the relation of bodies of thought more than it answers them.

[9] 246 a–b, 253 d–e.

Obviously, this interpretation of influence assumes we properly speak of it only when a view is adopted in significant part because it is commended by the authority of the writer advocating it. Influence in this sense would tend to exert itself, by definition, in more than piecemeal fashion: if one adopts Plato's views because they are those of a thinker whose stature is such that his views are accorded an almost indubitable rectitude, then presumably that thinker's views would merit adoption as a whole, or at least in large part. This kind of wholesale adoption of any Greek philosophy is precisely what we do not find in patristic theology. Take the Platonic tradition again as a case in point. Plato's epistemology goes hand in hand with his metaphysics. Plato's notion that we acquire knowledge through anamnesis presupposes not only forgotten knowledge, but an earlier existence, and hence some form of pre-existent soul, if not necessarily a full-blown doctrine of reincarnation. It also presupposes that real knowledge is not of the sensible, but the intelligible, since knowledge of what is most real is not acquired by gathering information through the senses. This epistemology correlates to a metaphysics, in virtue of which what is deemed most real are the Forms, whose immutability guarantees both their intelligibility and their utter distinction from matter, and which are therefore the proper object of human knowledge, sensible instantiations of these Forms being real in only a pale and derivative sense. The distinction of the sensible and the intelligible thus serves, not only to divide objects of knowing into two different categories, but to identify one of these as the proper object of knowledge and the philosophically more important.

The writers we shall survey appeal frequently to the distinction of the sensible and the intelligible, and one might be tempted to consider that they think in these terms because of their respect for Plato. The immediate difficulty with taking that position is that none of them adopted the theory of Forms; in other words, if prompted to make free use of a distinction employed in Plato's epistemology, they felt equally free to disengage the latter from his metaphysics. They also declined to adopt a central contention of the creation myth of the *Timaeus*, namely the notion that the Craftsman uses the Forms as patterns according to which he shapes the pre-existent matter he has to hand. This picture will not mesh with either of the creation stories in Genesis, and it was the Bible that the early church held to be theologically normative. Disengaged from the metaphysics and an hypothesis about the origin of particulars, Plato's sensible–intelligible distinction does no more than label a fact about the way human beings know. To know what an orange tastes like, you have to taste one. To know what justice is, on the other hand, requires more than experiencing punishment; one has to have a notion of right and wrong and of appropriate penalties for wrongdoing, for example, none of which is the direct product of sensory experience. Plato may certainly be credited with observing this basic fact of the way the world is and how human beings know, and with formulating its significance cogently, but to claim the distinction of the sensible and the intelligible belongs to him is rather like claiming Newton invented gravity.

If large problems attach to assigning influence to Plato himself, they mount as one moves chronologically closer to the ancient Christian world and to neo-Platonism, despite the fact that many accounts of patristic theology freely claim the influence of Plotinus and his followers. The immediate formal problem with these attributions is that the simultaneous development of the two traditions means it is frequently difficult to disentangle them so as to establish which might have borrowed from which.[10] The material problems are more numerous, if not more fundamental, beginning with the generally low estimation of matter throughout the neo-Platonic tradition, an appraisal that sits uneasily with the Christian doctrines of creation, anthropology, the Incarnation and the sacraments, not to mention the resurrection of the body.[11]

The differences between the Christian and Platonic traditions over the value and epistemological role of matter are rather obvious, but there are many other examples of views, the superficial similarity of which encourages the ready attribution of influence, but which on closer examination differ significantly. Take the notion of contemplation as a case in point. Those inclined to attribute consonance to influence might point to the absence of any such idea in the New Testament and on that basis claim that when Christians began appealing to it, it was because of their acquaintance with the Platonic tradition, whose concerns and sensibilities they then wrote into Christian theology. To get from the embryonic Christology and doctrine of the Trinity in the texts of the New Testament to what would count as Christian orthodoxy by the sixth century, however, one must allow for development, the maturing of root ideas in the collective mind of a community that both debated and worshipped. The same principle may apply just as legitimately to the

---

[10] Wallis 1972, 154–55, but cp. 2.
[11] Louth also points to some fundamental, indeed irreconcilable, differences between Christianity and Platonism (1981, xlii, xiv, 51).

church's understanding of theology and prayer. That is, just as early Christian theology freely borrowed terminology such as *ousia* and *hypostasis* from a Greek vocabulary that was to hand, but made a distinctly Christian use of it, so early Christianity may be seen to have made use of the notion of contemplation, albeit with a considerably modified meaning. The latter point is important, for it challenges any easy talk of influence. In the Christian tradition, as we shall see, theoria or *contemplatio* could designate activities as various as adoration of the Trinity or the study of scripture. The latter had no exact counterpart in the Greek philosophical tradition, because there was no comparable body of communally normative sacred writings.[12]

Moreover, the contemplation of God was not, for the Greek tradition, clearly an encounter with an Other. The Christian tradition's use of visual imagery – however incongruously applied to an immaterial deity – pointed to the fundamental opposition at the heart of Christian notions of consummation, of what would come to be called the vision of God (drawing on the Biblical tradition of seeing God as the culmination of spiritual experience): to gaze upon something assumes that what is beheld is not the beholder, but something she faces. If on the Christian account the telos of human existence is meant to be union with God, it is equally the adoration and contemplation of God.[13] In its eschatology, Christianity preserves the tensive relationship of union and distinction that runs through its theology as a whole, a principle informing the doctrine of the Trinity and Christology, as well as its anthropology.[14] Because the Christian understanding of the height of both spiritual experience and human development encompasses both a unitive dimension and the

---

[12] Although Burton-Christie (1993) notes that among Plotinus and his disciples, reading and interpreting the texts of Plato was essentially a religious exercise (51), this is at best a weak and isolated parallel to the church's use of the Bible.

[13] Consider, for example, the gloss of Iamblichus given by Pépin: 'la prière tire le divin en nous de son assoupisement, le met en pleine lumière et ainsi rend possible sa réunion au divin absolu' (1971, 11). In the Christian conception of contemplation, likeness to God is rather the basis that makes prayer possible, and although prayer may be conducive to some form of union with God, the latter could take place only on divine initiative and it would be an exaggeration to say it is ever conceived as taking place with an impersonal 'divin absolu'.

[14] Armstrong is quite content to call Augustine and Nyssen Christian Platonists (1979, 6.133), even as he acknowledges fundamental differences between Christian conceptions of the intellect, God and the human person and those of Plotinus (1979, 6.139). In this respect, too, note Festugière's contention that theoria is for Plato always linked to the theory of Forms (1936, 31). If so, the Christian notion of contemplation would have to differ significantly from the Platonic, given Christianity's refusal to adopt the theory of Forms. The difference between Festugière's account of Platonic contemplation and the Christian emerges clearly in his claim that for Plato, theoria represents a union between the soul and the Idea (1936, 89); for the Christian contemplator, the union is of the human person and the Trinity.

preservation of distinction, its notion of both the experience and the purpose of each differs from what they were in the various Greek philosophical systems and religions, even when the same language is used, and a similar pattern obtains in relation to almost any topic considered in this study. Those given to tracing verbal parallels between Christian texts and non-Christian philosophical ones rarely acknowledge the crucial factor in interpreting the significance of these parallels: that every text that recalls an older classical source also fits into the broader theological framework of the Christian work in which it occurs, and the structure into which a given idea is inserted is at least as important to its interpretation as the supposed provenance of the idea itself. The fact that the same terms, images or analogies are used by classical and Christian authors does not in itself indicate identity of conception, for once incorporated into a system whose assumptions and desiderata differ, the terms take on new meaning, being shaded by their context.[15]

If Plotinus' emphasis on contemplation bears a marked resemblance to the emphasis on it which we shall see in early Christian theology, the rarified atmosphere of his writings attests to the audience they were aimed at: the educated and leisured classes, a far cry from the majority of early Christians, and equally remote from the earliest Christian monks, the supposedly illiterate Copts of the desert. While it is true that monastic life demanded, if not wealth to finance it (as the philosophical life of Plotinus' ideal seems to require), then at least the willingness to renounce the creature comforts one can only have with either independent wealth or paid employment, it is equally the case that one need not have been educated in order to attain to the heights of prayer as Christians understood these. Anyone could pray; indeed, all were enjoined to do so, and just as the spiritual athletes of the desert spent a good deal of their time simply reciting psalms, so ordinary Christians were also able to learn to fix their attention on God by reciting set texts, and this form of verbal prayer was not considered unworthy, nor even clearly the mere threshhold of contemplation. The Christian conception of contemplation was

---

[15] Jaeger makes a similar point (in relation specifically to Origen's theology), namely that it is not enough simply to seek the philosophical sources of ideas; one must seek the structure of the thought as a whole (1961, 68). The Jaeger edition of the works of Nyssen (the editors of whose volumes are various) nevertheless relentlessly documents Platonic parallels. Similarly, the work of Pépin was much concerned to point to the supposedly neo-Platonic character of Christian thought, largely based on tracing parallels, although on occasion, he acknowledged how the selectively neo-Platonic conceptualities were employed (see his essay in O'Meara 1982). On occasion, the influence hunters resort to brute insistence on influence, even when they admit they cannot demonstrate it (see Dillon in O'Meara 1982, 23).

much broader than the Plotinian, a breadth correlating to the come-one-come-all character of the church.[16]

How then can we account for the adoption of the language of contemplation at all, with its notion of directing the soul's gaze to God in an overtly intellectual manner, given that any Biblical basis one might propose for it would be decidedly tenuous? The usual wooden appeal to neo-Platonic influence must eventually stumble on the fact that theoria in the sense of contemplation was used long before the neo-Platonists, not only by Plato, but also by Aristotle and Epicurus.[17] Even if we attribute the spread of the idea to the neo-Platonists, we would still have to postulate a reason for its absorption into Christianity: given that Christian thinkers need not have adopted it, why did they do so? Why appeal to this concept when so many others deriving from the Platonic tradition were rejected? One possible ground of its appeal was its compatibility with the creedal emphasis in Christianity. In holding that the parameters of communal and individual identity were determined in the first instance by baptism, a central feature of which was the confession of faith according to a set form, the church differed from most of the religions and philosophies on offer in the ancient world. To be a Christian meant assenting to certain propositions as true, as well as undergoing baptism in the triune name, and the church was adamant in rejecting syncretism; to accept baptism and profess the creed during the initiation rite meant disassociating oneself from other religions and philosophies. These hallmarks of identity reflect a Christian anthropology and soteriology, inasmuch as they presume the involvement of the whole human person in the initiation rite: the mind, grasping the content of the creed; the will, assenting to it; and union with Christ in body and soul in the sacrament of washing. However strong the appeal of Christianity to those on the lower rungs of the social ladder and to the unlettered, moreover, the fact that its initiatory lustration required a propositionally-formulated declaration of assent meant it contained an inescapably intellectual dimension, requiring as a condition of membership the grasp and profession of what it proclaimed to be true.[18] The significance of that act of

---

[16] Here I concur with Young (1997, 683).

[17] See the entry in Liddell and Scott's Greek-English Lexicon. Festugière acknowledges the significance of Aristotle when he calls the latter and Plato 'les apôtres de la contemplation' (1936, 18). How this claim coheres with his earlier contention regarding the thoroughly Platonic character of the Fathers' thought (see note 7) is left unclear.

[18] The intellectual dimension of Christianity, moreover, was not confined to the likeness posited in virtue of the assertion of the imago Dei, but was also based on declaration of certain propositions to be true, propositions which were taken as constitutive of the identity of those asserting

assent was underlined by the insistence that accepting this creed meant rejecting others, no matter what apparent similarities they bore. The baptismal liturgy not only addressed and involved the whole human person as a psychosomatic unity, but integrally linked intellectual understanding, assent and worship – which is precisely what contemplation is.[19] If one wished to pin Christianity's developing interest in contemplation on the influence of philosophical movements, notably neo-Platonism, one would have to take account of Christianity's habitual linkage of theology (even in its schematic creedal form), and prayer (even in its most vocal and stylised liturgical form). In other words, there are distinctive features of Christianity that would commend the notion of contemplation to it, and these as plausibly account for the pervasiveness of the concept in patristic theology as any authoritative appeal of Plotinus and his followers.

Another reason for wariness of the standard claims of influence is that their routine appeal to the Platonic and Stoic traditions oddly ignores some rather strong parallels to Aristotle and the presocratics. To begin with, there is Aristotle's generally positive view of matter and the substantial role he accords the senses in epistemology, both of which sit more easily in a Christian framework than their Platonic counterparts. The everlasting, unchanging, immaterial divine Mind in Aristotle's philosophy not only resembles the God of early Christian theology, but is identically conceived with respect to these attributes. Although Aristotle's divine principle neither creates nor envisages the cosmos, the First Mover is nevertheless the root of its rational order and intelligibility inasmuch as he is its final cause: the world is the expression of a tending towards the Mover.[20] Furthermore, only one animal also possesses the element which is divine, *nous*, and it is therefore human beings who are uniquely able to imitate God, notably by engaging in the act of contemplation.[21] The Aristotelian notion of contemplation bears a marked similarity to the Christian one, for example in holding that contemplation draws us as

---

them. Contrast the platonising maxim *ho nous gar hēmōn ho theos* (the mind is what is divine in us) found in the Iamblichan corpus but widely attributed to other authors (Pépin 1971, 8). In Christian theology, the human intellect can only be called divine (as indeed, Origen does call it) in the sense that it is the means by which we apprehend divinity, not in the sense that we are divine as God is with respect to at least this faculty. The intellect allows for communication and contemplation, but is not ontologically identical with divine nature.

[19] I would quibble, therefore, with Jaeger's contention that for Nyssen Christianity was not 'a mere set of dogmas but the perfect life based on theoria' (1961, 90). For Nyssen, it was both, for the two were complementary and even mutually inclusive.

[20] Lear 1988, 295.   [21] Ackrill 1981, 134.

close to God as we can approach, even though the structure of our knowing will always distinguish us from him.²²

It is moreover to Aristotle that we owe the conception of intellectual virtue,²³ which joins the notions of *ratio* and the good. In maintaining that the whole of the moral life is to be ordered to the life of contemplation as its end, Aristotle connects what Christians would call the ascetical and the mystical, and Christian theologians concur with Aristotle in holding that the acquisition of moral virtues opens the door to true contemplation. Aristotle's philosophy is thus oriented to both contemplation and practical ethics, engagement with the world, and, as such, bears at least as close a resemblance to early Christian thought as the more unworldly neo-Platonic systems which patristic theology is usually taken as resembling.

In a formal sense, too, Aristotle's philosophy is marked by features which would later characterise Christian theology, notably the drive towards systematisation. Aristotle aims to develop a systematic and comprehensive philosophy,²⁴ and in this respect resembles the awareness shown in early Christian theology of the implications of *ratio* for system, and for him, the human person is a by nature systematic thinker.²⁵ The significance of system in Aristotle's thought is not original to him, however, but hearkens back to the very beginnings of Greek thought, the presocratics. What we find in this philosophy of immediate significance to this study are not even conceptions of the intellect itself, but the simple yet radical assumption that discourse about divine and created things must be internally coherent and consistent, that is, that talk about God and the world is necessarily systematic. The roots of this drive towards system may be seen in Xenophanes, who objected to the undignified behaviour of the gods depicted by Hesiod (the standard source for Greek religion) and who established fittingness as a theological criterion.²⁶ In other words, both what we may attribute to the gods, and how they actually are and behave, corresponds to an intrinsic principle of godlikeness: the gods in fact conduct themselves as gods ought to do and we describe and think of them accordingly.

There are intimations of the significance of both mind and system in the thought of other presocratic philosophers, also. It is Heraclitus who inaugurates the notion of logos as a central concept,²⁷ yet, crucially for our

---

²² Lear 1988, 319.   ²³ *Nicomachean Ethics* Bk 6.   ²⁴ Ackrill 1981, 1.   ²⁵ Lear 1988, 134.
²⁶ Hussey 1972, 14.   ²⁷ Hussey 1972, 40–42.

purposes, logos is not for him only identified with the divine principle, but with the flow of rationality through the created order.[28] Like Xenophanes, Heraclitus is concerned that religio-philosophical discourse construct a model of the universe revealing it to be unified and orderly, and as such, the reflection of the divine mind.[29] A similar insight is found in Anaxagoras, who identified the cosmos not simply as the object of God's thought, but one whose intelligibility is guaranteed by the origin of its disposition in the divine mind.[30] Mind is central to Anaxagoras' conception of the divine yet more overtly, for in his philosophy 'mind' is the name of God.[31]

Around the same time as these propositions were being asserted, with their far-reaching implications, the development of Euclidean geometry furnished Western thought with the notions of axiom, definition and proof and the notion of reasoned argument began to develop.[32] Although patristic theology does not exhibit the interest in proofs evident in later Western theology, the earliest theologians knew that defining terms carefully not only serves heuristic and defensive purposes, but also enables the thinker to extrapolate from the known to the not-yet-grasped, just as the recognition of what an axiom is allows one to ground an argument in a starting point which is itself debatable. Both procedures would prove invaluable for Christian theology, the second because it permitted the theologian to reason from Biblical data without becoming mired in disputes over whether the Bible was in itself demonstrably true, and the first because it allowed for, among other things, the broader application of Biblical dicta. Both methods of reflection can only be theologically valid, however, if the ways of God do conform to *ratio*, and conform to it in ways that human beings can grasp and so truly reflect in human discourse.

These parallels between the significance of the intellect in patristic theology and its role in the presocratics and Aristotle are not invoked to substitute one set of putative influences for another, but rather to illustrate the difficulty of positing any particular thinker as the source of an idea: there may be a resemblance between A and B, but if C also resembles these, one cannot simply claim B as the source of A. One problem with the attempt to posit influence as the explanation for any parallel one might see between a claim in a patristic text and a similar one found in a body of philosophical writings is the Fathers' bricolage

---

[28] Armstrong 1977, 11. [29] Hussey 1972, 42 and 47. [30] Hussey 1972, 139.
[31] Hussey 1972, 138. [32] Hussey 1972, 4 and 15.

methodology: none of them takes a single school, let alone a single thinker, and uses that philosophical system as the consistent basis for a theology. By selecting a term here, a notion there, the Fathers display an opportunistic mentality that amounts to a form of virtual indifference to the status of their sources, a disregard bordering on disdain for the integrity of any philosophical system, of even the greatest of the Greek philosophers. Those commentators who see the Fathers' Christian judgement overridden by their enthrallment to 'the wisdom of the Greeks' not only fail to take full account of how much they reject or adapt, as well as how much they modify simply in virtue of the way in which they combine. Such judgements moreover rest on unexamined presuppositions about what is and is not authentically Christian, the latter being virtually defined by its non-overlap with any notion clearly derivable from Greek philosophy. If, to take the example of contemplation again, we do not see this as a major theme in the Bible, it must be Greek, and if Greek, somehow alien to Christianity. Such determinations often reveal more about the unacknowledged ecclesial sympathies of their authors, a prefabricated notion of what Christianity is, than they illumine about the theology of another age.

The patristic penchant for bricolage not only stands as a strong contra-indication to blithe ascriptions of influence to any one philosophical school, but also points again to one of the dominant features of both Aristotelian and presocratic philosophies: the significance of system. The theologians of the early church are systematicians, not in the sense that they order texts in ways that would later become conventional, but in the sense that they consider all that a Christian theologian might truly say will fit together into an intricate pattern of pieces which interlock because divine wisdom has fashioned them to do so. Their theological method and the content of their theology reflect the same underlying conviction of divine ratio, a ratio that must ultimately evoke the awe of contemplation.

SCOPE AND METHOD

Fully to sustain the theses I have articulated would require a comprehensive survey of patristic literature which is, for a variety of reasons (not least the lack of enthusiasm among publishers for lengthy manuscripts) impossible. What I have attempted to do instead is to examine some representative samples of patristic literature. I have confined the scope of the sample to works that are theological rather than exegetical, so Biblical commentaries and homilies are excluded,[33] and to works in Greek and Latin, since these languages supplied the body of theology that became most broadly influential in the later theological tradition. Although this study does not itself extend into these later periods, one of its concerns is with the distinctive character of early Christian theology; focusing on the Greek and Latin traditions indicates that the contrast between these and later Western theology is not attributable to a cultural rift deriving from the unfamiliarity of later theologians with the Syriac or Coptic traditions. A third principle of selection was to choose authors representative of differing theological stances and approaches, but drawn from across the first five centuries; we stop with John Cassian both for reasons of space and because his death around 435, just after Augustine's and roughly fifteen years before Chalcedon, provides a chronologically convenient halting point.[34]

The need to provide broad chronological coverage and to address the writings both of dogmatic/speculative theologians and ones more ascetically inclined should serve to explain the choice of most of the authors selected, but two authors in particular have been given slight treatment whom a reader might have expected to see covered more generously, namely Basil of Caesarea and Athanasius. Both receive some attention in the chapter on monastic writings, and so serve as examples of how authors who are often thought of as dogmatic theologians may equally be considered as ascetical theologians, as those, in other words, who operate in the realm now labelled 'spirituality'. The reason for not giving Basil full treatment in the chapter on Cappadocian theology was simply that the rich vein of material required that one of the three Cappadocians be omitted and Basil is of the three the least original dogmatician. Athanasius was not treated with the other Alexandrians simply because the treatment of the Cappadocians and of Augustine meant the fourth century was being covered in considerable detail, while the treatment of the earlier centuries needed more attention. Although speculation of course always has its dangers, I will nevertheless venture to say that I doubt the picture built up by the textual evidence would have been in any

---

[33] The exception is Gregory Nazianzen, whose theology is prosecuted largely in the orations; these are, however, not primarily reflections on Biblical texts.

[34] The dating of the Apophthegmata is uncertain, but both the Greek alphabetic collection and the Latin thematic one were likely to have been written down later than this. The sayings themselves, however, obviously predate their assemblage and transcription, but we can no more know by how much than we can date the written collections surely, so Cassian's death provides as suitable a notional *terminus ad quem* as any.

perceptible degree altered had Basil and Athanasius received the fuller treatment they merit.

The method of examining the issues has been that of a close thematic reading of a broad range of texts, seeking above all the systematic interconnections of the constituent ideas relevant to the subject. Some readers may find the detail of the documentation excessive; in response, I can only point to the numerous studies making large claims about the Fathers' work while providing few or no references to the reader interested in following up the idea, or puzzled at the way in which a familiar author's work has been characterised. The documentation provided here strives in the first instance to allow a reader to get back to the relevant texts and examine them for herself, and in recognition that some who might be interested in these issues may not have Latin or Greek, I have given references in forms which should allow the reader to locate the relevant passage in a standard translation, as well as in the original, even though this has meant resort in some instances to unconventional use of page numbers in particular editions.

A second ground for the degree of detail in the documentation is that the case being made is systematic: it depends on no single large chunk of text in an author's work, one which neatly states a theory (for these are scarce in patristic theology), but the broad patterns running through oeuvres, schools and centuries. I believe these patterns are reasonably clear, but they can only be shown to be so by pointing to a welter of detail. Furthermore, although the pattern is distinct enough, there are plenty of small qualifications that need to be made if one is to be true to the textual evidence, and I have tried to point to qualifying evidence and counterevidence wherever I have found it. I have not, however, generally given multiple references to support the same claim, although at many points in the argument such multiplication of supporting texts could easily have been supplied.

CHAPTER I

The dawn of Christian theology

Christian theology begins, not with a school of academic theologians, but with the writings of a group of authors who knew they might end their lives as martyrs and who in several cases did. Under the circumstances, one would scarcely expect a fully developed systematic theology, much less a sustained reflection on the life of the mind. Yet to a surprising degree, we find the same themes in the earliest Christian theology that we find in the sophisticated reflection of later ages. These themes are less fully worked out, yet their sheer occurrence in these earliest texts is a signifier of the centrality of the mind in patristic theology. Because we are dealing with a group of writers separated both geographically, and chronologically by as much as the span of a century, we will treat them individually rather than synthetically. Even so, a clear pattern emerges, in virtue of which the mind begins as a present theme and gradually grows in importance.

THE APOSTOLIC FATHERS

We have certain knowledge regarding the authorship of only two of the writings traditionally grouped together under the label 'Apostolic': those of Ignatius of Antioch and Polycarp of Smyrna. Moreover, what writings are included under the rubric 'the Apostolic Fathers' has differed, and the label itself is fairly recent.[1] If the grouping together of these texts derives more from considerations of convenience than any traditionally asserted consonance, yet they bridge the space between the New Testament and the writings of the Apologists, and as a group, share the character of transitional documents. Although there is something to be said against it,

---

[1] Its first use has been attributed variously to Cotelier in 1672 and Ittig in 1699 (see Quasten 1950, 40 and Louth 1987, 10).

we will here follow convention and treat these writings as a unit, albeit a not necessarily homogeneous one.

Perhaps the single most important indication in the Apostolic writings of where Christian theology is heading is the weight placed in them on Christ's role as teacher and bringer of knowledge. In part, this emphasis reflects the unflagging moralism of the earliest Christian theology: it is always as much concerned with exhortations to good behaviour as with speaking of the Source of goodness. At the most elementary level, the connection between human behaviour and the Teacher is nothing more than the passing acknowledgment that Christians are supposed to keep both the words and deeds of Christ in their hearts and before their eyes[2] or the simple use of the title 'Teacher' for Christ.[3] Here and there we find a more sophisticated approach. The list of titles of Christ in the Letter to Diognetus includes *nous,* but the referent is unclear, and some of the titles in this list seem appropriate only to one of the Persons (Father, for example, or healer).[4] For Ignatius, the significance of the Incarnation of the Word is the visible and apprehensible manifestation of the invisible God: Jesus Christ represents the mind [gnōmē] of the Father.[5] Ignatius does not dwell on this point, however; he fastens on the purpose perhaps dearer to his heart, and one of which he never tires, of the role of the bishop, establishing a simple analogy: as Christ represents the mind of the Father, so the bishop represents the mind of Christ. Obedience therefore devolves, not on some conception of ecclesiastical hierarchy per se, but on conformity to divine intellect. Given the importance of the latter, Ignatius' incipient apophaticism may seem surprising. He holds that the Word proceeds from the Father in silence,[6] and the paradoxical silence of this procession is reflected in the silences of Jesus of Nazareth, which are as eloquent as words.[7] On this note, Ignatius moves on to a theme dear to all these early writers: God's knowledge of our innermost thoughts. The precise logic of the connection between these two ideas, of Christ's silence and God's knowledge of our minds, is finally left unclear. All that is apparent is that for Ignatius, they were somehow linked.[8] Although Ignatius does not spell out his insight for us, we see here a glimmer of one of the constant themes of later theology: human nature and divine nature

---

[2] Clem 2 and Barn 21.   [3] Diog 9, Eph 15.   [4] Diog 9.   [5] Eph 3.   [6] Magn 8.   [7] Eph 15.
[8] There is a faint echo of the Ignatian notion of the silence of the Word in the Epistle to Diognetus, where the author asserts that God's providential design for the universe was known to the Son alone (Diog 8). In equally tantalising fashion, Ignatius seems to anticipate Augustine when he says that faith is the beginning of life, and love its end, and that the union of the two is God (Eph 14), though it would of course be absurd to claim that he is here thinking in specifically trinitarian terms.

are both intellectual, yet our minds are not equal to the task of grasping the divine.

If the Apostolic Fathers regard knowledge as important, it is because knowledge nevertheless provides a point of contact with God. In the Epistle to Diognetus, faith is more or less equated with knowledge of the Father.[9] As we saw with Ignatius, the letter posits an analogy between trinitarian relations and the Incarnation, though this time, the weight of likeness is taken cataphatically: as the Word was manifested in the world, so the disciples came to know the mysteries of God.[10] Although the Didache posits such knowledge at times in exclusively moral terms (as when it draws a parallel between turning from the teaching of God and a host of evils, from lying to infanticide[11]), elsewhere, it posits a quasi-sacramental account of knowledge much like that in the Letter, holding that wherever divine attributes are the subject of discourse, there God is present.[12] On this model, theology makes God present to the community, in much the same way as do the bread and wine of the Eucharist.

A more widespread sentiment is simply that wrong ideas harm and right thinking brings one closer to God. The harmfulness of erroneous doctrine is of course the constant refrain of Irenaeus, especially in *Adversus haereses*, but if we discount it there on the grounds that it is to be expected in light of his episcopal responsibility to refute heresy, we cannot similarly dismiss it in the Apostolic writings, which are not specifically polemical. Yet Ignatius warns against 'the strange plants of heresy'[13] and Polycarp warns against the stupidity of the mob and false doctrines.[14] The concern does not lie solely with false doctrine, moreover: the unity of belief and practice in the early church is evident in Ignatius' injunction to the Smyrnaeans to return to their right minds [ananpsai] by repenting.[15] If sin can cloud the mind, though, so can prejudice, and the Letter to Diognetus warns against clinging to the hidebound notions that can only lead to error.[16] Inaugurating a theme that we will encounter in many later writers, the same author portrays idolatry as a form of mindlessness, for idolatry is only possible because the worship it designates is of the insensible: the idolater must worship that which is irrational, because no rational being would put up with such nonsense.[17] Such worship turns out to be the carrier of a communicable disease: worship irrational things, the author warns, and you will grow like them.[18]

---

[9] Diog 10. [10] Diog 11. [11] Did 5–6. [12] Did 4. [13] Tral 6. [14] Phlp 7.
[15] Smyr 9. [16] Diog 2. [17] Diog 2. [18] Diog 2.

Both Ignatius and the Letter to Diognetus express sentiments that extend well beyond these negative injunctions, according something like an intrinsically sanctifying power to knowledge.[19] Ignatius claims both the limited usefulness of knowledge and, for his own part, knowledge of a quite breathtaking variety: the ability to comprehend celestial secrets and angelic hierarchies and the arrangements of the heavenly powers, though he notes that these things do not in themselves make a real disciple.[20] The author of the Letter, on the other hand, claims that the known truths of *ta theia* become 'a very paradise of delight', flourishing and yielding all kinds of fruit. In this garden of truths are planted both the Tree of Knowledge and the Tree of Life, which grow side by side because without knowledge there can be no life and without life no trustworthy knowledge.[21] The Letter to Diognetus stresses not only such knowledge, but its precondition, intelliegence.[22]

While such passages presage rather strikingly the tone of later Alexandrian and Cappadocian theology, they are less characteristic of the Apostolic theology than the simple appeal to obey the precepts of the moral life, a theme present in Clement, Polycarp, Barnabas, and the Didache,[23] but largely absent in the writings of Ignatius. If for other writers we imitate Christ by obeying his moral teaching, for Ignatius we follow by coming to possess the mind of the Father; since it is the bishops who in the first instance possess this mind [gnōmē],[24] we ought to obey them and the priests with undivided minds [dianoiai][25] and Ignatius is willing to claim this deep conformity to the mind [gnōmē] of God for himself.[26] This claim is not simple self-pleading, however, for he also recognises the conformity of other people's minds to God, including those of his addressees[27] (though of course he may be not so much describing what he observes to be the case, as enjoining what he wishes were true). The unity Ignatius frequently extols is very much an intellectual unity, not simply in the sense of the assent of each individual to the truth received and proclaimed by the church, but the union of those individuals with one another: 'Come, each one of you, and form a choir', he urges, 'every one of you; let there be a whole symphony of minds [homonoia]',[28] a unity which brings about participation in God. It is

---

[19] Barnard finds in the Letter a foreshadowing of the efforts of the Apologists, both in the way it presents the Christian faith as fundamentally rational, and in its concern to honour intellectual questions (1967, 3).
[20] Tral 5.   [21] Diog 12.   [22] Diog 2 and 21.
[23] Clem 2 and 13, Polycarp in Phlp 4, Barn 2, and the Did 1.   [24] Eph 3.
[25] Eph 20, Phil 1.   [26] Rom 8.   [27] Pol 8.   [28] Eph 4.

concerns of this kind that prompt his attack on private judgement,[29] rather than a wooden conception of ecclesiastical authority.

Although Ignatius stresses the obedience of Christians to their bishop more sharply and more clearly, others of the apostolic writings still lay a considerable weight upon obedience and submission to God. The irrational and inanimate world by its order manifests this docility,[30] but human obedience to God reflects both God's goodness in declining to use coercive means to quell our unruliness and, implicitly, our freedom.[31] Freedom itself implies a mind with the discernment to make use of it, yet only in Clement do we find a clear acknowledgement of the imago Dei, coupled with an exhortation to do as God wills.[32]

If the Apostolic Fathers do not take pains to stipulate the human mind, neither do they see tension between mind and body and there is little trace of suspicion of the body in their writings. Ignatius, it is true, exhibits a zeal to meet the lions that verges on the very seeking of martyrdom that the church later felt obliged to forbid. Yet when he claims that he will truly be Christ's disciple when the lions have ground his body so that there is nothing left of it to see,[33] he voices not so much a desire to annihilate the body per se, as a desire to imitate Christ in utter self-abandonment to the purposes of God, for the good of the church. For Ignatius, his own martyrdom is the ultimate way of celebrating the Eucharist, of uniting himself to Christ's passion by becoming that which is broken up and given for the benefit of the faithful. As the Eucharist proclaims God's presence to his people, so Ignatius' own death will become a form of discourse: 'by maintaining silence in my cause', he urges his readers, 'you can turn me into an intelligible utterance [logos] of God; but if you speak, then I will become [nothing more than] a voice'.[34] Here is the human answer to the silence of the Word's proceeding: by acceding to Ignatius' martyrdom without protestation, the faithful will allow his screams of anguish to be an intelligible utterance mirroring the wordless discourse of the Word at the Trinity's heart, logos imitating Logos. The body is not disregarded – clearly Ignatius is all too conscious of the pain he will shortly suffer – but its instincts are subordinated to the mind's guidance. Viewing Ignatius in this light helps in seeing the full

---

[29] Magn 7. [30] Clem 20. [31] Diog 7; Barn 2. [32] Clem 33. [33] Rom 4.
[34] Rom 2. Caveat lector: this translation follows the Greek of the Loeb edition, which SC relegates to a footnote and rejects, on the grounds that the play on *logos* and *ēchō/phōnē* is too subtle and therefore alien to this kind of text. The wording the SC editor does accept barely makes sense, however, and I have therefore preferred the Loeb; see text in SC 10, 126 and 128, and n. 1 on those pages.

significance of Polycarp's retort to the governor's telling him to recant, as the wild beasts are at hand: 'Why, then, call them up. It is out of the question to exchange a good way of thinking for a bad one, though it would be very creditable to change from wrong to right.'[35] Here we see, not bravado, but the expression of a deep conviction in the importance of abiding in the truth; the body serves the mind that knows and professes, rather than dictating by its fears. In the Letter to Diognetus, we find a passage requiring similarly sensitive interpretation, in which the author claims that the relation of Christians to the world is that of the soul to the body. The flesh hates the soul, but the soul nevertheless loves the flesh, as Christians love those who hate them. While the soul is imprisoned in the body, it holds the body together [synechei].[36] The flesh does not emerge from this analogy with its reputation unscathed, yet the predominant message is of love and care for the flesh.[37]

Perhaps the most significant difference between the Apostolic Fathers and all the later theology we will see is the absence of attention to contemplation evinced in these writings. The exception is Clement, who speaks both of a 'fixing' [atenisōmen] of the believer's thoughts on Christ,[38] and of the blossoming of understanding when the eyes of the heart are lifted up to the highest heaven.[39] He enjoins his reader to contemplate with the mind and look upon him with the eyes of the soul, visual imagery found elsewhere only in the Letter to Diognetus.[40] Any attempt to account for this absence must of course be conjectural, but it is hardly surprising, given the urgency of the circumstances in which these writers found themselves, busy as they were establishing churches before hastening to untimely deaths.

JUSTIN

Justin spans the period between the Apostolic writings, with their immediate concern for the health of the church in the face of martyrdom, and the theology written after the peace of the church, whose writers had the leisure to reflect upon less urgent issues than the prospect of their own imminent demise and the possible extinction of a fledgling church. Justin's interest focuses neither on martyrdom (though he was in fact

---

[35] MarP 11. [36] Diog 6.
[37] O'Hagan points to the strong emphasis on the resurrection of the body in 2 Clement: through redemption, human flesh is identified with the church, and he counsels continence because the parousia is in some way dependent on our acts (1968, 70).
[38] Clem 7. [39] Clem 36 and 19. [40] Diog 2.

martyred) nor on the living of an upright Christian life, but on the intellectual cogency of Christianity in the face of pagan critique. Themes that figure widely and significantly in later theology are scarce in his work: the sanctification wrought by knowledge, union with God through contemplation, wisdom and illumination, God's own knowledge and foreknowledge, idolatry, truth, the body, or indeed, the mind itself. Instead, we find an overriding preoccupation with questions concerning philosophy and proof, the grace that is needed to reach truth, the Christian conception of the intellectual life, anthropology and Christology.

Indeed, it is not in Clement of Alexandria, but in Justin, that we find the first extended reflection on the theme of Christ the Teacher. In the first instance, Christ taught the prophets and lawgivers of the Old Testament, as well as the philosophers who learnt from them; where these err, it is because they did not know the whole of the Word.[41] Elsewhere, Justin exhorts his interlocutors to learn from the Word. This teacher not only offers instruction that differs from that of the Greek philosophers, but by his teaching effects a different sort of moral and spiritual persuasion, one that drives away the passions that are destructive of the philosophical life and which even confers immortality.[42] Although Justin's purpose is apologetic, he offers an argument that anticipates Calvin's notion of scriptural truth as self-authenticating: 'The word of truth is free and carries its own authority, disdaining to fall under any skilful argument or endure the logical scrutiny of its hearers'; the truth is therefore to be believed because of its intrinsic nobility and the unimpeachable reliability of its source.[43]

If there is an important difference between Justin and Clement of Alexandria, it lies in the latter's almost exclusive focus on Christ as the bringer of wisdom, versus Justin's more thorough trinitarian grounding of the pedagogical principle. At some points, he can be read either as agnostic about appropriation or merely confused.[44] At other points, he appears to hold a fully figured doctrine of the Trinity: the Father, the Son, and the prophetic Spirit are worshipped and adored, known in reason and in truth.[45] Although, when asked to define God, his answers focused on immutability and causality, with no mention of mind or wisdom, he agrees with Plato that the mind alone is capable of perceiving God.[46] The Father is 'perfect in intelligence' and truth, and the role of the Incarnate Word is to reveal both himself and the Father. It is because

---

[41] 2 Apol 10. [42] Disc 5. [43] Resr 1. [44] Dial 61. [45] 1 Apol 6. [46] Dial 3.

of this role of revealer of the truth that the truth is self-authenticating in Justin's view: Christ is the proof of himself and all things.[47]

We reach this truth, then, not by valid argumentation, but through God's gifts, the greatest of which is the very faculty by which we perceive the truth: by means of the rational faculties God himself has endowed us with, he both persuades and leads us to faith.[48] More than merely endowing us with cognitive and moral capacities, the gift of the intellect specifically underwrites contemplation[49] and the sacramental life, for, like Gregory Nazianzen, Justin stresses that baptism is 'illumination' and that the rationale for the sacrament is that we will not be ignorant, but will have an illumined mind [dianoia].[50] Thus, baptism is the bath of repentance and knowledge of God[51] and Justin is even willing to deem knowledge of God and Christ a form of circumcision, thus extending his 'sacramental' system back into the religion of the prophets.[52] His linkage of intellectual illumination and a physical event follows from his anthropology, for Justin's resembles that of Aristotle:[53] human beings are rational animals composed of a body and a soul, the two together forming a composite, and only of this composite can humanity be predicated;[54] he goes on to say that the imago Dei means that we are of flesh,[55] presumably meaning that the flesh represents the element of unlikeness necessary to anything that is an image rather than the original.

Although he felt free to borrow from the Greeks, Justin's attitude towards philosophy and reason is complex, though its complexities might be summarised by describing it as philosophical supersessionism.[56] He has great respect for Greek philosophy[57] (though decidedly less for Greek religion), but regards the prophets, who had no need to use convoluted proofs, as having anticipated the philosophers and as having foretold Christ.[58] Christ, in Justin's view, is the only sure and useful philosophy.[59] Demonstration for Justin does not simply connote cogent reasoning, but the rancour of dispute; it is this habitual love of argument that he associates with philosophy, as much as any love of truth;[60] demonstration is

---

[47] Resr 1. [48] 1 Apol. 10. [49] 1 Apol 28. Contra Goodenough 1923, 217. [50] 1 Apol 61.
[51] Dial 14. [52] Dial 28. [53] On this point I differ from Goodenough 1923; see 214. [54] Resr 8.
[55] Resr 7. I see no grounds for Goodenough's claim that the soul is intrinsically intelligent, and that it is not the Spirit or mind which is the focus of personal existence, but the soul (1923, 213).
[56] In describing it as such, I differ from H. Chadwick's view that for Justin 'the gospel and the best elements in Plato and the Stoics are almost identical ways of apprehending the same truth' (1966, 10–11).
[57] Dial 2. [58] Dial 7. [59] Dial 8.
[60] Exhort 1. Patterson takes a more positive view of Justin's estimation of philosophy, claiming that his position implies that Christ is the bearer of that truth which the Platonists sought as the means of the soul's perfection and that philosophers thus have some share in the divine Word (1967, 35).

always of that which is in some measure uncertain, and that which is demonstrated always bears the mark of its uncertain provenance. Nothing is more powerful or trustworthy than the truth, which needs no demonstration.[61] His estimation of philosophical argumentation does not entail any rejection of reasoning per se, however: indeed, he regards the search for the truth in the Christian as *more* rigorous than that of the philosophers and their followers: he notes drily that scrutiny reveals that ideas that have passed for excellent are often in reality of a quite different sort.[62] In his more conciliatory moments, he comes close to placing the prophets and the philosophers on equal footing,[63] reserving his scorn for teachers of religion; 'what religious teachers do you have?', he asks sceptically, 'the poets?'. The latter, in his view, merely peddle foolishness.[64]

Because zeal alone will not allow one to reach the truth, Justin stresses grace more strongly than the Apostolic Fathers do. Divine truth cannot be perceived through human faculties, but only by the divine gift imparted to the saints.[65] As Ignatius likened the bishop's being in tune with God's precepts to a harp with its strings,[66] so Justin uses the image of a harp or lyre to describe the accord of the righteous person with the gift of grace from above.[67] It is the teacher's role, not to invent doctrine, but merely to transmit this gift which God has given.[68]

When it suits him, in the *First Apology* for example, Justin can acknowledge right thinking in pagan intellectuals in a way that could be taken either as merely flattering opponents with a proven proclivity to violence, or as seeking to exhort his opponents to a logical consistency they sometimes appear to lack. So he reminds his antagonists and potential persecutors that they are merely adhering to their own stated principles in accusing Christians only of those crimes that authentically count as crimes in the eyes of their law, and that they ought to abide by those principles, not out of some alien notion of charity, but for reason's sake.[69] There is both an intellectual and an ethical imperative here: it is incumbent on the lover of truth only to do what is right and to speak the truth.[70]

Not to act in accord with reason is to fall prey to passion. If persecuting Christians constitutes wronging those who are blameless, then such persecution merely proceeds from passion – so Justin turns the critique of irrationality directed against Christians back against those who laid the

---

Barnard also maintains that Justin made an utter distinction between theology and philosophy in the strict sense (1967, 27).
[61] Resr 1. [62] Exhort 1. [63] Exhort 1. [64] Exhort 2 and 11. [65] Exhort 8. [66] Phil 1.
[67] Exhort 8. [68] Exhort 10. [69] 1 Apol 2–3. [70] 1 Apol 2.

charges. His polemic against passion could be expected to sting those who had drunk deeply at the well of Stoic ethics, but Justin has a rather different notion of apatheia in mind. As the snake charmer can force the serpent from its nest, so the Word makes passions flee.[71] This cleansing and sanctification resembles what the later tradition would assert of baptism: it regenerates and lifts the stain of sin.[72] If Christ can be deemed a physician, in Justin's view, it is because he rescues us from our desires by a 'wise and temperate' rule.[73]

Justin's Christology, of course, identifies Christ with the same principle of reason (logos) that by definition inspires all who think and reason rightly:[74] he is the notable exponent of the so-called 'logos theology'. The exact claims and import of this theology have been disputed, but the association of the Logos with God's wisdom[75] and the fact that, at the Incarnation, the Logos becomes fully identified with the rational being point to the Word's identity as the rational element of divine being; Christ became the whole rational being: body, reason [logos] and soul.[76] The similarity Justin posits between ancient philosophy and Christian teaching rests, not merely on his unquestioned cultural assumptions or wishful thinking, but this Christological base.[77] Moreover, Justin is well aware of the differences between, for example, Plato's thought and the teaching of Christ.[78]

Oddly, in light of his Christology and frequent approval of pagan philosophy, Justin's doctrine of God evidences little interest in the mind. True, he is quick to defend both God's knowledge of Adam's whereabouts in the garden of Eden and Christ's foreknowledge of the Passion;[79] nevertheless, he omits any mention of mind in a list of divine attributes.[80] Where he exhibits interest in mind per se, it is the human mind filled with the love of God,[81] rather than the divine intellect, which he emphasises.[82] The Christological principle is reflected in an anthropological one. Later theology would forge a link between the two by asserting the imago Dei. Justin does not. His equivalent, both substantively and systematically, is the notion of the *Logos spermatikos*: 'Each [philosopher] saw in proportion to his share of the spermatic word . . . all

---

[71] Disc 5.   [72] 1 Apol 61.   [73] Resr 10.   [74] 1 Apol 5.
[75] Dial 61.3. I am grateful to Osborn for this reference (1973, 36).
[76] 2 Apol 10.
[77] For a detailed account of Justin's conception of the Logos, see Norris 1966, 42–45.
[78] Cp. 2 Apol. 13.   [79] Dial 99.
[80] 1 Apol 10. He does mention wisdom [sōphrosynē], however.   [81] Govt 1.
[82] Note Barnard's striking description of Justin: 'In Mary's womb the cosmic Reason had become available to men as a human being of flesh and blood' (1967, 117).

were able to see, if fuzzily, something of the truth in virtue the word [logos] implanted in them'.[83] This concept of the *Logos spermatikos* helps in interpreting the pleasantries of Justin's writing: he addresses the *First Apology* to Lucius 'the philosopher, the lover of learning [paideia]' and arranges in the *Dialogue with Trypho* to have himself greeted as 'Hail, O philosopher!'[84]

As the *Dialogue* makes clear, the aims of philosophy are much the same as those of theology and Christian piety: to create happiness and to provide the content and incentive for contemplation.[85] Justin disparages his former, and philosophical, self, not for any philosophical error, but rather for having become conceited enough to imagine he would at any minute be brought to the vision of God.[86] Yet Justin also makes clear that moral qualities are necessary to one who would see God and while he never states it directly, he implies that in this respect, Christianity has the advantage: 'O instruction that quenches the natural fire of the soul! The Word's power does not make us poets, learned philosophers or skilled orators, but makes mortals immortal, mortals gods'.[87] Greek philosophy, in contrast, leads only to inner doubt and sectarian squabbles.[88]

IRENAEUS

In passing from Justin to Irenaeus, we might expect to encounter a reduced interest in matters intellectual: Justin, after all, seeks to convince educated and philosophically interested pagans of the intellectual cogency of Christianity, whereas Irenaeus' energies are directed against the quasi-Christian gnostics, with their complex systems, and his work is polemical rather than apologetic. It is a small sign of the importance of Christian reflection on the intellect that we in fact see the reverse: the theme looms larger in the works of Irenaeus (and of Tertullian) than it did in earlier writing, and becomes progressively more deeply embedded in the system, and thus less exclusively concerned with the moral life and more focused on God.[89]

---

[83] 2 Apol 13.
[84] 1 Apol 1 and Dial 1. Although Justin does claim that the Logos is part of every human being in 2 Apol 10, he does not call the Logos 'the higher divine principle in man', as Goodenough claims (1923, 214).
[85] Dial 3. Cf. Norris: for Justin, philosophy is 'not so much "speculation" as it is a religious search for the vision of God' (1966, 30).
[86] Dial 2.   [87] Disc 5.   [88] Exhort 4.
[89] Contrast Roberts, who holds that Irenaeus deprecates too much speculation as to the nature of God, thinking it better to attain to nearness of God by means of love (cf. Haer 2.25 and 26; Roberts 1924, 59).

There is one important qualification to this claim that mind is becoming an increasingly important divine predicate, namely, that while intelligence is an obvious and key attribute of God, it remains largely implicit: in the lists of secondary predicates and in creedal statements, there is no mention of intellect.[90] This omission is significant and is by no means to be dismissed lightly; nevertheless, the *assumption* of mind as a key attribute becomes increasingly obvious and is on occasion explicitly stated, even if not in lists of predicates or in creedal statements. In addition to the acknowledgement of God's foreknowledge,[91] which we found in some of the apostolic writings and in Justin, now there is an acknowledgement of God's design on the universe: it is blasphemous to regard the universe as faulty or deficient, Irenaeus chides, given that it reflects the Father's mental conception and 'pre-formation' [mente conceptum est et praeformatum sic].[92] It is important to the bishop to preserve a unity of conception and creation, moreover: the *same* God who envisages the universe is the one who formed it.[93] What God conceives in his mind comes into existence exactly as he envisages it, and the world therefore exactly mirrors the divine mind – if he had wanted an immaterial world, that is what would exist;[94] God is no slave of necessity.[95] The absence of mind from the lists of predicates nevertheless does not prevent Irenaeus describing God, quite simply, as Mind; thus, God is all mind, all reason [totus mens, totus ratio], all active Spirit, all light;[96] the Father is Mind comprehending all things[97] and nothing escapes his knowledge.[98] Indeed, without specifically appealing to the notion of simplicity, Irenaeus clearly assumes it, and does so in specifically intellectual terms: 'The one who posits mind in God and ascribes to it a special origin of its own [prolationem propriam], declares him a compound being, as if God were one thing and mind another.'[99]

It is the function of the Word to make the utterly transcendent Father known to those for whom knowledge is life-giving and salvific, and Irenaeus delights in portraying the Incarnate Word in the paradoxical terms that will continue to be beloved of the later tradition: 'God took humanity up into himself, the invisible becoming visible, the incomprehensible being made comprehensible, the impassible becoming passible.'[100] The Word thus imparts knowledge of the Father,[101] and yet only the Father knows the Word.[102] The Incarnation however proves no

---

[90] Haer 2.1.1; 2.30.9; 4.prae.5. [91] Haer 2.1.1. [92] Haer 2.3.2. [93] Haer 2.3.2.
[94] Haer 2.3.2. [95] Haer 2.5.4. [96] Haer 2.28.4. [97] Haer 2.28.5.
[98] Haer 2.26.3 and 2.28.3. [99] Haer 2.28.5. [100] Haer 3.16.6. [101] Haer 4.6.1 and 5.
[102] Haer 4.6.3.

limitation on the Word; strikingly, Irenaeus maintains Christ's divinity even on the cross: 'the creation could not have sustained him [on the cross] if it were the product [emissio] of ignorance and defect... How could the fruit of ignorance and defect sustain him who contains the knowledge of all things and is true and perfect?'[103]

Irenaeus gives a trinitarian ground to the imperative towards human knowledge of God. Because Christ declares the pre-eminent knowledge of the Father, we too ought to have perfect knowledge of God.[104] This knowledge we cannot have of our own accord, however; it is impossible to come to knowledge of God without divine assistance and it is for this reason that Christ is sent to teach us.[105] 'God cannot be known without God' is indeed something of an Irenaean maxim.[106] and whatever function might be asserted of it in the context of anti-gnostic polemic, it serves an additional purpose in the context of Irenaeus' systematic theology, that of grounding the relation between God and humanity in significantly (though not exclusively) intellectual terms.

Despite the way in which knowledge of God and God's desire that we know him connect us to God, Irenaeus also acknowledges an important difference: because we are inferior to the Word and the Spirit, we lack [indigemus] knowledge of God's mysteries.[107] This link between the knower's mode of existence and the possibility of knowledge of God posits a link between epistemology and ontology whose sophistication anticipates much later theology. The impetus to seek God remains, even though many questions we have about the world are not answered in scripture; some questions just have to be left [cedere] to God, though this acknowledgement implies no deficiency in scripture itself.[108] The balance between assiduous seeking, even in the face of obstacles, and a counter-productive flailing is delicate: it is a mistake, in Irenaeus' view, to throw away that true and firm knowledge of God that is available to us by running after the answer to every conceivable question.[109] Some of these imponderables evidently concern the doctrine of God, for Irenaeus earlier maintains that one should know one's epistemological place and not seek to rise above the unsurpassable God. This form of modesty the bishop deems a preserving of the proper order of knowledge.[110] Those things which by divine decree lie within human capacities are however susceptible to increase through effort: daily study of such things (though,

---

[103] Haer 5.18.1. [104] Haer 2.28.8. [105] Haer 4.5.1. [106] Haer 4.6.4; cf. 4.20.5.
[107] Haer 2.28.2. [108] Haer 2.28.2. [109] Haer 2.28.1. [110] Haer 2.25.4.

implicitly, not those things God has placed out of our reach) renders knowledge of them not only possible, but easy.[111]

Despite his strong insistence on God's good pleasure in granting knowledge of himself, Irenaeus ultimately proposes a model of dynamic epistemological mutuality. He maintains on the one hand that to follow light is to receive light, so that those who are in the light do not themselves illumine it, but are rather illumined and revealed by it.[112] On the other, he holds to a notion of participation, so that those who see the light are in the light and partake of its brilliancy, and those who see God are in God and receive of his radiance. Participation in God means knowing God and enjoying his goodness.[113] The chief enabler of sight is not this light – which seems unlikely to be material – but the literal flesh-and-blood manifestation of the Word, who made the divine nature, which is beyond comprehension and boundless and invisible, visible and comprehensible to believers.[114] In accord with Irenaeus' strongly communal models of biblical interpretation and doctrinal formulation, his notion of illumination is also ecclesial: light is bestowed by the church, the seven-light candelabrum, which sheds illumination on the church and on the world at large.[115]

As we have already begun to see, Irenaeus resembles the later theological and spiritual tradition in his virtual equation of knowledge and sight. He also resembles later thought in equating both with the perfection and beatitude of the Age to Come: the vision of God is life-giving, and bestows immortality.[116] As with other patristic theology, the Irenaean holds the next life to stand in seamless continuity with this: 'The glory of God is a living human person and human life consists in beholding God.'[117] The 'eye' with which we do this beholding belongs to the mind, so Irenaeus anticipates the tradition of the spiritual senses, the chief inaugurator of which is Origen, although for the bishop, the visual imagery extends to include volition as well: it is with the eye of the mind that we experience good and evil and make the choice of better things.[118]

Freedom, indeed, is a key item of Irenaean theology: it figures in his anthropology, it reflects back onto the doctrine of God, showing forth God's goodness, and links God to humanity.[119] Freedom is nevertheless not the only component of Irenaeus' theology of the imago Dei. Just as his theology of history stresses that even the Fall shows God's wise forethought and ultimate plan to bring the whole creation to its intended

---

[111] Haer 2.27.1. [112] Haer 4.14.1. [113] Haer 4.20.5. [114] Haer 4.20.5. [115] Haer 5.20.1.
[116] Haer 4.20.6. [117] Haer 4.20.7. [118] Haer 4.39.1. [119] See, notably, Haer 4.37.3-5.

good, so the imago Dei subsists significantly in humanity's reflection of the harmony and order in the mind of God.[120] Irenaeus is less interested than many other theologians in the mind as the faculty in virtue of which we are above all said to be made in the image of God, but harmony and order presuppose intelligence, and, plausibly therefore, Irenaeus neglects to make much of the intellectual element of the imago because he simply assumes it.[121]

Because Irenaeus sees the Incarnate Christ as the perfection of the imago Dei,[122] he has a systematic base which helps him to avoid the suspicious attitude towards the body which we find in Origen, for example. The body is subordinate to the mind in Irenaeus' theology, inasmuch as the soul possesses and rules over it, but the body receives not only life from the soul, but inspiration.[123] Although the bishop views the body as slowing the soul down, his fundamental conception of their relation is of a positive interchange: the body is the instrument of the artist [artifex] which is the soul[124] and the soul even is said to teach the body and share with it the spiritual vision it has enjoyed.[125] One of the effects of the Fall which the Incarnation reverses is the derangement of both body and soul, so that the Incarnate Word forces the soul from its spiritual bondage in order that the soul may purify the body.[126] The model proposed in the latter passage apparently assumes that not even God incarnate could directly act on the body, yet elsewhere Irenaeus states starkly that the flesh is not destitute of participation in the constitutive wisdom and power of God,[127] which asserts a doctrine of fleshly deification as strongly as any to be found in the writings of the Fathers.

If God is incomprehensible to the mind [animo], he cannot be measured in the heart [corde], either.[128] Like many other later writers, Irenaeus does not make a sharp distinction between heart and mind, and the latter does not have the purely emotional connotations it does in our time. Thus Irenaeus worries that, for all the mind's centrality to the spiritual life, the mind could also become the occasion for vanity or ingratitude [ingratam mentem accipientes].[129] Despite these dangers, the mind is still accorded the status of that which permits perception of God and *ta theia*. Because the mind is our point of contact to God, that which

---

[120] Haer 4.38.3.
[121] Cf. Haer 5.6.1, where there is an extensive discussion of the imago, with no explicit reference to mind per se, but where he does cite Paul's dictum about the wisdom of the perfect (1 Cor 2.6).
[122] Haer 5.21.2. [123] Haer 2.33.4. [124] Haer 2.34.4. [125] Haer 2.33.3. [126] Haer 4.13.2.
[127] Haer 5.3.3. [128] Haer 4.19.2. [129] Haer 5.2.3.

draws us closer to God, it is also the devil's point of attack.[130] The problem with the gnostics, according to Irenaeus, is that their distribution of divine attributes over two cosmic powers eliminates the justice and intelligence of both.[131] It was not God's intention in endowing humanity with intellect that we should have reached unorthodox conclusions: reason, implanted in our minds [ratio mentibus infixus], reveals the truth, that there is one God and Lord of all.[132] Intelligence is not given to us that we can invent new gods and change the subject matter of faith, but so we can use reason rightly to discern the One Who Is.[133]

Even in a polemical work, such as *Adversus haereses*, the intellect is of such importance that meditation and contemplation, activities little related to dispute with heretics, also figure in significant ways: a sound mind [sensus sanus] meditates eagerly on these things which God has given the mind to understand.[134] Here Irenaeus links his usual concern for doctrinal and episcopal continuity with the concern for contemplative theology characteristic of later thinkers.

TERTULLIAN

With Tertullian, we move to a theology whose trinitarian underpinnings are becoming ever more developed and clearly articulated. Nevertheless, his Christology retains many of the features of earlier theology, in virtue of which the Word is conceived as the Father's Reason and the agent of creation, and as for Justin, it is important for Tertullian that the ancient philosophers also recognised such a logos.[135] Although he is capable of omitting any mention of mind, even when purporting to offer a 'definition' of God, he quickly moves on to extrapolate from what he evidently considers the leading divine attributes (supremacy and eternity) to others, which include reason, so the respects in which God is supreme are form, power and reason [ratione].[136] He links divine perfection to eternity and rationality, maintaining that the irrational is necessarily imperfect.[137] A similar pattern obtains in his treatise refuting Hermogenes. He expatiates at length on attributes such as unity and aseity and eternity,[138] and only much later gets around to stipulating wisdom, intelligence and knowledge.[139]

---

[130] Haer 5.24.3. The devil is said 'abstrahere mentem hominis'. [131] Haer 3.25.2.
[132] Haer 2.6.1. [133] Haer 1.10.3. [134] Haer 2.27.1. [135] Apol 20.10. [136] Marc 1.3.2.
[137] Marc 1.24.1. [138] Herm 5.1–2 and 6.2.
[139] Herm 18.1; cp. the assertion of rationality in Prax 5.2.

Mind, along with cognate notions, such as wisdom or rationality, thus appear most frequently as implicates of other attributes: nothing can be properly considered good but that which is reasonably good, he claims, and rationality, along with perfection, is further linked to order.[140] Indeed, one of the main problems with the Marcionite doctrine of God is that it portrays divine nature as irrational.[141] Against this doctrine, Tertullian does not quite propose one in which the divine mind per se is crucial, but he does stress God's wisdom and knowledge, both of which presuppose mind.[142] At times, he makes the connection between wisdom and mind explicit, as in *Contra Hermogenem*, when he writes of God as the one who established the cosmos by his wisdom and understanding, applying the efforts of these, as well as his mind [animi], his power, his word, his spirit, and his might.[143] The universe reflects the mind of God also by its beauty, a connection which tacitly presupposes an aesthetic in which beauty is linked to order and harmony.[144] Since Tertullian explicitly links order to wisdom,[145] there is a direct link between his aesthetic, his doctrine of creation and the assumption of divine nature as intellectual.

Tertullian differs from earlier writers in having a more fully developed notion of what mind is and how it functions. Indeed, he is the only one of these earlier writers to pen a full-length treatise on the soul, a practice that becomes more common in later centuries. His psychology is straightforward and clearly asserted: the mind [mens, which he glosses as nous] is that innate faculty by which the soul knows.[146] The rational element of the human person derives from God, who is himself rational in essence;[147] the irrational is linked to sin and the devil.[148] This analysis bequeaths him some awkward exegetical problems, such as accounting for Christ's impatience with the scribes and pharisees and his equally impatient desire to celebrate the passover with his disciples.[149] Nevertheless, it is to Christ we must look to understand how the irascible and concupiscible elements of the soul rightly operate in relation to the rational.[150] His Biblical fidelity causes him to modify the Platonic psychology on which he has been explicitly drawing: the irascible and concupiscible cannot be simply irrational, since we see them in Christ and since Paul himself allows for the concupiscible (the proof text for this

---

[140] Marc 1.23.1 and 6, and 1.24.1. [141] Marc 1.24.1. [142] Cp. Herm 18.20. [143] Herm 45.4.
[144] Herm 29.1. [145] Herm 18.5 and 20.2. [146] Anim 12.2. [147] Anim 16.1. [148] Anim 16.2.
[149] Anim 16.4. [150] Anim 16.5.

claim being 1 Tim 3.1, admittedly not what most of us would take as an example of raging desire),[151] so they are allowed in our own case as well.[152]

No more are the senses opposed to reason. The senses are not the source of the errors we make in trying to figure out the world around us. An oar looked at from above the water surface seems bent, but the problem lies not in the oar itself, which is straight, nor even in our senses, but in the sense we make of what we perceive [opinio], the root of which lies in the soul.[153] Both the senses and the intellect are integral to the soul; to employ the senses is to employ the intellect, and vice versa [intelligere sentire est].[154] Tertullian's opposition to heretics, such as the Valentinians, is founded on their unacceptable Platonism: they divide sensation from intelligence, the consequence of which is the separation of intelligence from its spiritual source and sense knowledge from its animal source. Although he admits of a distinction between corporeal and spiritual things, he does so grudgingly,[155] and refuses on the basis of a difference he considers all but inconsequential to allow that the senses perceive the material and the mind, the intelligible; for him, the mind is above all the faculty which perceives the spiritual, yet it is merely an instrument of the soul.[156] Moreover, the senses cannot operate in isolation from the mind, and the mind is said to be exercising sensation when it is thinking.[157] Although from one perspective, the mind is superior, it is so because its object is superior to the object of sense; in any intrinsic sense, the intellect is not superior, since it is dependent on the senses to reach the truth.[158] He concludes Chapter 24 of his treatise on the soul with a round denunciation of key tenets of Platonism (the unborn soul and anamnesis) on the basis of his rejection of Platonic epistemology: the whole structure collapses once one demonstrates (as Tertullian believes he has) that the mind and the senses operate together to produce knowledge. If he seems Aristotelian in his stress on the senses, he nonetheless roundly declares himself opposed to Aristotle on the grounds that the latter will not allow that the mind undergoes emotions.[159] The dominant category in Tertullian's psychology is finally not the mind but the soul. The mind is a component of the latter, but is is not the faculty that is *capax Dei*, in the first instance: God always speaks to the soul, moving it so that the mind may also turn to him.[160] It is altogether natural to the soul to be

---

[151] Anim 16.6.   [152] Anim 16.5.
[153] Anim 17.5ff; his argument here is specifically directed against the Epicureans.
[154] Anim 18.3.   [155] Anim 18.6.   [156] Anim 18.5.   [157] Anim 18.6.
[158] Anim 18.11; a summary of the whole position may be found in Anim 18.13.
[159] Anim 12.5.   [160] Anim 13.3.

rational, since its origin is of the creator; as such, irrationality is a consequence of the Fall,[161] though a permanent one, much like the debility of the will.

Tertullian's anthropology is worked out in significant measure in relation to infants, these presumably standing for human nature in its most basic state. Already in the womb, the infant begins to grow with its full complement of faculties of sensation and intelligence, and the fact that babies are capable of affection is a sign that they possess intelligence.[162] At times, he is so concerned to endow the soul with intelligence that he elevates it almost to the level of God: from the moment of its birth it is endowed both with intellect and even a measure of foreknowledge.[163] If his allowance for intellectual subtlety in infants seems to glorify human nature, it seems part of a larger generosity, for he also accords knowledge to trees and intelligence to logs.[164] However considerable the endowments of nature, however, Tertullian does not go so far as to deny the need for grace, of which knowledge is a gift[165] and one can only know the truth of human nature from God; no other source is trustworthy.[166] Indeed, it is safer to be ignorant, in the absence of revelation, than to rely on human presumption.[167]

He nevertheless extends beyond this anthropology worked out at the level of nature with only fleeting references to grace to one which embeds grace more deeply in the system, proposing a psychological image of the divine Trinity that in cursory form anticipates Augustine's. Addressing Praxeas (or perhaps at this point, simply the reader), he remarks: 'The Word is a second person within you... through which in uttering speech you generate a thought.' Obviously, there is a worrisome element to this suggestion; it appears to leave us caught on the horns of a dilemma, in virtue of which either rationality renders us incipiently triune (though there is no mention of the Spirit), or the distinction of Persons in the divine Trinity little differs from the way faculties are distinguished in us. Tertullian is aware of the first problem, for he quickly insists on the distinction of the Word from an ordinary human being,[168] though he gives no sign of seeing the second.

Tertullian's strong emphasis on corporeality, however, drives a wedge between his theology and any incautious form of the *analogia entis*: 'What

---

[161] Anim 16.1. [162] Anim 19.9. [163] Anim 19.8. [164] Anim 19.4 and 19.6. [165] Pres 14.2.
[166] Anim 1.6. [167] Anim 1.6.
[168] Prax 5.6–7. His argument here is a fortiori: if we, made in the image of God, have a word within us which is distinct from ourselves, how much more distinct must God's word be from him [quanto ergo plenius hoc agitur in Deo ...]?

else is a human being but flesh?', he asks, reminding his reader that humanity was made from dust. For this reason, it is not accurate to say God breathed us into being: we were moulded, as befits those whose 'fabric' is of flesh rather than of spirit.[169] Alongside this frank insistence on corporeality stands a doctrine of the imago whose essential traits are mind and will,[170] although he seems more interested in the will than the mind.[171] He links the will, not to the mind, but to goodness, arguably the key attribute of God for him,[172] so that we image God by being good as God is good, freedom being the condition of the possibility of this goodness.[173] Despite the general lack of grounding of will in the intellect's ability to envisage choices, Tertullian on occasion does connect the two, albeit rather loosely: 'as a rational being, capable of intelligence and knowledge, be restrained within the bounds of rational liberty [libertate rationali], subject to him who subjected all things to himself'.[174] Elsewhere, he simply includes intelligence amongst a long list of attributes related to the image (though not clearly constitutive of it). The image possesses the lineaments of true divinity, such as an immortal soul, freedom, and mastery over itself, as well as a measure of foreknowledge, reasonableness, capacity for understanding and knowledge. Nevertheless it remains an image and an image, however expressive of the reality it imitates, still lacks intrinsic power [motum].[175] Hence he can claim that grace is stronger than nature, overpowering it to the point that even the free will is subjected to it.[176] He does not explain how freedom, an endowment so crucial to his anthropology, can continue to function systematically if he does away with it on occasion, but though this claim makes it difficult to see the overall consistency of his thought, it does testify to his conviction of the power of grace.

The body has for Tertullian many of the same connotations that it has for later writers – without it, we would not be afflicted with some of the more troublesome passions – but his view is in some respects more positive. To begin with, the body is intrinsic to humanity; second, it is the soul's instrument.[177] The view he proposes is merely scriptural, he claims: in the scriptures, the flesh is blamed only because without it the soul could not commit sins of concupiscence, intemperance, cruelty or idolatry.[178] This scriptural view is contrasted unfavourably with the Platonic one: for the latter, the body is a prison, while for Paul, it is the

---

[169] Marc 1.24.5. [170] Marc 2.9.4. [171] Marc 2.6.3. [172] Cf. Marc 1.25.1, 2.6 passim.
[173] Marc 2.6.5. [174] Marc 2.4.5. [175] Marc 2.9.5. [176] Anim 21.6. [177] Anim 40.3.
[178] Anim 40.3.

temple of God.[179] Tertullian nevertheless concedes an important point to the Platonist: by enclosing the soul, the body obscures and sullies it,[180] and death is therefore a purification, a release from the bondage of the flesh.[181] His willingness to posit a disembodied afterlife in the period between the individual's death and final judgement might be taken as significant in positing an incipient doctrine of purgatory. Tertullian's portrayal of this intermediate state however differs markedly from the medieval Western one; there is the briefest of allusions to remedial exercises for the saved,[182] and apparently no separation of these from the damned. The real significance of Tertullian's Hades lies not in its tenuous anticipation of later doctrines of purgatory, but its anthropological import, for at this point he suddenly departs from his earlier insistence on psychosomatic unity holding that the soul's separation from the body at death does not prevent it from rejoicing or being sad as it awaits either resurrection or damnation.[183] Whatever problems of overall coherence are created by this sudden allowing the soul independence from the body (and describing that independence as a release), it does not in itself indicate the intrinsic sinfulness of the body, for he acknowledges that there are many forms of sin which are proper to the soul alone, and for which the body is in no way culpable.[184] Like his near-contemporary, Origen, Tertullian was drawn towards asceticism, yet, like Origen, bodily imagery occasionally creeps into his writing, precisely at the point when he speaks of mind; thus he can speak of the Word's proceeding from the Father, 'in a way peculiar to himself, from the womb of his own heart'.[185] Nevertheless, his lengthy speculations about Hades in the treatise on the soul are followed by the briefest of mentions of the resurrection.[186]

The picture he presents in other treatises veers in a more positive direction as far as the estimation of the body is concerned. In the treatise on the resurrection, he portrays the body's functioning as the soul's useful servant, although it is not on that account base, for if the soul is the body's master, being governed in this way is the body's glory.[187] His conviction of the unity of body and soul, at least in this life, is such that he can call the flesh the 'pivot' of salvation, arguing that if the flesh is the soul's consort in this life, it must also be its co-heir in the next.[188] He can also speak of a resurrection of the mind [animo], in virtue of which we are no longer alienated from God.[189] His conviction of psychosomatic unity

---

[179] Anim 53.5. [180] Anim 53.5. [181] Anim 53.6. [182] Anim 58.8. [183] Anim 58.5.
[184] Anim 58.6. [185] Prax 7.1. [186] Anim 58.8. [187] Resr 7.10. [188] Resr 7.13.
[189] Resr 23.4.

is such that he insists that spiritual growth takes place only in the flesh: whatever is done in the heart is done by the soul in the flesh, and with the flesh and through the flesh.[190] Despite his willingness in his treatise on the soul to see the body as a hindrance, in the treatise on fasting he locates the fundamental problem in the soul: those who are wound up in the care and will of the flesh cannot please God, although that does not mean that those who are embodied cannot please him.[191]

Although Tertullian in several respects foreshadows the later tradition in the importance he accords mind, he displays much less interest in the mind's role in prayer and contemplation, despite the fact that he penned a treatise on prayer. The latter is essentially an exposition of the Lord's Prayer to which is appended a series of brief remarks on practical issues such as posture and dress, places and times for prayer. Perhaps Tertullian's concern for these reflects the uncompromising insistence on psychosomatic unity evident elsewhere in his theology. One could as plausibly maintain, though, that his theology of prayer simply lacks the depth and subtlety of later treatments (although he anticipates these in his brief remarks on mental distraction in Chapter 12). In Tertullian, then, we have the curious phenomenon of a theology which is doctrinally significantly advanced beyond that of the Apostolic Fathers, but which is, if anything, less subtle in its analysis of the spiritual and less concerned to connect matters of spirituality, theology, or even (and despite his reputation for personal ascetical rigour) ascesis and theology.

If the absence of attention to ascetical theology is surprising, it is no more so than the fact that in Tertullian, we see no marked general rise in interest in matters pertaining to the intellect, despite his greater philosophical sophistication and more developed trinitarian theology. It is tempting to conjecture that there is a correlation between the weak interest in ascesis and contemplation on the one hand and the lack of a heightened interest in the intellect on the other, but such a judgement would be impossibly speculative. Moreover, while Tertullian's interest in the intellect is not proportionately greater than, say, the Apostolic Fathers' (for his writings are voluminous and theirs, tiny), he remains important for the sustained attention he gives in his treatise on the soul to the question of the mind's relation to the body and the senses. We see also a greater embedding of the issues in a theological system: the role of the intellect in anthropology is more fully worked out, as are the implications of asserting the imago Dei. If mind in God remains largely

[190] Resr 15.3. [191] Fast 17.6.

implicit (attendant upon the assertion of wisdom or order in creation, for example), Tertullian nevertheless insists on the human mind's function as a mirror of divine nature, as well as the medium by which human beings are brought into relation with God.

Although later writers possess more fully elaborated doctrines of sanctification (and ascetical theologies), the earliest theologians still provide significant indications of the importance these issues will come to have: Ignatius sees the Eucharist as the means of God's intelligent self-expression in creation; Justin presages the later tradition in seeing baptism as illumination; the Incarnation bestows life-giving knowledge in Irenaeus' theology; and Tertullian can speak of a resurrection of the mind. Intellectual regeneration and growth have thus been established as an important constituent of the doctrines of sanctification and consummation. If, in these earliest Christian writings, we do not find an interest in themes pertaining to the intellect that fully equals the intensity of the later writers we will survey, we do find most of these themes accurately foreshadowed, even at this embryonic stage of the tradition's development. The concern to portray divine nature as rational and human nature as not only rational, but divinely created to be so, and to sketch out the relation of mind to body and knowledge to sanctification, all surface from the very dawn of Christian theology, a testament to the significance of the theme throughout the period.

CHAPTER 2

Early Alexandrians: Clement and Origen

Origen begins what is arguably the first Christian systematic theology by declaring his intention to build a system out of principles, in order to produce a body of doctrine, constructed by clear and necessary arguments.[1] The foundations of this system are, it seems, based on the scriptural memory of Christ's teaching,[2] although Origen gives a creed-like summary of the Bible's salvation history that seems closely indebted to a Rule of Faith.[3] At one level, his purpose is no more than that of any systematician, to provide an orderly account of what is implicit in the Bible's welter of narrative, law and poetry, and so to quell disputes in the church.[4] The opening words of the treatise, however, reveal a broader purpose: 'All who believe and are sure that grace and truth have come by Jesus Christ and that Christ is the truth... receive the knowledge which calls us to lead a good and blessed life from no other source than the very words and teaching of Christ.'[5] Knowledge, then, is the key to living, not only in this world, but, as 'blessed' hints, in the Age to Come. The point that this knowledge comes from Christ does not merely follow from some predetermined methodological principle: the issue is not just right warrants for theological arguments, but the personal correspondence of God and humanity. This intellectual encounter of God and humankind becomes the great theme of *On First Principles* and is writ large also in the *Contra Celsum*.[6]

---

[1] PArch 1.Prae 10. Crouzel denies emphatically that *On First Principles* is any kind of *summa* and is generally hostile to the notion that Origen's theology is systematic (1989, 46 and 168). However, at key points, Crouzel's argument presupposes a system, for example, when he argues that a particular interpretation of Origen's doctrine of the Fall would do violence to his doctrine of God (1989, 16). Cf. also the sarcastic aside on p. 365. Daniélou's view closely resembles that of Crouzel on this point (1989, 312).

[2] PArch 1.Prae 1.   [3] PArch 1.Prae 4.   [4] PArch 1.Prae 2.   [5] PArch 1.Prae 1.

[6] Cf. Daniélou's claim that Origen's theology is a speculative theory of the way mind is illumined by gnōsis rather than a description of mystical experience, and that therein lie its limitations (1955, 297).

At the heart of Origen's conception of the intellect lies the notion of a correspondence between the eternal, invisible and divine on the one hand, and the temporal, sensible and human on the other. The distinction between created and Uncreated is central to most Christian theology, of course, and certainly to patristic theology, but in Origen's thought, it is the counter-weighing principle, the correspondence of God and the specifically rational beings, which looms almost as large. God is simple intellectual nature [intellectualis natura simplex],[7] unspeakably surpassing all that can be thought and exceeding the power of the human mind to conceive.[8] Nevertheless, it would be inconceivable that other minds would have any source other than God, and so, qua source [fons] of all intellectual existence,[9] God must bear some relation to all other intellectual beings, divine transcendence notwithstanding.

We will return to the nature of the correspondence of rational beings; for the moment, we remain with Origen's conception of divine nature itself. Part of what distinguishes God from all other rational beings is that the chief attributes of God differ in kind, and not only in degree. Origen is fond of pointing to God's essential goodness, holiness, and so on, as contrasted with the creature's accidental possession of these qualities [in haec enim sola trinitate, quae est auctor omnium bonitas substantialiter inest].[10] A second difference in kind is that God is purely intelligible, perceptible only to mind, a notion that emerges most explicitly in *Contra Celsum*,[11] but is also implicit in *On First Principles*. Part of the reason for insisting that divine nature is solely intelligible is to secure divine simplicity,[12] and part is to avoid idolatry, a concern which particularly characterises the *Contra Celsum*,[13] but which is also hinted at in the treatise on prayer.[14]

---

[7] PArch 1.1.6. The Latin of the quotation signals a perennial difficulty in the interpretation of Origen's thought, namely the state of the primary texts. An account of the problem can be found in Crouzel (1989, 37–49); he approves Daniélou's suggestion of making broad use of all the work, checking texts against each other for consistency (48), which is essentially the method of the present study.
[8] PArch 1.1.5.   [9] PArch 1.1.6.   [10] PArch 1.2.13; 1.5.3; 1.6.2; 1.8.3.   [11] 4.20; 7.37.
[12] PArch 1.1.6.   [13] 3.34; 5.35; 7.64.
[14] 23.3, 28.10 and cf. the related concern to avoid anthropomorphism. Origen's analysis of the irrationality of sin takes perhaps its most subtle form in his condemnation of idolatry. Growth in understanding is the rational soul's discarding the image it once thought to be God's (CCels 3.40). Wisdom persuades the worshipper to turn from statues, for example, and to ascend instead to God (CCels 5.35). More than being irrational, veneration of images or prayer to them actually impedes knowledge of God: it is quite impossible, Origen declares flatly, to pray to images and to know God (CCels 7.65). Clement also condemns idolatry, but does so as a matter of general principle, rather than as a specifically irrational activity (cf. Prot 4 and 10). Cf. also Crouzel: for Origen, every sin is both adultery and idolatry, adultery because it is infidelity to the sole lawful Husband and idolatry because it takes the perceptible creature for the heavenly realities themselves (1989, 123).

Some qualifications are nevertheless in order. If God possesses holiness in a radically different manner from the way we do, he does not possess intelligence in this unique fashion: mind is not essential to God and accidental to us, but essential to both divine and human nature. Second, if divine nature utterly exceeds the reach of our mind, it apparently also exceeds even the divine mind, for the Trinity is said to exceed the comprehension even of eternal intelligence.[15] Origen however never seems entirely certain of the extent to which he wishes to identify mind with divine nature: the Lord of the universe either is mind or transcends mind.[16]

The exposition of the doctrine of the Trinity is heavily dependent on Origen's stress on mind, for it is above all the need to assert wisdom in God that suggests a plurality of divine hypostases. Scripture asserts wisdom in God; Origen claims wisdom must have hypostatic existence,[17] and the hypostasis of divine wisdom is the Son.[18] Origen's reasoning at this point is somewhat shaky, inasmuch as his premises are neither as incontrovertible as he seems to believe, nor does his conclusion follow as necessarily from them as he implies. Nevertheless, his insistence on the point reveals something of the importance of mind as a divine attribute in his thought.[19]

His Christology is yet more strongly marked by a proclivity for stressing mind. The begetting of the Son is an essentially intellectual process, an act of will proceeding from mind.[20] The nature of this act, intellectual and volitional, secures the unity of substance of the First and Second Persons.[21] Having warded off any suggestion of Arianism, however, he creates for himself another sort of problem, for the Son's identity as Word stipulates, in Origen's view, that there is nothing in him perceptible to the senses [*verbum enim est filius, et ideo nihil in eo sensibile intelligendum est*].[22] While this claim by no means invalidates a later assertion of the Incarnation, it does hint at a larger problem with Origen's overwhelming stress on the intellect, namely a wariness of the sensible

---

[15] PArch 4.4.1.   [16] CCels 7.38.
[17] The Latin is *substantia*, but later in the same passage Origen glosses *hypostasis* as *substantia*; for clarity's sake, then, the translation *hypostasis* has been used.
[18] PArch 1.2.2.
[19] Berchman adumbrates Origen's doctrine of the Trinity in markedly intellectualist terms in (1992, 236).
[20] PArch 1.2.6. Daniélou sees Origen's doctrine of the Logos differently; he claims that the role accorded the Logos in Origen's theology of the spiritual life anticipates the devotional tradition centring on the humanity of Jesus, such as is found in Bernard and Bonaventure, rather than the spirituality of Nyssen, Evagrius or Denys (1955, x).
[21] PArch 1.2.6.   [22] PArch 1.2.6.

and material that sometimes seems to border on docetism and Manichaeism.[23] There is an advantage in his privileging of the mind though, since it allows him to give more content to the notions of Word and Wisdom than most later theologians have done. The Son's role as Image of the Father is to reveal the Father.[24] The precise nature of this revelation is not specified; certainly, Origen's thought is not that this revelation should be equated with the Word's enfleshment, for he insists that the Son is the invisible image of the invisible God.[25] As the true image of God, the Word expresses the Father's substance and so makes God known,[26] interpreting and offering to rational creatures the secrets of wisdom and the mysteries of knowledge.[27]

The Word is a mediator, then, but a mediator of an essentially intellectual kind, one who trains the human eye to the light of God, a mediator between humanity and the light.[28] Certainly, the Logos is the one who heals from the worst of diseases, sin,[29] but he also heals that infirmity of mind that comes of not knowing the truth.[30] Not only healing, but wisdom, comes from the Word, although these are not purely the Word's gifts, inasmuch as becoming wise – even rational – depends also on the rational creatures' exerting themselves to imitate him.[31]

This Christology does not, however, fully exploit its own riches. Origen is remarkable in the development of doctrine for positing a human soul in Christ long before the Apollinarian controversy.[32] He is even at pains to insist that the nature of Christ's soul was the same as that of all souls,[33] though it of course clung to God when the others did not at the Fall. Nevertheless, he does not press this point to assert some variety of *communicatio idiomatum*, in virtue of which human nature is regenerated through the contact of the human soul with the divine Word; it is always the Word that illumines and heals all other human minds and souls, rather than the communication of the effects of the regenerated human soul in Jesus to all other souls in virtue of a solidarity of human

---

[23] Cf. Karen Jo Torjesen's claim that in Origen's thought, the Logos is made accessible to humankind not in the form of flesh, but doctrine (1987, 376).
[24] PArch 1.2.6. Cf. Widdicombe's view that, for Origen, to know God fully is to know God as Father (1994, 2).
[25] PArch 1.2.6. [26] PArch 1.2.8.
[27] PArch 1.2.7. Cf. Widdicombe's claim that the Son is the model of our knowing and loving God; we share in the Son's continuous uninterrupted contemplation of the depths of the Father and the Father's eternal delight in his Son becomes ours as well (1994, 118); thus, it is not accurate to say that for Origen, the Father is unknown, because he is known by the Son (47).
[28] PArch 1.2.7. [29] CCels 4.15 and 8.72. [30] CCels 3.60. [31] PArch 4.4.4.
[32] See, for example and notably, PArch 2.4.3; cf. also CCels 3.29. [33] PArch 2.6.5.

nature.³⁴ It is the *Word* which descends into holy souls and makes them friends of God,³⁵ illuminating minds with the knowledge of the Father,³⁶ rather than such friendship's being forged by the commonality of Jesus' soul and ours. One explanation of this failure of a supremely systematic mind to forge a felicitous theological connection is that at times Origen perhaps leans towards a kind of proto-Nestorianism: 'the person and essence of divine being in Jesus', he writes, 'is quite different matter from that of his human element'³⁷ and he claims that the Word suffers nothing of the experience of body and soul,³⁸ although he can simultaneously assert that the man Jesus participated in the Logos.³⁹ There are, too, distinct traces of some form of subordinationism in Origen's Christology.⁴⁰ Moreover, so convinced is he of divine transcendence that he occasionally compromises the reality of the Incarnation: he characterises the ascent of the soul to the Father as the ascent of the mind rather than the body.⁴¹

Clement's conception of the mind closely matches Origen's.⁴² He is surer of the identity of God and the mind – God is being and mind, in his view, and this is the ground of his role as the ultimate teacher.⁴³ Nevertheless, God ultimately lies beyond all such affirmations: no one can adequately name or express the divine nature, and even in naming God 'mind' we do not do so.⁴⁴ This point may appear rather unremarkable; certainly, few modern people would say one had adequately named or described God in calling him 'mind'. What makes this claim of Clement's striking is the list of titles in which the appellation 'mind' is included: one, good, absolute being, and even Father, God, Creator and Lord. If 'mind' does not adequately encapsulate divine nature, it nevertheless ranks alongside the most basic Biblical and philosophical titles for God and this status is itself an important index of the mind's significance in early Alexandrian theology.

---

³⁴ He does assert *communicatio* insofar as the soul of *Jesus* is transformed by its union with the Word; cf. CCels 3.41.
³⁵ CCels 4.3. ³⁶ CCels 6.330. ³⁷ CCels 7.16. ³⁸ CCels 4.15. ³⁹ CCels 7.17.
⁴⁰ Thus, at least, is Koetschau's text: the SC edition omits this passage entirely, as being of insufficient authenticity. Cf. PArch 1.3.5 and the suggestion we ought not to pray to the Son because he is begotten in Pray 15.1.
⁴¹ Pray 23.2.
⁴² Osborn pleads that the canon of patristic theology ought to be expanded backwards to include the second century, arguing that key Christian notions, such as the idea of God as being, good and mind, the *archē* of physics, ethics and logic, come from Clement (1992, 34).
⁴³ Str 4.25. H. Chadwick goes further, claiming that the Father has no other function in Clement's theology than to be the ground of being; see Armstrong 1967, 179.
⁴⁴ Str 5.12.

Clement's theology is on the whole rather less theocentric than Origen's, however. In part, this difference may be explained by the fact that Origen wrote in overtly systematic fashion, locus by locus, while Clement did not, and that Clement's trinitarian thought is not as developed. More than the doctrine of God, Clement is interested in Christology, a Christology that is overwhelmingly exemplarist: Jesus is above all the Teacher, not only in *The Teacher*, as one would expect, but also in *What Rich Person Is Saved?*,[45] the *Stromateis*,[46] and the *Protreptikos*,[47] and the prominence of Christ's pedagogical role speaks eloquently of the role of the intellect in Clement's theology.

Clement frankly identifies the Word of God with the intellect:[48] the distinctive form of both God and humanity is the mind that characterises both. The rational nature of the Word is linked to his passionlessness: as the Word is impassible,[49] so those who are the image of Mind ought to strive to imitate his passionlessness.[50] Clement's equation of sin with irrationality[51] correlates with his conviction that deliverance from sin cannot be won without a teacher,[52] so that the effect of this teaching is for Clement closely connected to healing from vice and passion.[53] Yet Christ the Teacher works not simply to exhort, but to transform; what he effects in us is above all regenerative [ho anagennōn ton anthrōpon].[54]

Remarkably, for all its pronounced intellectualism, Clement's Christology also has a place for the body: Christ is the good teacher, and the wisdom and word of the Father, the physician and saviour who heals body and soul.[55] Indeed, Christ is admirable in every respect, and even though Clement here quotes Isaiah ('He had neither form nor comeliness', 53.2), he claims Christ was possessed of beauty of both body and soul; his was a true beauty, however, one not visible to the eye.[56] Because the Word was made flesh, he exhibits virtues that are both contemplative and practical.[57] The emphasis on the practical side of the Saviour's mission can on occasion even eclipse his role in transforming the mind: Clement claims that the Teacher's mission is practical, and not

---

[45] 2.936 P. [46] 6.9. [47] 1.7P. [48] Str 6.9. [49] Str 6.9; Paed 1.2. [50] Str 1.9.
[51] Paed 1.2. [52] Paed 1.1. [53] Paed 1.2.
[54] Prot. 11.90P. Cf. H. Chadwick's claim that for Clement, Christ is the uniting principle of all the separate fragments of knowledge (see Armstrong 1967, 170).
[55] Paed 1.2.
[56] Paed 3.1; cf. Str 2.5. Clement here contrasts the beauty of *sarx* with the true beauty of *sōma*, yet also speaks of the *sarx* as *athanaton* (immortal), so his paradox cannot be entirely explained by the *sarx–sōma* distinction.
[57] Paed 1.3.

theoretical, his aim being to improve the soul rather than teach, to train for a life that is virtuous rather than intellectual.[58]

If the Saviour can be deemed beautiful, this beauty is no doubt that of a perfect image. Like that of Origen, Clement's theology of the imago Dei entails Christ's being the image of the Father and humanity's being merely the image of that image, or imitators twice removed from the source.[59] Christ possesses both the image and the likeness of God, and we, the image alone,[60] and it is the task of the Word (for Clement has little to say of the Spirit), to restore the tarnished likeness by providing the teaching and example that enable us to fashion ourselves after him.

The Christological focus of Clement's work seems to overwhelm the doctrine of God as a whole, so that attributes in other theologies appropriated to the Spirit are here associated with the Son. Wisdom, for example, often seems to be generically divine;[61] certainly, its provenance is solely divine.[62] More specifically, however, Christ himself is wisdom.[63] Elsewhere, Clement seems to undermine the identification of Christ with Wisdom by claiming wisdom is sold in heaven, purchased with the true coin which is the Word,[64] suggesting that wisdom is that which is obtained through Christ, rather than being Christ himself.

For all its modulations and subtleties, the pattern in both Origen's and Clement's thought is clear: intellect and rationality are key attributes of God. Indeed, when one considers the other commonly-invoked divine attributes, intellect might well claim to be the root of them all. Impassibility, for instance, follows from rationality, inasmuch as the passions are contrary to reason. Goodness and holiness turn out to be the qualities of one who always acts rightly and wisely. Simplicity is linked to intellect inasmuch as what God is simply is intellectual being. If Clement differs from Origen in not grounding his system as thoroughly in the doctrine of God, their commonality lies in a picture of God painted almost entirely in intellectual hues.

Both Clement and Origen also want to say that the human person is made in the image of God and from this point and from the assertion of intellect in God follows the stress on mind in their anthropology. Both theologians assert considerably more than the inescapable – and empirically evident – fact that human beings have minds, for both want to claim we have been given minds expressly for the purpose of communion with God. Not only to know, but to be known is the property of

---

[58] Paed 1.1. [59] Paed 1.2 and 1.12. [60] Paed 1.12. [61] Str 7.7.
[62] Str 6.18. [63] Str 6.7. [64] Paed 2.3.

intellectual existence,[65] and since God is such an intellectual being, there must be knowers to know him. Of course, one might say that God himself is the requisite knower, though neither Origen nor Clement seems much concerned with this kind of affirmation of divine aseity.

The worry that the mind might be taken for a body looms large for Origen, and on the basis that we are able to understand, remember and contemplate divine doctrines he attacks the notion that the mind is a body.[66] The correspondence of God and humanity establishes a central point of anthropology, therefore: that even the human mind is incorporeal. In rejecting Stoic substance metaphysics on this point, Origen allows himself to develop a doctrine of participation that will not imperil his doctrine of God, which will not, in other words, create the systematic conditions under which it might be possible to predicate corporeality of God because minds are taken to be corporeal.

All rational beings, he claims, are partakers of the Word.[67] This assumption implies, as Origen acknowledges, that God is at work in sinners as well as saints, but this is a corollary he must accept if he wishes to maintain a divine monopoly on intelligence. In fact, he is willing to go further, claiming that even non-rational beings participate in the Father.[68] He does not, however, predicate wisdom of the non-rational beings in quite the same way as he does of the rational, nor does he impute to the other animals the desire to know God's truth. Human beings, in contrast, burn with this desire,[69] and God would not have implanted such a desire in us had it been impossible for us to know the causes of things and the design of the universe. Human beings are made to be knowers and their knowledge encompasses both God and creation. If the existence of divine intelligence requires the positing of knowers, the opposite is also evidently true: arguing in reverse fashion, Origen seeks to establish the co-eternity of the Word from the indisputable existence of other rational beings: 'How could rational beings exist, unless the Word or reason had existed before them?', he asks.[70]

Clement, too, wants to assert a correspondence between God and humanity, but, unlike Origen, tends to assert this resemblance only of human beings and asserts it in rather more substantial terms than Origen does. He writes: 'The other works of creation he made by command alone, but the human person he formed by his own hand and breathed into her something of his own.'[71] In the *Protreptikos* he is willing to claim

---

[65] PArch 1.1.8. [66] PArch 1.1.7. [67] PArch 1.3.6. [68] PArch 1.3.6.
[69] PArch 2.11.4. [70] PArch 1.2.4. [71] Paed 1.3.

an apparent continuity of substance, something of the divine's being instilled in us not only in virtue of our humanity *tout court*, but also in virtue of a willingness to dedicate ourselves to the life of the mind.[72] So, while there is an innate communion between humankind and heaven, it is darkened by ignorance; erroneous theology turns us from a heavenly way of life [ouraniou diaitēs],[73] and this variability implies that it is the better part of virtue to strive to assimilate ourselves to the Image.[74] Nevertheless, for all his stress on human striving, the dominant themes emerging from Clement's theology are of God's work, of our adoption as children of God, and the attendant assertion of an innate correspondence between us and God: 'As soon as [God] conceived the thought, we became his children.... he concerns himself with the human person herself, focusing all his care on her, regarding her as his greatest work, placing her soul under the direction of intelligence and temperance, and adorning her body with beauty and grace'.[75]

Although he does not express himself in the (perhaps recklessly) substantial terms that Clement uses, in addition to the innate endowment of the imago Dei, Origen is willing to posit further a kind of continuing participation in God as the ground of various human faculties: the Father gives the gift of existence, holiness comes from the participation in the grace of the Spirit, and participation in Christ confers rationality.[76] The assertion of this participation stands alongside appeal to the image and Origen seems to regard the Word's status as image as the basis for asserting the participation of rational creatures.[77] He does not specify the relation between what we can anachronistically call nature and grace, or between the work and the effect of the Son and that of the Spirit, or indeed, even seem to see a potential problem in not sorting out these matters. However a reason for holding that rational creatures necessarily participate in the Spirit is readily extrapolable from the system itself: Origen does not envisage a rational being without will, and it is in virtue of the latter that the creature participates in the Spirit. Indeed, one can, through the assent to evil and adoption of wicked modes of life, become a participant in evil spirits as well,[78] and since every rational being has been said to participate in the Holy Spirit, it would appear to be possible simultaneously to participate in God and the demons – another problem Origen does not attempt to resolve.[79]

---

[72] 6.59P. [73] Prot 2.21P. [74] Paed 1.2. [75] Paed 1.2. [76] PArch 1.3.7–8.
[77] See, for example, PArch 2.6.3. [78] PArch 3.3.3.
[79] Bertrand maintains that the mind itself is threatened with becoming impure, because it is capable of losing itself as the demons did (1999, 361).

Participation in the Trinity nevertheless is said to endow human beings with certain distinctive qualities. The immortality of the soul, for example, is attributable to the eternity of the Trinity in which human nature has a share.[80] While Origen grants that there can be differing degrees of participation in the Trinity,[81] a quality like eternity does not admit of variation by degree, and so we must assume that all souls participate in the Trinity, at least in this respect, in unqualified fashion. In other respects, the degree of participation in God seems to vary so that, for example, the intellectual virtues such as prudence and wisdom show the marks of the divine image in the person possessing them.[82] Clement, in contrast, attributes immortality not to participation in God's eternity, but to an entitlement based on the possession of knowledge.[83] It is this knowledge (rather than the faculty of intellect itself) that distinguishes us from other animals; without knowledge of the Word and the attendant illumination, we would be no different from the birds, fed and fattened up for the sole purpose of dying.[84] For all these differences, there is a common denominator in Clement and Origen, namely that such definitively human endowments as immortality are linked, via the intellect, to particular Persons of the Trinity, although the precise reasoning used by each theologian is different.

Both Origen and Clement are careful to specify the ways in which humankind resembles and does not resemble other animals. Origen, for all his relentless interest in mind as a key attribute of both God and humanity, does not claim that the soul is what distinguishes us from the beasts, as one might expect. Some of the other animals possess imaginations, for example: the spider envisions the web she will spin.[85] Origen is willing to allow the spider her imagination despite his definition of a soul as an existence possessing imagination and desire [substantia phantastikē et hormetikē; the Greek terms are used in the midst of the Latin text].[86] This view does not disrupt Origen's system because he posits, not the soul, but the faculty of reason, as that which distinguishes the human from the other animals. All living creatures, even aquatic life, have souls;[87] the human animal has something else in its nature besides soul with its imagination, however, and this is reason.[88] It is reason that allows us to choose rightly between the different courses of action we can envisage with the imagination, and the beasts are therefore not deemed capable of moral reflection or action.

---

[80] PArch 4.4.9.   [81] PArch 4.4.9.   [82] PArch 4.4.10.   [83] Str 6.8.   [84] Prot 11.87P.
[85] PArch 3.1.2.   [86] PArch 2.8.1.   [87] PArch 2.8.1.   [88] PArch 3.1.3.

However much God exceeds us, we cannot deem ourselves worms in comparison with him, because we possess reason, reason originates from the Logos, and we can therefore never be utterly alienated from God.[89] Origen's insistence on the dignity of human nature in its distinction from the other animals also leads him to reject Plato's doctrine of reincarnation. It is unthinkable that rational beings should be reborn as irrational animals, and he accordingly rejects Plato's view of the matter.[90] The fact that this is the only argument Origen gives against the Platonic doctrine of the transmigration of souls – of the many Christian arguments he might have made – indicates the power of the notion of the intellect in his work.

Although only humankind is said to be made in the image of God, since reason is the sole possession of human and heavenly beings (and *probably* God, Origen says, in a puzzling moment of uncertainty),[91] all living creatures are said to possess souls, and, having these, to be capable of feeling and movement.[92] The distinctive quality of rational beings is that they have motion *through* themselves, that is, that they are self-propelling.[93] The rational beings differ also in that God is said to become 'all in all' in them, but not in irrational animals.[94] Although God cannot be said to indwell evil or lifeless things in any sense, Origen does appear to be suggesting that rationality is the faculty in virtue of which sanctification and consummation are possible.

The most significant similarity between human beings and the beasts is that both are animals, as both Origen and Clement freely acknowledge, their stress on the intellect notwithstanding. As Clement notes, the irrational animals fight, breed and die, and these things, being in accordance with their nature, cannot possibly be unnatural to us.[95] Both theologians nevertheless accord the body a frankly secondary status. For Origen, the body is at best a kind of warehouse in which the soul is stored: 'A human being is a soul using a body, the soul being called the inner person [anthrōpos]';[96] or the clothing [idumentum] in which it is garbed.[97] Likewise, in Clement's view, one cares for the body, not as an end in itself, but only for the sake of the soul[98] and the effect of the Word's teaching is to bring us away from external things, attending to the

---

[89] CCels 4.25. [90] CCels 3.75; cf. 8.32. [91] CCels 4.85. [92] PArch 2.8.1.
[93] Pray 6.1. [94] PArch 3.6.2. [95] Str 7.4.
[96] CCels 7.38. R. Williams claims that for Origen, the soul as such cannot be the organ of salvation, because it is not really *capax Dei*. In his view, *nous* and *psychē* never become interchangeable; *nous* always remains the superior part of the soul (1985, 134 and 136). Cf. Crouzel on Origen's trichotomic anthropology and mind as the higher element of the soul (1989, 88).
[97] PArch 2.3.2. [98] Str 4.5.

body instead of to the mind.⁹⁹ However, at least for Clement, secondary status is not per se demeaning: the soul is humanity's better part, so it is not to be deemed good and the body bad.¹⁰⁰ Although Clement clearly privileges the body, he does not view it as a barrier to holiness; the flesh must be sanctified [hagnidzein], but the soul's eye must also be cleansed.¹⁰¹

Origen's view of the body approaches the more frankly disdainful. While he, too, defines human beings as rational animals,¹⁰² and identifies the animal nature as one composed of a unity of body and soul,¹⁰³ he is notorious for regarding embodiment as a consequence of the Fall; having lost the inclination to virtue,¹⁰⁴ or, as the anathemas would have it, having wearied of contemplation,¹⁰⁵ the pre-existent souls acquired bodies. Likewise, though he chastises some for their failure to articulate a sound doctrine of the resurrection,¹⁰⁶ Origen's own doctrine has been criticised for sometimes at least appearing to deny the resurrection of the body, substituting for it the soul's continuation in a kind of ethereal existence: 'Those who in the end shall be subjected to God will lay aside their bodies.'¹⁰⁷ Thus Koetschau; the Latin text, followed by the editors of the *Sources chrétiennes*, omits this passage, including instead a section in which Origen sharply criticises the notion of a bodiless existence. Elsewhere, he firmly acknowledges a resurrection of the body,¹⁰⁸ and this view is even to be found in one of Koetschau's fragments. A further complication is that in the Latin text of *On First Principles*, where Origen speculates about the nature of the next life, he writes, interpreting 1 Cor 7.31, 'The fashion of this world will fall away'; 'it is difficult for us to explain

---

⁹⁹ Paed 2.1.
¹⁰⁰ Str 4.26. Torjesen maintains however that Clement thought the soul was not created perfect, but only with the capacity for virtue; it is through the acquisition of virtue that the soul acquires the resemblance to God that makes possible the perfect contemplation of God (1987, 372).
¹⁰¹ Paed 2.1. ¹⁰² PArch 1.5.2. ¹⁰³ PArch 1.1.6. ¹⁰⁴ PArch 1.8.4.
¹⁰⁵ PArch 2.8.3. This text comes from the anathemas of Constantinople II and, as such, is of questionable authenticity. They are taken as accurate representations of Origen's views by some, notably Koetschau, although not by others, such as the editors of the SC text of *On First Principles* (cf. no. 253, the commentary on Bks I and II, pp. 206–8, n. 27). ¹⁰⁶ PArch 2.10.3.
¹⁰⁷ PArch 2.3.3. Indeed, Dorival claims that the passages in Origen's works that support his endorsement of the resurrection of the body employ the concept of 'flesh' in a non-carnal sense (1987, 310). Osborn, however, claims that in Origen's thought, rational beings need bodies for life and movement and that the original creation was of rational beings who are only separable from their bodies in thought (1987, 364). Crouzel also insists that the body is what characterises the creature for Origen, and that he regards the Trinity alone as incorporeal (1989, 90, 182 and 241; cf., however, p. 259). Cf. also Widdicombe's claim that mind, as Origen perceives it, is the ontological opposite of bodily nature and therefore is especially fitting as a description of God (1994, 23).
¹⁰⁸ PArch 2.10.8.

this world, lest someone get the impresssion that we were affirming the existence of certain imaginary forms that Greeks call ideas. For it is certainly foreign to our way of thinking to speak of an incorporeal world that exists solely in the imagination or the insubstantial region of thought; and I do not see how the Saviour could come from such a place, or the saints go to it.'[109]

If it is difficult to conclude anything about Origen's view of the human body from his uncertain doctrine of the general resurrection, his broader view equally resists any easy summary. The body has a value, qua dwelling of the rational soul, that demands respectful treatment.[110] Nevertheless, embodiment is a humiliating condition,[111] and the body is a hindrance to the contemplative and holy life inasmuch as it provides a constant source of temptation.[112] Origen's distrust of the body is not a form of Manichaeism, or a simple rejection of matter as evil or unnecessary. There is dispute over whether Origen believed that all souls are incorporeal with respect to their proper nature,[113] given that this view does not accord with the claim that life without a body is found in the Trinity alone and that it is only in thought that material substance is separable from rational creatures.[114] The latter text may be an interpolation of Rufinus' and if one takes it as such, then Origen's system could be said consistently to portray embodiment as a punishment that can finally be eluded by the virtuous. For the editors of the *Sources chrétiennes*, Origen's position is easily explained as holding that the soul itself is essentially incorporeal, but is always 'clothed' in a body of some sort.[115] Yet Origen is still willing to admit the possibility that the soul inheres in the seminal particles of the body itself (the origin of the soul being a *dubitum* on which the church had not yet expressed herself),[116] a view that would dignify the body considerably, as well as perhaps pleading its continued existence in the next life. However the problem of ascertaining Origen's view of the body with any certitude will likely remain intractable, barring a miraculous discovery of the complete Greek text. Nevertheless, in claiming that the body is properly speaking a dead

---

[109] PArch 2.3.6. Before this passage (in 2.3.3), Koetschau introduces a Greek fragment, which agrees with the testimony of Jerome (Ep. ad Avitum 5). In this section, Origen speculates that in the next life, all will lay aside their bodies and bodily nature will dissolve away into non-existence, only to emerge again if the rational beings fall a second time (PArch 2.3.3). The SC edition does not include this text, and the usual difficulties obtain in determining how accurately it represents Origen's views.
[110] CCels 8.30.   [111] CCels 6.17.
[112] PArch 1.8.4; cf. 3.4.4. The Greek version of this text is in Koetschau, but not the SC edition.
[113] PArch 1.7.1.   [114] PArch 2.2.2.   [115] Vol. 2, p. 105, n. 4.   [116] PArch 1.prae.5.

thing,[117] Origen does no more than subscribe to the usual patristic anthropology, in virtue of which the soul animates the body and the body's death comes about as a result of the separation of the body from this animating principle, a notion that does not denigrate the body, but simply makes it dependent on the soul.

The notion of inter-dependency governs more than the relation of the constituents of human nature, for Origen and Clement portray human beings as innately social; as Clement says, 'God has created us sociable and righteous by nature',[118] and however many later theologians would disagree with the second of these assertions, few would dispute the first. Here, too, the relentless intellectualism of the early Alexandrians manifests itself, for the social element of human nature devolves on its rationality. Origen, indeed, espouses a notion of solidarity that asserts unity of substance: all rational beings come from one lump of dough [phuramatos/natura].[119] At times, this commonality appears to be acquired rather than innate, for every mind that shares in the intellectual light is said to be of one nature with every other mind which shares this light.[120] Perhaps Origen means to designate by these assertions no more than the commonality of those with similar capacities, but it seems more is intended, and if so, then what in later centuries is called human nature is for Origen a unity of substance possessed in distinct individuals in virtue of their having an intellect, and, perhaps, of their directing their mind to a common end.

Whatever similarities there exist among human beings, Origen and Clement are nevertheless both at pains to insist on differences among people as well, usually in terms that sound shockingly elitist to modern ears. Origen, for example, can state bluntly that it is not just anyone who can partake of divine wisdom;[121] one must first learn to make the all-important distinction between the sensible and the intelligible[122] and this finesse does not come readily to all. Clement verges on a kind of hermeticism: 'our tradition is not held in common or open to all', he writes, and it is therefore unnecessary to 'keep secret "the wisdom uttered in a mystery"'.[123] He descends into crude disdain when he complains of the difficulty of presenting complex arguments to those who are 'like pigs in their lack of education'; admittedly, the image derives from Jesus' sayings

---

[117] PArch 3.4.2. This view seems to be Origen's, though the text is a little more ambiguous.
[118] Str 1.6.   [119] PArch 3.1.22; cf. CCels 3.69.   [120] PArch 4.4.9.   [121] CCels 6.13.
[122] CCels 7.37; cf.7.46.   [123] Str 1.12 [1].

(Mt 7.6), but Clement is not above extending it to describe the people he himself must teach.

The frank elitism of the early Alexandrians is nevertheless somewhat tempered by the recognition of the need to preach the gospel to 'all sorts and conditions' of people. 'Let the educated, the wise and the discerning come', writes Origen, 'but let the uneducated, the ignorant and the boorish come also; for the Logos promises them healing, if they will only come, and makes all worthy of God'.[124] Apparently answering criticism, he says, a little defensively, that Christians do everything they can to see that their assemblies include the uneducated,[125] though he adds that the teaching is modified when simple people are present to conceal the more profound truths. He wavers between the high-minded aim of educating everyone to the full extent of their ability,[126] and apparently despairing of really teaching the simple folk any theology and counselling them instead simply to trust themselves to God.[127] However little the masses may be able to understand and however little Origen seems confident of his ability to teach them, he trusts that they have been 'delivered' from their lack of education.[128] A similar tension prevails in Clement's thought, so that he can both justify the rudimentary catechesis by claiming that the Lord himself did not reveal to the people in the street what was not for them,[129] yet also recognise that it is possible to have faith while being illiterate.[130]

The meticulous hierarchy of intelligence echoes the careful gradations of Origen's cosmological hierarchy, and his disinclination to glorify God by despising humanity arises not from any unduly sanguine view of human nature, but from his high view of one of the key attributes of God, namely mind. Origen's cosmology and doctrine of the Fall constitute one of the most original, as well as the most problematic, parts of his theology. It is an indication of the significance of the intellect in his theology that these are also loci where the intellect plays a decisive role. Because of the controversy about, and eventual condemnation of, Origen's thought on these subjects, the relevant sources are corrupt: we have the anathemas of Constantinople II, whose reliability as guides to Origen's thought is disputed, along with Rufinus' Latin translation of *On First Principles*, whose theology was possibly altered to shield Origen from as much censure as bowdlerising could. What is common to both the anathemas and Rufinus' text is, broadly, the notion that the Fall was

---

[124] CCels 3.48. [125] CCels 3.53. [126] CCels 6.13–14. [127] CCels 4.9.
[128] CCels 6.14. [129] Str 1.1. [130] Str 1.6.

the result of a lessened desire for participation in God, with this participation being conceived in largely intellectual terms. As Jerome presents Origen's views, the Fall represents a conversion of mind to soul, a loss of original dignity of the mind.[131] In a fragment of Greek text, however, Origen (admittedly in obviously speculative fashion) maintains that the body is not primary, but was created at intervals on account of falls that happened to rational beings, and that when these are restored to perfection, their bodies dissolve into nothing.[132]

The charge of the anathemas is slightly different. On this account, Origen believed that the original creation was entirely immaterial and all the rational beings in it formed a numerical unity, both because of their identity in essence, power and energy, and by their union with and knowledge of the Second Person, the Word. This mass of bodiless minds united to God and to each other was engaged in the love and contemplation of God, and the Fall occurred only when they tired of intellectual adoration. Embodiment not only follows as the direct consequence of this failure of attention in this account, but the kind of body a creature acquires was attendant on how fully it inclined to turn its mental gaze from God, so that some gained bodies composed of a fine substance, and others, bodies of something more crassly material.[133] The anathemas concur with Rufinus in additionally claiming that fallen minds were called souls, and from this concurrence, one can either conclude the general reliability of the anathemas as a guide to Origen's views, or maintain that the latter cannot be validly inferred from concurrence on a single point. That the original creation was incorporeal is attested by Jerome, whose witness on this point Koetschau takes to be unquestionably reliable and which he accordingly inserts into the Greek text;[134] the *Sources chrétiennes* editors, as per their usual policy, omit it.[135] Origen

---

[131] PArch 2.8.3. Ep ad. Avitum 6, cited in Koetschau's text at PArch 2.8.3. SC does not accept the bald statement 'Mind when it fell became soul', but does accept formulations that are only slightly more oblique that occur earlier in the same section of text.

[132] PArch 4.4.8.

[133] Inserted into Koetschau's text of PArch 2.8.3; cf. his text of PArch 2.1.1. Even Crouzel, whose interpretation of Origen usually differs markedly from that of the anathemas, acknowledges that for him there is a link between sin and earthly corporeality (1989, 215); cf. also Daniélou, 1955, 218.

[134] 3.6.1.

[135] In this connection, we see Origen's curious depreciation of the soul – 'mind when it fell became soul' (PArch 2.8.3; this text comes from Jerome, but the same idea is expressed almost identically in Rufinus' Latin text (PArch 2.8.3) and is accepted by Crouzel and Simonetti). Coming as they do from Rufinus (perhaps) and the anathemas respectively, these ideas may not be those of Origen himself, but if they are taken as consonant with those views which we can be certain are his, then he elevates both mind and will above the level of soul, regarding the latter as the product of the degradation of the former.

regards himself as having Biblical support for his notion of the mind's superiority to the soul. Citing 1 Cor 14.15, 'I will pray with the Spirit; I will pray with the mind also', he concludes tentatively and conjecturally, as he often does, that Paul associates the mind rather than the soul with the Holy Spirit, so that it is the mind and not the soul which is *capax Dei*.

In the *Contra Celsum*, in contrast, Origen asserts that the entire intricate order of creation is God's work, and not just the rational soul,[136] which implies that the soul is God's handwork also, and not the unfortunate result of human error. The *Contra Celsum* also evidences no suggestion of the material order as fallen in its origin and very nature. The whole world is the temple of God[137] and no substance or thing in it is evil, strictly speaking.[138] Even the demons are the fruit of the divine intelligence and design, not inasmuch as they are demons, certainly, but inasmuch as they, too, are rational beings. The non-rational elements of the cosmos, while not evil, are nonetheless clearly subservient; all else was created to serve the rational beings and their intelligence.[139] The non-rational creation's secondary role in the schema indicates the rational beings ought to turn their attention away from what is created (away, that is, from both anything that is below them and from themselves) and towards the supreme God.[140]

In Origen's view, the object of creation is the restoration of the rational beings to a state of communion with God. The highest good is to become as far as possible like God; it is towards this goal that all rational nature is progressing.[141] The process of growth towards God is one of consistent cleaving to virtue, but this virtuous living is conceived of in rather intellectual terms, for it is a matter of doing everything according to reason.[142] It is our capacity for virtue and wickedness that makes us worthy of praise or blame,[143] and we are worthy of progressing to the beatitude of the divine things [*ta theia*] and being drawn towards the Logos according to the degree to which we have kept our rational nature pure.[144]

Cleaving to God and living virtuously means rightly using the will, and one of the most important elements of the Alexandrian anthropology is the free will.[145] Because both are convinced that salvation comes to those

---

[136] 4.54. [137] 7.44. [138] 4.66. [139] 4.78. [140] 3.81. [141] PArch 3.6.1.
[142] CCels 4.29. *Panta prattein kata ton logon*; SC translates *logon*, not as reason, but as Logos, while H. Chadwick translates 'reason'. The Greek is of course inherently ambiguous.
[143] PArch 1.3.8. [144] CCels 6.44.
[145] Cf. Crouzel: human freedom is one of the controlling ideas of Origen's theology (1989, 211); the same could be asserted of Clement.

who strive for righteousness, and indeed, perfection, the assertion of free will is crucial to their soteriology, moral theology, doctrine of sanctification and eschatology. For both theologians, the will is dependent on the mind inasmuch as by means of the will one effects what has first been conceived by the mind. The capacity for sin, therefore, only properly speaking arises in one who has a mind: we can only be said to sin if we first share in the Word and are capable of understanding.[146] Thus all rational creatures are capable of good and evil;[147] this capacity seems in fact a defining characteristic of the genus. Once the capacity for sin is acquired (presumably at the point at which a child reaches the age of reason), actual sin occurs when one fails to adhere to that which reason ordains.[148]

Part of the reason for the insistence on human freedom derives from the desire to avoid portraying God as a tyrant; the Logos rules no one who does not want him as Lord, says Origen.[149] Clement goes one step further, not simply asserting that freedom of the will is attendant on the intellect, but extolling the liberty of the mind itself.[150] Clement however posits a double transaction of intellect and will: on the one hand, he regards reasoned reflection as the guiding power within us, the pilot of the soul;[151] on the other hand, he claims that in contemplation the will leads the way and the powers of reason are naturally the servants of the will.[152] There is not so much contradiction here as a chicken-and-egg problem that admits of no resolution: one must envisage that which one wishes to do before one does it, yet one must will to envisage it in the first place. The condition of willing and thinking anything whatsoever, of course, is freedom, and so, like Origen, Clement quarrels with those who would deny human freedom;[153] freedom, for Clement, is the ground of virtue.[154] Yet freedom and the intellect exist in a symbiotic relationship: Origen speculates that the intellectual light of human beings comes from their freedom,[155] so that intellect is at once freedom's ground and the product.

If in this life, we focus unduly on the wrong things, failing to direct our minds [*motus animarum*] to God, God will withdraw from us.[156] Yet, although ridding ourselves of evil apparently lies within our own powers, ascending to God requires God's assistance. Thus Origen can contrast human means and divine ends, praying that he will treat his subject not

---

[146] PArch 1.3.6.   [147] PArch 1.8.3.   [148] PArch 1.5.2.   [149] CCels 8.15.   [150] Rich 14 943 P.
[151] Str 2.11.   [152] Str 2.17.   [153] Str 2.3.   [154] Str 5.1.   [155] CCels 5.10.
[156] PArch 2.9.2. The Latin here might be translated as 'souls', but both Butterworth and the SC editors instead use 'minds' (French: *intelligences*).

with the aid of merely human wisdom, but by receiving the mind of Christ.[157] Here he seems to express a classic doctrine of synergy: we do not rise to the perfect contemplation of God unaided, but God does not give the assistance needed for growth to those who will not make an effort of their own. For all his affirmation of human capacities, Origen is well aware of human contingency: the goodness in us is not ours by nature, but is the fruit of the Creator's generosity: what they are is not theirs properly and eternally, but is given by God, on loan, as it were.[158]

For all the early Alexandrians' emphasis on striving and self-improvement, their theologies are by no means devoid of a doctrine of grace. Origen seems flatly to contradict the general tenor of his theology when he writes: 'It is not within our power to put away wickedness . . . . it is the work of God . . . something due entirely to divine grace'.[159] The contradiction is only apparent, for as he goes on to explain, this grace takes the form of a knowledge implanted in those who come to knowledge, taking away their stony hearts and wickedness and enabling them to walk in the way of the divinely-given commandments,[160] though it is not entirely clear whether grace is bestowed in order that we may keep the commandments we have been given, or whether knowledge of the commandments wholly constitutes this grace. However insufficient human will may be for us to attain our end, we are not perfected without some effort on our own part,[161] yet, as is clear from his discussion of the will and freedom, neither are we perfected as the result of our own efforts. Origen is content to allow the synergistic paradox without attempting to solve it.

Origen's doctrine of grace becomes most insistent in connection with his doctrine of the knowledge of God. Both *On First Principles* and the *Contra Celsum* are punctuated with assertions of Origen's own inability to answer his opponents and his disavowal that any competence to do so comes from within himself. He can answer Celsus only if God helps him and Christ dwells in his soul,[162] and he acknowledges his need of divine assistance if he is to write his treatise at the beginning or end of almost every book.[163] For all the high role of the mind in Origen's works, he is well aware of the human mind's fragility and, especially, its inadequacy to the task of theology.[164] For this reason, he not only acknowledges his

---

[157] CCels 5.1. [158] PArch 2.9.2. [159] PArch 3.1.15.
[160] PArch 3.1.15, quoting Ezekiel 11.19–20. NB Crouzel's equation of purity of heart with purity of mind and his claim that the virtue most closely associated with knowledge is purity of heart (1989, 101; cf. also 142, on the equation of bodily chastity with purity of heart).
[161] PArch 3.1.19. [162] CCels 2.128. [163] CCels 1.71; 2.79; 4.1 and 99; 5.1; 7.1; 8.1.
[164] PArch 1.1.9.

need for grace, but proclaims his willingness to conform the mind to the 'rule of piety'; only then will his work escape being merely a composition depending on mere human eloquence.[165] Indeed, even with diligence and a mind enlightened by the gift of grace, no one will be able to satisfy the mind's desire to understand or reach the end of theology.[166] Origen's acute awareness of his own intellectual frailty is evident, too, especially in *On First Principles*, in his stress in the preface to Book I on the teaching of the church and the Rule of Faith, as well as in his forthrightly stated willingness to stand corrected: 'For our part, we ask to be allowed to mention these things, but as hypotheses to be discussed and then rejected';[167] likewise, he leaves it to the reader to choose between the two views of the body he has discussed.[168] Impelled at once by the desire to explicate the faith and to acknowledge his own weakness, he can do no more than admit he has not done justice to his subject,[169] a problem particularly acute in relation to the doctrine of God. Clement's synergism is perhaps formulated more lucidly when he says that if God saves us against our will, this is an act of force, but when he saves us when we choose, this is an act of grace.[170]

Though Clement is less likely to plead his own inadequacy or invite his own correction, he insists fully as much as Origen does on the necessity of grace if the mind is to reach its goal.[171] Not without grace, he says, is the soul winged and not without grace does it soar;[172] if he here borrows a well-worn Platonic image, his insistence on grace is characteristically Christian. Clement, moreover, speaks of a form of direct divine inspiration at which Origen only hints. He distinguishes between someone's talking about truth and truth's giving an account of herself, the first being the mere likeness of truth and the second, its actuality.[173] Grace, it seems, is a tutor of immediacy, by means of which we understand the Unknown God.[174]

Although Origen sounds at times breathtakingly semi-Pelagian by the standards of later orthodoxy, he does not think we attain to virtue and to God solely through our own effort. We are constantly being instructed and trained by heavenly powers,[175] or at least, those who have not completely given themselves over to a dissolute life are so instructed. Origen even speculates that perhaps such mental training continues into the next life, so that those who have devoted themselves to the pursuit of wisdom in this life, and thereby purified their minds, will be further

---

[165] PArch 4.3.14. [166] PArch 4.3.14. [167] 1.8.4. [168] 3.6.9. [169] PArch 1.1.9.
[170] Rich 21 947P. [171] Str 5.1. [172] Str 5.13. [173] Str 1.7. [174] Str 5.12. [175] PArch 1.6.3.

improved in an intermediate (purgatorial) stage of the next life, advancing to a still richer understanding of the truth.[176]

One implication of the early Alexandrians' insistence on the mind's gracing is for theological method. Obviously, both Origen and Clement make use of classic techniques of argumentation and are reliant on ancient philosophy to make their case. Origen justifies these props (though the fact that he does so indicates his awareness that they are potentially objectionable) by noting that Paul did not include argumentation among the things that separate us from Christ,[177] yet he can also declare his contempt for anyone whose beliefs are shaken by either Celsus or plausibility in argument.[178] Origen is not, however, asserting a supra- or a-rational Christianity over against a rational Greek philosophy, but rather bewailing the latter's speciousness;[179] Paul knows, says Origen, that there are impressive doctrines in Greek philosophy which are convincing to most, but nevertheless not true.[180] At one level, the cleverness of these arguments is largely irrelevant given, as Origen notes drily, that most people are not keen on rational thought anyway.[181] Those who do not incline to the life of the mind can still come to faith in Christ, but to do so requires good fortune; in the absence of luck, there is no substitute for vigorous examination of the relevant evidence.[182]

Origen's ambivalence about the Greeks' tools of argumentation emerges in a single passage of the *Contra Celsum*, where in one breath he claims that writers endowed with divine power accomplished far more than if they had merely resorted to logical argument, and yet, in the next, commends Christian doctrine for being in accord with universal notions and therefore capable of changing people's minds.[183] Nevertheless, there is no other cure for human argumentation than more of the same; as he notes wryly, doctrines opposed to the truth are destroyed by God's truth,

---

[176] PArch 2.3.1.   [177] CCels prae 3.   [178] CCels prae 4.
[179] I therefore cannot concur with Kobusch, who claims that for Origen, Greek philosophy is the reflective form of human reason (1987, 442). An additional problem with philosophy is that it cannot cure the one ill that really matters: sin (Crouzel, 1989, 158). Daniélou considers that Origen regarded philosophy as a participation in this world, whereas faith was a participation in the real world (1955, 73).
[180] CCels prae 5.   [181] CCels 1.9.
[182] CCels 3.38. Note the difference between Daniélou and H. Chadwick on Origen's conception of the relation of the Bible and philosophy. For Chadwick, while philosophy is not indispensable for receiving the truth of revelation, logic is of great utility in defending Christianity (Armstrong 1967, 185), while for Daniélou, scripture was the centre of Origen's life and he studied philosophy only as an aid in gaining a better understanding of God's word and to enable him to explain it to his contemporaries (1955, 131).
[183] CCels 3.39–40.

so we need words to root out ideas contrary to the truth.[184] The alleged effects of argumentation, however, vary considerably on Origen's account. On the one hand, sincere devotion is never disquieted by plausible arguments, any more than it is shaken by fatigue, pain or fear of death.[185] On the other hand, the doctrines of truth, rightly stated, are capable of effecting moral reformation.[186]

We can distinguish in Origen's thought an attitude towards what one might call debaters' tricks, and perhaps also philosophers' tools, and reason itself; since the latter comes from the Logos, Origen can scarcely oppose it.[187] Those who wish to honour the Logos may do nothing irrational, he maintains,[188] and this presumably includes not only resisting the passions, but also refraining from making poor theological arguments.[189] If Origen is willing to disagree with Celsus' contention that God is not attainable by reason,[190] it must be because he cannot envisage any faculty by which we would attain to God other than the mind. To be sure, God is not attainable by the naked human intellect, but because the Logos comprehends the Father, it must be the case that the Father can be grasped by those to whom the Logos reveals the Father. Because of this heavy insistence on divine aid, it is not surprising that Origen maintains theological truth does not admit of demonstration based on appeal to the senses, so if, for example, we are to reach the conclusion that the heavenly bodies are created, it is only reason, and not the senses, that could lead us to do so.[191]

Clement's attitude towards argumentation shows few of the ambivalences or subtleties of Origen's. At pains to distinguish between demonstration proper and mere syllogism, where the conclusion is validly deduced from premises that may or may not be true,[192] he displays no

---

[184] CCels 7.1. In a rather obscure argument, Origen maintains that constructing doctrine according to recognised criteria of rationality is an inescapable requirement of the Christian theologian, for if the world has an appointed end, anyone who constructs Christian philosophy will have to argue the truth of her doctrine with arguments from scripture and reason (CCels 4.9).

[185] CCels 4.26.   [186] CCels 4.4.

[187] Origen's theology is notorious for being speculative, but less well-known for the limits Origen places on speculation. His is a speculation of 'the gaps': speculation is deemed licit where the Bible and the Church do not answer a particular question clearly. Crouzel notes the way in which Origen's theological method was misunderstood when he was anathematised: those who condemned him had no sense of theology as an exercise – *gymnastikē* – as Origen did (1987, 283).

[188] CCels 8.9.

[189] Indeed, Joseph Trigg argues that appealing to institutional authority is not a real option for Origen because his own principles require that dispute be settled by rational argument (1992, 54). This view perhaps underestimates Origen's own affirmation of ecclesial authority in methodological statements in *On First Principles*, however.

[190] CCels 6.65.   [191] Contrast, however, the view of Roukema (1999, 23).   [192] Str 8.3.

interest in merely syllogistic argumentation. Nevertheless, he does not distrust logical argumentation in general, apparently seeing no possibility of non-syllogistic reasoning's resulting in rhetoric that is merely clever rather than true: demonstration from points admitted to points disputed produces belief, he claims outright.[193] Moreover, unlike Origen, he is willing to allow the validity in a theological context of argument from premises derived from sense-perception.[194] He is also much more likely to acknowledge the compatibility of the classic forms of argument and the Christian faith. One can give a definition, he asserts, of anything of which one possesses knowledge,[195] and he does not seem to anticipate the objection that this implies one can define, and so comprehend, God. Dogma is a logical conception, he claims, and a conception is a state of assent of the mind.[196] Clement here evidences none of the apophaticism and ambivalence regarding the use of logic that we see in later Greek theology; the truth is knowable, he says,[197] and so his work demonstrates that the intellectualism we see in mainstream patristic theology can take quite different forms, some tending to affirm the value of reasoning and logic, some tending to deny.

The Alexandrians' conception of mind shapes their notion of theological method, even though they agree in taking the highest view of mind, yet differ in the conclusions they reach regarding method. Origen affirms that he will construct a rational system, one that uses elementary or foundational principles and cogent arguments to produce a single body of doctrine consisting of theorems that follow logically from axioms.[198] Furthermore, he will extrapolate from the visible to the invisible.[199] In affirming a form of what might loosely be called natural theology, he seeks to ground his system in something more reliable than human feelings, namely in the Creator's own works. His purpose is nonetheless quite different from that of the Enlightenment thinkers who made natural arguments for the existence of God, for he declares that the faith is not something that needs to be proved by human reason, and that his purpose in pursuing particular points is only to follow the inquiry where it logically leads.[200] The line between the two is very fine, of course, and Origen does not trouble to explain where he would draw it. It seems to run between the differing sorts of intention, the desire, which he

---

[193] Str 8.3. Cf. H. Chadwick: Clement develops Philo's thesis that philosophy prepares the mind for revealed theology, but is much more interested than Philo is in logic as an indispensable mental skill (Armstrong 1967, 168–69).
[194] Str 8.4.   [195] Str 8.6.   [196] Str 8.5.   [197] Str 8.5.
[198] PArch 1.prae.10.   [199] PArch 2.6.1.   [200] PArch 2.6.2.

implicitly repudiates, to look intellectually strong in the eyes of the world, and the rightful wish to inform inquirers about the faith in a way that is readily graspable, this latter purpose being one also of catechesis, and hence not one a Christian teacher could plausibly reject. What he wants, however, is to present the truth clearly, not to manufacture cleverness. If the tired techniques of human demonstration were actually convincing, then the exposition of faith that made use of them would seem to rest in human wisdom, rather than in the power of God.[201] Some human acumen is needed, though, simply because of the difficulties inherent in the interpretation of the Bible. The scriptures have a hidden meaning; their content is the outward form of the mysteries, the images of divine things;[202] this is the meaning Origen delighted in expounding in his commentaries and homilies. In pursuing 'divine things' in the sacred page, he investigates, not the original authors' intention, but the mind of Christ himself and this, Origen notes, requires grace.[203] Although he neglects explicitly to acknowledge it, it also requires intelligence, skill and careful thought. No matter how often he explicitly eschews reasoning, he proves his estimation of it in the very way he argues.

Clement is on the whole less insistent on hidden meanings of scripture and the consequently oblique methods needed to interpret it rightly, yet admits the enigmatic quality of some of Jesus' utterances. Nevertheless, the sayings which he simplified for the disciples' benefit possess a depth of thought that requires the investment of even greater mental effort than the most mysterious teachings.[204] Despite all of these difficulties inherent in scripture and its interpretation, Clement regards his 'demonstration' as sure to lead to the truth because it derives from scripture, and indeed claims that it is this sort of argument that *alone* leads to truth.[205]

Clement seems overall less interested in deriving theology from scripture than in the appropriate uses of philosophy, although what he calls philosophy includes what would today be termed theology. 'Philosophy' as he uses it can also mean a synthetic system of truth which, taking the good from each of the philosophical schools, combines with the truths of religion and piety.[206] Because philosophy is true, it must be of divine provenance,[207] since there is no source of truth in the world other than God. Clement indeed equates denying philosophy's divine provenance with denying God's sole causality of all that is and God's knowledge of particulars,[208] although the first of these claims would not

---

[201] PArch 4.1.7. [202] PArch 1.prae.8. [203] PArch 4.2.3. [204] Rich 5, 938–39P. [205] Str 2.11.
[206] Str 1.7. [207] Str 1.7. [208] Str 6.17.

hold had Clement more clearly distinguished primary from secondary causality. While philosophy no more encompasses or comprehends the truth than does the human mind itself, it can still function as a useful preparation[209] and can even make human beings righteous,[210] thus preparing the way for faith.[211] By sharpening the mind through its exercise in investigation, moreover, philosophy prepares the mind to rest in Christ.[212] However valuable this preparation, though, philosophy never has greater significance than this for Clement: it is a searching for truth which contributes to our understanding of truth but is not itself the sole cause of our grasp of the truth.[213] The trace of wisdom that is to be found in philosophy is like Promethean fire, stolen from its true source and rightful home.[214] The source of the truth which philosophers have stolen – in fragments – is the Bible and Clement is sufficiently convinced of this point that he bluntly calls the Greek philosophers 'robbers and bandits'.[215] The primacy of revealed wisdom is evident also in Clement's claim that Plato relied on Moses for his legal theory.[216] The church's scriptures are not merely older than the philosophical writings of the Greeks, according to Clement; the latter are directly dependent on the former, their doctrine having been plagiarised [paracharassontas].[217] However, even when he is not directly attributing the truths of philosophy to a Biblical source, he cannot seem to resist using Biblical imagery to account for it: philosophy, he claims, was especially given to the Greeks as their peculiar covenant,[218] although he still views it as given as a stepping-stone to Christ. Even this theft was providential, however, having occurred not by accident, but by divine dispensation [theias oikonomias].[219]

For all his approval of and recourse to philosophy, Clement still does not seem to regard it as a necessary tool of the Christian theologian. It is not a *sine qua non*, he maintains, because the education of Christians is undertaken by Wisdom herself and even illiterates can understand theological teachings through faith.[220] The informing issue on this point seems to be the sufficiency of Christ's teaching; to claim that philosophy adds something to it constitutes an implicit admission that the full truth is not revealed in Christ.[221] The complete and true philosophy is not that of the Greeks, therefore, but the 'foreign' one of the Bible.[222] In one important respect, moreover, Greek thought is fundamentally

---

[209] Str 1.16. [210] Str 1.4. [211] Str 7.3. [212] Str 1.5. [213] Str 1.20. [214] Str 1.17. [215] Str 1.17.
[216] Str 1.25. [217] Str 2.1. [218] Str 6.8. [219] Str 1.19. [220] Str 1.20. [221] Str 1. 100 [1].
[222] Str 2.2.

misguided: our goal in life is not contemplation of the heavens, as the whole 'choir' of philosophers claim,[223] but contemplation of God, the summit of the mind's activity in the view of both Origen and Clement. Some philosophy, then, is valuable, inasmuch as it is simply the cultivation of right reason, which in turn is nothing other than rational righteousness and the avoidance of the irrationality of sin.[224] The cultivated and thoughtful Christian (Clement's 'gnostic') knows to use philosophy prudently, avoiding its excesses. Even the pursuit of what is best in philosophy, however, ranks below higher intellectual pursuits: philosophy is the preferred occupation of one's leisure, to which one turns as relaxation from higher pursuits.[225] It is no mere pastime, nevertheless, but the verbal expression of *ratio*, for Clement's description of philosophy bears a distinct resemblance to Origen's description of his task in *On First Principles*: both are fundamentally systematic enterprises [orthōs sophian technikēn].[226]

The rarified atmosphere of the Alexandrians' discussions of philosophy and theological method never creates the kind of other-worldliness one tends to find in philosophical texts, in part because they never lose sight of the importance of love. If divine aid is vital for the right working of the human mind, it is equally necessary for the will. The will is also the faculty through which we love, and for Origen, at least, love proves determinative of salvation – curiously so, given the prevailing intellectualism of his thought.[227] Rational creatures participate in God in proportion as they cling to him in love.[228] The anathemas would also have it that the cooling of love brings about the Fall in Origen's view, for it is in consequence of this failure to love God rightly that the rational beings come to be called souls.[229] Whether or not this was his own view, he certainly makes love central to both the drama of salvation and the Christian life. Perhaps because of the positive value he accords love, Origen seems less worried about the passions than Clement is. He stresses, of course, that it is possible to live virtuously and, with his characteristic systematic impulse, points out that to deny as much is to impugn the Creator.[230] Wrongly ordered loves (passions such as lust, for example) can be driven out by a single word; hence Christians need not

---

[223] Prot 4.55.   [224] Paed 1.13.   [225] Str 6.18.   [226] Str 6.7.
[227] Note, however, Crouzel: 'L'acte de connaître n'est pas seulement vision ou contact direct, ni même participation, il est l'union dans l'amour du connaissant et du connu' (1985, 324). He similarly insists in his monograph that because Origen's theology is always synthetic, knowledge is the same as love and union (1989, 99).
[228] PArch 2.6.3.   [229] PArch 2.8.3.   [230] CCels 3.69.

have recourse to hemlock and other such depressant devices.[231] This triumph of mind over recalcitrant flesh is not the achievement solely of the intelligentsia, for the masses who are ruled by their passions are also converted,[232] this conversion presumably leading them towards a more virtuous and less passion-ridden life. Because the passions are regarded as an affliction, relief from them is viewed as a form of healing, Christ is seen as the physician who heals the wounds of our souls.[233] Later theology would also consider that humanity stands in need of healing, but would regard the illness as sin, conceived of in exclusively spiritual terms. Origen's conception of healing as specifically healing from passions, and of the passions as the consequence of the mind's loss or surrender of ascendancy, means that healing is of a specifically mental disorder.[234]

Clement, less inclined to appeal to love, is also a much more strident critic of the passions than Origen is. He declares: 'He who does not will to root out the passion of the soul kills himself.'[235] Optimistically, perhaps, he regards the attainment of virtue and the acquisition of salvation as the reward of knowledge.[236] Even emotions such as cheerfulness are suspect and the Gnostic Christian ought not to share them.[237] Rejecting any suggestion of Aristotelian moderation, Clement states that knowledge produces, not the calming or reduction of passion, but impassibility itself.[238] Clement is able to accord love a place in his generally anti-emotional system because he severs it from any connection with desires. Love is a relation of affection, he claims, and it is impossible that the one who has been made perfect in love and who feasts on the limitless joy of contemplation should be subject to such trivial emotions allied with pleasure, pain and fear. At times, Clement seems resolute in his conviction that the Christian can root out the passions unaided and control them, apparently without any external assistance, other than that perhaps implied by the mind's being fixed on God.[239] Elsewhere he not only allows for the work of God, but insists upon it: of the wounds of fear, lust, grief and so on, Jesus is the only healer.[240] Clement's stark disavowal of the emotions nonetheless does not preclude a role for love in his

---

[231] CCels 7.48.   [232] CCels 2.79.
[233] CCels 4.15. In Crouzel's view, for Origen apatheia means, not the eradication of the passions, but finding an Aristotelian mean (1985, 13).
[234] Note that whatever credence Origen gives to controlling the passions, he uses the word apatheia very rarely; cf. Somos 1999, 365 and Crouzel, 1989, 7. Both Somos and Crouzel agree that Origen rather favours the concept of *metriopatheia*, or restraint of the passions (see Somos 1999, 371 and Crouzel, *loc. cit.*)
[235] Str 7.12.   [236] Str 7.12.   [237] Str 6.9.   [238] Str 6.9.   [239] EE [Stählin 3.221].
[240] Rich 29; 952 P.

thought, though it is a minor role compared to the one it has in Origen's oeuvre.

Origen's conviction that perfect sanctification comes of directing the mind towards God prescribes also his attitude towards occupying the mind with other things. We simply do not have time to pursue the eternal things when we are obliged to bother about the needs of the body.[241] In pointing to the necessary connection between intellectual pursuits and the leisure needed for contemplation, Origen might be taken as displaying elitism, but he does not in this respect denigrate the body so much as show how it distracts attention from what is salvific and sanctifying. The mind as well as the body requires constant exercise if it is to grow strong and increase in magnitude.[242] Like Irenaeus, Origen believes that it is natural for us to grow and develop and while he does not look upon the earlier stages of human development with the same fond and indulgent gaze as the bishop, neither does he condemn human infancy as such.

The ultimate growth is of course towards the perfection of paradise and Origen's theology is constructed always with the next life in mind; Clement is overall less interested in either sanctification or eschatology. His understanding of what it means to be holy, however, closely resembles Origen's. The virtues include knowledge of the truth,[243] and both inclination towards right conduct and the desire for truth are linked in being identified as God's greatest gifts.[244] The good of creation is restored through the gift of the commandments, through which the soul learns to choose what is highest.[245] Clement provides for a sort of natural virtue, a virtue that is not the product of instruction and learning, but education still speeds its acquisition.[246] Clement views the virtues as so closely linked together that a person who possesses any one of them and also has revealed knowledge can be said to have any one of them.[247] Because of these close linkages, the person who experiences the virtues as a whole also has salvation.[248] As with Origen, sin is for Clement in the first instance a form of thoughtlessness, of irrational behaviour. Self-control [engkrateia], or continence, consists in never going beyond the conclusions of right action.[249]

Clement allows a greater role for the body in his understanding of sanctification inasmuch as he points to baptism as key to our growth towards God. In keeping with the use of the early church, he calls

---

[241] PArch 3.4.4. [242] PArch 1.1.6. [243] Rich 3.937 P. [244] Str 1.6. [245] Str 1.6.
[246] Str 1.6. [247] Str 2.18. [248] Str 2.18. [249] Str 2.18.

baptism 'illumination' [phōtismos]. The sanctification that comes with the Spirit's descent in baptism bestows illumination and perfection, making illumination the immediate effect of baptism, which leads in turn to adoption, perfection and, ultimately, immortality.[250] Indeed, baptism is the 'one grace' of illumination and the illumination we receive is knowledge [gnōsis]. Clement comes close here to suggesting that a virtual infusion of knowledge accompanies baptism, though he also links growth in knowledge to the Eucharist: we are fed by the blood and milk of the Lord, which are symbolic of his passion and teaching. Having been regenerated in Christ, he nourishes us with the milk of the Word, milk that swells out of breasts full of love.[251] In two ways, then, we are brought into relationship with the one who saves and teaches: we are redeemed by his passion and regenerated by baptism into his death and resurrection; yet the salvation he brings is continually made efficacious through nourishment when we are fed with his blood and milk.

The teaching of the Word is thus allied to the spiritual nourishment of the Eucharist and growth in knowledge of God is thereby not only deemed spiritually salutary, but acquires a quasi-sacramental character. The superiority of this instruction to every worldly philosophy is obvious from the fact that it is the loving God himself who is our Teacher.[252] Listening to the Word is closely linked to being imprinted of the Redeemer's saving life;[253] hearing, then, is already a mode of conformity to God and meditating on the Saviour's life allows us to walk in his footsteps. Distinguishing between virtue and vice is accordingly as simple as discerning the difference between the rational and the irrational:[254] he defines Christian conduct as the operation of a rational soul using the body, in accordance with right judgement and desire for the truth, the body being the soul's natural ally.[255] The Word is a healer, but the saving medicines he administers are rational ones.[256] The life of a Christian can thus be seen as an orderly system of reasonable action.[257]

For Clement the mind proves the relentless guide to right behaviour: one can escape sensible light, but not the mind's light.[258] This light directs us to avoid both large and serious sins such as adultery and fornication, but also such infringements of good breeding as hiccoughing and sneezing at banquets and scratching the ears[259] – the last two attend unbridled fornication, in his view. Such mundane virtues all form part of the soul's study, the end of which is God and in the cause of which

---

[250] Paed 1.6. [251] Paed 1.6. [252] Paed 1.7. [253] Paed 1.12. [254] Paed 1.13.
[255] Paed 1.13. [256] Paed 1.12. [257] Paed 1.13. [258] Paed 2.10. [259] Paed 2.7.

nothing is to be deemed bad but that which is contrary to right reason.[260] Clement wishes always to maintain a tight relationship between the bottom and top rungs of his system of virtues, because the link between them is wisdom: practical wisdom follows knowledge and seems to be higher than ordinary knowledge, for Clement calls it 'divine knowledge'. Self-control, while a good in itself, can be found in those who merely philosophise; practical wisdom, in contrast, exists in those who are deified,[261] for if virtue is divine, Clement reasons, so must be the knowledge of it.[262]

Origen's doctrine of sanctification displays both his exaltation of mind over body, but also his tendency to reach for physical images to describe spiritual experience. Christ's gift to us is that our thoughts can be engaged with God rather than with objects of sense.[263] For this reason, education and intelligence can only be of help in the Christian life.[264] Like Clement, Origen reaches for the imagery of physical nourishment to explain the effect of God on the mind: the living bread is distributed to the mind[265] and the saints thus partake of the spiritual and rational food,[266] a transformation which is effected by the renewal of their mind.[267] Origen acknowledges with a hint of awe the greatness of the gift we have been given in virtue of having a mind: it is superior to any endowment of the other animals, a gift that enables us to overcome wild animals physically much stronger than ourselves.[268] The mind is also central to one of the activities that distinguishes human beings from the other animals, namely prayer; it is with the mind, aided by the Spirit, that we pray.[269] We pray by shutting the eyes of sense (that is, by closing the mind to distractions), with the mind ascending beyond this world.[270] If the mind is sufficiently exercised, it can ascend to the eternal power of God,[271] although Origen recognises the possibility of its becoming sterile.[272]

The salvation wrought by Christ affects the mind, and not just the soul or some spiritual aptitude conceived as independent of any particular human faculty.[273] It is the carnal mind in us that is destroyed [phronēma tēs sarkos],[274] and conversely, the consequence of being blinded in one's mind is that one will not be able to see the Father of mind, the Creator.[275] Despite the fact that Christ heals those sick in mind and illumines the

---

[260] Str 6.14. [261] Str 6.15. [262] Str 6.15. [263] CCels 3.34. [264] CCels 3.49.
[265] Pray 27.9. [266] Pray 27.11. [267] Pray 22.4, quoting Rom 12.2. [268] CCels 4.78.
[269] Pray 20.1 and 2.4. [270] CCels 7.44. [271] CCels 7.46. [272] Pray 13.3.
[273] Cf. Crouzel's view that the distinction between the spiritual and the intellectual is not clear in Christian antiquity generally: you get to God one way or another (1989, 56).
[274] CCels 7.22. [275] CCels 38.

mind of those who are already pure,[276] each one of us is responsible for the evil in our minds.[277] Purity of mind can therefore be maintained only by mental discipline, so it comes as no surprise that he claims we should come to prayer straining not the eyes but the mind,[278] hence his glossing of the command to pray in secret (i.e., presumably in accordance with Jesus' injunction in Mt 6.6) as praying in the mind itself.[279]

Discipline alone will not bring illumination or sanctifying knowledge of God; thus Origen's epistemology expresses greater confidence in the reliability of God's self-disclosure than in human methods of argumentation.[280] All knowledge of the Father is revealed by the Son and made known by the Spirit,[281] and to be separated from this knowledge of God is to be immersed in an ignorance that the Bible describes as the outer darkness – thus Origen's interpretation of Matthew 8.12. To those to whom the Spirit has revealed spiritual knowledge, in contrast, the Spirit provides comfort; knowledge of God delivers the one who receives it from misfortune and subsequently implants blessedness.[282] Unlike Clement, however, Origen recognises the epistemological implications of his doctrine of God: if God is without beginning, he cannot be comprehended.[283] The analogy seems as much temporal as spatial, for Origen says that as far as the understanding stretches out, the ability to understand recedes endlessly.[284] Using language that will be later also adopted by Gregory Nyssen and the Pseudo-Denys, he maintains that God hides himself in darkness from those who cannot bear his radiance.[285] In contrast to later theologians, though, Origen is astonishingly tentative on the question of human capacity to know God: it is possible, he says, that the knowledge of God is beyond the capacity of human nature;[286] Nyssen, for example, grounds the gap rather on the divine side, in infinity. Origen does not seem altogether sure on this point, however, and his uncertainty sits uneasily in the context of his affirmations of the systematic implications of divine eternity and infinity.

If knowledge of God did lie within human capacities, it still would not lie within every human being's capacity since personal holiness is also determinative. To know God, one must be pure in heart,[287] and even

---

[276] CCels 3.61. [277] CCels 4.66. [278] Pray 31.2. [279] CCels 8.74.
[280] Cf. Crouzel's claim that Origen constantly asserts the unknowability of the Father, but that unlike Plotinus' One, the Father reveals himself, according to Origen (1987, 431).
[281] PArch 1.3.4.
[282] CCels 4.6. Cf. Crouzel's assertion that for Origen, knowledge is an improvement on faith in that it affords greater evidence, a direct perception through the five spiritual senses of the reality of the mystery: it is a true experience of God present in the intellect (1989, 113).
[283] PArch 3.5.2. [284] PArch 3.5.2. [285] CCels 6.17. [286] CCels 7.44. [287] CCels 6.369.

refrain from marvelling at the light of the sun, moon and stars: one must rise above all these created things.[288] A relationship of mutual conditioning therefore exists between moral progress and knowledge of God: there can be no progress apart from knowledge of God and purity of heart is the prerequisite of such knowledge.[289] Nevertheless, knowing is per se proper to rational beings: 'Nothing else is more suitable for incorporeal, and above all, intellectual nature than to know and be known', Origen writes,[290] and while this passage concerns the Trinity, there are obvious implications for human knowledge of God as well. He describes an intra-Trinitarian movement of the divine Persons' mutual knowledge, thereby avoiding any suggestion of the intelligible God's being dependent on creation in order to be divine. One important entailment of this construal of rational nature proceeds from its attribution of a constant activity of knowing and being known to intellectual nature, which stipulates the possibility of relation between the divine Persons: we were in a particular sense made for each other, made for a certain relation of regard (to borrow a phrase from Aquinas).

If Origen can on occasion seem unwise in the extent to which he is willing to allow that humankind is capable of knowledge, Clement goes yet further, saying in a phrase that may be no more than colourful (though undoubtedly even as such unfortunate in its implications), 'we can get possession [ktēsasthai] of God through knowledge and apprehension'.[291] For all his confidence in our ability to know God, even by means of human skills such as logic and demonstration, he ultimately grounds this possibility in God's *will* that we know him.[292] Learning and knowledge are the end for which we were made, the object of our birth;[293] knowledge of God is the end for which, above all others, we were made[294] and it is this knowledge which itself confers on us the end of salvation, namely immortality.[295] Conversely, ignorance of God is death; life is only to be had with full knowledge and love of God and growth into his likeness.[296] While conferring immortality, however, knowledge itself is the higher thing: if we had to choose between knowledge of God and everlasting salvation, the Christian 'gnostic' would unhesitatingly choose knowledge, although the question is of course purely hypothetical, since

---

[288] CCels 5.10.
[289] PArch 3.1.24. O'Cleirigh examines the relation between mystical and natural knowledge in Origen's thought and concludes that while there is undoubtedly tension between the two, it is more accurate to say that mystical knowledge perfects, rather than replaces, natural knowledge, at least prior to union with the Logos (1987, 350). Cf. Crouzel (1987, 432).
[290] PArch 2.4.3. [291] Rich 7; 939P. [292] Str 4.6. [293] Str 3.9. [294] Str 6.8.
[295] Str 4.6. [296] Rich 7; 939P.

the two are inseparable as far as Clement is concerned.[297] Eternal life has a particular significance (and one which argues its own necessity, for all of his willingness to conjecture it out of existence), inasmuch as no one in this life has been able to apprehend God visibly.[298] He even equates knowledge with salvation outright when he declares that it is by knowledge we are translated from slavery to adoption.[299] Such claims only make sense in a Christian context if one takes into account that 'knowledge' does not have the associations it has in our day; here it denotes something not narrowly informational, but rather, relational.

No more does Clement ally faith exclusively with the mind's activity. Faith is both a concise knowledge of essentials[300] or is roughly equated with knowledge,[301] and a form of ascent of the soul.[302] At times, he joins both faculties, as when he declares that faith is a voluntarily made hypothesis [hypolēpsis].[303] Like other varieties of knowledge, the starting point of faith is sense perception (here he gives Theophrastus as his authority,[304] just as he later cites Plato as his authority for the view that faith is the mother of the virtues).[305] Elsewhere, faith seems more like a hyperlogical faculty: it travels through the world of perception, overtaking hypothesis and hastening straight to the truth itself.[306] Faith has the additional advantage of being able to arrive at first principles; indeed, the First Cause [archē] is reachable only by faith.[307] If faith seems to endow the human person with superhuman capacities, it is because it is itself superhuman, a form of grace that enables its recipient to climb to heights of understanding that science cannot scale.[308] Yet faith resembles other forms of human inquiry in that it can be both scientific demonstration and conjectural,[309] either built up logically from what is known and given, or speculative – though Clement gives little idea of what such speculative faith would be. More characteristically, he simply allies faith with truth; he approvingly cites Plato's view that to lack faith is either to love falsehood deliberately, or to love falsehood inadvertently, which is a form of senselessness.[310]

Part of the reason knowledge itself is accorded salvific status for Clement is that it is in his view inextricably connected to virtue: works follow knowledge as the shadow the body.[311] Virtues such as patience and self-control are all therefore deemed to be elements of knowledge.[312] So when Clement poses the rhetorical question, 'what is full knowledge

---

[297] Str 4.22. [298] Str 5.1. [299] Str 7.13. [300] Str 7.10. [301] Str 2.4. [302] Str 5.13.
[303] Str 2.6. [304] Str 2.2. [305] Str 2.5. [306] Str 2.4. [307] Str 2.4. [308] Str 2.4.
[309] Str 2.11. [310] Str 2.4. [311] Str 7.13. [312] Str 2.4.

[epignōsis]?', the answer is, inevitably, 'godliness [theosebeia]'.³¹³ Here is another chicken-and-egg problem, however, for we come to know the will of God by doing it.³¹⁴ Clearly, though, living badly, and especially yielding to the passions, effectively blocks out any knowledge of God.³¹⁵ As the tree is known from its flowers, so the way one lives one's life is in fact an accurate indicator of one's knowledge of God, or lack of it.³¹⁶ More starkly, Clement can even suggest that anyone who does not have knowledge of God is wicked.³¹⁷

It is not merely that we cannot do the good without knowing it; we cannot persist in the good without right knowledge, for knowledge produces practice and practice produces habit and disposition.³¹⁸ If in this respect Clement sounds like an Aristotelian, he quickly dispels the impression, for the end of habit is not the perfect mean of moderation, but impassibility.³¹⁹ Perhaps because knowledge is a habit, Clement claims it can never become ignorance; knowledge of what is good is firm and unchangeable.³²⁰ He is also prepared to speak of the turn away from the passions toward knowledge in quite radical terms; just as death is the separation of the soul from the body, so knowledge is a separation of the spirit from the passions, a rational death [logikos thanatos].³²¹ To knowledge also belongs the supreme perfection of assimilation to Christ: by means of the Word, we become word-like.³²²

Clement's high estimation of knowledge is evident from the fact that, unlike most patristic authors, he prizes it beyond even wisdom. Knowledge [gnōsis] differs from wisdom [sophia] in that the latter is the result of teaching (and not the opposite, as one might expect); all wisdom is knowledge, but not all knowledge is wisdom.³²³ Knowledge therefore seems to be the broader and the higher category. This comparative devaluation of wisdom is all the more surprising given that Clement is willing to a large degree to characterise knowledge as the product of logical investigation: true knowledge cannot be overthrown by a process of reasoning, as ignorance can.³²⁴ At one point, Clement flatly states that God is not apprehended by the science of demonstration,³²⁵ a claim consistent with his earlier assertion that first principles are in general not demonstrable,³²⁶ but in tension with his identification of knowledge with demonstration.³²⁷ Nor does he shy from identifying this demonstration

---

³¹³ Prot 9.71P. ³¹⁴ Str 1.7, citing Jn 7.17. ³¹⁵ Str 3.5. ³¹⁶ Str 3.5.
³¹⁷ Str 5.10. ³¹⁸ Str 6.9. ³¹⁹ Str 6.9. ³²⁰ Str 7.12. ³²¹ Str 7.12.
³²² Str 7.10. ³²³ Str 7.10. ³²⁴ Str 2.17; 2.2; 2.10. ³²⁵ Str 5.12. ³²⁶ Str 2.5.
³²⁷ Str 2.11; cf. 7.16.

with the traditions of 'true philosophy', claiming further that it is founded on faith.[328]

What Clement understands by 'demonstration' is a reasoning from some principle to another. Demonstration is demonstrably right when its reasoning is valid; it cannot in itself be proved, however, because first principles cannot be proved. It is for this reason he claims God cannot be apprehended by demonstration, but only by the grace of faith.[329] When one reasons from principles that are entirely sane, such as the revealed truths of scripture, then the demonstration will be as sound as the argument from the principles itself; the scriptures themselves require interpretation (a point that was obvious to the Fathers, though some later theologians would insist scripture is self-interpreting). The scriptures bestow a God-given knowledge; yet with the synergism characteristic of the Greek Fathers, Clement claims God's gift comes to us through our comprehension, and through the true illumination of logical investigation.[330] Right first principles and sound reasoning are not by themselves enough, for there can be no knowledge of God without faith, nor faith without knowledge of God.[331] Hence, Clement is careful to distinguish the salvific knowledge that is his chief concern from 'bare theory'. The kind of knowledge that interests him does not derive from some solitary and genial deduction, but is a 'kind of divine understanding', a light engendered in the soul from obedience.[332]

For all Clement's elevation of knowledge above wisdom, both our early Alexandrians have a high view of the latter. Origen tends to identify it with the Second Person of the Trinity. For him, the Word is called wisdom because the latter reveals to other beings – and not just rational beings, but the whole creation – the meaning of the mysteries and secrets contained in the wisdom of God; wisdom is therefore an interpreter of the mind's secrets.[333] Wisdom and knowledge are thus for Origen distinct but related; along with truth, they are indeed the only sure realities in the world.[334] Yet wisdom has a regulating function *vis-à-vis* knowledge: we need wisdom to pull down the proud thoughts that are a form of self-assertive rebellion [hypsōmata] against the knowledge of God.[335] Moreover, not all wisdom comes from God and it is important to distinguish between divine and human wisdom,[336] a point on which Origen and Plato agree.

---

[328] Str 2.11. [329] Str 2.4. [330] Str 8.1. [331] Str 5.1. [332] Str 3.5. [333] PArch 1.2.3.
[334] CCels 3.72. [335] CCels 4.1. [336] CCels 6.13.

Clement, despite his lower estimation of wisdom, nevertheless makes greater use of it as a category. He claims that wisdom is open to all (this despite the prevailing elitism of his thought), and even loves humankind.[337] Despite its divine provenance, however, wisdom can be augmented by the study of philosophy,[338] and has its beginning in education;[339] notably, Clement's support for this opinion is scriptural (Prov 1.7). If he does not see the tension later ages would anguish over, between reason and revelation, it is because he views wisdom as natural only to the divine,[340] although it can be imparted to creatures. More, it is indisputably a means of apprehending things divine and human,[341] a form of knowledge of things divine and human that is absolutely certain and hence it can be equated with faith when it is devoid of speculation.[342] Nevertheless, though wisdom is nothing but knowledge or science,[343] God can never be known to human wisdom, and for this reason even Moses finds himself forced to enter the darkness. Here, too, we see yet again the deep connection always maintained in Alexandrian theology between the motions and habits of the mind and those of the will and virtue. Clement equates wisdom as both the object of the desire for philosophy and as rectitude of soul, reason, and purity of life,[344] though later in the same chapter he simply identifies Christ with wisdom. The connection of wisdom [phronēsis] to the virtues is not only that it apparently produces virtue, but also it is of this genre of thing that virtues are, namely a habit.[345] 'Wisdom' does not characterise actions that are wise, but is in the first instance a disposition to act wisely.

Clement's view of sanctification seems on the whole more narrowly conceived in moral terms than Origen's and Origen displays a stronger tendency to orient his doctrine of sanctification towards the Age to Come. The highest stage of spiritual development in this life is for him not solely to do as God does, to imitate him, but participation in God; in this respect, Origen stands in the mainstream of patristic theology. He conceives of this participation in dynamic terms: God is always giving a share of His Spirit to those who partake of him.[346] No more than other endowments are, this one is not equally distributed; there is a diversity of participation in the Trinity, Origen claims, varying in proportion both to the capacity of mind and the assiduousness with which it seeks God.[347] Origen maintains this point even though he subscribes to the rather odd view that the minds that share intellectual light are of one nature with all

---

[337] Str 1.1. [338] Str 1.5. [339] Str 2.7. [340] Str 2.9. [341] Paed 2.2. [342] Str 6.17 and 6.7.
[343] Str 4.3. [344] Str 6.7. [345] Str 7.11. [346] CCels 6.70. [347] PArch 4.4.9.

other minds that share in that light.[348] Even though this participation is 'earned' by exertion and desire, it is nevertheless participation itself that makes us wise and spiritual, wisdom coming from participation in the Son and holiness from participation in the Spirit.[349]

Origen vacillates on the subject of a purgatorial state following death, sometimes entertaining the possibility that the end of this world is immediate, with no provision for a purgatorial state. What is significant for our purposes in this speculation is not whether Origen ultimately concludes for or against some sort of purgatory (the state of the texts makes this difficult to determine), but the strongly intellectual character of the purgatory he envisages. Healing will occur in this state,[350] and the improvement to which we will be subjected will doubtless be very painful, but on the whole, this purificatory state seems like a sort of graduate school of theology where those who have majored in wisdom up to the intermediate level can now pursue more advanced thought.[351] On occasion, Origen does not even distinguish between instruction and purity: to be instructed is to become purer in mind.[352]

When completely purified of its vices, the mind will no longer be conscious of anything but God: it will think God and see God and God will be all to it.[353] Not surprisingly, Origen conceives of paradise in overwhelmingly intellectual terms: it will be like a lecture theatre, where the saints will be taught by God himself about creation and its rationale.[354] This happy state will be immediately granted to those who were utterly pure in doctrine, morals, and mind; only these will not have to undergo a preliminary purification by fire.[355] The divine gift given to those who have lived purely is undivided love of God, and to abide in this love is our blessed end,[356] for eternal life is the end toward which God orders every rational soul.[357] For all its intellectualism, however, Origen's notion of union with God in the next life differs sharply from forms of neo-Platonism, inasmuch as in his vision, union with God entails no suppression of the individual.[358]

The height of spiritual development nevertheless remains for both Origen and Clement contemplation, an activity ambiguously allied with both earth and heaven, with this age and the Age to Come.[359] For Origen,

---

[348] PArch 4.4.9. [349] PArch 4.4.5. [350] PArch 2.10.6. [351] PArch 2.11.7. [352] PArch 2.3.1.
[353] PArch 3.6.3. [354] PArch 2.11.7. [355] CCels 5.16. [356] CCels 3.81. [357] Pray 29.13.
[358] Crouzel, 1989, 261. Note that Daniélou in any case declines to call Origen a Neo-Platonist (1955, 78), although he also notes Porphyry's claim that Origen was always reading Plato (*ibid.*, 79).
[359] Cf. Lefeber: 'In Origen's view, prayer is the most decisive act for us to participate in God in order to be saved' (1999, 33).

this contemplation is not simply the summit we reach, but the means by which we ascend: we are made wise and educated by mystical contemplation, he asserts.[360] Yet 'sheer contemplation' of God is also the *terminus ad quem* of human aspiration.[361] Contemplation in Origen's thought stands in sharp contrast to concern for this world, however, and in discussing it, Origen sometimes betrays a degree of otherworldliness that sits in a not entirely comfortable relation to his Christianity.[362] We are, he instructs, to despise all transitory things and seek instead those that are invisible; to see that which is unseen, he says, with a delightful oxymoron that hints of his doctrine of the spiritual senses.[363] He cites the authority of his teachers for the notion that we should dispense with all that is sensible, urging people to contemplation of invisible things, a contemplation he equates with the blessed life, living with God and the friends of God.[364] Elsewhere he can accord a little more good to the material world doomed to decomposition, as at least forming steps to the contemplation of the nature of intelligibles.[365] If sensibles can function as the objects of contemplation, the senses nevertheless have no necessary role in it: the mind is able to contemplate with the naked intellect and reason.[366] This form of intellectual discernment can be called perception, and even though Origen uses the term 'perceive' with some hesitation, here is another hint of his notion of the spiritual senses.

Clement's conception of contemplation seems in many respects less rarefied than Origen's. The desire for it is kindled in our soul by scripture and this fire directs our sight to contemplation.[367] Contemplation is above all a way of life and in particular the fitting way of life for the Christian 'gnostic': it was for this that we were created. Our frame (skeleton) was formed upright so that we might contemplate heaven[368] and contemplation is the wise man's end;[369] hence like Nyssen, Clement points to Moses as the archetypical contemplator.[370] To be a 'gnostic' of the kind Clement extols, that is, to be a Christian gnostic, one must practise contemplation.[371] Contemplation thus separates the reflective from the non-reflective; quoting Plato, Clement agrees that the one who

---

[360] CCels 2.6. [361] Pray 9.3.
[362] Contrast Daniélou, who notes that all Origen's terms to describe the Christian in ecstasy are borrowed from the *Phaedrus*, yet he holds to the notion of contemplation as something that eludes the philosophers but is granted to unlearned Christians (1955, 109). Likewise, Widdicombe points out that Origen differs from the Platonic view of contemplation inasmuch as for him, contemplation is properly not of the Forms, but of the divine hypostases (1994, 45).
[363] CCels 3.47; the image is borrowed from 2 Cor 4.18. [364] CCels 3.56.
[365] CCels 7.46. [366] PArch 1.2.2. [367] Str 1.1. [368] Str 4.26. [369] Str 6.7.
[370] Str 5.12. [371] Str 5.1.

contemplates lives amongst his fellows as a God among human beings.[372] Yet the capacity for contemplation is also virtually definitive of what it means to be human: it is this, along with self-restraint and life itself, that is common to mortal nature and contemplation, Clement hints, is the most excellent of all.[373] Like Origen, Clement recognises that contemplation is a luxury not all can afford: poverty renders it – and virtue as well – more difficult.[374] If neither offers a solution to this unhappy state of affairs, they can scarcely be faulted for pointing to a perennial fact of human societies.

Clement does not however disdain to make what one could call utilitarian arguments in contemplation's favour. In the contemplative life, the worshipper attends to herself also, benefiting from the activity by being drawn closer to God.[375] The 'gnostic' Christian's whole life is a holy festival: engaged in contemplation, she unites herself to the divine choir with constant recollection.[376] Contemplation moreover has enduring effect: the one who engages in it retains the permanent power of the objects of contemplation in her soul,[377] and so the permanence of contemplation is one of the gifts for which one prays when one has reached the peak of the spiritual life,[378] for the end envisaged by the gnostic Christian terminates in contemplation.[379] What else, he asks, is incumbent on the rational creature than the contemplation of the divine and human?[380]

The significance of contemplation points to the strongly intellectualist strain in these early Alexandrians' doctrine of God, anthropology and doctrines of sanctification and consummation. One of the most important common threads running through their theology and contributing in large part to its cohesion is just this stress on the intellect, yet in Origen's thought in particular, as we have seen, the appreciation of the mind is accompanied by a rather negative view of the body. This, at least, is the conclusion one would reach if one only attended to what he asserts. If one looks systematically at the language in which he couches his assertions, one might see his theology in a slightly different light.[381] For Origen's most vividly evocative epithet for the mind is 'the divine sense'. This

---

[372] Str 4.25. [373] Str 4.3. [374] Str 4.5. [375] Str 4.23.
[376] Str 7.7. The notions of the gnostic's life as a holy festival and of union or instruction by a divine or mystic choir appear twice in this chapter.
[377] Str 7.7. [378] Str 7.7. [379] Str 7.13. [380] Paed 1.12.
[381] Cox makes an analogous point to the argument I will make here: in her study of 'bestial imagination' in Origen, she notes that Origen does not advocate a renunciation of the sensuous world, but rather an embrace of that world as an 'enigmatic bearer' of the kingdom of heaven (in Hansen, 1985, 65).

sense, he claims, is superior to all other senses.[382] This point is adduced in favour of the conclusion that the mind is not a body, admittedly, but what it chiefly indicates is that Origen prefers to describe and extol this incorporeal faculty using bodily imagery.[383] Traditionally, Origen has been interpreted as holding a doctrine of the spiritual senses, and in many texts is indeterminate as to the precise identity of these senses. If, for example, one reads the *Contra Celsum* without the light shed from *On First Principles*, one encounters a text such as 'There is a certain divine sense found now only by the person who is blessed',[384] and might perhaps assume that this sense comes of having ascended spiritual heights. *On First Principles*, however, warns against such an interpretation. Commenting on Matthew 5.8, one of the Beatitudes, Origen asks, 'What is it to "see God in the heart" other than to understand and know him with the mind?',[385] and he even formulates a general rule, claiming that both the Old and New Testaments repeatedly use 'heart' when they mean to designate the mind.[386] Origen's chief proof-text for this point, one he seems never to tire of citing, is Prov. 2:5b, which in the Septuagint reads, 'You shall find knowledge of God', but which Origen cites as 'You will find a divine sense'.[387] The application of this text indicates, in Origen's view, that the names of the sense organs are often applied to the soul,[388] and this principle in turn provides the key for interpreting much of Origen's talk of the senses. So, for example, when Origen speaks of the divine voice being heard only by those whom God wishes to hear it,[389] he is not alluding to a spiritual or mystical experience of supernatural phenomena, but to God's informing the mind, an interpretation validated by his assertion a little further on in the same passage that God's utterances are heard by a superior sense. It is this superior sense that *On First Principles* allows us to gloss *tout court* as the mind.[390]

Auditory imagery has of course often been used in the Christian tradition to convey the notion of divine inspiration, but Origen interprets the mind's encounter with God in terms of many senses. The sense of

---

[382] PArch 1.1.7 *bis*.
[383] For this reason, I cannot concur with Daniélou's view that Origen's contrast of the sensible and intelligible worlds is connected to the notion of a transcendent God who cannot be known except by a mind set free from the senses (1955, 106).
[384] 1.48.   [385] PArch 1.1.9.   [386] PArch 1.1.9.   [387] Cf., for example, PArch 1.1.9 and CCels 7.34.
[388] PArch 1.1.9.   [389] CCels 2.72.
[390] Daniélou's interpretation is a little different. He claims that the spiritual senses are put into operation by the Word and correspond to rational spiritual experiences, all concerned with the Word present in the soul; they are thus bound up with the perfection of the spiritual life (1955, 308).

taste, for example, is appealed to in texts where Origen speaks of the mind: being nourished by the food of wisdom, a nourishment that is capable of restoring the imago Dei to its state of perfection.[391] The surrounding text forms an extended meditation on spiritual growth, expounded through images of eating and nourishment.[392] At the end of Book II of *On First Principles*, Origen returns to this imagery, and in an extended simile even describes the mind as feeding – moderately, and on appropriate foods – in the state of perfection. In all respects, he says, this food must be understood to be the contemplation and understanding of God.[393]

The most consistently privileged of the senses is neither hearing nor taste, but vision; in this respect, Origen initiates the main strand of subsequent Christian mysticism and mystical theology.[394] Unlike those Christian thinkers who incline to view the Incarnation as God's self-manifestation in a form comprehensible to embodied rational beings, Origen's elitism and spiritualising prevail even in a Christological context. Even after the Incarnation, he claims, Christ's divinity is most evident to those who have 'sharp eyes' in their soul.[395] Clarity of mental vision is not a natural endowment, but rather the gift of the Spirit; mixing two kinds of sensory images, Origen says such vision is the result of the Spirit's touch [aphēs].[396] Elsewhere, he credits the Logos with giving the power of sight.[397] The same eyes of the mind that in prayer are lifted up from preoccupation with mundane things[398] are those that gaze on the glory of the Lord,[399] the Invisible and Intelligible who can be perceived only with the intellect.[400]

Early Alexandrian theology gives unmistakable notice of the significance of intellect in patristic thought, at every level: systematic, methodological, ascetical. In the work of Origen, the stress on mind and contemplation seems accompanied by a devaluation of the body and although at times, this distrust constitutes an exhortation to discipline, at others it extends further. Against Origen's tendency to disparage the body, however, we must place in the balance his use of bodily and sensual

---

[391] PArch 2.11.3.
[392] For an extended examination of images of nourishment in *On Prayer*, see Noel, 1992, 481ff.
[393] PArch 2.11.7.
[394] According to Rowe, at times in Origen's works the language of seeing is used to denote the process whereby Christ introduces human beings to the Father (1985, 140).
[395] CCels 3.14. [396] CCels 7.4. [397] CCels 7.39. [398] Pray 9.2. [399] Pray 99.
[400] Clement does not make any appeal to a divine sense, as Origen does, but he does employ sensory imagery in connection with the mind, imagery which is usually of the oral/nutritional kind. See, for example, Rich 34 and Prot 10.

imagery. This imagery cannot be dismissed as merely decorative and therefore unimportant; to do so would be not only to ignore the high level of literary and rhetorical sensitivity in the world of the Fathers, but also the perennial fact of Christian theology: that its tradent is above all the word, the scriptural word, the liturgical and creedal word, and the words of theology and individual prayer. To dismiss figurative language would be to consent to a form of apophaticism which Christianity has never accepted, in virtue of which theological ideas and the constituent truths of the faith can be separated from human language. Whatever the limitations of the latter, and irrespective of the value, even necessity, of silence, the word has always its place, and its particularities – the diction, argumentative forms, poetic speech an author uses – must be heeded and taken into account as part of the text's meaning. Doing so in the case of Origen means adjusting any hasty conclusion of hostility to the body and also allows us to see a much greater resemblance between his theology and that of Clement, which, while less sensual in its texture, is also less marked by any apparently overt hostility to the body.

CHAPTER 3

Cappadocian theology: Nazianzen and Nyssen

With the Cappadocians, we re-enter the world of Alexandrian theology, for they are in many ways most fully Origen's heirs. Although we will see many of the same themes that appeared in the theology of the early Alexandrians, the thought has been refined, Origen's skittishness about the body being less in evidence, and new theological themes – such as infinity – doing greater systematic work. The lines of continuity nevertheless appear far more clearly than does any evidence of breakage, and this fact testifies not only to the constancy of our theme in patristic theology but also to the relatively small impact of contemporary controversies on its overall shape: despite the very different concerns of one figure's arguing against gnosticism and another against Arianism or Eunomianism, within their theological systems the significance of the intellect remains largely the same.

More surprising than the low impact of these latter controversies is the slight effect of the Apollinarian, whose relevance to matters touching the intellect is more immediate. There are several factors that may account for the relative lack of energy around this issue in the thought of Nazianzen and Nyssen. The first is that although both assert a rational soul in Christ for the most part neither is directly disputing with Apollinarius and they accordingly assume a human mind in Christ rather than argue for it vigorously. A second factor is that Apollinarius was not narrowly concerned with mind in Christ but with the role of the Word as the vivifier of the hypostasis of union. His opponents did not so much insist on a human mind or will as on a human soul (though they certainly took mind and will as constituents of the soul). Even after the official condemnation of Apollinarius in 381, it took centuries for the church fully to grapple with the problems attendant on asserting two centres of consciousness in a single subject. The Cappadocians touch on issues such as the growth of Christ's knowledge, or his ignorance of the details of judgement, but do not really wrestle fully with the problem of a finite intellect united to one that is infinite, an omission surprising in light of both the Cappadocian sensitivity to the systematic implications of their thought and their strong interest in the doctrine of God.

The best arrangement in any oration, maintained Nazianzen, is to begin from God and end in God,[1] and that conviction might well be taken as the overarching rubric of Cappadocian theology. Most of the characteristics of this theology can be systematically traced to the particular character of its doctrine of God and the Trinity: the centrality of infinity among divine attributes in Nyssen's theology, for example, becomes the major premise from which he derives much of his doctrine of sanctification and consummation.[2] Infinity does much less work in Nazianzen's theology, while a trinitarian dynamic figures prominently to an extent it does not in Nyssen's thought, yet the ensemble of attributes the two Gregories consider important is essentially consistent.

Of the two, Nyssen is on the whole fonder of lists of divine attributes, each of which functions as a capsule doctrine of God, a miniature of the divine nature, and a mostly predictable one. God is immaterial, invisible, formless, ungenerate, everlasting, imperishable, immutable 'and all such things'.[3] This list consists almost entirely of privative attributes, which some might regard as consistent with the supposedly marked apophaticism of Cappadocian thought, and especially of Nyssen's. He soon chases this list with another, this time of positive qualities – goodness, kindness, holiness[4] – and if the first list could be accused of an unseemly indebtedness to Greek philosophy, the second derives from scripture. The Biblical pedigree obviously matters to him: elsewhere he is at pains to show his doctrine is not merely consonant with scripture, but derives directly from it, even though he becomes markedly more reliant on what are strictly speaking titles rather than attributes (shepherd, fountain, king and so on).[5] Notably, Nyssen also affirms that divine nature is fundamentally intellectual [noēton].[6]

---

[1] Or 2.1.

[2] Mühlenberg (1966) rightly notes that infinity does not for Gregory represent the pinnacle of perfection (21). This observation in no way obviates its systematic centrality, however. The centrality of infinity to a doctrine of God that in other respects resembles that of Origen indicates the cautiousness of Cappadocian appropriation of the latter's thought. As Mühlenberg also notes (81), Origen rejects infinity as a property of the divine specifically on the grounds that God is *nous*; on his account, if God were infinite, he would not be able to think himself. Rationality and infinity are thus taken to be logically incompatible, a vew with which Nyssen does not concur.

[3] CEun 75b/J.1.153. References to Nyssen's works are, unless otherwise indicated, by page number in NPNF and volume and page in Jaeger's Greek.

[4] CEun 82b/J.1.174.   [5] CEun 119b/J.2.365.

[6] HumP 24.2/F250. The Latin title for this treatise is usually given as *De opificio hominis*. The most recent edition is that of Forbes (1855), where he gives it as *De conditione hominis*; I have used an English translation of the conventional title. References are to chapter and section number in

Even as he affirms these positive, easily graspable names and qualities, though, Nyssen insists on God's transcendence of all human conceptualities, on the grounds of other seminal divine attributes: because God is simple, uniform, incomposite, he is also unutterable, beyond names, images and conceptualities, all of which betray what they seek to designate by themselves reflecting the composite order from which they derive. The mind's quest to capture God in words is thus a chasing of what is hidden.[7] Still, this apparently futile piling up of predicates that can never represent what is simple nevertheless constitutes a search of like for like, for besides being goodness and truth, God is reason [logos][8] and the human mind seeks its archetype in its Maker. That likeness provides the notional ground for the very enterprise of Cappadocian theology.

However much God transcends us, therefore, there are hints in Nyssen's theology that the possibility of an orderly and coherent doctrine of God is grounded in this affirmation of God's very nature as rational. All divine attributes are those of a transcendent being, yet this transcendence does not license a theology of inappropriate or arbitrary predication, nor a truncated doctrine of God. Every fitting attribute must be included in this doctrine, and all of these attributes must be properly related to one another.[9] Divine nature is therefore essentially rational both in the sense that it is shaped in accord with a *ratio* and that this *ratio* announces itself and is recognisable as such to the rational creature.

Nazianzen, on the whole less fond of catalogues of attributes, also inclines less towards lists that are either wholly philosophical or wholly Biblical. Whether or not the conventional wisdom is true in maintaining that Nyssen's mystical theology centres on darkness, while Nazianzen's centres on light, it is certainly true that light is a central category in the latter's theology and a key attribute of God: God is light, so pure as to be inapproachable and yet simultaneously that self-communicating light which enlightens the mind.[10] God can only illumine minds because he is himself Mind: are not mind [nous] and reason [logos] (among others) names of the first nature?, he asks.[11] However, even positive attributes are linked to divine unknowability: God's goodness is beyond all goodness[12] and, most fundamentally, his simplicity places him beyond the compass

---

NPNF and to page numbers in Forbes' Greek, because Forbes' enumeration of the chapters and those of NPNF do not concur.

[7] 2CEun 298a/J.1.365   [8] Inf 380a/J.3.3.93.
[9] CtOr 301/J.3.4.62. References to the *Catechetical Oration* are by page numbers in Hardy and Jaeger.
[10] Or 2.76.   [11] Or 28 13.
[12] Or 2.76. Goodness here is 'kalon', the sense of which could, of course, also be 'beauty'.

of human experience.¹³ In making this point, Nazianzen uncovers the veiled apophaticism of any doctrine of simplicity: as its underlying meaning is essentially negative ('simple' means 'not composite'), so in stating the utter distinction of the Uncreated from creation, the assertion of simplicity does little more than name divine unlikeness.¹⁴

Nyssen maintains a similiar balance of the positive and negative ways, although his apophaticism is more pronounced. His conviction of the correspondence of the human mind to the divine nevertheless means that there always remains open some possibility of apprehension: although God cannot be perceived by the senses, and though he transcends all reason, human thought can barely touch [thingganei] the inapproachable and lofty divine nature.¹⁵ This correspondence seems ultimately to devolve on God's own intellectual nature, although Nyssen's strong sense of divine transcendence leads him to make the point with what one could only call diffidence. He is more confident of the possibility of speaking of God according to operations, some of which are intellectual: God can be understood as the mental operation of conception [hē tou nou hēmōn pros tēn katanoēsin tōn ginomenōn synergia],¹⁶ although he is not himself a conception [epinoia],¹⁷ so not what is envisaged or envisageable by our minds, but the very act of Mind engaging in thought; divinity is mind and word [nous kai logos].¹⁸ Despite the fact that God transcends all thought, he constantly prompts us to think of him: he is the Being who transcends all existences, yet is the source of all the beauty and majesty of creation, and contemplation of that very creation only spurs new thoughts of God in us, each of which must be interpreted in the light of wisdom.¹⁹

Nazianzen, too, adverts to mind as a key attribute of God on the basis of his effects. If, in order to commune with God, the human mind must retire into itself and withdraw from sensible things, this can only be because God is intelligible, and indeed is intelligence itself, the source of the light that illuminates human minds.²⁰ Thus far, the schema seems no more than Platonic. However deep the stream of ancient philosophy may

---

¹³ Or 45.3.
¹⁴ The strains of apophaticism in Nazianzen's theology, as well as the basic assumption of his doctrine of illumination – namely, that we need assistance from without – mean that he does not differ significantly from the standard non-Christian epistemology of his era, pace Bergmann (1995), 211: likeness grounds our *capacity* to know God, but not the fullness of knowledge we ultimately have. Gregory's position is more than a 'dynamic' interpretation of the Platonic theory (214): it confines its relevance to the sphere of potentiality.
¹⁵ 2CEun 264a/ J.1.265. ¹⁶ 2CEun 281a/J.1.315. ¹⁷ 2CEun 267a/J.1.274. ¹⁸ HumP 5.2/F130.
¹⁹ 2CEun 309a/J.1.396. ²⁰ Or 12.4.

run, in Nazianzen's thought it becomes fully trinitarian: to creatures of sense ordered to the sensible, the Incarnate Son speaks, illumining the visible world; to those who think, it is God who speaks, the highest of objects of thought, and the one that satisfies the most searching minds.[21] The trinitarian theology and the Platonic notion of *nous* (if that is what it is) marry: 'Divinity [theotēta] is one nature in three personalities [idiotēsi], intellectual [noerais], perfect, self-existent.'[22] The simultaneous use of the via positiva and via negativa evident in Nazianzen's doctrine of God figures also in his doctrine of the Trinity. The Word is the 'offspring of the great mind', who is the Father; the Word is the Father's speech, related to him as word is to mind [hōs pros noun logos].[23] Although divine nature itself lies beyond human intellectual grasp, the Word expresses that nature, and as such, is equally light and wisdom.[24] However, even though the incarnate Word presents divine nature in a form graspable by embodied creatures, it is finally the mind that leads us to God: reason [logos] comes from God, who implants the same capacity in us as a kind of 'first law' of our being.[25]

For Nazianzen the Incarnate Word is divine because even after appearing on earth in visible form, he retained that which is perceived by mind [dia to nooumenon]:[26] intelligibility has come to be regarded as a definitive characteristic of divinity. The Incarnate Word takes on an intelligent soul for the sake of the human soul, so that like may be purified by like. At first glance, it seems that intellect is what the Word acquires at the incarnation, in order to communicate to human beings; in fact, it is Christ's intellectual soul which mediates between the infinite and uncontainable God and finite flesh.[27] The connection is made more explicit in the second of the theological orations, where Nazianzen notes that reason proceeds from God and, having been implanted in us, proceeds back to God through visible things;[28] it is our mind and reason that are Godlike [theoeides] and divine [theion].[29] To attain to the mind of Christ, therefore, is at once to be admitted to the hidden treasures and to be able to impart these to others,[30] although he can also maintain a tempering apophaticism: 'since God's nature is ineffable, we will honour it with silence'.[31]

For both Gregories, possession of an intellect not only locates the creature in relation to God, but also constitutes a cosmic ordering principle, stipulating a schema that endured as the standard until at least

[21] Or 21.1. [22] Or 33.16. [23] Or 30.20. [24] Or 45.30. [25] Or 28.16. [26] Or 30.21.
[27] Or 45.9. [28] Or 28.16. [29] Or 28.17. [30] Or 2.96. [31] Or 28.20.

the High Middle Ages, in virtue of which God is uncreated, rational and immaterial; the angels, created, rational and immaterial; humanity, created, rational and material; and the beasts created, irrational and material. Thus for Nazianzen, the element of human nature that is created in the image of God and the highest faculty of that nature is the power of intelligence.[32] We are related to God especially through the Second Person, the Word, who is the constituting and creative [systasis kai ousiōsis] power of every reasonable soul[33] and who prefers nothing to rational and speaking creatures [tōn logikōn].[34] This linkage is reflected on the human side by the fact that every rational nature longs for God, even though it is unable to grasp him [katalabein].[35] We were created rational and hasten towards the Word by means of the Word [dia logou].[36] While Nazianzen seems to agree with Nyssen's view (which is also the conventional one), that intellect is what distinguishes humankind from the other animals, his schema is slightly more nuanced inasmuch as he acknowledges degrees of knowledge among the 'beasts': the natural knowledge of even the irrational animals is something to marvel at, and while some animals are completely devoid of any kind of learning, others have natural skills that put them on a par with the cleverest human beings.[37]

Nyssen distinguishes humanity from the beasts much more sharply. He repeatedly defines the human person in Aristotelian fashion, as a rational animal[38] or with analogous formulae, as when he declares reasoning [to logikos] and mortality to be the leading characteristics of the human person.[39] The intellectual dimension of the angels' nature makes them somewhat like our siblings,[40] and while the devil is truly kin only to falsehood, Nyssen admits that demonic nature is still intellectual and incorporeal.[41] Although the other animals can be said to possess some sort of knowledge (that which originates in the senses) Nyssen does not

---

[32] Plagnieux (1951) speaks of 'ce pouvoir prodigieux d'atteindre au divin: nous, noēsis, dianoia' (145).
[33] Or 30.20. [34] Or 28.11. [35] Or 28.13. [36] Or 25.1. [37] Or 28.23–24.
[38] CEun 109b/J.2.336; Soul 51/K42. When citing texts from this treatise, I have ascribed to Nyssen himself the views espoused in the work by Macrina, since hers are taken as authoritative in the dialogue. References to this treatise are by page in Roth and Krabinger.
[39] HSp 317b/J.3.1.93.
[40] LM 1.47 and 2.209. References to *The Life of Moses* are by book and the section numbers of Daniélou's *Sources chrétiennes* edition, which were adopted by Malherbe and Ferguson in their Classics of Western Spirituality translation. I consulted both Jaeger and Daniélou's texts, but finding no differences between the two that matter for the purposes of this study, have cited using Daniélou's section numbers, since these render the task of locating the relevant passage much easier in both the Greek and the translation.
[41] CEun 156b/J.2.65.

marvel at this as Nazianzen does; rather, he stresses the inferior quality of their knowledge and the fact that they lack the capacity for contemplation as the reasons they were not allowed on Mount Sinai. If no human being but Moses was privy to the theophany there, no matter: at least some representative of the human race was, and this fact signifies our privileged position as those who are able to contemplate what is intelligible and not only what is sensible.[42] The superiority of the rational animals to the others is even invoked to counter Eunomius' mistaken notions of trinitarian procession, as when Nyssen points to the creation of humanity last of all the animals as an indication that what comes after is not necessarily inferior.[43] Nevertheless our embodiment, which entails kinship with irrational nature, means that we are subject to irrational passions.[44] We are accordingly caught between the horns of a dilemma: we act on the impulses of the passions because we are tempted downwards by our animal nature, but unlike the irrational animals, we are morally accountable because we know what we are doing.

If Nyssen's opinion of the value of the non-intellectual parts of the soul seems variable and even contradictory, he displays no such lack of consistency in his portrayal of the mind's relation to God. Intellectual essence is godlike [theios],[45] and as reasoning and intelligent creatures, human persons both retain a likeness to God and show themselves to be the work of God.[46] Rational natures were indeed created for the very purpose of manifesting the divine, and as such, rational nature is a kind of cosmic container [angeion] of good things.[47] We can discover what is proper to the soul by applying the simple test of asking what is proper to divine nature – what belongs essentially to the first must also belong to the second.[48]

As we have seen, both Gregories argue from God's effects in the created order to at least implicit, and sometimes explicit, doctrines of God. The basis of this line of 'bottom-up' reasoning is the 'top-down' movement of creation, the divine initiative whereby God gives to the rational creature the means to perceive nature that is sheerly intelligible, which is the capacity for communion with the Trinity. The theology of the imago Dei, a theological commonplace in the Christian tradition long before the Cappadocians, is one of the lynchpins of their system, yet is articulated in largely atomised fashion: explicit appeal to it appears much more

---

[42] LM 2.156.   [43] CEun 132a/J.2.401.   [44] HumP pref 18/F110.
[45] Inf 375a and b/J.3.3.77 and 78.   [46] Virg 357a/J.8.1.298.   [47] Soul 87/K98.   [48] Soul 51/K42.

frequently in Nyssen's work than Nazianzen's[49] but in the Nyssenian corpus figures largely in his treatise on anthropology, *On the Making of the Human Person*.

Nyssen's thought on the imago, however conventional in its general outline, displays some significant tensions that indicate how deeply he appropriated and thought through the theological implications of the doctrine. He provides a summary of it near the opening of his anthropological treatise. The soul is rational, and although the mind that makes it so functions, in rational animals, by means of the senses, the mind itself is not part of the body: the body is no more than the outward form of this mind which serves its needs.[50] If the body exists to further the ends of the mind, to what end is the mind given? The opening encomium of the treatise, addressed to his brother Basil, makes clear that creation 'after God' – which appears to consist in making right use of the divine gift of likeness – enables human persons to complete the movement from the Uncreated to the rational creature through returning to God in contemplation.[51] Both the mind and the human person are therefore defined by this contemplative end.

The imago does not for Nyssen subsist solely in the mind, but also in freedom from sin [parrēsian][52] and beatitude: human nature is the image of the transcendent beatitude, marked with the beauty of goodness from which it came.[53] Likeness in this instance names a form of participation: the

---

[49] The notion of a correspondence between humanity and God – that we were created to be *capax Dei* – surfaces at some points in Nazianzen's work, but the actual language of the imago figures much less frequently. In Or 2.74, he refers to the human person as an image of the Good, but he uses not eikōn, but eidōlon. He does use eikōn in Or 3.7 (cf. Or 40.10 and 32). Ellverson (1981) notes his use of kat' eikōna in Or 1.4, 2.22, 6.14, the image itself being Christ (25, n. 59). Cf. also Or 40.10 and 32 and 'I had a share of the image and did not keep it' (Or 45.9). Nazianzen appeals far less often to the theology of the imago Dei, although he does acknowledge that the human soul comes from God, is divine and presses to return to him.
[50] HumP pref 9/F108.   [51] HumP pref [precedes 1]/F103-4.
[52] LP 5.71/J.7.2.59. References to this treatise are by the number of the sermon, the page number of the translation and the volume and page number of Jaeger's Greek. Here I differ from Cavarnon (1955), who maintains that humanity resembles God in possessing reason as a governing principle, which he identifies outright with the soul (140-41). Similarly, Fedwick claims that the seat of resemblance with God is in *nous* (1994, 369), and Balthasar (1989) claims the image is *nous kai phronēsis*, accompanied by the whole range of virtues (66). While it is true that will is logically dependent upon mind, Gregory's thought allows neither for the possibility of a mind able to act without a distinct capacity to will, nor for a godlike mind somehow lacking in freedom. Meredith seems closer to the mark in holding that freedom and virtue are important elements of Nyssen's theology of the image, though the intellectual element is always prominent (1989, 42). Völker (1955) regards the mind as the prime bearer of the image (68), though, on this point as on so many others, he sees the ubiquitous influence of Platonism (73).
[53] Beat 1.88/J.7.2.81. References are to sermon and section number in ACW and page number in Jaeger.

divine alone is blessed and we only share in God's blessedness through our similarity to it.[54] Mingled with the conviction of likeness and its enormous significance, ontological and salvific, is the equally deep conviction of dissimilarity, but that unlikeness derives in part from the participatory nature of the likeness.[55] There is always and necessarily a difference between an image and an archetype, but in the anthropological treatise the difference amounts to opposition in certain respects: the image which is the human person is mortal, passible and shortlived, whereas the archetype is immortal, pure and eternal.[56] In fact, humanity bears a double imprint: of the divine beauty (which similitude exists in the mind), and of brute nature (evident in the passionate impulses which are the manifestations of irrationality).[57] This irrational element does not exist in us contrary to the divine plan, however. It was God who mingled with his own image an element of the irrational; the reference here is not to any deliberate installation in us of passions, but of human sexual distinction and generation, which has no counterpart in divine nature.[58] While by modern standards Nyssen's identification of the irrational with the feminine may be distasteful, the link to Genesis 1 is significant, for it stipulates that the image, in all its complexity of likeness and unlikeness to its archetype, exists by divine will that it be so and it cannot therefore be dismissed as unfortunate. Moreover the connection of irrationality and the feminine by no means constitutes a denial of intellect in women. The image of God is not in part of our nature, nor in only some of the human race: all human beings possess the power of understanding and deliberating, and all are consequently made in the image of

---

[54] Beat 1.90/J.7.2.82–83. Likeness is not always portrayed in terms of participation, however, and certainly the imago Dei is not inevitably an instance of such; on this point I differ from Harrison (1989), who regards both image and likeness as a form of participation (23). Her article gives a valuable bibliography of material on the imago (see n. 1).

[55] Meredith (1989) maintains that the divine character of the image is comprised of both moral and intellectual elements which together make up the divine image, and if any element is missing, the image is impaired (he cites Migne 44.137b, which is HumP 5.1). Gregory does list both moral and intellectual qualities, but the text cited does not quite extend to claiming all these are the necessary condition of being in the image of God.

[56] HumP 16.4/F196.   [57] HumP 18.3/F216.

[58] HumP 22.4/F236. Thus I differ rather sharply from Balthasar (1988), who reads Nyssen as attributing all passion to the Fall and as saying that to return to what we were before it, we must leave behind sexuality, birth, nourishment and bodily growth (73, citing Soul [in PG 46] 148b–149a). Subsequently, Balthasar concedes (his term) that passions themselves are not the cause of sin (74–75), but rather sin resides in the use we make of them. Still later, he maintains that in Soul, Nyssen seems to waver between two incompatible positions, the idealist definition of soul given by Macrina, which does not seem to admit of the passions, and a more moderate view which stressed the indispensable role of the passions (79). Gregory, he says, is wary of tidy, one-sided positions (79) – indeed he is, which is why Balthasar's first assessment overstated the case.

God.⁵⁹ Nyssen's anthropology wobbles on this point, moreover, for the theology of the *Catechetical Oration* is rather different: being a copy of the impassible, Adam was by nature without passion, so passibility is a consequence of the Fall, rather than femininity, and as such, is contrary to God's intention for creation. The imago here seems to have no negative connotations: Adam's form was beautiful, since he was created in the image of archetypal beauty.⁶⁰ This beauty further possesses the character of the divine in that it is deathless: death affected the sentient part of the human being, but not the inward, which is the divine image.⁶¹

Alongside this restrained theology, in which the imago exists in a tensive relationship with characteristics utterly different from, even at odds with, the divine, stands a theology of unqualified affirmation. The term 'image' comprehends all the divine attributes;⁶² indeed, what constitutes the image is that it fails in none of the attributes we perceive in the archetype: if, therefore, one of the attributes we contemplate in the divine is incomprehensibility of essence, then the image must imitate this quality in some way also.⁶³ The assertion here is not a momentary lapse on Nyssen's part, for he makes analogous claims in *On the Soul and Resurrection* and *The Life of Moses*.⁶⁴ In the first, the given point of resemblance however lies in the character of intellect: we mirror the incomprehensibility of divine nature inasmuch as the very nature of our own minds escapes us.⁶⁵

For Nyssen, the theology of the imago Dei grounds in particular the divine beauty which is the reflection of the divine beauty in the human rational soul. God, on this account, is both the beauty we contemplate with unspeakable happiness, and the artist who on the canvas of the human person paints a portrait resembling his own beauty.⁶⁶ This beauty has something of the character of virtue,⁶⁷ but also of Mind and of Love:⁶⁸ 'Since the most beautiful and greatest good is divine nature itself... we say that the mind, as being in the image of the most beautiful, itself remains in beauty and goodness [both rendered by forms of to kalon] as long as it participates as far as possible in the likeness of the archetype.'⁶⁹

---

⁵⁹ HumP 16.17/F206.   ⁶⁰ CtOr 280/J.3.4.25.
⁶¹ CtOr 283/J.3.4.30. McLelland claims that Nyssen develops the thought of the early Alexandrians in that while Origen, for example, emphasised the mind as image, for Nyssen, the image includes virtue, 'indeed, makes it decisive' (148). I am not inclined to equate apatheia with virtue to the extent that McLelland seems to, nor to see apatheia, or virtue itself, as clearly less important to Nyssen than to Origen.
⁶² CtOr 276/J.3.4.18.   ⁶³ HumP 11.3/F158.   ⁶⁴ Soul 45/K32 and LM 2.318.
⁶⁵ HumP 11.4/F158.   ⁶⁶ HumP 5.1/F128.   ⁶⁷ HumP 5.1/F129.   ⁶⁸ HumP 5.2/F130.
⁶⁹ HumP 12.9/F168.

The soul's role as governor of the psychosomatic unity that is the human person clearly requires that intellect be one of its constituents, or it would not be able to discern the good; actively choosing the good requires an additional but closely related faculty, namely the will. At times, Nyssen appears to privilege will over mind, as when he maintains that freedom from any kind of necessity constitutes the greatest of all divine gifts: as virtue is voluntary, freedom is the precondition of all virtue and wisdom.[70] Elsewhere he simply points to the necessity of their relation: every being possessed of a rational mind is meant to be governed by an autonomous and free will.[71] On occasion, the relation is so close that the two seem virtually conflated: 'the movements of our soul are shepherded, like sheep, by the will of knowing reason' [tō boulēmati tou epistatountos logou].[72]

If the lower orders of creation are subject to the mechanical laws of nature, those endowed with free will are not, at least not to the same degree, and there is a world of difference between these states.[73] The soul's impulses are largely involuntary, and as such, in themselves morally neutral; what turns these random promptings into virtues or vices is free choice but free choice guided by reason acting as the charioteer.[74] The ability rightly to conceive of the good, and, having perceived it, to act in accord with it, does more than permit the flourishing of virtue: it makes us godlike in the sense that we are both sovereign and creators, so the highest freedom is to be master of oneself,[75] and the exercise of the rational will [proairesis] even means that we are in some sense our own parents, giving birth to ourselves.[76] However significant the human will is, on this account, intellect maintains an inescapable logical priority.[77]

Nazianzen gives less attention to the will than Nyssen does, but essentially holds a similar view of its significance although he does not spell out with equal clarity the will's necessary dependence on the mind (perhaps because the point seems so obvious to him as to make it unnecessary to state explicitly). Freedom [proairesis] is the ground of any act that could count as meritorious, as well as anything whatsoever that is of enduring value [asphalestaton].[78] The involuntary results from oppression and although he does not make the point, he scarcely needs

---

[70] HumP 16.11/F202; cf. CtOr 309/J.3.4.76. [71] LP 4.61/J.7.2.49. [72] LM 2.18.
[73] CEun 73b/J.1.147. [74] Soul 57/K52. [75] Beat 8.173/J.7.2.169. [76] LM 2.3.
[77] Völker (1955) notes that sin is an intellectual mistake, citing *De mortuis* and the *Catechetical Oration* (see 87 and n. 8).For a generally illuminating treatment of freedom in Nyssen's work, see Harrison (1992), who neatly encapsulates the chicken-and-egg nature of the relation of will and intellect (139–76, esp. 165).
[78] Or 2.15.

to: oppression, being neither meritorious nor enduring, is incompatible with divine goodness.[79] The intrinsic connection between freedom and merit also has an anthropological ground: godliness belongs to those who are willing, not those who are overpowered.[80] The absence of desire to overpower is an essential attribute of God, just as freedom is the precondition of the rational being's enlightened choice of the good, and more, the ground of the bond between the two.

The strong assertion of the soul's relation to God necessarily presses the question of how the body fits into the schema and, on the whole, Nazianzen's theology lays greater weight on the psychosomatic unity of the human person. As in Nyssen's thought, the soul mediates between the divine and the flesh,[81] and while Nazianzen has no doubt that corporeity is essential to human nature (we are 'double-made', of body and soul[82]) he does regard the body as an impediment to both contemplation and holiness: the darkness of the body is placed between us and God, and so the flesh constitutes something of an obstacle to discovering the truth.[83] Nevertheless, those in the body cannot but think through the medium of the body; the fact of our embodiment means that we cannot conceive of even objects of pure thought [tōn nooumenōn] apart from material objects.[84] This epistemological consequence of embodiment is part of the rationale for the Incarnation: Christ's body enables bodily creatures to apprehend the incomprehensible.[85] Christ's soul mediates between his body and the divine nature,[86] a new union [hē kainē mixis] that both saves the now-soiled image of God in humanity and grants immortality to that which is most passable and mutable, flesh [sarx];[87] indeed, in the New Adam, death is slain by the flesh [again, sarx],[88] an affirmation of the goodness of the body, albeit a rather curious one.

Nazianzen's love of paradox manifests itself in his treatment of the relation of body and soul, for despite his conviction that the flesh impedes spiritual progress, he insists on the body's full participation in the spiritual life. In his sermon on Pentecost, for example, he says that the festival is not to end, but is now to be kept in a bodily way.[89] The soul's advantage over the body is moreover only relative, for if God cannot rightly be spoken of by the physical uttering of words, neither can he be conceived of by the mind [nōi].[90] The chief difficulty in humankind's approach to God, therefore, is not the darkness of the flesh, nor even the frailty of the human intellect; it resides in the first instance in the sheer

---

[79] Or 2.208. [80] Or 12.5. [81] Or 38.13. [82] Or 40.8. [83] Or 28.4 and 12. [84] Or 28.12.
[85] Or 30.21. [86] Or 2.23. [87] Or 45.9. [88] Or 39.13. [89] Or 41.18. [90] Or 40.5.

ineffability of God himself. If God eludes us entirely, as does no other object of thought, other theological questions scarcely offer themselves as easy intellectual exercises: great effort is required to grasp how the soul is united to the body, the mind to soul, or reason [logos] to mind [nous], to name just a few examples.[91] Human language itself is a form of embodiment which must be endured as a burden by the bodiless divine nature towards which it gestures, and Nazianzen can only comfort himself with the thought that if the Word stooped to taking on human flesh he can probably endure human words as well.[92] The paradox emerges also in Gregory's adoption of bodily imagery, in the manner of Origen: the nourishment of the Word must be eaten with the hidden things of the mind, where he shall be given up to spiritual digestion [pepsin].[93] Guarding the purity of the body – through custody of the eyes, for example – matters, but the mind [dianoia] must also be virgin, not roving or wandering about.[94]

Nyssen's theology of the body and soul bears many of the same marks as Nazianzen's. The soul is that which is godlike, having a natural affinity for the divine; the soul is joined to the divine through its purity and so adheres to what is proper to it.[95] The union of body and soul necessitates a mediator between the two, different as they are, and so the soul must first be blended with the sensitive faculty.[96] The connection of body to soul is however both innate (the way God created us to be) and moral (something effected and affected by the human person's exercise of the will). It is itself mysterious, beyond the power of human language adequately to describe or the mind to envisage,[97] yet despite their fundamental difference, nothing hinders the soul from being present to the body.[98] The anthropological grounding of psychosomatic unity is matched in Nyssen's thought, as in Nazianzen's, by a Christological base: the union of divine and human natures in Christ parallels the union of body and soul in the human person, although this principle grounds, not a heuristic analogy, but the mystery of the hypostatic union: if we cannot even understand ourselves, we should not expect to grasp the

---

[91] Or 29.8. [92] Or 37.2. [93] Or 45.16.
[94] Or 37.10. The treatment above indicates my marked disagreement with Ellverson (1981), who cites two passages in proof of Gregory's 'very negative attitude to corporal existence' (27). She acknowledges that other passages reveal a more positive stance, but she still maintains he has a 'double attitude' (34), and that overall, he considers the body a burden (29). It seems to me that she overstates the case significantly, by underestimating how much of the problem Gregory sees is the result, not of the body's inherent badness, but the soul's failure to govern it rightly.
[95] Soul 77/K84. [96] HumP 8.5/F142. [97] HumP 15.3/F194. [98] Soul 48/K38.

Christological mystery either.⁹⁹ On the whole, though, Christology does not do as much work in Nyssen's anthropology as it does in Nazianzen's. It is not the Incarnation which effects a kind of *communicatio idiomatum* between the human body and soul but humankind's very creation.¹⁰⁰

The chief point at which Nyssen's anthropology differs from Nazianzen's is the former's more vivid sense of the soul's volatility. If bodily suffering is related to our fluctuating natures [tōi rheustōi tēs physeōs],¹⁰¹ then the blame for these fluctuations lies in the first instance with the soul rather than the body: the body does not so much tug the soul downwards, away from its natural inclination towards what lies above it, as the soul succumbs to the temptations of its own lower desires; the soul can be attracted to and seduced by as little as custom¹⁰² and it can exist in both fleshly and spiritual states (following Paul in 1 Cor 2.14, 15).¹⁰³ One might expect to see this susceptibility as lodging in the soul conceived in some way as to exclude mind (for Nyssen carefully distinguishes the two),¹⁰⁴ yet he makes clear that the mind itself is equally vulnerable. Capable of gazing on heavenly things, it is equally prone to looking downwards, expending its energy on gluttony and worse.¹⁰⁵ True, these impulses derive from the body, but the mind can resist them: if one does not live for the flesh, then one will not suffer mishaps on account of it.¹⁰⁶ Borrowing a well-worn image from ancient philosophy, he compares the mind's guidance of the body to a driver's use of reins to steer a chariot.¹⁰⁷ The mind, then, is the governing principle, not only of the lower powers, but of the soul as a whole; the soul finds its perfection in the intellectual [noeron] and the rational [logikon].¹⁰⁸ Intellectual energies can be dulled [amblunesthai] by bodily conditions, and indeed even incapacitated, but the mind always retains a certain independence.¹⁰⁹ That autonomy is parsed notably in terms of self-determination in relation to God: the soul becomes godlike [theoeidēs] when it resists the downward pull of the worst in its nature.¹¹⁰ In this respect, too, Nyssen's account characterises the image of God as both a natural endowment and an alterable state, for through love the soul becomes an accurate image of God, conformed to the properties of divine nature and attached to its beauty.¹¹¹ If this motion and resultant conformity can be summoned through sheer attentiveness and force of will, it is helped by the soul's natural affinity for the divine.¹¹² Although this schema, articulated in *On*

---

⁹⁹ CtOr. 288/J.3.4.39.   ¹⁰⁰ LP 4.61/J.7.2.49.   ¹⁰¹ CtOr 285/J.3.4.34.   ¹⁰² Virg 353b/J.8.1.286.
¹⁰³ CtOr 281/J.3.4.27.   ¹⁰⁴ Soul 51–52/K44.   ¹⁰⁵ Virg 350a/J.8.1.272.   ¹⁰⁶ Virg 351a/ J.8.1.276.
¹⁰⁷ Virg 368a/J.8.1.332.   ¹⁰⁸ HumP 15.2/F192.   ¹⁰⁹ HumP 12.8/F166.
¹¹⁰ Soul 79/K88.   ¹¹¹ Soul 79–80/K88.   ¹¹² Soul 83/K90.

the *Soul and Resurrection,* seems in danger of dispensing with any explicitly salvific work on God's part, the *Catechetical Oration* makes clear that, through the sacraments, both body and soul are united to Christ and so transformed.[113]

With humankind's transformation comes also the possibility of a regenerated creation; in asserting this cosmic dimension of sanctification Nyssen resembles Irenaeus. As the soul mediates between the immaterial God and the material body, so humankind mediates between God and the irrational life of 'beasts' [tēs alogou kai ktēnōdous zōēs].[114] Nyssen muses aloud in his fourth sermon on the Lord's Prayer as to why the rational creation should be divided into the corporeal and the incorporeal, and conjectures that it was so as to bring the whole creation into relationship with itself and to effect the mutual indwelling [metousia] of each part in the other.[115] The work of reconciliation extends not merely to parties that are by nature alien to one another but to those which are actively hostile. Nyssen does not view the material and the immaterial in this light, but he does see the human person as a battlefield of sorts, where the war of flesh and spirit is constantly being waged. It is the human person herself who is the peacemaker in this conflict, creating harmony by subjecting both parties to the dispute, body and mind, to the higher law of God.[116]

Nyssen nevertheless makes clear that whatever tension may arise in us as a result of our corporeal nature, the problem is not a necessary opposition of body and soul, fundamentally different though the two undoubtedly are.[117] Perfect bodily life is seen in human nature, because of its rationality,[118] and it would scarcely be possible for corporeity to achieve perfection only when united to intellectual nature if the two were fundamentally at odds. Indeed, the very existence of such an entity as a rational animal shows that the body must be a suitable instrument for reason;[119] in particular, human hands are fitting servants of intelligent nature, the wise creator having given them to us so as to give raw reason a particular advantage.[120] He acknowledges that the Biblical and

---

[113] CtOr 318/J.3.4.93. [114] HumP 16.9/F200. [115] LP 4.61/J.7.2.48–49. [116] Beat 7.165/J.7.2.160.
[117] This point is well made by Hart (1990), who notes that when Nyssen speaks of the soul's being debased by its involvement with the flesh in Virg 5.1–15, he does not mean the latter is evil or debased in and of itself, or that its needs may not be satisfied, but that the soul should not satisfy itself in an animal way (463).
[118] HumP 8.4/F140.
[119] HumP 8.8/F144. Gregory literally says that the body must be made fit [kataskeuasthēnai] for the rational faculty.
[120] HumP 8.8/F148.

philosophical notions of the human person do not exactly concur (the scriptural view being presented in figurative language, though no less intellectually rigorous for that), but seems at times content to adopt the view of 'profane learning' which sees the spiritual and appetitive parts of the soul placed beneath its intellectual part, supporting it so that even if human nature is not defined by faculties such as perception and nutrition,[121] all work together to draw the person towards participation in the good.[122] Elsewhere he takes a dimmer view; in *On the Soul and Resurrection*, for example, he maintains that reason conflicts with these faculties and the soul yearns to be rid of them as quickly as possible.[123] Nyssen does not himself resolve these contradictions; his readers can only note the tension in the thought and decide for themselves which line of thought seems most consistent with the overall pattern of his theology.

Although in Nyssen's theology we see one of the most ambivalent presentations of the relation between body and soul and a distrust of the kind of knowledge which originates in sense perception, he remains one of the inheritors of the Origenistic tradition of the spiritual senses. He speaks of 'mental senses' [ta tēs psychēs aisthētēria][124] and the perception of beauties above the material [tēn tōn hyperkosmiōn agathōn katanoēsin].[125] Visual imagery and analogies predominate heavily in this schema, one hint of Nyssen's intense and abiding interest in contemplation.[126] Very occasionally, he employs images related to the other senses: the 'perfume' of Christ,[127] the voices of the saints,[128] the sweet fragrance of the life of the priest[129] and the richly sensuous passage in *The Life of Moses* describing the heights of contemplation: 'When you conquer all enemies... cross the water, are enlightened by the cloud, sweetened by the wood, drink from the rock, taste of the food above... you are instructed in the divine mystery by the sound of the trumpets'.[130] Appeal to the senses other than sight figures rather rarely on the whole, however, the net effect of which is that Nyssen's prose leaves the reader with the impression of a more purely cerebral world than either Origen's or Nazianzen's.

Moreover, Nyssen more frequently disavows the value of sense experience. The senses mislead,[131] he states flatly, and at times he

---

[121] Soul 52/K44. [122] LM 2.96. [123] Soul 52/K44. [124] CEun 155b/J.2.61.
[125] Inf 378a/J.3.2.86–87.
[126] E.g., Virg. 355a/J.8.1.290, 348b, J.8.1.267; 350b/J.8.1.275; 2CEun 264a/J.1.265–66; HumP 10.3/F152; LM 2.189.
[127] Virg 369b/J.8.1.338. [128] Beat 6.151/J.7.2.145. [129] LM 2.286. [130] LM 2.315.
[131] Virg 351b/J.8.1.278.

associates them directly with irrationality.¹³² The senses are not even reliable guides to the material world: so the discerning mind does not rely on the eyes to interpret the world around it.¹³³ Quite aside from the senses' propensity to mislead by mistaking appearances for reality, the very objects of sense perception have the potential to hinder the seeker after the things above and the prototype of all beauty.¹³⁴ Accordingly, the emotional and sensual worlds must be resisted; one must seek to escape them and live solely for the Spirit.¹³⁵

Nyssen however balances these negative estimations of the senses with straightforwardly positive assessments of their value. Although his anthropology is generally less holistic than Nazianzen's, he recognises the interdependence of mind and body in the processes of learning and knowing. The mind works by means of the senses,¹³⁶ so some notion of truth comes to us through sensible things;¹³⁷ moreover, through the senses the union of human nature with mind takes place.¹³⁸ Consequently, the true and perfect soul is one by nature, the intellectual mingling with our material nature through the agency of the senses.¹³⁹ In one respect, the mind is even dependent upon the senses, for rational power cannot enter bodily life except through perception.

By means of perception, the soul becomes associated with traits joined to perception – passions – which, surprisingly, Nyssen in this instance says do not work solely evil in us.¹⁴⁰ The problem with the senses lies therefore not in any intrinsic danger associated with sense perception, which, along with thought and the ability to discern good from evil, is a divine gift;¹⁴¹ if the senses can lead astray, it is not because they are maleficent in themselves. The senses can become enslaved, but when they do so, the root of the problem lies in the failure to exercise the intellect.¹⁴² If the senses are troubled and so bring about misfortune,¹⁴³ the problem lies in the soul's consent to be led astray. Thus in great souls, such as Elijah and John Baptist, taste is simple and unspoilt, the ears free from distracting noise and they maintain custody of the eyes, so attaining serenity.¹⁴⁴

It remains, then, that the senses are necessary for the embodied creature to interpret the material world, but however necessary and good this knowledge may be, it does not count as the highest.¹⁴⁵ The world of sense

---

¹³² LM 2.156 and 161. ¹³³ Virg 355b/J.8.1.291. ¹³⁴ 2CEun 259a/J.1.252.
¹³⁵ Virg 350b–51a/J.8.1.276. ¹³⁶ HumP pref 10/F108. ¹³⁷ CEun 202a/J.2.190.
¹³⁸ HumP 13.5/F178. ¹³⁹ HumP 14.2/F190. ¹⁴⁰ Soul 56/K52. ¹⁴¹ LP 5.82/J.7.2.71.
¹⁴² LM 2.46. ¹⁴³ Soul 71/K76. ¹⁴⁴ Virg 351b/J.8.1.279.
¹⁴⁵ Pace Wilken (2003), who straightforwardly characterises Nyssen as a Christian Platonist 'who believed that what was "truly real" was to be found not in material things but in a spiritual realm accessible to the mind alone' (238). Knowledge of the intelligible is higher, in Nyssen's view, but

perception is the finite world, marked off by boundaries, and thus essentially unlike God, whose leading property for Nyssen is infinitude;[146] divine nature can therefore only be known in the impossibility of perceiving it.[147] This characteristic insistence on infinity and its systematic consequences leads Nyssen, on occasion, vigorously to deny any kind of even analogical knowledge of God, yet although he maintains that the visible beauty we appreciate in this life does not furnish us with any idea of that which is invisible and formless,[148] there is still some trace of a natural theology in Nyssen's thought, inasmuch as our eyes become interpreters of the omnipotent wisdom contemplated in the universe.[149]

While Nazianzen shows faint traces of Nyssen's ambivalence towards the senses and the sensible, his thought on these issues for the most part coheres more successfully with the rest of his theology. The human mind [logos] both shares in sense and retreats away [systelletai] from sense.[150] There is no tension or opposition here; rather, the working of the mind reflects its object in any given process of perception. Thus God is to intelligible things what the sun is to the sensible world: the latter lights up what is visible, the former, the invisible world.[151] Moses may have been capable of withdrawing from the senses and perceiving the inapproachable and immaterial deity, but hardly anyone else could have, hence the Incarnation: Christ empties himself [kenoutai] and so becomes comprehensible [chōrētos].[152] The implication is clear: if the cosmic Word wills to cater to corporeity and material beings' need for a sensible God, then there cannot be anything fundamentally wrong with sense perception. Natural theology is consequently more to the fore in Nazianzen's thought than in Nyssen's: our eyes beholding nature tell us both of the existence of God and that God is the cause of all that is created and sustained in life.[153] If mind and sense are distinguished from each other, each has a rightful place and fitting role,[154] and in some circumstances the perceptible even exceeds the sheerly intelligible in value, for the beauty of visible things exceeds that of mere words, Nazianzen declares (though we might be forgiven for wondering at a rhetorician's sincerity in making this claim in the middle of a carefully crafted oration). When Nazianzen exhorts us to purify the senses, therefore,[155] it is not because he shares

---

that does not mean the sensible is unreal. Wilken subsequently notes Nyssen's reverence for relics, apparently seeing this devotion to the mattter as an exception to his overall Platonism. I would take it not as an exception to the rule, but a qualification that, along with other textual evidence, suggests his Platonism was much more tempered – less of a rule, then – than Wilken suggests.
[146] LM 1.5.   [147] CEun 70a/J.1.137.   [148] Virg 355a/J.8.1.290–91.   [149] Soul 34/K16.
[150] Or 28.22.   [151] Or 21.1.   [152] Or 37.3.   [153] Or 28.6.   [154] Or 38.11.   [155] Or 45.14.

Nyssen's uneasiness about the material and sensible, but simply because in his view the whole person needs purification if she is to approach God.

The relation of body to soul, and the mind to the senses, correlates with a broader pattern observable, not just in the microcosm of the human person but in the cosmos as a whole, the distinction of the sensible from the intelligible. This is fundamental to Nyssen: it is the ultimate division of all being,[156] and the distinction is in turn connected to modes of knowledge, that is, whether we know through bodily organs or through the mind. The distinctions proper to the sensible world have no place in the intelligible world,[157] and for this reason, it is impossible to know the visible from the invisible.[158] The converse does not hold true, however, for material beauty can function as a stepping-stool [hypobathra] upon which we climb to gain a view of intellectual beauty.[159] This process is not so much a matter of logical deduction, as a leap that defies logic; by means of the beautiful things that are seen [dia tou phainomena kallous], one can imagine [analogisasthe] the beauty of the invisible prototype.[160] If imagination proves stronger than the imprint of sense impressions alone, it is because the senses need the governance of the mind; the two exist in a symbiotic, yet hierarchically ordered, relation, with the body like a musical instrument which the mind plays.[161] Because the gulf that separates the sensible from the intelligible is very great – they are opposites[162] – it is not surprising that small-souled people will become immersed in perceptible things, and shut off the vision of intelligible things.[163] However, Nyssen admits that the gap between the sensible and intelligible has been bridged by the ultimately Intelligible: God united

---

[156] CEun 60a/J.1.105.   [157] CEun 60b/J.1.106.   [158] CEun 75b/J.1.153.
[159] Virg 355b/ J.8.1.292. For this reason, I question the judgement of Daniélou (1953), that for Nyssen the sensible is not part of human nature, the real nature being the image of God which was in the beginning (132).
[160] 2CEun 273a/J.1.291.
[161] HumP 12.8/F166. Because the body is integral to the scheme, I consider distinctly overstated Völker's thesis that Nyssen's theology is strongly influenced by Platonism, in virtue of the distinction between the sensible and the intelligible (1955, 23ff). The terminology is of course used by Plato and his successors, but that in itself does not mean Nyssen is borrowing from them conceptually. Völker considers the concepts can be rendered in more strictly Biblical fashion by the contrast created–uncreated (24), yet the term 'uncreated' is no more Biblical than 'intelligible', even as both concepts are compatible with the notion of God as spirit, which does have Biblical grounding. 'Intelligible' as applied to divine nature designates no more than the idea that the ways of God may be understood, but not perceived by the senses, a conclusion as easily reached on the basis of the scriptures as of Plato. The same kind of problem is evident in Völker's claim that the notion of *analogia entis* 'wird also streng durchgeführt' (29), supposedly also evidence of Platonism – although the only evidence of Nyssen's appeal to this concept is the use of the term *analogia* tout court, with no equivalent of *entis* anywhere in sight.
[162] CtOr 278/J.4.21.   [163] Soul 31/K10.

with both elements of our nature,[164] and divine nature produces a like blending in us, a union whose effect extends through all creation.[165] Our very means of gaining knowledge of God – scripture – speaks to us only through the senses: we would not be able to learn what the divine and intellectual nature seeks to communicate to us if not through voice and word, perceived by ear and eye. Just so, while David might have known by divine inspiration [tēn tou noēthentos didaskalian] (which is presumably non-sensory), he could only convey that experience to others through speech and hearing.[166]

Nazianzen, however, also takes pains to distinguish the visible from the intelligible,[167] even calling creatures that gather knowledge via the senses 'utterly alien' to intellectual natures, of which God is of course one, although it was God who called these alien natures into being.[168] If the origin of the distinction lies in divine intention that there be such disparity in the universe, that does not mean the sensible is straightforwardly of use in the soul's quest to contemplate the divine, for Gregory commends his friend Basil for having tempered every sense and controlled every limb.[169] The problem as Nazianzen sees it does not lie simply in the nature of matter, but in undesirable properties in some way associated with it; doctrines, constructs of thought, can be carnal and base, so he exhorts his readers to abandon the world of sight and rise up to the world of thought [tois nooumenois] proper.[170]

The Cappadocians, like the earlier authors, assume that this rising up requires the assistance of the ultimate object of the quest, God. They do so, not with the lurking fears of Pelagianism that would plague the later Western tradition, nor the insouciance about emphasising human striving which besets much of Eastern theology, but simply because it would not occur to them that the Infinite lies within the natural reach of the finite. The central issue for them is not guarding against extravagant claims of human capacities, but the union of the knower and the known: knowledge is for them (as it would later be for the Pseudo-Denys) a unitive force and one sees the imprint of this concern in their doctrine of grace. Nazianzen has less to say directly of grace than Nyssen does, but he still presupposes its need for all his theology.[171]

For Nyssen, the advent of grace is overwhelmingly associated with the Spirit: it is out of love for humanity that the latter arranges for myriad conceptions of the divine to reach us, coming from many sources. The

---

[164] CtOr 293/J.4.48.   [165] CtOr 279/J.4.22.   [166] 2CEun 290a/J.1.341.
[167] Or 30.15.   [168] Or 45.6.   [169] Or 43.62.   [170] Or 29.18.   [171] Or 28.31.

fruit of the implantation of all of these is a generation of word from mind,[172] a process clearly mirroring the procession of the Son from the Father. The Spirit's aid is needed rightly to understand scripture,[173] and indeed every intellectual nature, angelic as well as human, is governed by the ordering of the Spirit, for the soul is linked by its intellectual and invisible nature to angelic life.[174] Nyssen knows of people who do not realise that their intellectual capacity and attainments come from God's generosity, but their problem is described not so much in terms of theological as spiritual error: they fail to marvel at the divine gift and fall prey to sophistry as a result.[175] The *ratio* of what is believed, the tradition received from the Fathers, must be sought from God; those able to see this logic of faith are endowed with grace, and persons of faith ought therefore to give thanks to the bestower of the gift.[176] The gratuitous quality of the knowledge we have through faith means that even when we cannot reason our way to the solution of theological problems, we should hold firm to the tradition received from the Fathers. Subject to delusion, we need medicine for our souls, and this healing knowledge of truth comes explicitly through generosity of the Saviour.[177] This knowledge is never however extraneous, a *donum superadditum*: the gifts of mind and reason, though imparted through a 'godlike grace' [theocidē tina charin], are rightly thought of not as given, but implanted [metadōkē].[178]

As grace is particularly associated with the Spirit in Nyssen's writing, so does light lie particularly within the Spirit's gift. The Second Person is identified with light itself: the Only-Begotten is the 'reflection of glory';[179] Gregory maintains, echoing scripture. To this light, which is the Second Person, no one can however draw near who has not been illumined by the Spirit.[180] If Christ alone is identified with light, however, illumination can come as the gift of any of the Persons. Thus illumination is a gift of the Spirit,[181] yet Nyssen reminds us that the grace of light must come equally from the Father, the Son and the Spirit.[182] The Spirit not only enlightens, thereby making the saints luminous, but also purifies; as a consequence the human mind becomes so filled with radiance that it emits light and itself becomes a light.[183] The process of enlightenment

---

[172] CEun 115a/J.2.351–52. [173] CEun 139b/J.2.18. [174] Eust 329a/J.3.2.12–13.
[175] 2CEun 258b/J.1.250. [176] Abl 331b/J.3.1.38–39.
[177] ChrM 127/J.8.1.41. The authorship of this treatise has been disputed, not all commentators accepting Jaeger's attribution to Nyssen. The evidence in favour of its authenticity is strong enough to warrant inclusion here, in my view, although deleting references to it would not alter the overall pattern I trace. References are by page in FC and volume and page in Jaeger.
[178] HumP 9.1/F148. [179] CEun 114b/J.2.351. [180] Eust 329a/J.3.1.13.
[181] CEun 140a/J.2.18. [182] CEun 133b/J.2.406. [183] Virg 356b/J.8.1.295.

nevertheless retains the synergism characteristic of patristic doctrines of grace: light is never forced upon the soul: those who are hostile to the light cannot keep their souls in it.[184]

On the whole, however, Nyssen is less concerned to specify the source of illumination than simply to dwell on its effects. Light is associated above all with truth;[185] yet also with virtue: thus the lives of the saints are like lights instructing those of lesser sanctity.[186] This radiance may not be restricted to the extraordinary; some, Nyssen notes, continue in darkness, driven by evil pursuits, while others become radiant with the light of virtue,[187] but the life of every Christian must be illumined with the ray of true light, and the virtues themselves are rays of 'the Sun of Righteousness' streaming forth that we may be illumined.[188] Conversely, failing to be true to the light causes one to fall into vice: to attempt to represent the ineffable light in the debased currency of human words is to lie[189] (here, too, Gregory claims a scriptural warrant), for how can we, he asks, have worthy conceptions of the light beyond?[190]

Because the light which bathes humankind in its radiance exceeds our knowing, Nyssen will often pair light with darkness. Sometimes his doing so is merely contrastive, but frequently he mixes metaphors of darkness and light to deliberate theological effect. Following in the steps of Moses, one can be enlightened by the cloud and so draw near to God in the impenetrable darkness,[191] yet the bush he saw in the desert was ablaze with a light given, not only for him, but also for us.[192] Likewise, although his vision at the summit of the mountain was only of the back parts of God, the mount of contemplation is lit up by rays of true light,[193] light which illuminates all who contemplate. Although Nyssen employs the imagery of illumination less often than Nazianzen does, its significance for him becomes clear from the way he mixes visual and auditory images. The grace of light which Moses receives is distributed to all his senses, so that his hearing, too, is illuminated by rays of light. Similarly, the purified heart is instructed by means of silent illumination of the thoughts that transcend speech.[194]

While Nazianzen affirms that the unity of the Trinity's operations means that to conceive of any one of the Three or to speak of God means being illumined by them all,[195] like Nyssen, he both identifies light with

---

[184] CEun 226a/J.2.254.　[185] LP4.62,/J.8.2.50; LM 2.19.　[186] Virg 357a/J.8.1.297.　[187] LM 2.81.
[188] Perf 103/J.8.1.184–85, quoting Mal 3.20/4.2. References are by page in FC and volume and page in Jaeger.
[189] Virg 355a/J.8.1.290.　[190] Beat 3.111/J.7.2.104.　[191] LM 2.315.　[192] LM 2.26.
[193] Beat 1.85/J.7.2.77.　[194] CEun 137a/J.2.9.　[195] Or 40.41 and Or 39.11.

divine nature generally and appropriates it to particular persons of the Trinity. Light is one of Christ's titles;[196] he is light above light,[197] the first light,[198] who is called light because he is the brightness of souls purified by word and life.[199] As in Nyssen's theology, the Spirit bestows light; yet Nazianzen goes farther, also identifying the Spirit with light.[200]

Nazianzen also associates light with knowledge[201] and more specifically, graced knowledge. That light simply stands for a form of intellectual apprehension, of truth that is given rather than attained, is clear from the way he mixes visual and auditory images: 'Let us enlighten our ears ... and our tongue.'[202] It gives freely of itself [phōti phōs charizomenous] to bring us to the knowledge of the highest truths,[203] and as for Nyssen, this illumination benefits not only the individual believer, but the whole church.[204] The connection between the enlightened individual and the greater Body of Christ is baptism; although it was a commonplace of the early Church to think of baptism as illumination or enlightenment, Nazianzen makes more theological hay of this notion than perhaps any other patristic writer. Baptism is called illumination because of its splendour, and even to know its power in itself constitutes enlightenment. It brings the perfecting of the mind and the remodelling [syntheseōs] of the whole person.[205] The high degree of intellectualism in Gregory's conception of the effect of the sacrament becomes clear when he speaks of his own baptism: 'I cannot bear to be unenlightened after my Enlightenment, by marking with a false stamp [paracharassōn] any of the Three into whom I was baptised'[206] – thus runs one rationale for his rejection of Arianism.

Equally, though, illumination accompanies purity of life. 'Be purified', he urges, 'that you may stand as perfect lights beside that great light';[207] indeed a godly life [bios ho entheos] is itself light.[208] Typically, this spiritual or moral purity is linked to intellectual rectitude: he summarises the gist of his first theological oration as 'the theologian must be pure, in order that light may be apprehended [katalambanētai] by light'.[209] Even the resurrection provides light only in the degree that the mind [dianoia] is purified.[210] The self-diffusing quality of material light forms the analogical basis for an embryonic ecclesiology.

Because Christ is illumined, we may shine forth in companionship with him[211] and therefore illumination is to be shared, not hid under a bushel.[212] The light that unites us to the Trinity which is the source of

---

[196] Or 2.98 and Or 29.17. [197] Or 37.4. [198] Or 40.10. [199] Or 30.20.
[200] Or 41.9; 31.29, 'light' here rendering autophōs; Or 12.4. [201] Or 31.21. [202] Or 40.38.
[203] Or 41.6. [204] Or 5.35. [205] Or 40.3. [206] Or 34.11. [207] Or 39.20. [208] Or 30.20.
[209] Or 28.1. [210] Or 40.45. [211] Or 39.14. [212] Or 12.6.

light bids the theologian share with others light he has received, the worship of the Trinity.[213] Light breaks upon the church like dawn, gradually, and this property of light to reveal itself by degrees serves to explain the development of doctrine, in particular the late advent of the doctrine of the Spirit's divinity.[214]

For both Gregories, then, the theology of light becomes a mechanism for articulating the intellectual self-giving of the Trinity and the diffusing of divine knowledge through the cosmos. It is not only a play of metaphor or a rhetorical embellishment so much as a piece of systematic sinew, a fact that the modern reader may miss, given that light has ceased to figure in systematic theologies. If light represents the self-communication of pure goodness and truth, the passions represent the revolt of irrationality and disorder. Nyssen's theology of the passions – which encompasses both the dogmatic and the ascetical – departs from a clear schema of divine, human and brute attributes. The infinite must by nature be passionless, simply because passions wax and wane and the infinite does not admit of increase and decrease.[215] The same conclusion of passionlessness must be reached departing from reflection on divine immutability,[216] but also the assertion of divine purity, since Nyssen regards passion as a stain [kēlis].[217] Thus, the passions belong properly to the nature at furthest remove from the divine, that of the beasts, the irrational animals. What become passions in us are animal instincts of self-preservation that become frustrated in some way,[218] and as such, could not be evil in themselves (an element of Nyssen's theology whose importance we shall see shortly), yet it is our commonality with irrational nature that leaves us vulnerable to being assailed by the passions,[219] specifically because of the way we are generated;[220] the problem lies not in the inherent wickedness of sex, but the fact that the procreative process cannot be wholly subjected to the rule of reason.

The passions therefore correlate to the embodied, rather than the intellectual and spiritual, side of our nature, although the problem does not lie in the body itself.[221] The impulses connected to the passions reside

---

[213] Or 31.33.   [214] Or 31.27.   [215] 2CEun 257a/J.2.247.   [216] Soul 93/K110.
[217] LP 2.44/J.7.2.30.
[218] HumP 18.2/F214. For this reason, Fedwick's view that apatheia is the main characteristic of the soul regenerated through baptism (1994, 365) scarcely seems credible: the baptised will always struggle with the passions, as long as they have reason to have doubts about their own self-preservation.
[219] HumP pref 18/F110.   [220] HumP 30.30/F316.
[221] Here and in the following analysis, I thus differ sharply from John Cavarnos, who attributes the passions almost entirely to the flesh (a term which he seems to use interchangeably with 'body'

in our miserable life (i.e., here on earth),[222] a life made miserable, not by the good divine gift of a body, but of the poor human decision to indulge it inappropriately. The weakness of passion spreads like a film [lēmē] over the life of one who lives in an atmosphere of material indulgence,[223] so not bodily existence per se, but a fleshly life, is subject to the passions.[224] In the sinful passions there is a certain bond between soul and body (that is, a relation of equality, rather than the correct one of ruling principle to subordinate), and an analogy between bodily and spiritual death.[225]

As there are echoes of the Stoic notion of the *hēgemonikon* in Nyssen's notion of the intellect, now we will see how it informs his conception of the passions, although, as Figura rightly points out, Nyssen's conception of the passions differs significantly from that of the Stoics inasmuch as its goal is the soul's governance of them, rather than complete submission.[226] The passions often overwhelm the intellectual part of the soul:[227] when reason lets go of the reins of the chariot drawn by impulses, the latter are turned into passions,[228] and uncontrolled passion becomes a fierce and raging master to servile reasoning [tō andrapodōdei logismōi].[229] More insidiously, the passions apparently tempt the mind to action contrary to its own nature, prompting it to base movements; these, personified, are said to beset human nature.[230] Devoting one's soul to the will of the flesh results in the mind [dianoia], the most immaterial element of human nature, becoming paradoxically carnal.[231] At times, it seems that carnality is not a state into which some minds fall, but one element or characteristic of mind that lies within us all: we have a 'fleshly mind' [sarkos nekrōsas] and sacrifice consists in mortifying it.[232] Elsewhere, the problem seems much more external: the mind can fall prey to human deceit [apatē],[233] impassioned thoughts [tas empatheis tēs dianoias],[234] or simply lack of tutelage.[235] Enslavement to the passions forecloses any possibility of union with God, but only such enslavement can alienate the human soul from God. Although the passions are potent, however, they cannot of themselves gain control of any human being; only when reason consents to be overthrown can the passions gain the upper hand.[236] What allows us to raise ourselves above the passions is the noble spirit in us,

---

and which he interprets Gregory to be saying will ultimately be freed). See Cavarnos (1976), esp. 63 and 78.

[222] LP 4.62/J.7.2.50.   [223] Virg 354b/J.8.1.289.   [224] HumP 28.4/F278.   [225] CtOr 284/J.3.4.31.
[226] 1987, 32.   [227] HumP 12.3/F162.   [228] Soul 57/K52.   [229] LM 2.129.   [230] LM 2.125.
[231] Soul 76/K80.   [232] LP 3.46/J.7.2.32.   [233] Beat 2.104/J.7.2.97.   [234] LP 1.28/J.7.2.12.
[235] CEun 248b/J.2.311.   [236] HumP 18.3/F216.

which has the power to elevate our thoughts, a possibility apparently always lying within our reach.

In addition to a reasoning mind, therefore, we need a will determined to ignore the sleeve-tugging impulses which always threaten to turn into something worse, for cleansing from the passions occurs only through a deliberate act of the will [dia proaireseōs energeitai].[237] Prompted by misery, we allow ourselves to forget the divine gift of reason, and so passion is 'plastered over' the flesh, obscuring the beauty of God's image within us.[238] Thus, when Nyssen says that passion is a conformity [homoiōsis] of the soul to the irrational,[239] he is not speaking of a conformity imposed by an external force but the soul's own self-accommodation to what is inherently alien to it. Because it lies within us actively to turn from our gross thoughts and passionate longings towards the simple, immaterial Beauty, the emotions that prompt the passions cannot be considered good or bad in themselves, but only become negative forces through the active volition of those who have them.[240] Nevertheless the will is to be exercised, not as a tyrant stamping out all emotion, but precisely as an enlightened ruler; hence Nyssen's reading of the beatitudes, where the praise of meekness is not a command for the absolute absence of passion, but rather, moderation.[241] Maintaining such equilibrium comes about only through the exercise of the rational mind, for Nyssen insists that impulses of desire and anger come not from the body, but the soul, and therefore from what is intellectual in us[242] and therefore the body cannot be blamed for the sometimes brutish behaviour of human beings.

The voluntarist element of Nyssen's theology seems to chafe slightly against the prevalent imagery in his writings of the passions as a disease or a stain, since these are most often things we can do little to prevent. Nevertheless, although Nyssen can speak of the passions as a disease of

---

[237] CallC 88/J.8.1.140. References are by page in FC and Jaeger.
[238] HumP 18.6/F218.   [239] HumP 28.4/F280.
[240] Soul 60/K58. Wilken (2003) argues that Nyssen's conception of the passions is linked to his understanding of love: 'the passions prepare the way for the love of God' (298; cf. 299–303). While Gregory undoubtedly has positive things to say of love, the textual evidence Wilken cites leaves me unconvinced of the connection he claims to the passions, and even of the centrality of love in Nyssen's thought. Love may indeed rank first among the commandments in Nyssen's view, as Wilken points out (301), but that in itself does not demonstrate its centrality in the overall theological framework.
[241] Beat 2.103/J.7.2.95–96.
[242] Soul 49/K40. Here Gregory is the speaker, but in Macrina's subsequent response, she does not dispute the point, only denying that the passions are definitive of rational nature.

youth,[243] the fact that the worst of these is pleasure [hēdonē][244] indicates that he does not think we are merely victims of forces beyond our control: prayer has the power to deliver from this affliction, as the disease of any passion can be appeased by reason [dia tōn logismōn katapraunei tēn noson].[245] If God delivers up to passion those who do not know him,[246] then it lies within our powers to make the saving profession of faith. If the passions assault our nature,[247] as the Egyptians did the Israelites, then they can be put to death in the water,[248] in this instance, the water of baptism, for it is this water which washes away the stain of passion on the soul.[249]

A life enmeshed in the passions obviously could not acquire the likeness of the impassible divine nature to which it is our proper calling to be united,[250] and we must therefore approach the holy mountain of the contemplative and spiritual life free from passion, and undue concern for the body.[251] Not only purity is related to freedom from passion, therefore, but even more so, blessedness.[252] Freedom from passion is the beginning of a life of virtue,[253] and virtue is analogous to God.

Nazianzen has far less to say of the passions, but what he does follows closely the lineaments of Nyssen's thought on the subject. Passion is not will,[254] and is even opposed to the rational element in us. The passions can be restrained by temperance [sōphrosynēi] using the gift of reason to overcome pleasure and the brutish instincts raging within us.[255] We can choose to follow Christ the Teacher or be our own teachers, but, either way, must work to excise [tmēthēnai] the passions, both bodily and spiritual.[256] The connection between passion and reason is not only that rule by the passions indicates reason has been usurped, but that those who portray the passions as inevitable or good have made a fundamental category error. This was the problem of the Greeks: not only their philosophy was wrong, but also their religion, for they made even the gods advocates of the passions.[257] Both Gregories, then, treat the connection between passion and irrationality systematically, from the assertion of impassibility in the doctrine of God, in consequence of divine nature's being supremely intellectual, to an ascetical theology urging moderation.

---

[243] LP 1.29/J.7.2.14.   [244] LM 2.301.
[245] Beat 2.104/J.7.2.97.   [246] LM 2.75.
[247] Literally, kakias, or evils, but the examples Gregory gives are all of states he usually describes as passions, such as anger, pride and envy.
[248] LM 2.125.   [249] CtOr 324/J.3.4.103.   [250] Beat 1.90/J.7.2.82.   [251] LM 1.42.
[252] CtOr 317/J.3.4.491.   [253] CtOr 280/J.3.4.24.   [254] Or 29.6.   [255] Or 45.18.
[256] Or 37.21.   [257] Or 39.7.

At all these levels the treatment of the passions signifies the import of the intellect in their theologies.

In a sense, for the Cappadocians, the working out of the mind's relation to God comes through the life of virtue, and the activity of the intellect is thus conceived of as inseparable from that of the will. It is important to their theology, therefore, to have an anthropological basis for claiming virtue lies within human reach. Nothing in our constitution is opposed to virtue, Nyssen maintains,[258] and indeed, zeal for virtue is the only truly existing thing [pagion ti esti kai enupostaton].[259] Resisting the passions does not merely lead us to a morally neutral position, but is actively a work of virtue, so the rational faculties are the parents of virtue.[260] The movement from merely resisting passion to actively possessing virtue is almost a matter of course: if reason assumes sway over the emotions, each of them is converted into a form of virtue.[261] That is why Nyssen can regard all virtue as springing from the union of two intellectual habits, justice and wisdom.[262]

However, Nyssen sometimes portrays virtue as a preparatory stage in the spiritual life, specifically, the antecedent to knowledge of God.[263] Thus the people of Israel were not ready to receive the theophany until they were purified, not only by the sprinkling of water, but by chastity. In the post-Biblical era, Christ renders the holy mountain accessible through virtue, and there gives not only the vision of divine power, but an actual share in it, so the people are brought into kinship with divine nature [eis syngeneian].[264] Because virtue and participation in God are identified, Nyssen predicates infinitude of virtue as he does of divine nature: possession of virtue is not circumscribed, and, conversely, whatever is marked off by boundaries is not virtue.[265] To be virtuous, then, is to resemble divinity in one of the characteristics proper and unique to divine nature.

Virtue consists both in certain kinds of knowledge and in right action; it is, as it were, the middle term between soul and body. So religious

---

[258] CtOr 292/J.3.4.45. [259] Beat 4.126/J.7.2.120. [260] LM 2.4.
[261] HumP 18.5/F218. [262] CtOr 297/J.4.54.
[263] Thus I differ from Bebis (1966–67), who holds that virtue, ascent and contemplation are the 'trilogy' of the ascetic life and the basis of the mystical life of the Christian, with virtue being equated with, first, faith and knowledge of God, and second, moral 'achievements' and purity of life (380). His overall characterisation of LM stresses its apophatic element to the point of making unknowing seem inherently holy (392–93), a conclusion which he can reach, I think, only because his schema as a whole understates the significance of mind, in part because of the subsuming of knowledge under the heading of virtue. For Daniélou, virtue is a participation in the very life of God, which permits us to know something of him; this he calls 'cette doctrine de la connaissance de Dieu dans le miroir des vertus' (1953, 99).
[264] LP 2.35/J.7.2.20. [265] Beat 4.127/J.7.2.120–21 and LM 1.5.

virtue is divided into what pertains to the divine and what pertains to right conduct,[266] a statement which Gregory later glosses, clarifying that the first of these components of virtue ('what pertains to the divine') is faith.[267] Because knowledge looms so large in this account, he maintains that the one road to divine life for the virtues is knowing what the name of Christ means; the will's conformity to this knowledge comes second.[268] The ordering of the anthropology is therefore preserved in the ethics and ascetical theology: mind is logically prior to will, and the lower appetites are to be subordinated to the rational appetite, which is the will – that is why, for Nazianzen, philosophy can open the way to virtue and blessedness.[269]

Nyssen, in contrast, often seems to match his ambivalence about the body with an almost equal hesitation with respect to the mind. His writings are full of references to the multifarious ways in which human minds can go astray, betraying God's good intentions for them. The mind [ennoia] that attempts to conceive of God can do so only if it resolutely frees itself from carnal conceptions of such matters as generation.[270] At times, Nyssen portrays the problem as moral, the mind's becoming bent by its own habits: through wrong thinking [gnōmē], it is misled; such is the consequence of espousing heresy.[271] On other occasions, he virtually equates wrong thinking with insanity. The mind which entertains theologically incongruous ideas (such as the imperfection of the Holy Spirit) falls into madness [paraplēxia].[272] Not only theology, but also the spiritual life is endangered by the mind's susceptibility: those who babble nonsense when they pray suffer from a mental illness [tēs kata

---

[266] LM 2.166.   [267] LM 2.192 and 198.
[268] Perf 101/J.8.1.181. Nazianzen's treatment of virtue is slight. He takes for granted that keeping the commandments means purifying the flesh, and that where there is purification, illumination necessarily also enters in (Or. 39.8), but beyond this, seems little interested in the subject.
[269] Or 25.1 and 25.10.
[270] CEun 93b/J.1.207. Gregory uses a variety of terms designating mind and intellect (for example, *dianoia* and *psychē*, in addition to *nous*). Daniélou (1953) maintains that he prefers *dianoia* to *nous*, since the former better designates a faculty than the latter (267). Daniélou may be correct, although he provides no hard evidence for the claim and it could of course only be established by a careful gathering of statistics. The fact that Gregory, like the other Fathers, seems little concerned to make fine distinctions among the terms he sues (for example, by defining them), suggests that the actual terminology makes little difference to the overall structure of his theology. Balthasar (1988) makes the even stronger assertion that 'Plotinus' realm of "*nous*" finds itself excluded from the domain of reality [in Nyssen's thought]' (19). It is not quite clear what Balthasar means by this claim. He claims Origen identifies *nous* with the Logos and that 'Christian metaphysics' assigned *nous* an intermediary place between the Father and the soul, but that this position proved untenable, and although Augustine tried to maintain it, Nyssen abandons it. He gives no references to primary texts to support any of these claims.
[271] CEun 112a/J.2.343.   [272] HSp 318a/J.3.1.94.

noun autōn arrōstias]²⁷³ and the consequence of the mind's predisposition to the passions [dia tēs empathous diatheseōs] is no less than the alienation [allotriōsis] of the soul from God.²⁷⁴

Falling into disease, ignorance or depravity is easy enough, but is not the only option for the human mind, whose mutability also offers the possibility of health. If corrupt minds exist, so do lofty ones: these look up, while grosser intellects look down.²⁷⁵ True sobriety of mind [sōphrosynē] embraces the emotional as well as the strictly intellectual dimensions of human existence, for it consists in self-control, through the exertion of intellectual virtues such as wisdom or prudence.²⁷⁶ The other virtues also have a role: temperance ensures the mind never dwells on seductive pleasures, taste in particular.²⁷⁷ Not only pleasure can derail the intellect, however; hardship can have a similar effect, and it is the clear-seeing mind that is deflected from its path by neither.²⁷⁸ The fact that it is specifically intellectual virtues which curb the mind's baser instincts indicates that even in his most sceptical moments, Nyssen remains firmly within the Origenistic theology of the intellect.

When discussing the temptations which assail the mind, Nyssen speaks as if resistance lies well within human powers; in the context of the mind raising its gaze, however, he tends to stress the need for divine assistance. In its natural state, the human mind is not so much corrupt, as immature, this immaturity being one reason for its need for divine assistance: the Lord strengthens its weakness, helping it to grow out of infancy, as a kind of prelude to the perfection which will come with the resurrection.²⁷⁹ Because the mind should be governed [dioikeisthai] by God,²⁸⁰ the devout accept, not their own conclusions, but the nobler ones of the Spirit.²⁸¹ More strongly still, Nyssen can refer to the intellect's accepting doctrinal 'orders' from God, believing what is required of it,²⁸² strong language from one whose ethics bears the deep mark of voluntarism, but this view is corrected by Macrina, who points out that such an attitude towards the soul would imply hostility to virtue. The extent of the mind's autonomy may simply be an area where Nyssen could not reconcile conflicting insights which all seemed to him to have some ground: of itself, the human mind has no power to move towards the good (at least as long as it does not turn away from pleasure).²⁸³ Our material nature

---

²⁷³ LP 1.29/J.7.2.14.   ²⁷⁴ LP 1.31/J.7.2.16.   ²⁷⁵ Virg 350a/J.8.1.272.   ²⁷⁶ Virg 364a/J.8.1.320.
²⁷⁷ Virg 366b/J.8.1.329.   ²⁷⁸ Virg 349b/J.8.1.271–72.   ²⁷⁹ HumP 25.7/F256.
²⁸⁰ HumP 12.13/F172.   ²⁸¹ HSp 317b/J.3.1.94.   ²⁸² Soul 29/K6.   ²⁸³ Virg 352a/J.8.1.280.

can be governed by the mind, which is in turn governed by God, as long as the body does not become perverted from its own nature and so alienated from the mind.[284] The mind [nous] discriminates between the truly good and the only apparently so[285] but its capacities are limited, so we cannot even grasp the nature of our own generation.[286] Our minds are still at the foot of the holy mountain, without further guidance unable to ascend to the summit and the divine theophany.[287] In the third sermon on the Beatitudes, the Word guides; elsewhere the need is for the inspiration of the Spirit: the Spirit 'bears witness with our Spirit' and that means the Spirit dwells [engignomai] in the mind of the faithful.[288] Just so, it is the human cognitive capacity [tōi nooumenōi] that makes it possible for Christ to be present to his disciples after the ascension.[289]

The pattern is complex, but it is clear that the power of mind for Nyssen therefore inheres fundamentally in the divine, not the human, intellect.[290] The human mind resembles that of its creator,[291] but conformity to the divine image is affected by the supreme beauty.[292] Desire for what is beautiful elevates the mind (here, phronēma) so as to effect our conformity to the beauty of the divine image,[293] the divine nature [theiotēs] which is fundamentally intellectual [noēton],[294] mind [nous] and word.[295] The human mind resembles its archetype even in incomprehensibility: for all the power of our minds to know other things, they cannot know themselves.[296] Yet the created mind images not divine essence itself, but the divine power of wisdom, and the limitations of resemblance stipulate the limitations of human meditation on the divine: we apprehend not God's qualities, but his energies or effects.[297] The mind cannot attain to that which is [oute gar hē dianoia kathikneitai tou ontos], however sublime the thoughts we may think about it.[298]

---

[284] HumP 12.13/F172. [285] CtOr 298/J.3.4.56. [286] CtOr 313/J.3.4.83.
[287] Beat 3.106/J.7.2.98–99. [288] CEun 191b/J.2.161. [289] CtOr 312/J.3.4.81.
[290] The interpretation here parallels Harrison's analysis of the role of faith in Nyssen's thought. On her reading, he does not contrast all knowledge with faith, plumping for faith as the better means to God, but only knowledge in the Eunomian sense. Knowledge is bounded by what the mind can contain, but faith moves beyond the boundary, bridging the gap between the created and the uncreated (Harrison 1992, 67). The question which Harrison does not answer directly is: with what do we have faith? Her analysis of faith revolves around the relation of knowledge and love (see esp. 81), which implies the engagement of the intellect, inasmuch as it seems inseparable from will.
[291] HumP 11.4/F158; Soul 45/K32. Nyssen does not, however, reason solely from divine to human nature. As Barnes points out, in HumP, he argues that just as the mind is one despite its multiple faculties and diverse operations, so God is one, and Barnes remarks upon this appearance of an Aristotelian psychology in the heart of a supposedly thoroughly Platonic author (1994, 11).
[292] HumP 12.9/F168. [293] HumP 18.5/F218. [294] HumP 24.2/F250. [295] HumP 5.2/F130.
[296] HumP 11.4/F158. [297] Beat 6.147/J.7.2.141; cp. 2CEun 265b/J.1.270. [298] Beat 1.88/J.7.2.80.

Divine assistance bridges the divide remaining between humanity and God, a gap inherent in the fact that humankind is a kind of middle term between the divine and the animal. Nyssen regards the mind as fully integrated into our animal nature, but it is not enclosed within the body's parameters, which suggests he does not regard it as a bodily organ at all.[299] It is not confined within any one part of us;[300] rather, it empowers and gives itself to every sensory organ,[301] receiving from these the kind of knowledge that lies within their power to impart,[302] yet in gathering information about what is external to the body via the body, the mind remains aloof.

Nazianzen's view of mind shows fewer signs of conflict: what is godlike within us is mind and reason [nous kai logos][303] and he acknowledges that even the mind is not so godlike as to escape any threat of corruption, though he seems on the whole less preoccupied with the distinction between lofty and lowly minds than Nyssen. He goads his listeners, asking how long they will be 'hard-hearted and coarse-minded [that is, coarse in dianoia]?'[304] but immediately before this galvanising rhetorical question, he rapturously recounts the state of the soul that has shaken off the fetters that held it down and bound the wings of the mind, becoming one in spirit and mind and God. The problem does not seem rooted in differing types of minds, carnal and sublime, as in Nyssen's thought, but in the need to discipline oneself against laziness. Elsewhere, Nazianzen makes clear that the mind's problem lies not so much in the mind's corrupting itself, as in its being usurped by that which is alien to it: the Greeks (which seems a way of designating philosophy as a discipline, rather than any cultural or national group) implanted improperly a tree of knowledge in us, causing our removal away from the Tree of Life; far from making us more intelligent, this supplantation carried away the mind and the ruling power in us, opening the door to the passions.[305] Because he does not view the mind itself as susceptible to illness, even when he rebukes his opponents for their mindset [dianoian],[306] he falls short of any claim of fundamental putrefaction of the mind itself.

Although on occasion his glorification of mind over matter acquires sharply dualistic overtones, as in an extended passage in his oration on

---

[299] CtOr 287/J.3.4.38.   [300] HumP 15.3/F194.   [301] Soul 38/K20.   [302] HumP 10.7/F157.
[303] Or 28.17. Ellverson attempts to distinguish between *nous* on the one hand (which she translates as 'mind') and reason or intellect on the other (*logos* or *dianoia*), but admits that Nazianzen's usage is 'not totally fixed or coherent' (1981, 23). It is not fixed, certainly, though there is no reason to assume that a fluid use of these terms is necessarily incoherent, as she seems to do.
[304] Or 7.22.   [305] Or 39.7.   [306] Or 27.1.

Athanasius, where he speaks of 'those who, being yoked to matter, become mired in the mud and so are unable to look at the rays of truth',[307] he portrays mind and sense as not so much fundamentally at odds with one another as simply distinct. Each remains within its own boundaries; each bears within itself the magnificence of the creative Word. They are opposites and do not mingle, but do not seem to work against each other.[308] We are therefore 'mingled worshippers' [proskynētēn mikton] who belong fully to the visible creation, but only partly to the intellectual, suspended halfway between greatness and lowliness.[309]

The balancing act in Nazianzen's work takes place not so much on the occasion of two kinds of mind, as in relation to the capacities and limitations of the human intellect. The point of our having a mind is to conceive of God, but reflection on divine nature encompasses a variety of activities, not solely formal theology; the chief purpose of the festival of the Holy Lights, for example, is to bear God in mind,[310] apparently an effort in sustained awareness rather than determined cogitation. Nevertheless, the illuminated state of one's mind, indeed its divine quality, shows in theological acumen, such as knowing the Spirit is God.[311] Even lesser sorts of knowledge, such as awareness of the power of baptism, are a form of enlightenment.[312] However elementary the knowledge Nazianzen countenances as varieties of enlightenment, he still considers the mind's affinities as lying beyond the things of this world: it yearns to transcend corporeal things and consort with the incorporeal, longing, as every rational creature does, for God as the first cause (for the mind's proper object is God)[313] even though it is unable to grasp him. Significantly, the real peril lies not in this limitation itself, but our refusal to accept it; we chafe against this disability, growing impatient, and in so doing, becoming vulnerable to turning to visible things for a glimpse of God, so opening the door to idolatry.[314]

The distinction between the Cappadocians' view of intellect itself and the uses to which it is put escapes easy characterisation, simply because of their tendency to qualify an overwhelmingly positive estimation of the mind with warnings about the possibilities of its misuse. For Nyssen, therefore, heretics like the Manichees fall into their errors through a species of absurdity [atopia, a favourite word of Nyssen's],[315] and fallacious reasoning not only captivates Eunomius and his followers, but causes them to deceive others.[316] Consequently, the insulting tenor of

---

[307] Or 21.2. [308] Or 45.7. [309] Or 38.11. [310] Or 39.11. [311] Or 41.6. [312] Or 40.1.
[313] Or 28.22. [314] Or 28.13–14. [315] CEun 83b/J.1.178. [316] 2CEun 256a–b/J.1.244.

their discourse Nyssen attributes, not to any want of charity, but sick minds [arrōstia kai dysklēria psychēs].³¹⁷ Failure in reasoning results in non-intellectual sins as well: lack of training in reasoning can lead to gluttony.³¹⁸ To abandon reason therefore means sinking into licentiousness, but more, the very denial of one's humanity as a result of which we become animals [boskēmata].³¹⁹ The connection between failures of reason and carnal vice goes back to the mind's role as the ruling principle. Reason should hold the reins of the chariot; when it lets go of them, the chariot not only runs out of control, but the charioteer is dragged behind it, a stark image illustrating not only how impulses are turned into passions, but the way in which, once successful in usurpation, they damage the intellectual faculties themselves.³²⁰ This grim state of affairs is always avoidable, however, for even though it lies beyond our nature completely to eradicate the passions, reason still remains stronger than passion.³²¹

In the devout reasoner [tais dianoiais tōn eusebōs logizomenōn], apparent logical difficulties, such as the First Person's identity as both Father and Ungenerate One, can be held together³²² so reason, far from assailing piety, aids it; hence reason, along with desire for a virtuous life, can purify the soul.³²³ Notably, even the Fall cannot so damage reason as to render it helpless: the archetypal beauty of humanity is disfigured by sin, but reason [logos] counsels us to wash it off.³²⁴ Reason looms so large in Nyssen's thought as to constitute a lens through which he reads Old Testament passages, which from a modern perspective are unlikely vehicles for his intellectualising parables: Abraham, father of the faithful, set out on his travels, which in Nyssen's description seems overwhelmingly a journey through the undiscovered country of the mind, his journey of reasoning taking him far beyond the wisdom of his countrymen,³²⁵ so that he was led to grasp the power of God, his goodness and his infinity.³²⁶

Despite this overwhelmingly sanguine appraisal of reason, Nyssen retains a firm awareness of its sheer limitation. Divine nature lies above all the speculative powers of human reason,³²⁷ reason [tōn logismōn] furnishing only a dim [amudran] and imperfect [brachutatēn] understanding of God, and even the Incarnation, the most tangible form of divine self-disclosure, defeats reason's powers of investigation.³²⁸ More

---

[317] 2CEun 313a/J.1.406. [318] Soul 71/K76. [319] LM 2.302. [320] Soul 57–58/K54.
[321] Beat 2.103 and 104/J.7.2.94–95. [322] CEun 91a/J.1.198. [323] Soul 96/K114.
[324] Virg 358a/J.8.1.300. [325] 2CEun 259a/J.1.251. [326] 2CEun 259b/J.1.253.
[327] 2 CEun 260a–b/J.1.254–55 passim. [328] CtOr 288/J.3.4.39.

generally, though, human reasoning lacks muscle (it is 'atonos'),[329] wavering and doubting.[330] Because of the unreliability of human reasoning, Nyssen insists on the necessity of aid from without: logical reasoning alone will not lead us to correct doctrine,[331] so Christians rely on scripture as the normative rule of truth,[332] along with the tradition received from the Fathers.[333] Nyssen's doubts about the reliability of human reason correlate with a high estimation of the role of scripture. He contrasts it with trivial and base notions of our own.[334] Unlike errant human reasoning, scripture can guide the Christian thinker to the safe harbour of divine will.[335] Its language may be figurative, but it gives 'scientific understanding' of the nature of soul – though admittedly, on this point, profane learning is also correct.[336] However scripture's value seems to lie not so much in the information it provides, as the direction in which it merely gestures. Its role is preparatory, telling us what to accomplish before we approach the mountain of divine knowledge [tōi tēs theognosias orei].[337]

For all its caveats, however, Nyssen's theology reflects his firm conviction that there is reason in God (literally, God is not 'alogon'),[338] and this reason, along with wisdom, governs all things.[339] His basic anthropology is equally clear: the power of human reasoning is a work of God.[340] Along with the capacities for laughter and for knowledge, the reasoning faculty [to logikon] is proper to humanity;[341] thought and reason [to dianoētikon te kai logikon] are the distinctive properties of our nature.[342]

Nazianzen's view of reason and reasoning bears a marked similarity to Nyssen's, though it is not elaborated in as much detail. Less inclined to identify reason as what properly characterises either divine or human nature, Nazianzen nevertheless affirms that reason proceeds from God, who implants it in us, so along with mind, reason is godlike and divine.[343] Reason is also peculiarly associated with the Word: it is because we belong to the Word that we escape irrationality.[344] Reason further gives us the power to escape the worldliness associated with the flesh, for it is reason that leads the soul up towards God, giving it wings.[345] Reason in Nazianzen's thought is also the rider of the hard-mouthed horse of the passions, the one that must take care not to be thrown by an unruly

---

[329] HumP 26.1/F266. [330] LM 2.243. [331] Soul 29/K6. [332] Soul 50/K40.
[333] Abl 331b/ J.3.1.39. [334] ChrM 128/J.8.1.43. [335] LM 1.11. [336] LM 2.96. [337] LM 2.152.
[338] CtOr 270/J.3.4.8. [339] CtOr 275/J.3.4.16. [340] 2CEun 275a/J.1.298.
[341] 2CEun 256a/J.1.244. [342] Soul 56 and 57/K50. [343] Or 28.17. [344] Or 6.4.
[345] Or 37.11. Here the Platonic parallel is unmistakable; see *Phaedrus* 246.

mount – but it does this, paradoxically, by keeping within its limits and philosophising only within proper bounds.[346]

Reasoning can therefore be a threat and Nazianzen may be on balance more concerned about this prospect than he is encouraged by reason's capabilities. As with Nyssen, there is keen awareness of the limitations of human reasoning; how, he asks, can you rightly conceive of [hypolēpsei] the deity while relying on the approximations [ephodois] of reason?[347] Quite aside from its limitations, reason is additionally susceptible to outright deception – even the desire for God, surely unambiguously good in itself, can be deceived by reason, hence his fear that some absurd [atopos] reasoning may come in[348] and his railing against bitter reasoners about divine nature.[349] Idolators endowed with a rational nature and who have even received divine grace still go astray,[350] so he counsels that faith should lead us rather than reason [logos] – that will at least teach us reason's feebleness [to asthenes].[351] Reason, if sovereign among human faculties, is never autonomous: those who reason can lean upon nothing but the will of God.[352] Such statements lead themselves to two quite different conclusions: on the one hand, one might take them as evidence that human reason avails little unless helped by God; on the other, they may be seen as yet another systematic ligament expressing the relation of God and humanity via the intellect.

The Cappadocians display little such diffidence when it comes to wisdom. In Nyssen's writings, a few ironic references appear to 'the wisdom that has made humanity foolish' [tēn mōrantheisan sophian],[353] which differs utterly from the beliefs of Christians; although he can also give credit where it is due, acknowledging the truth of the Epicurean teaching that it is the mind which sees and hears,[354] showing himself to be quite content to adopt pagan conceptualities when he finds them correct. Minor digs at secular learning aside, both Gregories hold an unambiguously positive view of the matter. They identify wisdom both with the second divine hypostasis and with divine nature itself. So for Nyssen, Christ is God's wisdom[355] or simply wisdom[356] and for Nazianzen the Word and the Saviour are identified with wisdom,[357] God is wisdom (Nyssen)[358] and wisdom is another name for the First Nature (Nazianzen).[359]

---

[346] Or 27.5. [347] Or 28.7. [348] Or 37.15. [349] Or 45.26. [350] Or 28.15. [351] Or 28.28.
[352] Or 28.26. [353] CEun 226a/J.2.255. [354] Soul 38/K20. [355] Abl 334b/J.3.1.49.
[356] CEun 101/J.2.312; CEun 141a/J.2.22; CEun 210b/J.2.214. [357] Or 29.17; Or 30.2.
[358] Beat 1.87/J.7.2.80. [359] Or 28.13.

Most often, however, wisdom is associated not with divine nature but its effects, particularly creative and providential ones. Thus, Nyssen affirms that it was by wisdom that God made all things[360] and that through it even evil can be induced to cooperate with the good.[361] This providential governance is so obvious in Nyssen's view that everyone must acknowledge that reason and wisdom govern all existing things[362] and create harmony among the strongly opposed elements of the sensible world.[363] That harmony is evident particularly in the orderly arrangement of the heavens, which displays divine wisdom for all to see.[364] Although the gift of wisdom enables us rightly to understand all else and so to grasp something of their Source, we can no more comprehend wisdom itself than we can grasp divine nature.[365] The dual emphasis on wisdom's manifestation in creation and the appropriation of wisdom to the Second Person indicates that Nyssen conceives of it more as a divine power working *ad extra* than as an attribute chiefly constitutive of divine nature (as immutability is, for instance). In Christ, wisdom and power are woven together, and because this is so, he is the one through whom all things were made; contemplation of these indescribable wonders leads us to worship the wisdom of that maker,[366] so the Incarnation itself reveals divine wisdom, particularly its linkage to goodness and justice.[367] Nyssen's theology contrasts with Nazianzen's in this respect, for on the latter's account wisdom bears its fruit in the created order, but he tends more to associate this wisdom with the First Person, who creates the harmonic cosmos through his Word.[368]

The chief effect of wisdom, however, displays itself in human beings, to whom wisdom is imparted. Particular persons are singled out as notable examples of wisdom; for Nyssen, Paul[369] and for Nazianzen, his own father,[370] but for the most part, the concern is to assert wisdom's more general inspiration. Nyssen stresses wisdom's connection to other virtues: it does not come apart from other gifts of the Spirit,[371] for it is linked particularly to another virtue classified as intellectual by Aristotle, namely prudence.[372] The tenor of an Aristotelian ethic is suggested also in Nyssen's notion that wisdom shows the middle way between extremes.[373] Wisdom on Nyssen's account therefore functions in something of the

---

[360] 2CEun 290b/J.1.343. [361] Nyssen, Inf 380b/J.3.3.95. [362] CtOr 275/J.3.4.16 rep.
[363] CtOr 278/J.3.4.21. [364] LM 2.168. [365] Soul 34/K16. [366] Perf 101/J.8.1.182.
[367] CtOr 300/J.4.60. [368] Or 2.74–75. [369] CEun 86a/J.1.184. [370] Or 18.16.
[371] CEun 140a/J.2.18. [372] LP 3.50/J.7.2.36; Virg 363b/J.8.1.319.
[373] LM 2.289. Heine (1975) downplays the roots of Gregory's ethic in preceding philosophy, claiming his emphasis on both belief and conduct derives from the prior Christian tradition in the first instance (123–25). The evidence he presents certainly indicates there was such an ecclesiastical

way in which prudence does for Aristotle, as a controlling and guiding principle, a meta-virtue: the virtuous person is one who has been taught by wisdom,[374] so wisdom enables the acquisition of other virtues. The more sheerly intellectual effect of wisdom emerges in the claim that the apprehension of the truth comes particularly through the power of wisdom,[375] although the conviction of the unbridgeable gap between the finite intellect and the infinite object appears in this context, too. Although wisdom is 'begotten' in the faithful, and so is unmistakably a work of grace,[376] interpreting, describing or explaining the divine essence remains a form of wisdom in which we are unlearned [amatheis].[377] The one who is enamoured of wisdom can only cleave to the true wisdom, God, like a bridegroom to his beloved.[378]

Despite Nazianzen's having had more formal education than Nyssen, including a better grounding in philosophy, his thought bears little trace of Aristotelianism in his treatment of wisdom and he shows less interest in it overall, beyond the occasional rehearsal of Biblical commonplaces (Ps III.10, 'the fear of the Lord is the beginning of wisdom').[379] When he links wisdom to other virtues, it is to holiness more generally;[380] it is not possible, in his view, for wisdom to remain within the subject, as knowledge does, for we cannot participate in wisdom without living it [anastraphentas].[381] In this respect, he mirrors Nyssen's portrayal of wisdom chiefly as a power, rather than a divine attribute.

Despite the fact that knowledge[382] may be purely mundane or secular, its connotations in Cappadocian theology tend markedly to the positive. A great many uses of the word in Nyssen's works occur in the phrase 'knowledge of God' (the genitive being objective – i.e., designating our knowledge of God), although the connection of knowledge to the Fall is also acknowledged: Adam and Eve were forbidden, not only knowledge of evil, but of good as well.[383] Still, eating the fruits of the Garden of Eden grants both knowledge and eternal life[384] in Nyssen's view, and for Nazianzen as well, the associations of the Tree are by no means wholly negative: the problem was not that its fruits were eaten, but that they were not consumed at the right time.[385]

---

tradition, but does not demonstrate that Nyssen had not also been exposed in some way to Aristotelian ethics, to which aspects of his thought do bear a strong resemblance at times.
[374] Inf 377b/J.3.2.85.   [375] CEun 140a/J.2.18.   [376] CEun 141b/J.2.18 and 142a/J.2.25.
[377] CEun 146b/J.2.38.   [378] Virg 366b/J.8.1.328.   [379] Or 21.6.   [380] Or 2.45.   [381] Or 4.113.
[382] The Gregories use gnōsis, epignōsis and epistēmē, with little concern to differentiate between them or define their parameters.
[383] Virg 359a/J.8.1.304.   [384] CtOr 276/J.3.4.18.   [385] Or 38.12.

Nyssen's epistemology ranges very widely. His notion of knowledge includes what is gathered from organs of sense,[386] but also of divine things. Verna Harrison points out that because of the general structure of human knowledge in Gregory's thought, in virtue of which we know the manifestations of things [epinoiai], but never their essence, divine incomprehensibility parallels the incomprehensibility of created things, even though the problem is greater and more fundamental in the former case, in virtue of the ontological distinction of God and humanity.[387] Knowledge of divine things therefore undergirds all other forms of knowledge, ensuring their rectitude. Accordingly, some knowledge can only be attained through the 'touch' of reason and through knowing that what one seeks transcends knowledge.[388] Religious knowledge [tēs eusebeias hē gnōsis], in particular, comes to those who receive it as light,[389] rather than attempting to manufacture it for themselves. It can be given from above by the saints[390] and it can come after a process of purification from sensual and irrational emotion,[391] or more starkly, winning victory over these assailants.[392] Accordingly, Nyssen explicitly acknowledges that there is no one path to knowledge of God.[393] Such knowledge as we do have only approximates what we seek: true being is inaccessible to human knowledge [epignōsis],[394] although less radically, Nyssen will admit that what evades us is not any sort of knowledge whatsoever, but a stretching out and encompassing what exceeds knowledge (i.e., comprehension).[395]

Unfortunately, knowledge of God is not all that evades us: we do not grasp the nature of our own minds, either, and Nyssen is blunt enough to ask the obvious question: how can someone who is ignorant of herself have knowledge of something above herself?[396] One response might be that we turn to knowledge God himself gives in scripture, but Nyssen's view of the latter is surprisingly sober: the scriptural account of creation is no more than a beginner's introduction to knowledge of God himself,

---

[386] HumP 10.3/F152; cp. Soul 38/K20.   [387] Harrison 1992, 59.   [388] 2CEun 264a/J.1.265–66.
[389] LM 2.162.
[390] CEun 136a/J.2.5. As McGuckin notes, tradition for Gregory consists not only in formal education but is also a charismatic matter related to the enlightenment of particular saints (2001, 289, n. 327).
[391] LM 2.157; here knowledge is theognōsis.   [392] LM 2.152.   [393] 2CEun 298a/J.1.365.
[394] LM 2.235.
[395] 2CEun 256a/J.1.243. It does not, however, fit neatly into any scheme based on later notions of 'mystical': it is not possible to determine from the texts whether Nyssen himself had had 'mystical' experiences and so the debate about whether his notion of knowledge of God is based on such personal experiences is in my view unhelpfully speculative. For a summary of the battle and its contenders see Stritzky (1973), 67–70.
[396] 2CEun 262a/J.1.260.

indicating by sensible objects what lies beyond them.³⁹⁷ The operations [energeiōn] of God can therefore give us some idea of that which ultimately evades our knowledge.³⁹⁸ What cannot be fully known can nevertheless be adored, and in a passage which foreshadows Augustine, Nyssen writes: 'the life of the superior nature [tēs anō physeōs] is love, since the beautiful [to kalon] is in every respect lovable for them that know it... knowledge becomes love, because that which is known is by nature beautiful'.³⁹⁹

Nazianzen shows much less interest in the question of knowledge, certainly in the subtleties of religious epistemology. Knowledge [epistēmē] feeds the ecclesiastical flock⁴⁰⁰ and full knowledge [epignōsis] is a great light.⁴⁰¹ The rhetor's concern to communicate manifests itself in the almost shocking assumption behind his question 'how long shall we... withhold from others the full [knowledge of] divine nature [tēs teleias theiotētos]?'⁴⁰² If the idea that anyone could have such knowledge, let alone pass it on to others, seems breathtakingly overconfident, it is perhaps because of what Nazianzen takes knowledge to be: simply beatitude [makariotēs],⁴⁰³ and it is unthinkable that blessedness should be withheld from the saints.

There is little difference between the estimation of knowledge and thought or thoughts (usually, noēma or logismos) in the theology of either Gregory; neither seems much concerned to distinguish the process of reflection from its fruits, or the fruit of teaching.⁴⁰⁴ In Nyssen's view, thought comes in many varieties: it can be profane [bebēlos],⁴⁰⁵ empty [koilōn] and base,⁴⁰⁶ pure [katharas],⁴⁰⁷ prudent and farsighted,⁴⁰⁸ virtuous,⁴⁰⁹ and even sublime.⁴¹⁰ Nevertheless, although the gift of thought comes from God,⁴¹¹ and the purification bestowed by the Spirit enables high thought,⁴¹² and despite the fact that estrangement from evil comes about only at the prompting of thought [tēi tēs dianoias hormēi],⁴¹³ and that thought [enthumion] is one of three characteristics of the life of Christ (along with action and word [praxis and logos]),⁴¹⁴ thought no more attains its ultimate object than knowledge does. It seems that reason

---

[397] 2CEun 273a/J.1.292. [398] Eust 328b/J.3.1.11.
[399] Soul 81/K90. I see no basis for Fedwick's claim that a knowledge of being [gnōsis tōn ontōn] is 'the supreme end of religion for Gregory' (1989, 349, citing Jaeger).
[400] Or 2.117. [401] Or 38.2. [402] Or 12.6. [403] Or 23.305.12.
[404] Indeed, translations often render epinoia as 'knowledge', when it more strictly corresponds to 'reflection' or 'thought'.
[405] LP 3.47/J.7.2.33. [406] Beat 1.85/J.7.2.77. [407] Perf 109/J.8.1.193. [408] LM 2.7.
[409] LM 2.97. [410] Beat 3.112/J.7.2.104. [411] LP 5.82/J.7.2.71. [412] LP 3.56/J.7.2.44.
[413] CallC 88/J.8.1.140. [414] Perf 120/J.8.1.210.

[logismos] can nudge thought to pass beyond the senses and so to reach intellectual nature,[415] but divine nature still transcends all cognitive thought [gnōstikou noēmatos].[416] Human thought simply cannot search out the nature above us which we seek.[417]

Nazianzen estimates the value of thought rather more highly; for him, God as the highest of all objects of thought is the one who gave substance to the intelligible world.[418] Indeed, God is the most beautiful of all objects of thought [tōn nooumenōn],[419] of whom we should think more often than we draw our breath.[420] Nazianzen's notion of thought therefore anticipates his notion of contemplation: in his theology the two scarcely differ.

As knowledge and thought can be of the good or not, and work for the good or not, so doctrine, dogma or teaching can be similarly ambivalent. For Nyssen, what is at stake in adhering to right doctrine is no less than life and salvation itself. The one who confesses that the Trinity is uncreated enters into life,[421] and the spiritual life depends on correct apprehension of the truth: the rule of piety is fixed by the right dogma of the faith.[422] Church teaching therefore in some sense compensates for our intellectual finitude: we need no knowledge beyond the capacity of our feeble and limited creaturely minds, for the teaching we have been given suffices for salvation;[423] but these doctrines must be precisely given, not manufactured, for if doctrines can be divine [theōn][424] and mystical [mystagogia or mystikōn],[425] they can equally be profane [tois exōthen logois][426] or even evil.[427] Nevertheless, even those doctrines rooted in pagan philosophy can transmute into fully Christian teaching: such doctrines are the 'pious offspring' [ho eusebēs tokos] of their pagan parent.[428] On the whole, though, Nyssen tends to contrast pagan reasoning with scriptural truth; the teaching of the gospels and scripture should not be in any way disturbed by the fact that there are doctrines which commend themselves to the sages 'who are without' [tōn exō sophōn].[429] This suspicion of wisdom 'from without' announces a theme

---

[415] Beat 2.98/J.7.2.90.   [416] LM 1.47.   [417] Beat 3.111/J.7.2.104.   [418] Or 45.6.   [419] Or 28.30.
[420] Or 27.4 (5 in Hardy).   [421] CtOr 322/J.3.4.100.   [422] ChrM 128/J.8.1.42.
[423] CEun 103b/J.2.319.   [424] CEun 80b/J.1.169 and CEun 144a/J.2.30.   [425] LM 1.46 and 56.
[426] LM 2.12.   [427] LM 2.161.   [428] LM 2.40.
[429] CEun 226a/J.2.255. His misgivings about pagan thought are one of several reasons to be wary of the enterprise of influence-hunting for traces of classical philosophy in his work. Stritzky (1973), for example, while careful to acknowledge the differences between Nyssen's thought and that of the ancients (see e.g., 25, 96–97), nevertheless maintains he can only be understood against the backdrop of pagan thought (110). Although notions of the human person as image, for example, are to be found in Plato, it is far from clear that Nyssen's use of the concept could not be wholly accounted for on the basis of the authority of Genesis (see 13ff.). Finding textual evidence of parallels does not suffice; there needs to be textual evidence of approval of the philosophical

which persists in the Eastern tradition up to the end of the Byzantine period, and what is merely germinal in the fourth century becomes full-blown antagonism by the fourteenth. However, Nyssen recognises that even scripture does not contain answers to every question about the things of God; for example, it contains no doctrine of divine nature ('scripture' here is theopneuston phōnēn).[430] Sheer reasonableness moreover commends itself to the believer and the unbeliever alike: those who do not accept Christian teaching do not, as a consequence of their disagreement, suppose divine nature to lack rationality, and that admission in itself will make Christian teaching intelligible to them.[431]

For Nazianzen, in contrast, dogma and doctrine have less positive significance, though they are also categories he works with less often than Nyssen does. Somewhat disingenuously (given the sophisticated reasoning and learning displayed in the *Orations*), he says that some need to be fed with the milk of simple doctrines,[432] though admittedly, this counsel seems a concession to the less advanced or less intellectually adept, rather than constituting some sort of general principle. More harshly, he calls upon the divine binder and looser for help in solving the tortuous knots of the Eunomians' dogmas[433] – as if his own thought were not on occasion challenging to follow. Characteristically, he vents his scorn in a rhetorical question, asking those whose teaching on the Trinity does not measure up to his standards 'where did you get this from? from what teachers of dogma or myths?',[434] seemingly equating the two in a way that it would be hard to imagine Nyssen doing. Nevertheless he lauds the fathers of Nicaea for establishing firm doctrinal boundaries (perigraptōn horōn te kai rhēmatōn tēn theologian).[435]

The Cappadocians therefore display divergent attitudes to their predecessors in the Greek philosophical tradition and use the terms 'philosophy' and 'philosophise' in markedly divergent ways. For Nyssen, the terms are often associated with pagan, and false, teaching. For Nazianzen, they serve as ways of distinguishing what would now be called Christian theology in its various forms. Nyssen's view teeters between the positive and the negative; Nazianzen's stands firmly on the side of the positive.

Nyssen can summarily dismiss the major lights of Greek intellectual history: Plato's *Cratylus* is 'nonsense' [phluaria[436]] and in *The Life of Moses*, the childless daughter of Pharaoh is taken to represent profane

concepts in question, and not merely an assumption of unconscious assimilation or inadvertent borrowing.
[430] 2CEun 261a/J.1.257. [431] CtOr 270/J.3.4.8. [432] Or 2.45. [433] Or 29.21.
[434] Or 31.18. [435] Or 25.8. [436] CEun 291a/J.1.344.

philosophy.[437] Even if one applies oneself to higher philosophical matters over a long period of time, that effort will barely lead one to apprehend what true being is,[438] although, as we have noted, Nyssen's scepticism in this instance is no greater than his doubt that any form of intellectual effort is of much use in attaining to ultimate truths. Moreover, as noted, although pagan philosophy is supposedly barren, Nyssen claims in the same treatise that it can have pious offspring. Although there is strictly no need for the Christian theologian to engage in philosophy,[439] the philosophical life is full of goodness, even though austere and uncongenial,[440] a form of surgery [iatrikēs] for the soul.[441] Still, at times Nyssen's use of the term 'philosophy' overlaps with Nazianzen's, so that it virtually equals 'theology': the virtuous draw those enslaved by deceit to the freedom of the philosophical life.[442] Likewise, he maintains that practical philosophy should be joined to contemplative philosophy – the practical here seeming to connote something like moral and ascetical theology, and the contemplative, mystical theology.[443]

Nazianzen's view, more straightforwardly positive, forthrightly declares philosophy to be the greatest and most difficult of professions.[444] Likewise, he claims that one has only two choices: either to be a philosopher oneself or to honour philosophy, unless one wants to end up lapsing into irrationality.[445] True, he surrounds the subject with certain caveats; to begin with, not everyone is fit to philosophise.[446] Then again, when he speaks of philosophy, he does not mean to designate the Greek luminaries of the past: no need to mourn his departed brother Caesarius, for he did not make a show of his knowledge of Plato and Aristotle or make use of specious [pithanotētas] arguments[447] – this despite the fact that Gregory himself frequently has recourse to the terminology and methods of ancient logic.[448] His objections to pagan philosophy also spring from substantive quarrels, however; he ties emanationism to Greek philosophy, yet rejects it, not for its roots, but because he believes it to be

---

[437] LM 2.10–11. According to Ruether (1969), Nazianzen's writings evidence direct knowledge only of Plato and Aristotle, his knowledge of the Epicureans, Stoics and Cynics being anecdotal and his knowledge of neo-Platonism being non-existent (26–27). Ruether claims his neo-Platonism was inherited from Origen, and Nazianzen *therefore* assumed these ideas to be Christian (27). She does not consider the possibility that he found these ideas worthy of expression and adoption because he thought they were true, and therefore compatible with Christianity.
[438] LM 2.23. [439] CEun 66a/J.1.124. [440] LM 2.193. [441] Virg 368b/J.8.1.335.
[442] LM 2.68. Ludlow (2000) maintains that for Nyssen *philosophia* indicates both an academic discipline and a monastic or ascetic lifestyle. The evidence she cites in favour of this assertion is drawn entirely from *The Life of Moses*, however, and I am not sure that Gregory's usage elsewhere is equally clear.
[443] LM 2.200. [444] Or 7.9. [445] Or 25.1. [446] Or 27.3. [447] Or 7.20. [448] Or 29.13–14.

wrong.[449] The deeper problem with philosophy, to the extent that Nazianzen sees one, relates to its practioners' propensity to hubristic overreaching. At times, philosophy itself supplies the parameters of proper reasoning, which Gregory is careful to say the church by its practices does not overstep when studying divine things.[450] One may philosophise only in such subjects as lie within one's own reach and within the grasp of one's audience.[451] Philosophy has something to do, therefore, with rhetoric: Christian philosophy can be assisted by eloquence [logoi],[452] but equally can be defeated in its suasive purpose if the speaker wantonly abuses language [epēreazō].[453] Some subjects, however, lie permanently beyond the bounds of propriety for philosophy even to attempt to address: one may philosophise about the world, matter, soul, Christology, eschatology, but in this life, can engage in divine discourse only a little.[454] As Nyssen does, Nazianzen therefore views philosophy as encompassing a wide range of subjects, covering both the contemplative and the practical[455] and, perhaps surprisingly, the latter even includes the care of souls; this is the branch of philosophy which Nazianzen declares is too high for him;[456] a perhaps realistic self-appraisal from a man who could at times be a prickly character.[457]

Cappadocian attitudes to formal argumentation and logic displays many of the same traits as their views of reason and philosophy, maintaining a delicate balance between scepticism and approval. Nyssen's chastisements of misuse of formal reasoning by his opponents (especially the unfortunate Eunomius) vary from finding flaws in the validity of their logic, to scorning their very use of logic. Most frequently, he attacks their use of syllogistic reasoning, faulting (with an element of inconsistency) both the validity of the syllogisms they construct and their employment of syllogisms *tout court*. Eunomius supposedly cannot construct a valid syllogism,[458] yet his argument suffers from its very use of syllogism in the first place, which 'tramples' [embateuontes] divine being.[459] More generally, he is taken to task for substituting assertion for argument[460] as well as for failing to demonstrate the logical necessity of the implications he claims for Nyssen's own position and engaging in straw man

---

[449] Or 29.2. [450] Or 2.5. [451] Or 27.3. [452] Or 43.13. [453] Or 27.6. [454] Or 27.9. [455] Or 4.113. [456] Or 2.78.
[457] Despite the positive qualifications which surface in his work, his overall evaluation of philosophy is cautious, to say the least, and for this reason, it seems implausible to say that it was for him and his brother Basil 'axiomatic' to equate the Christian with the monk and the monk with the philosopher, as Ruether does (1969, 15).
[458] CEun 87b/J.1.187–88 and 89a, J.1.192–93. [459] CEun 188b/J.2.152. [460] CEun 56b/J.1.92.

argumentation.⁴⁶¹ At times, Nyssen descends to simple accusations of sophistry and quibbling, rather than relying on hardnosed exposure of the errors of his opponents' reasoning.⁴⁶² However error-ridden Eunomius' arguments, they have the potential to deceive through ingenuity of their argumentation – as Nyssen's apparently do not.⁴⁶³

Although he affirms the necessity of logical consistency [to akolouthon ho logos],⁴⁶⁴ and scathingly mocks Eunomius for lack of it,⁴⁶⁵ he also pronounces logic to be important to reach the truths of divine nature.⁴⁶⁶ Nevertheless, he declines to provide confirmation of his argument through syllogism on the grounds that such reasoning is unreliable, a suspect means of demonstrating truth.⁴⁶⁷ A syllogism may convince some people, but Nyssen maintains that scripture is more sure,⁴⁶⁸ hence the excoriation of Eunomius for failing to construct an argument based either on scripture or on probable arguments [tēs tōn eikotōn logismōn akolouthias].⁴⁶⁹

When he does not fall into the trap of resorting to cheap debater's tricks to score rhetorical points off his interlocutors, Nyssen can mount tight critiques of their arguments which demonstrate his own fluency in the techniques of formal argumentation, predicate logic, for example⁴⁷⁰ or reductio ad absurdum [kataskeuazein to atopon].⁴⁷¹ He seems quite content to accept the conclusions of logical reasoning when the reasoning is sound,⁴⁷² and he is willing to make use of such inferential reasoning for his own purposes.⁴⁷³ How can this more positive appraisal of the value of logic cohere with the bitter repudiations characteristic of the *Contra Eunomium*? Nyssen's thought shows an awareness of a fundamental problem of Christian theology, as vexatious for contemporary theology as it was in the fourth century: how can one hold together two apparently opposing theological truths, the first being the utter ontological distinction of the Uncreated and the created, with its implications of the incapacity of human thought and speech for its divine object, and the second being the value one must allow to human discourse and reasoning, if any theology, catechesis, preaching or worship is to be possible and if

---

⁴⁶¹ CEun 80a/J.1.167.　⁴⁶² CEun 92a/J.1.201; 101b/J.2.313; 116b/J.2.355.　⁴⁶³ CEun 221a/J.2.240.
⁴⁶⁴ 2CEun 258a/J.1.248.　⁴⁶⁵ 2CEun 281b/J.1.316.　⁴⁶⁶ HSp 322a/J.3.1.104.　⁴⁶⁷ Soul 51/K42.
⁴⁶⁸ Soul 58/K54.　⁴⁶⁹ CEun 130b/J.2.397.
⁴⁷⁰ CEun 92a/J.1.201; 99a/J.1.221; and 2CEun 256a/J.1.243.
⁴⁷¹ CEun 82a /J.1.173 and 110a/J.2.337. Gregory acknowledges the charge that can be brought against his assertion that Eunomius' position implies Manichaeism [alla tauta men isōs bebiasmenēn echonta tēn tou atopou kataskeuein], but the translator of NPNF is correct in deeming the structure of his argument a reductio.
⁴⁷² CEun 165b/J.2.90.　⁴⁷³ CtOr 269/J.3.4.6.

we are to acknowledge the divine gift to humanity of rationality and language? Clearly, one must agree with Nyssen that training in logic will not in itself allow one correctly to apprehend reality,[474] but on his own principles, can he consistently maintain that one must wean oneself from the human application of words when we think of God?[475] Obviously, if Nyssen meant human language never rises to theology's task, he would not have written any theology at all, let alone the *Contra Eunomium*. A hint of the position he sees himself as taking may be found in his (ironically Aristotelian) references to a 'middle way' [mesotēta].[476] In reasoning as in morality, wisdom lies in the avoidance of extremes. Thus it is possible to make use of logical argumentation without placing such confidence in it as to imagine divine nature can be somehow captured by the inexorable forward march of a syllogism.

Nazianzen's views of argumentation concur substantially with those of Nyssen. He accuses his opponents of inventing recherché arguments [aneuriskōn logismous] and resorting to tricks of logic,[477] as well as sophistry and illegitimate recourse to syllogisms,[478] and declares himself to have answered the intricacies of his opponents' arguments by the power of the Spirit, thereby responding to their objections and exposing their misuse of scripture.[479] Yet Nazianzen seems more able to acknowledge his own use of the very means employed by his opponents. 'Let the syllogisms be woven [plekesthōsan]', he says, 'he is either unbegotten or begotten.'[480] He is able – apparently without sarcasm – to acknowledge merit in an antagonist's argument,[481] and frankly acknowledges that every sort of discourse entails the argumentational strategies of establishing one's own position and overturning that of one's opponent.[482] Still, the very subject matter of theology curtails the use of reasoned discourse and logic: 'when we prefer the power of reason [logos], putting faith aside... then the weakness of our argument [logos] does not match the importance of the subject'.[483] Philosophy is fine, then, but it, along with disputation [philoneikon] in general, must be kept within proper bounds,[484] and faith must complete any theological argument.[485] Although Nyssen makes explicit appeal to a 'middle way', Nazianzen seems to walk it with greater ease.

Nowhere is Nyssen's 'middle way' more evident than in his treatment of language and analogy; here the balancing act that sometimes borders

---

[474] CEun 220a/J.2.238.   [475] CEun 93a/J.1.204.
[476] CEun 284b/J.1.325; LM 2.288; Virg 352b/J.8.1.282.   [477] Or 29.6.   [478] Or 5.30.
[479] Or 30.1.   [480] Or 31.7.   [481] Or 29.6.   [482] Or 29.1.   [483] Or 29.21.
[484] Or 27.5.   [485] Or 29.21.

on outright self-contradiction is successfully executed. Speech [logos] is the greatest of God's gifts to us,[486] yet those who keep the eye of the heart clear condemn all human utterance as powerless to represent that which they have apprehended.[487] On the other hand, God's self-expression in the sending of the Word is a form of communication, one adapted to the limitations of our nature, which makes divine mysteries intelligible to us,[488] so that there can be no question of merely dispensing with and eschewing language. Although words applied to God have their own distinctive meaning, this significance does not stand in opposition to the ordinary meanings of the words,[489] and the relation of ordinary language to the higher varieties is analogical. As long as we avoid the mistake of identifying entities which are no more than similar,[490] we can conceive of God by analogy [kath' homoiotēta] and so be driven to a yet higher conception of God's reason.[491] The validity of analogy holds for conception as well as language: the present life offers an analogy [analogias] of future life[492] and something as material as sunlight can by its beauty allow us to grasp the beauty of real light.[493]

Although it is impossible that the good things above sense experience should be revealed by proper names, despite our lowliness we can learn about them in ways appropriate to our nature, for if it were not so, beatitude would altogether escape us.[494] God himself adapts to us, speaking our language, like a tender mother echoing her baby's whimpers.[495] The reason we name God derives from God himself,[496] for although he is above every name he has many names,[497] this immaterial nature nevertheless needs no name; not for God's sake, then, but for ours are these given in scripture.[498] All words may be inadequate to thought, of course, but in the twofold movement behind all utterance – rightly conceiving the object in the first place and then uttering it verbally – it is preferable to get their basic conceptions [dianoiai] right,[499] the implication being that there is some form of mental apprehension which escapes the problems associated with language itself.

For all their ambivalence about the limitations of the human intellect and thought, and for all their reputation for apophaticism, therefore, the Cappadocians by no means advocate the *via negativa* in any emphatic

---

[486] 2CEun 292b/J.1.350. [487] Virg 354b/J.1.288. [488] Beat 2.98/J.7.2.90–91.
[489] Abl 332b/J.3.2.42. Words applied to God each have a distinct meaning designating attributes of the divine nature rather than the nature itself.
[490] Soul 45/K32. [491] CtOr 270/J.3.4.2. [492] Inf 377a/J.3.2.83. [493] Inf 377b/J.3.2.85.
[494] Beat 2.99/J.7.2.91. [495] 2CEun 292a/J.1.348. [496] 2CEun 290a/J.1.342.
[497] CEun. 221b/J.2.242. [498] 2CEun 289b/J.1.341. [499] 2CEun 308a/J.1.394.

way; indeed, they show an awareness both of the limitations of negation and the impracticability of veiling all discourse in silence.[500] Nyssen, for example, faults the Eunomians for imagining they can define the substance of God any better through negation than affirmation [to tinos aphairetikon noēma],[501] since divine nature surpasses every concept [epinoia][502] and we cannot even comprehend ourselves;[503] the acknowledgement of the limitations of negative predicates does not solely concern theology in the narrow sense of doctrine of God, therefore. Gregory declares that he renounces even investigation of 'the ways of the universe' on the grounds that these are beyond explanation.[504] Renunciation proves the husk of a movement that remains fundamentally affirmative, for silence is in its own way doxological: 'we have learnt to honour with silence what transcends speech and thought'.[505] The tendency in Nyssen's theology is therefore more straightforwardly to honour the apophatic impulse.

Nazianzen's view of the matter manifests greater doubt about the consolations of apophaticism, although he too sees some value in it. Piety consists in silence, he maintains. His clearest disavowals of the value of speech concern statements pertaining to the doctrine of God, whose name is ineffable, and whose nature and begetting alike must be honoured in silence.[506] Nevertheless, although Nazianzen says he wishes to forbid disputation about God [theologein], the fundamental difficulty does not lie in talk itself, even talk about God; problems arise only when this talk is unseasonable [akairian] or immoderate [ametrian].[507] Both speech and silence can honour God,[508] and he further proposes the rather odd compromise between apophaticism and cataphaticism of uttering mysteries 'mystically'.[509] However on occasion he issues sharp rebukes against certain kinds of naive apophaticism: the one who eagerly pursues the self-existent will not stop at saying what he is not, but *must* go further and state what he is.[510] As for those who point to scriptural aporias as warrant for theological agnosticism or woolly thinking, Nazianzen counsels them to look at the inner meaning of the sacred page, so as to see

---

[500] Thus I differ once again from Völker (1955), who views Nyssen's theology as the strong outworking of an apophatic theology (30).
[501] CEun 96a/J.1.213.   [502] Beat 6.146/J.7.2.140.   [503] 2CEun 261a/J.1.258; HumP 11.2/F156.
[504] CtOr 288/J.4.40.   [505] CEun 147a/J.2.39.   [506] Or 28.20.   [507] Or 27.5; Or 3.7.
[508] Or 12.1.
[509] 'Mystikōs', which Hardy translates as 'under one's breath', though Nazianzen probably means something more like 'in a manner appropriate to a mystery' (whatever that is, exactly); see Or 27.5.
[510] Or 28.9.

there hidden beauty and be illuminated with the light of knowledge.[511] Our knowledge may be partial, our language inadequate, but the One of whom we speak is the God of presence and self-disclosure, not of absence and withdrawal, and this consideration must rule out the more adamant forms of the via negativa as a Christian theological option.

Although the insistence on the infinite's elusion of the finite belongs more characteristically to Nyssen than to Nazianzen, both take epistemological account of this fundamental difference between the Uncreated and the created. In its simplest form, Nyssen's view amounts to little more than a quasi-quantitative pointing to the difference between God and humanity: Abraham, for Nyssen one of the paradigmatic knowers of God, stretched farther than anyone, yet still knew that God exceeded all his capacity for knowledge,[512] and finitude, though never identified with sin by Nyssen, does open the door to foolishness and error.[513] A finite nature [to tē physei brachu] simply cannot rise above the limits imposed by nature[514] and our knowledge does not extend to comprehension of what transcends limit.[515] Human reason cannot stretch out far enough even to take in the whole of creation, so the cloud in Exodus that led the people of Israel is beyond comprehension;[516] even the mind's most busy and ambitious strivings do not permit it to get to the end of the Infinite, the creative power itself,[517] and not only divine nature proper, but attributes such as its greatness exceed our intellectual capacity.[518] Although the incomprehensibility of divine nature is often linked to infinity in some quasi-spatial or quantitative sense,[519] Nyssen associates it with other divine attributes as well, such as holiness,[520] love and beauty.[521] Even the Word, whom Nyssen so often affirms became flesh that material beings might know something of their immaterial maker, even so, is not comprehended, for if he were, he would not share in the infinite divine nature.[522] There is simply no faculty in human nature adequate to comprehension of divine nature,[523] however openly nature is manifested.

Nyssen qualifies this basic position in some significant ways, however. First, what escapes comprehension may lie within the reach of apprehension: Abraham apprehended God's power and goodness and even his infinity.[524] Furthermore – and surprisingly – Nyssen on occasion allows for some form of comprehension. We can comprehend the essence of mind by reflecting on various properties of divinity and draining them of any

---

[511] Or 31.21. [512] 2CEun 259a/J.1.253. [513] Soul 44/K30. [514] 2CEun 292a/J.1.348.
[515] 2CEun 256a/J.1.243. [516] LM 1.30. [517] CEun 69b/J.1.135. [518] CEun 147b/J.2.40.
[519] HumP 12.3/F162. [520] HSp 323b/J.3.1.107. [521] Soul 81/K90; Virg 354b/J.8.1.290.
[522] CEun 154b/J.2.58. [523] 2CEun 257a/J.1.245. [524] 2CEun 259b/J.1.253.

corporeal associations.⁵²⁵ More surprisingly, he concedes that reason can supply us with a dim and imperfect grasp of the divine nature,⁵²⁶ and that the myriad names of God allow us to gain some glimmering of comprehension.⁵²⁷ In both these cases what is designated by the English term 'comprehension' functions paradoxically, even oxymoronically: it is in the nature of comprehension to be more than a clutching at the dim or the merely glimmering, and Nyssen's very gesturing towards the idea in such contexts indicates its limitations. His concern strictly to circumscribe the possibilities of theological affirmation is evident in the taxonomy he gives of what does come within reach of comprehension [katalēpsin]: things which occupy space and have a beginning and an end, and mutable things.⁵²⁸ The complexities of Nyssen's thought in this regard lead to sharp disputes among readers of *The Life of Moses* especially. Lieske and Koch argue that Gregory provides for some sort of direct apprehension of God in this life, which has the character of mystical union, interpretations which Heine adamantly rejects. Heine denies that the treatise contains any teaching about union with God, 'intuitive knowledge of God and therefore, it lacks the characteristic marks of mysticism'.⁵²⁹

Infinity always does less systematic work in Nazianzen's thought than in Nyssen's, but the substance of what he says does not differ markedly. The gap between the Uncreated and the created seems less absolute on Nazianzen's than Nyssen's account. God is a great, limitless, Sea of Being,⁵³⁰ and if he were comprehensible in thought [dianoiai katalēpton], he would be circumscribed in nature,⁵³¹ yet of his own desire he breaks through the barrier erected by the utter distinction of his nature from ours. The Incarnation, not surprisingly, represents one such divine initiative, the Word assuming that which he was not so that the Incomprehensible might be comprehended [chōrēthēi],⁵³² but the Incarnation is not the unique instance of such divine condescension. On Mount Sinai it seems that it is not only Moses who sees God, but in some way, all of humankind: we are drawn up from cognitive abasement in order that the Incomprehensible may in some degree, as far as it is safe, be comprehended by mortal nature.⁵³³

Although infinity does more systematic work in Nyssen's theology, Nazianzen's analysis of it may be more refined. Infinity, on his account, can be considered from two points of view, which he ironically terms

---

⁵²⁵ Soul 45/K32. ⁵²⁶ 2CEun 263a/J.2.263. ⁵²⁷ 2CEun 264a/J.1.266.
⁵²⁸ 2CEun 308a–b/J.1.395. ⁵²⁹ Heine (1975), 110–11 and 114. ⁵³⁰ Or 38.7. ⁵³¹ Or 28.10.
⁵³² Or 39.13. ⁵³³ Or 45.11.

'beginning' and 'end'. When we look upon phenomena individually and see in them the infinite and the unapproachable we call the infinite nature unoriginate; if we look at the whole, we call the divine 'Eternal and so, endless'. In either case, consideration of divine infinitude prompts some further knowledge.[534] Here Nazianzen might be seen as approaching Nyssen's epecstatic notion of apprehension, where knowledge of God resembles a corridor of endless doors opening forever onto new vistas. More distinctively his own is Nazianzen's awareness that our inability to comprehend God is its own kind of knowledge and is a positive thing: what we cannot comprehend moves us to wonder.[535] The emphasis here is not so much on knowledge yielding to bare silence, as the fullness of contemplative praise.

The nexus of divine and human minds looked at from the perspective of potentiality is the imago Dei; from the perspective of actuality, it is contemplation. Contemplation is related to the imago inasmuch as it numbers among the defining characteristics of human persons: the faculty of contemplation and discernment is proper to the godlike part of the soul.[536] Along with judgement and the seeing what is [tōn ontōn epoptikēn] it is proper and natural to us,[537] for we have a natural desire to contemplate the good.[538]

The core of Nyssen's doctrine of contemplation has two foci: the activity in its more sheerly intellectual (and what we would today call theological) dimension and in its more spiritual one (which we would call prayer).[539] These merge, as we shall see, this fusion being one of the great strengths of the Cappadocian theology, and of the patristic tradition generally. I would not, however, concur with Fedwick's view that the state of prayer as *theologia* by far surpasses the mere contemplation (theoria) of God.[540] First, I see no evidence that Nyssen ranks *theologia* above contemplation, nor that he equates *theologia* with a state of prayer, and while Fedwick cites Nyssen, the passages he quotes seem to have no direct bearing on these particular chasms. On the more strictly intellectual side, as we will see, the activity often designates a process of theological extrapolation, for Nyssen's notion of contemplation essentially

---

[534] Or 45.4. [535] Or 45.3 and Or 38.7. [536] Soul 77/K84. [537] Soul 54/K48.
[538] Beat 6.148/J.7.2.142.
[539] Daniélou's valuable discussion of the terrain distinguishes finely amongst differing senses of the word (1970, 1–17); however, he places relatively little emphasis on theoria as the equivalent of either theology or a form of prayer. Daniélou notes a sharp decline in Nyssen's use of the term in the later ascetical treatises and concludes that he gives the notion far less importance than either Evagrius or Nazianzen (17).
[540] 1994, 377.

commends the practice of thinking through the systematic implications of doctrine. In his view, to contemplate the infinity of the Father leads to the conclusion that the Son is also infinite – and therefore, of course, divine.[541] More broadly, contemplation can designate no more than considered or orderly reflection – so an argument can be said to contemplate [ho logos etheōrēsen],[542] and contemplation can mean reaching correct conclusions or seeing the full implications of a given position [syntheōretai].[543] The process of contemplation also includes grasping the connection between the Old and the New Testaments, the old and the new covenants,[544] a movement which is also essentially systematic in its force, or simply meditating on scripture.[545] Knowing when not to make connections can be equally important, however; for example, one avoids Christological error by knowing to contemplate the properties of divine and human nature separately, without confusing them.[546]

Here already is an indication that despite the overwhelmingly positive associations of theoria, Gregory does not shy from admitting that even in the act of contemplation the intellect can be exercised to negative ends. Hence Eunomius is acknowledged (ironically, no doubt) to be skilled in contemplation,[547] and Gregory can accordingly point to its limits: 'How will the contemplation of the maker of the sky procure a solution to the question, immaterial, invisible, formless, ungenerate, everlasting, incapable of decay and change and alteration, and such things, as He is?'[548] What Nyssen regards as the very summit of theological reflection, apprehension of Being, both yields to and resists the contemplative reach of the human subject. The soul thrives on contemplation of true Being, as if nourished by good food,[549] although, as we have seen, in Nyssen's view we apprehend only God's goodness, and not his essence.

The treatment of contemplation therefore summarises the delicate balancing act that is Nyssen's epistemology. However much contemplation may seem to designate ordinary, if rigorous, intellectual activity, he frequently enjoins raising one's gaze above the level of the mundane and superficial.[550] Contemplation allows one, like David, through thought alone [dia monēs tēs dianoias] to leave the body and enter the realm of

---

[541] CEun 154b/J.2.58. [542] CEun 93b/J.1.207. [543] CEun 102b/J.2.316. [544] LM 2.151.
[545] LM 2.135, 2.191, 2.217. Thus the second part of LM is simply titled 'Theoria', a meditation on the spiritual significance of the Israelites' journey out of Egypt. Daniélou distinguishes between several different types of theoria (liturgical, scriptural and mystical), distinctions which seem questionably grounded in what Nyssen himself says, though the former acknowledges that the various types of theoria are finally diverse aspects of the same reality (1953, 163).
[546] CEun 180b/J.2.130. [547] CEun 88b/J.1.192. [548] CEun 75b/J.1.153. [549] Inf 377b/J.3.2.85.
[550] Beat 1.85/J.7.2.78. reps.

the sheerly immaterial and intellectual.[551] Nevertheless, a species of natural theology (albeit a very diluted one) also appears in Nyssen's writings. While contemplation most essentially operates on the purely intelligible, the soul can use contemplation of the sensible world as a springboard, as when it marvels at the heavens.[552] In 'looking' to Moses and the cloud that led the people of Israel as guides, one can advance in contemplation. Whether or not this form of 'gazing' really constitutes, in its meditation on a real person, a movement from the sensible to the intelligible is debatable, of course. In a passage that appears only a little later in *The Life of Moses*, Nyssen declares that the exclusion of the irrational animals on the mountain signifies the superiority of knowledge derived from the contemplation of intelligibles over knowledge coming from sense perception,[553] but in both cases, consideration of some actually once-existing thing (animals in both cases) gives rise to the contemplation which takes one further. This interpretation concurs with what is directly stated in the *Contra Eunomium*, that some people can only elevate their thoughts to God by means of sensible things.[554] The opposition of the sensible and the intelligible is never absolute, however: we can simultaneously stretch out to the limits of the universe and contemplate heaven.[555]

Here is a hint of another balancing act of which Gregory's readers are observers: the tensive relation of human striving and various forms of aid, all of which ultimately originate on the divine side. Religious knowledge comes to us as light, but we progress by dint of diligence, through discipline, apprehending reality more and more, and so approach more nearly to contemplation proper; only then are we able to see what in divine nature we are able to contemplate.[556]

The preconditions of contemplation are thus the preconditions of all theological and spiritual activity, as far as the Cappadocians are concerned: grace (which includes the aid that comes through scripture), assiduity and actual purity, for only the devout mind [ho eusebēs logos] contemplates rightly.[557] The mark of the contemplative life is decorum or modesty [euschēmosynē];[558] this is why Nyssen can describe his treatise *On Virginity* as a 'sketch [hypographē] of the contemplative

---

[551] Virg 354b/J.8.1.290.   [552] CtOr 287/J.3.4.38.   [553] LM 2.156.   [554] CEun202a/J.2.190.
[555] Soul 47–48/K36–38.   [556] LM 2.162.
[557] CEun 94b/J.1.210. As Leys notes, contemplation for Nyssen is not philosophical, but theological. It may be going too far, however, to suggest as he does that it is *not* reflection, but rather prayer (1951, 51); for Nyssen, it seems to be both.
[558] On Pilgrimages [=Letter 2] 382b/J.8.2.14. Like the treatise on infant deaths, this treatise may be spurious, although it is included among the letters in the Jaeger edition; the same caveat and allowance noted for Inf apply here, too.

life'.⁵⁵⁹ One form of modesty is the willingness to accept the help we need, since characteristically, for Eastern theology, this acceptance of aid cannot be sheerly passive, but always requires a complementary exertion on our part: so although difficulty in contemplation can be overcome by God's light and Christ illumines the darkness by the brilliant light of his teaching, the vision of glory comes only to the pure in heart.⁵⁶⁰ The relation of divine and human striving is thus one of fluid reciprocity. Virtue of some sort and degree necessarily precedes contemplation, but can also provide its subject, so those who wish to be priests must both contemplate virtue and bring their own bodies to the altar themselves becoming the sacrifice.⁵⁶¹ Indeed, God not only aids contemplation, but apparently engages in it himself: he surveys all things, discerning our thoughts and entering us by his power of contemplation.⁵⁶² This divine contemplation is even trinitarian, since the Spirit cooperates [synergein] with the faithful for understanding and contemplation⁵⁶³ and the Word contemplates.⁵⁶⁴ The *circumincessio* of divine contemplation is mirrored by the communal dimension of theoria on the human side; as O'Connell observes, contemplation is not given to privileged individuals for their own enjoyment, but in order to teach, heal and lead others.⁵⁶⁵

The Old Testament provides Nyssen with many human models of great contemplators: Moses, David⁵⁶⁶ and also Abraham. The latter soars above those things perceptible to the senses, from beautiful objects to the 'harmony of the heavens' [tēs euarmostias tōn ouraniōn thaumatōn] to the archetype of all beauty.⁵⁶⁷ Even in lesser athletes of prayer, beauty often provides the link between the contemplation of sensibles and intelligibles. The soul turns its powers of affection from material things to the intellectual contemplation of immaterial beauty [epi tēn noētēn te kai aulon tou kalou theorian].⁵⁶⁸ To arrive at such heights means not only turning one's attention from sensory things, but apparently also to be robbed of one's physical powers: the divine beauty, lacking shape, form and colour, is contemplated in unspeakable bliss.⁵⁶⁹ Physical disorientation is evident, too, as Gregory shifts from the imagery of height which he constantly uses, speaking of gazing from a high ridge onto an immense sea, to the 'vertigo' [ilingon] of the soul that is drawn to the depths which is contemplated in the words 'no one shall see God and live'.⁵⁷⁰ Is God 'up' or 'down'? – nowhere and everywhere, Gregory answers, giving in the

---

⁵⁵⁹ Virg 343a/J.7.1.248. ⁵⁶⁰ LP 2.36/J.7.2.21. ⁵⁶¹ LM 2.191. ⁵⁶² Abl 333a/J.3.1.44.
⁵⁶³ CEun 133a/J.2.405. ⁵⁶⁴ Beat 4.123/J.7.2.116. ⁵⁶⁵ O'Connell 1983, 323.
⁵⁶⁶ 2CEun 265a/J.1.269. ⁵⁶⁷ 2CEun 259a/J.1.252. ⁵⁶⁸ Virg 351a/J.8.1.277–78.
⁵⁶⁹ HumP 5.1/F128. ⁵⁷⁰ Beat 6.143/J.7.2.137.

very motion of his prose a sense of that vertigo which is seemingly some form of mystical experience. So contemplation is linked to prayer and the deepest intimacy with God, and the effect of prayer said to be union with God, so that we become what we contemplate.[571] That is why the heart can stand as a symbol of contemplation,[572] because the activity of theoria, while clearly intellectual, encompasses much more than the modern world would associate with the intellect.[573]

Much of Nazianzen's notion of contemplation concurs exactly with Nyssen's, but he has his own distinctive emphases. Overall, his interest in contemplation does not seem as great as Nyssen's and there may thus be some justice in Špidlík's view that Basil is the classic instance of contemplation and that Nazianzen stands between the two, harmonising them.[574] Divine nature is self-contemplation.[575] Although he insists that contemplation is of intelligibles rather than sensibles, and even constitutes a means of distancing oneself from matter,[576] Nazianzen also links contemplation to a form of natural theology: it is a searching of all things, for the sheer delight of it (the 'deep things of God' admittedly come first).[577] Thus contemplation is, with action, also one of the components of every philosophy.[578] Like Nyssen, he regards contemplation as a form of theological reflection, though his account of this tends to the more rigorously intellectual, a teasing out of the significance of what would today be considered technicalities, such as the procession of the Persons of the Trinity, and the attributes of divine nature.[579] For Nazianzen theoria

---

[571] CallC 84/J.8.1.135.   [572] LM 2.200.

[573] The foregoing discussion, including its textual references, indicates where and why I differ from the estimation of Meredith (1989) that *On the Soul and Resurrection*, in offering an ideal of contemplation of the beautiful as the end of life, differs from the view in *On the Making of the Human Person* and the *Catechetical Oration*, the first having a 'rigidly intellectual' conception of the nature of the soul (50). Contemplation as a consummate activity is an ideal widely dispersed in Nyssen's work, and encompasses much more than sheerly intellectual activity, though this element is always crucial to it.

[574] 1971, xi.

[575] For a discussion of the intellectual background of this idea and references to Nazianzen's work, see Ruether (1969, 131).

[576] Or 21.2.

[577] Or 43.65. Hence I think Ruether (1969) goes too far in maintaining that 'man's encasement in matter offers a great obstacle to this withdrawal to the noetic world' (150). Nazianzen's anthropology is not so dichotomous, nor is the created mind 'separated' from the Uncreated in the first place.

[578] Or 4.113.

[579] Or 2.38. Winslow (1979) distinguishes between the distinct meanings of *theologia* in Nazianzen's work. The first designates the doctrine of God, while the second designates the activity of the Trinity in the *oikonomia* (30). Winslow later cites with approval L. Stephen's claim that Nazianzen's theology is primarily conceived as soteriology (Stephen, 1938, 38). This determination underestimates its contemplative dimension. Winslow himself seems closer to the mark when he

often designates meditation on scripture: by meditating on the whole of both Testaments of the Bible, one grows rich in contemplation.[580] It can also designate any turning over of theological affirmations in one's mind, such as the titles of Christ,[581] or indeed the whole subject matter of theology, from divine nature itself to the Incarnation.[582] Like Nyssen, Nazianzen nevertheless considers that there are theological subjects barely within the reach of even this, the highest activity of the human mind, though characteristically, he takes a slightly more optimistic view than his friend: divine being, while not utterly beyond the pale of human capacities, must be left to those who truly have the mind of God and are advanced in contemplation[583] – and it appears that Gregory himself is not one of these.

This latter implied disavowal of his own excellence provides a cautionary context for remarks that modern readers might otherwise take as insufferably overweening. He warns against the danger of approaching certain subjects if one numbers among those (the majority of us) who are unworthy of contemplation and impure.[584] However, this admonition does not state that to be of the multitude is necessarily to be excluded from contemplation, nor does it assume that the multitude consists of the uneducated: Gregory is simply urging those who have not dedicated themselves to the spiritual life to avoid making theological pronouncements. Those who are incapable of taking in the subject matter of contemplation are 'evil and savage' beasts, which seems to imply that all human beings have some capacity for contemplation, unless they abandon themselves to vice.[585] The choice set before all of us is stark: spirituality or depravity, but most of those who turn from evil and savage behaviour will nevertheless end up midway between those who are utterly dense and those with a high aptitude for contemplation, and Nazianzen numbers himself among these theological and spiritual mediocrities.[586]

While contemplation must designate an activity that is largely solitary, in this as in all else in the church, our lives depend upon one another and Gregory's conviction of this point argues against his being taken simply as an aristocratic intellectual snob. He is heartened in his own resolve to proclaim the truth by the support of his friend Basil's theology and

---

asserts that *theologia* is best understood as 'a process by which the activity of God and the searching human quest become one' (33), in the process of which the distinction between the two types of theology is effaced.
[580] Or 21.6. [581] Or 2.98. [582] Or 45.15 and 30. [583] Or 28.9.
[584] Or 28.2. [585] Or 28.2. [586] Or 45.12.

contemplation.[587] Although the truly advanced in contemplation seem to be hermits,[588] contemplative spirits ought not to be cut off from the common life of cenobites.[589] Therefore, contemplation and thought of God [theōrēmasi kai noēmasin] are meant to be lamps which illuminate the whole church.[590] In part, Gregory's position on this issue concerns not solely the nature of contemplation itself, but the vocations of those who contemplate, for he clearly seeks to bridge what was in his time the divide between the active, ordained ministry and the ascetical life of prayer and retreat from the world which was the province of monks.[591] Thus it was Athanasius' gift to reconcile the solitary with the communal life by showing that the priesthood is capable of a sort of philosophy [philosophian][592] but he made good use of his exile by going to Egypt, to the holy and divine homes of contemplation – the sketes of the desert – where Christians live more to God than any others.[593] The ultimate model for this simultaneous engagement with and withdrawal from the world must be God, who is the chief of all contemplators, to whose self-contemplation the trisagion attests.[594]

The Cappadocians present us with a schema that is in many ways paradigmatic. In their thought we find cautions, doubts and even contempt for too-readily sanguine appraisals of the human mind and human intellectual endeavour alongside a deep conviction of the intellectual nature of God, the centrality of the mind as a human faculty, and a moral and ascetical theology insistent upon the mind's governance of the body and the will, and its fulfillment in contemplation. The strains, which on occasion approach the status of virtual contradictions, reflect the depth in which they wrestle with the fundamental issues, but the tensions are contained within a framework that maintains coherence. In significant part, that coherence is the product of the strongly systematic drive consistently evident in Cappadocian theology, and in combining an impetus towards system with an equally persistent tendency towards contemplation, Cappadocian theology gathers together and intensifies the traits of patristic theology as a whole.

---

[587] Or 43.67. [588] Or 2.29. [589] Or 43.62.
[590] Or 5.35. Plagnieux (1951) claims that theology is such a near-relative of contemplation in Gregory's thought that the two are almost identified (108 and 159). He takes pains to stress that theoria is in no way opposed to praxis in Nazianzen's thought (143–44).
[591] McGuckin 2001 *passim*. [592] Or 21.19. [593] Or 21.19. [594] Or 38.8–9; cp. Or 45.4–5.

CHAPTER 4

Augustine

Augustine presents us with a complex phenomenon: a thinker in whose work the intellect is as central as it is to the Alexandrians and Cappadocians, but one whose approach is in the end decidedly different: the theme is pervasive and yet Augustine makes it his own. The complexity of his treatment is evident in the first instance simply because the intellect is the point at which many of his most cherished concerns intersect: wisdom and truth; illumination; the relation of body and soul and of this life and the next; the human person and the persons of the divine Trinity; beauty; virtue and vice; the hierarchy of being; contemplation and union with God. Augustine's treatment is conventional in the centrality of intellect to the overall scheme and the role accorded contemplation. Its distinctiveness subsists in its strong emphasis on love – and the consequent need to work out its precise relation to the mind – and the degree to which the theology as a whole is governed by the doctrine of the Trinity. The dominance of trinitarian theology in turn lends a markedly personalist flavour to the work that is less prominent in other writers in this period, and which is the distinctive note of Augustine's theology.

So strongly systematic is Augustine's theology that it becomes difficult to separate out any one strand from any other, so we begin at the centre of the knot, which is arguably the notion of order. Order is more important to Augustine than to perhaps any other Christian theologian, and because it is not, per se at least, a standard theological locus, neither its centrality to Augustine's theology, nor its significance for his conception of the intellect, is self-evident. Order is the governing principle of Augustine's cosmology: his universe is a duly arrayed hierarchy stretching from God, through the angels, to humanity and the other animals, and finally to plants and the inanimate world. Order is central to his ethics: the virtuous life is one in which the body is rightly subordinate to the will, as the will is to the intellect, and is also the linchpin of his aesthetic: the well-ordered is beautiful and the beautiful is well-ordered. Finally, what dictates the place of mind in the doctrine of God, the anthropology and the doctrine of sanctification, is again order. Consequently one could scarcely overestimate the importance of this theme to his theology as a whole. While the hierarchy establishes a great deal more in Augustine's thought than the role and value of the intellect, it is nevertheless to the hierarchy that we must turn in order to grasp more precisely how intellect fits into the broader scheme of his theology.

Augustine does not deliberate on the value of the hierarchy; it is an assumed good in his thought. We may conjecture, however, that it is no more than the elaboration of two fundamental facts of his theology, divine transcendence and the dynamism of divine self-giving, both of which give some indication of the role of the intellect in the hierarchy. Every attribute that Augustine predicates of God reveals divine transcendence; most, though not all, also manifest God's generosity. The summit of the hierarchy is God and inasmuch as intellect is predicated of God, intellect is also a faculty in respect of which God transcends all else: 'In him and with him we venerate the truth, who is in all respects like him, and who is the form of all things that have been made by the One . . . . To spiritual minds, it is clear that all things were made by this form which alone achieves what all things seek after.'[1] Intellect reveals both God's utter transcendence and the generosity of his self-giving; the prologue to Book 9 of *On the Trinity* concludes:

What we have to avoid is the sacrilegious mistake of saying anything about the trinity which does not belong to the creator but rather to the creature, or which is fabricated by vain imaginings.

In places he specifies the nature of the fundamental differences between creature and Creator: God is eternal and creation temporal;[2] the creature is material, while God is not.[3] At other times he dispenses with reasons altogether and simply asserts the vast disparity between God and ourselves,[4] particularly in respect of the mind.[5]

While there are divine attributes that point solely to transcendence – notably simplicity – intellect is not of this kind. Intellect both distinguishes God from all else and signifies God's generosity, for the existence of minds other than God's is due to the extravagance of divine giving. Thus, for instance, the goodness of creatures is divine goodness given freely away, or, with reasoning more subtle, human apatheia is divine

---

[1] VRel 55.113. [2] Trin 14.4. [3] Trin 1.27. [4] Trin 15.11 and 39. [5] Trin 5.1.

impassibility communicated to creatures who are passible and mutable, a point we shall explore more fully.

Intellect is a transitive divine attribute in two distinct senses. First, in having minds, human beings have been endowed with a divine faculty, and one that is shared with only one other class of creatures, the angels; intellect is a gift God chose to shed abroad in the universe less widely than existence or goodness, for example. Second, the faculty of the intellect is both a condition without which a human being could not be this kind of creature and the dynamic principle that, on the creaturely side, makes possible the divine–human relation. The most obvious, and indeed the principal, way in which this giving, receiving and consequent transformation in the creature takes place is divine self-disclosure, the prerequisite for which is that the creature be able to understand it. For Augustine, the Bible is certainly the sine qua non of our knowledge of God, but it is far from being the sole means by which we know God. It is through a constant process of self-giving – which takes many and diverse forms – that humanity is brought to know God. God's self-disclosure is both specific (the illumination of the individual, as well as the general revelation of scripture) and transformative (to know God is become like God to some degree). The knowledge of God is thus for Augustine the beginning, middle and end of sanctification – but it is only a rational being who can receive such knowledge.

The governing principle of the hierarchy, then, is that intelligent beings surpass the non-rational beings.[6] If we are superior to other animals [pecores, the 'beasts'], it is because we have minds and they do not, at least not in Augustine's view.[7] The possession of intellect does not in itself guarantee goodness, for the demons are also rational.[8] Intellect appears at first glance not to be the sole determining factor of the position of any class of creatures in the hierarchy, then, both because goodness obviously matters and also because part of the reason we rank between the angels and the 'beasts' is that we are mortal[9] – at least, this principle holds true after the Fall and before the inauguration of the Age to Come. The root problem with mortality is not simply that life is a good and death therefore a privation of good, but that mortality necessarily implies

---

[6] CD 11.16; NBon 1.   [7] LArb 1.8.18; cf. NBon 5 and FSym 4.8.
[8] CD 8.16. This determination cannot be established definitively from the text. Augustine attributes this view to Apuleius, but in a lengthy dispute with the latter over the nature of demons (CD 8.17–22) he does not deny this point, and as it fits with his overall cosmology (CD 5.11), the view may be attributed to Augustine, albeit somewhat speculatively.
[9] CD 9.13.

change. Mutability, too, at first glance seems to have nothing to do with the intellect, until we note that one of the respects in which the divine mind is superior to ours is that its truth is immutable.[10] If it seems that Augustine has added a principle (mortality) to intellect to determine order in the hierarchy, this impression proves on closer inspection to be misleading, for while he does assume that divinity necessarily entails immutability, his essential point is that God does not deviate from truth and thus never ceases to be or to behave as a rational being. Inasmuch as there are demons, the angelic intellect presumably cannot be accorded this status of unvarying rationality; inasmuch as human beings fall prey to cupidity, we cannot be said to be entirely rational either. Intellect that is always true to itself is the essential divine attribute, then; immutability simply follows from this principle.

The top of the hierarchy is important, then, because it is in the divine mind that intellect appears in its truest form. Why predicate mind of God at all? In the first instance, because knowledge is predicated of God: 'If there were a mind endowed with such great power of knowing and foreknowing that all the past and all the future were known to it as clearly as I know a familiar psalm, that mind would be wonderful beyond belief.'[11] God's knowledge is, of course, of this nature; indeed, his knowledge is yet *more* wonderful and mysterious.[12] The perfection of his works testifies to the perfection of his knowledge[13] and perfection of knowledge in turn indicates perfection of mind. One of the glories of this perfect Mind is that it could exist unto itself, and yet chooses to create: God is both Mind and the creator of minds and is therefore to be praised.[14] Here we see a recurring trait of Augustine's theology: so strong is his sense of the connection between God and creation – and especially between God and humanity – that there are very few divine attributes that he can discuss for long without implying their communicability. If we praise God for our minds, we are also implicitly acknowledging God's mind. One signification of divine intellect, therefore, is worship: if we worship God, it can only be because he is worthy of awe. One of the most immediate ways in which we are prompted to such reverent wonder is the beauty and diversity of the universe, which in turn testifies to God's knowledge, which is in turn a sign of intellect.

Because human persons and God are both intelligent beings, there is an important link between them, a connection central to Augustine's thought, as we shall see. Nevertheless, mind is also what distinguishes

---

[10] Conf 6.17; cf. VRel 31.57.   [11] Conf 11.31.   [12] Conf 11.31.   [13] CD 11.21.   [14] CD 11.21.

God radically from all creation, including the intelligent beings.[15] The philosophers are wrong, therefore, in assuming that God and the human mind are of the same nature.[16] God is not simply higher on the scale of intellects than we, but the Intellect than which there is no greater.[17] Because God is the supreme mind, he can be identified with truth itself[18] and with wisdom itself.[19] Perhaps because God's mind is qualitatively different from ours, Augustine can refer to God as the Divine Intelligence,[20] whereas human beings are described only as having minds, rather than being minds.

As much as with truth, the mind of God is identified with beauty.[21] Both God and mathematical symbols belong to the realm of intelligible things[22] – mathematics being one of Augustine's favourite examples of the sheerly intelligible and non-sensible – and yet the intelligible beauty of God is superior even to the truths of mathematics.[23] Here, too, both awe and communicability are implied: divine beauty is, as it were, the manifestation of God's mind to human minds, and our ability to perceive beauty is a function of our having been given intellects. As mind, truth and wisdom, God is not only beautiful, but the one who communicates beauty: 'he who journeys towards wisdom beholding and considering the whole created universe, finds wisdom appearing unto him graciously... and his eagerness to press along that way is all the greater because he sees that the way is made beautiful by the wisdom he longs to reach.'[24]

Wisdom is one of the many aspects under which God communicates himself, but in the course of explicating these connections, Augustine never loses sight of the sheer transcendence of the divine mind. The identification of wisdom with God both posits a connection between the divine and the created realms and distinguishes God from humanity: 'Our knowledge ... is vastly dissimilar to [God's] knowledge. What is God's knowledge is also his wisdom, and what is his wisdom is also his being or substance.'[25] While the doctrine of simplicity to which Augustine alludes here became a commonplace of Western theology, we need to note it carefully, for this doctrine is what prevents Augustine's strong conception of the imago Dei and his search for vestigia Trinitatis from compromising the distinction between God and creation. One of the governing rubrics of his notion of mind is therefore the vast qualitative

---

[15] VRel 36.67.   [16] CD 8.6.   [17] LArb 2.6.14.   [18] LArb 2.15.39; Conf 3.6.   [19] CD 8.1.
[20] CD 10.11.   [21] NBon 6.   [22] Sol 1.8.15.   [23] Sol 5.11.   [24] LArb 2.17.45.
[25] Trin 15.22. Cf. F. Bourassa: 'la difficulté qu'éprouve la raison devant une telle proposition [la doctrine de la Trinité] vient de sa propre faiblesse, que seule peut surmonter la Vérité divine reçue dans l'Église' (1977, 686).

difference between God's mind and ours. On the one hand, our knowledge of God differs from our knowledge of all other things;[26] on the other hand, God's knowledge is utterly unlike ours.[27] One element of this difference is that our minds are fully adequate to very little: our feeble reasoning powers are defeated by God's words,[28] let alone divine nature itself. While we have knowledge of the truth, God's truth and wisdom always exceed us,[29] and therefore our minds are dependent on God's help.[30] It is no exaggeration to say that the insistence on grace for which Augustine is notable in the patristic period is intimately tied to the centrality of the intellect in his thought.

Augustine's conception of the intellect is always inherently dynamic, positing a constant transfer of knowledge and wisdom from God to humanity. A particularly favoured image for this transaction is illumination. Our wisdom is illumination and we become wise, not of ourselves, but as the Giver of Light illumines us.[31] Hence God is aptly styled 'the Intelligible Light', by which intelligible things are themselves illumined.[32] If the imagery of light suggests initially the divine intellect's self-communication, 'intelligible light' is more broadly allusive, for it seems that our knowledge of God is of the one who illumines. Perhaps the bishop simply echoes the psalmist, 'in thy light we see light'. Perhaps, however, we might at least tentatively suggest that here again is evidence of the kinetic quality of mind in Augustine's vision; the light that enables us to see thereby not only making itself intelligible, but bringing us to see that it is itself intelligible and intelligent.

Augustine's notion of God as truth is also of this variety. Truth itself presides over our minds, dwelling within us.[33] As the result of God's gift of truth, we see God as truth. The divine mind is unmistakably transcendent, and yet, as the Fathers loved to say of Christ in Mary's womb, the infinite and uncircumscribable condescended to be confined, in this case, to the small compass of the human mind. This intimate connection Augustine also describes as teaching, pre-eminently (as one would expect) in *The Teacher*. While it might seem that mere teaching is quite distinct from the more radical 'indwelling', for the early Augustine at least, this is not so. If we are to call no one on earth 'teacher',[34] it is because God stands in relation to the soul as its primary teacher. Within the practical injunction to heed God alone, then, nestles a principle of humanity's relation to God. Augustine writes: 'our real teacher is he who is to be

---

[26] Sol 4.10–5.11. [27] CD 11.21. [28] CD 21.5. [29] LArb 2.13.35 and 2.14.38. [30] CD 1.25.
[31] LArb 3.24.72; PMer 1.10 and 37–38. [32] Sol 1.1.3. [33] Mag 11.38. [34] Mag 14.46.

listened to, who is said to dwell in the inner man, namely Christ, the wisdom of God'.[35] The logic of the relation of teaching and indwelling is significant, for it is not teaching that brings about indwelling but rather, teaching comes as a *result* of indwelling.[36] Christ teaches, not only because of this kind of union within the human person, but also because of the hypostatic union of natures in *his* person.[37] This indwelling of wisdom, of Christ, is possible only because we are *capax Dei*, the seat of our capacity being the mind: 'every rational soul heeds this wisdom, but to each is given only as much as she is able to receive'.[38] Augustine does not entertain the speculative question of whether God could bestow wisdom on a creature lacking a mind, but he never predicates wisdom of an irrational being. We may safely assume that while the dynamic of intellectual exchange between God and humanity – on which much else in the system depends – rests on the fragile stem of the imago Dei.

As we have seen, a key element of Augustine's understanding of the divine intellect is its voluntary creation and sustenance of other intellects. In moving from the theology proper to his anthropology, we merely delineate the working out of his doctrine of God. The imago Dei is such a commonplace of classical Christian theology that it is easy to forget its import: if rationality is a key attribute of God and we somehow mirror God, rationality must be a key attribute of humanity as well. Augustine follows the tradition before him in locating the image, not only in the human soul, but specifically in the mind.[39] The connection between rationality and the image lies not only in a posited similarity to God, but also in a potential receptivity.[40] Indeed, after the Fall, we can only be said really to exist in the image once the spirit is regenerated by the grace of baptism, which will eventually also bring about the regeneration of the body.[41] The whole process of regeneration is due to a discarding of carnal *mind*, however.[42] As he notes in the *Soliloquies*, God is the light of those made in his image.[43] Divine illumination is not generic, and the communicability of the divine mind is predicated (whether of necessity or merely in fact) on the existence of receptive intellects. What it means to be one of the latter is to be made in the image of God, which is implanted in us in our rational soul.[44]

When, therefore, he maintains that in virtue of our rationality the universe reaches the height of beauty and does so despite our sin,[45] he is

---

[35] Mag 11.38. [36] Mag 14.16. [37] CD 11.2. [38] Mag 11.38. [39] CD 11.2; CRud 18.29.
[40] CD 11.2; cf. SpLt 37 and 47. [41] PMer 2.9. [42] PMer 2.11. [43] 1.4. [44] CD 13.24.
[45] LArb 3.15.43.

saying that we are beautiful because we reflect the perfect beauty of God. Augustine can at times express essentially the same idea without directly using the language of the image. For example, he says that those things that are pleasing to the senses are so because we perceive in them harmony or proportion (or as he puts it, they are governed by number). To contemplate them with delight, therefore, is a mental act[46] and one we can only engage in because the laws of beauty rest within us.[47] If God is beauty and we recognise the beautiful as such because it in some sense indwells us, then the capacity for God may be said to have been imprinted upon us, a capacity that is also a likeness. Not the traditional terminology of the imago is crucial for Augustine, but the reciprocity of intellect. Beauty, like Mind, is self-communicating but the beautiful can only be appreciated as such because of mind. Although Augustine does not appeal directly to divine simplicity as often as later Christian theologians, particularly the medievals, do (Conf. 4.16 being a rare explicit reference), this notion often hovers just below the surface of the text, and what other attributes reduce to is often, as they do here, God's intellectual nature.

In the earlier works, Augustine is apparently more Platonic on this point. In *The Teacher*, for example, he describes learning as a process, not of being taught by another, but as the result of contemplating things with the inner light of truth.[48] Even in his latest works, however, as his anthropological pessimism drives him further from a Platonising sensibility, he claims that God speaks to the mind through direct impact of the truth, to anyone capable of hearing with the mind, and one must doubt, therefore, that his doctrine of illumination can be explained as the mere residue of a youthful fancy for pagan philosophy.[49] The truth of things is manifested through divine agency, even when conveyed by the words of one person to another.[50] Both the innate capacity and its actualisation and development through the action of God are necessary, and both are God-given. Not surprisingly, then, Augustine regards intelligence as entirely good[51] and knowledge as entirely good because it comes through reason and intelligence.[52] The mind, as we have noted, that which distinguishes human beings from other animals, is our highest faculty and that which is exceeded only by God himself.[53]

While the imago Dei provides the basis of all human relating to God, in Augustine's thought the image is never static. Its dynamism consists

---

[46] VRel 30.56. [47] LArb 2.16.41. [48] 12.40. [49] CD 11.2. [50] Mag 12.40. [51] LArb 1.1.3.
[52] LArb 1.17. [53] CD 11.2.

both in its status as the condition of the possibility of any intellectual growth towards God and in that the image itself grows in likeness to its prototype. The image is the point of departure in a transformative process of growth towards God: 'the image of God will achieve its full likeness of him when it attains to the full vision of him'.[54] What accomplishes this transformation is the mind's turning toward God: 'This trinity of the mind is not really the image of God because the mind remembers and understands and loves itself, but because it is also able to remember and understand and love him by whom it was made. And when it does this it becomes wise.'[55] The image of God in humanity is therefore both given and yet to come,[56] but the fact of some sort of likeness in nature is the foundation upon which grace works to bring us to glory.

> Anyone who has a lively intuition of these three [the Trinity] (as divinely established in the nature of his mind) [quae tria in sua mente naturaliter diuinitas instituta quisquis vivaliter perspicit] and of how great a thing it is that his mind has by that which even the eternal and unchanging nature can be recalled, beheld and desired – it is recalled by memory, beheld by intelligence, embraced by love [reminiscitur per memoriam, intuetur per intelligentiam, amplectitur per dilectionem] – has thereby found the image of that supreme trinity.[57]

The perfecting of the image is largely a process of bringing order into disorder, for the principle of hierarchy applies not only to the rational soul's relation to the God who dwells within, but also to the ordering within the person. The governing rubric is that the body derives its existence from the soul, as the soul does from God; the soul is therefore superior to the body,[58] as God is to the soul.[59] Right order implies the body's subservience to the mind: the body is the tool or servant [famulo vel tamquam instrumento] of the soul.[60] Within the soul itself there is also a hierarchy, the mind being its superior part, where wisdom and virtue make their home.[61] The principle here parallels that of the hierarchy of being: since the body is that which we share with lesser creatures, it is to be subordinated to the mind, which we share with higher beings.[62]

---

[54] Trin 14.24.   [55] Trin 14.15.
[56] Cf. Edmund Hill: 'The image is something we have to realise, to construct in ourselves; it is something which sin has defaced and grace is operating to restore' (1971, 79). Cf. also Gilson, who maintains the image of God in the soul is for Augustine the ever-present possibility of participation [in God] (1960, 219).
[57] Trin 15.39.   [58] LArb 3.5.16.   [59] Cf. also VRel 12.25.   [60] CD 10.6; cf. FSym 10.23.
[61] CD 9.6. 'Pars animi superior ... in qua virtus et sapientia'. The context here is a discussion of demons, but this claim is presented as a given.
[62] CD 19.14.

The fact that we are privileged in being endowed with rationality is the reason the mind is to govern all else in our nature.

The anthropological hierarchy, the order within the human person, should not be taken as implying denigration of its lower levels; the body is neither inherently evil, nor sinful, in Augustine's view, though it is corruptible. The soul ought to govern the body, Augustine maintains, but he insists upon the body's fundamental goodness, even when the soul abdicates its responsibility to rule, to the extent that he is willing to claim that rejecting the body is tantamount to rejecting divine truth.[63] The body, moreover, plays an important role in humanity's coming to know God. In the first instance, we are able to understand the eternal and spiritual by means of the physical and temporal – that, at least, is the view of the mid-career work, *On Christian Teaching*.[64] In the later *City of God*, Augustine's concern is to claim that God speaks not to the senses, but to the understanding; this is a correlative of the eternal quality of this speech.[65] Yet further on, he adamantly rejects the notion that intelligible things are apprehended with the mind's vision, but material things only by the senses.[66]

At first glance, it seems his thought on this point not only changes, but is in its later stages self-contradictory. *On Christian Teaching*, the earlier work, seems to make the senses valuable – perhaps even indispensable – for knowledge of God; the later *City of God* at once seems to deny their role and affirm it. On closer inspection, however, there is a consistent principle informing these dicta. Embodied creatures can know something of God through the senses, through knowledge of creation; God, however, is able to understand embodied creatures even though he has no body. Two principles are at work. First, all beings know in accordance with their state, the embodied through the senses and the purely intellectual through the intellect. We ascend to God as embodied creatures and God descends to us as an intelligible being. If the latter formulation seems suspect because it appears to obviate the Incarnation, Augustine affirms earlier in the same chapter[67] that we will see Christ in the *flesh* in the next life – this is what he takes John Baptist's quotation of Isaiah 40:5 in Luke 3:6 to mean. 'In the flesh', however, means we will see Christ incarnate, rather than with our corporeal eyes: 'we shall see God by the mind [spiritu]',[68] and it seems that we will see Christ in this fashion also. In this life, on the other hand, we need and use the senses in the usual way, even when attempting to grasp the mystery of God. Second, a purely

---

[63] CD 14.5.   [64] 1.4.   [65] CD 10.15.   [66] CD 22.29.   [67] 22.29.   [68] CD 22.29.

intellectual nature is not epistemologically disadvantaged for it, too, can know material things. There is still a hierarchy of knowledge – we may rise to knowledge of the eternal through the temporal – and God's self-disclosure is still primarily an intelligible rather than a sensible phenomenon, yet the higher beings are not deprived of knowledge of the lower. What this complex of texts indicates is that Augustine consistently privileges the mind, without denying the fact, indeed the goodness, of human embodiment. In the next life, all who were embodied before death will be embodied again, their souls united to their bodies as God intended. Yet the body is largely rendered superfluous, no longer supplying the data of sense experience it once did, but being supplanted in this role by the mind.

In claiming that the mind must govern the body, then, Augustine does not intend to demean the body, nor does his schema render it redundant. On the contrary, he may be taken as acknowledging the importance of the body in the spiritual life: the mind is not such that it can function independently, without being affected by the flesh to which it is joined. The life of the person depends on the unity of body and soul, and without this unity, there can be no life of the mind. Mere existence, however, is scarcely the destiny of the person created in God's image, for knowing is greater than existing or living.[69] On this point, Christians and pagans agree.[70] Nevertheless, there is a specifically Christian reason for this fact: reason is known by reason.[71] Our highest function is not only the one in respect of which we are like God, but the one that enables dynamic relation with God, a point which we will examine more fully in due course. While the mind never expires, as the body eventually will, it has one serious drawback that the body does not have: its capacity to corrupt. The body is, of course, corruptible, but it actively corrupts neither itself, nor others. For all the elevated status of the mind in Augustine's thought, he accords it the dubious distinction of a no more than tenuous desire for the good and the sinister capacity to wreak havoc by spreading corruption.

While Augustine clearly regards the human mind highly, therefore, his is a qualified approval, and he is also well aware of the human mind's frailty and fallibility. In the first instance, the human mind's mutability inspires a certain vulnerability, to the taunts of unbelievers, for example, who wound the believer's mind as blows would the body.[72] Our intellectual frailty appears in the weakness of our powers of reason even to

---

[69] LArb 2.3.7.   [70] CD 7.3.   [71] LArb 2.18.51.   [72] Pat 8.

such mundane ends as logic;[73] for higher purposes, the mind's inadequacies are even more apparent. When dealing with the more speculative points of the faith, Augustine is always quick to point out that the view he advances is tentative, because such things cannot be discerned by the human mind in this life.[74] The logic of the hierarchy indicates that as goes the mind, so go the lower faculties. Thus it is that the bodily senses suffer from two sorts of weakness: not only are they capable of being deceived, and useful in any case only for understanding that which is itself carnal; even sensory knowledge is dependent upon the mind, for the senses need the mind's interpretative capacity[75] and thus when the mind is disordered, *all* our mechanisms for gathering and sorting information inevitably suffer. While rationality is a good, it does not of itself confer wisdom; as Augustine notes tersely in *On the Freedom of the Will*: 'It is one thing to be a rational being, another to be a wise man.'[76]

Part of our intellectual inadequacy lies in our inability even rightly to understand ourselves, let alone others: 'When my mind speculates upon its own capabilities, it realises that it cannot safely trust its own judgement, because its inner workings are generally so obscure that they are only revealed in the light of experience.... Our only hope, our only confidence, the only firm promise we have is your mercy.'[77] If, from this formulation, it sounds as if God were the last resort of the desperate in an intolerable situation, Augustine provides a more positive version of what is essentially the same insight in the *Soliloquies*, when he writes: 'God, to whom we have committed ourselves, will doubtless lend his aid.'[78] The explicitly Christian dimension of the Augustinian conception of the intellect is not only that the human intellect is defined in relation to God in virtue of the imago Dei, but that the intellect requires the continued sustenance of God and that God, always the generous Giver, is always ready to lend his aid to those who seek the truth. Grace in the Augustinian system pertains not only to the will, therefore, and to our preservation from sin in its most obvious sense, but to the mind and its failure to contemplate; 'the mind must be healed so that it may behold the immutable form of things'.[79] Even when failure to contemplate is not considered a sin, strictly speaking, it still constitutes a falling short of the

---

[73] CD 2.1.   [74] Mort 20, for example.   [75] Mag 12.39.   [76] 3.24.72.
[77] Conf 10.32.   [78] Sol 2.6.9.
[79] VRel 3.3. This quotation comes from a question Augustine hypothetically puts to Plato, but we may take it as evidence of his own view since in 3.4 he claims that Plato's desideratum has now come to be.

heights of the human vocation. Augustine makes precisely the same point in *On the Trinity*:

> From myself indeed I understand how wonderful and incomprehensible is that knowledge of yours with which you have made me, seeing that I am not even able to comprehend myself whom you have made; and yet a fire burns up in my meditation, causing me to seek your face always.[80]

The acknowledgement in the context of this work is significant because it argues against any attempt to claim the investigation of the vestigia in *On the Trinity* constitutes an exercise in natural theology. To acknowledge this is not, nevertheless, to deny all traces of what one might loosely call natural law in Augustine's work. In the late and generally anthropologically pessimistic *Enchiridion*, Augustine notes that rational creatures recoil from falsity.[81]

Our intellectual capacities are not only frail, but also impaired by sin.[82] While not all ignorance leads to error – and in some instances ignorance is preferable to knowledge – error only ever comes from ignorance and we should accordingly exert ourselves to avoid it.[83] Elsewhere, he is even more dubious about the effects of sheer ignorance on the will[84] and the mind's infirmity.[85] One can also misuse the intellect, being so filled with one's own opinions that there is no room to meditate on God's thoughts[86] and Augustine enjoins us to resist the carnal senses and the impressions the mind forms of them[87] and to live, not by our own standard of truth, but by God's,[88] clearly assuming that it is possible for us to be sufficiently deceived as to create our own standard.[89] Substituting human for divine standards is essentially a rejection of right order, that is, of the body's subservience to the mind. When that right order is disrupted, the life-giving principle ceases to give life, and death, both spiritual and physical, results. Although the body is neither inherently evil nor sinful in Augustine's view, its vulnerability to corruption makes it helpless before a wayward soul, and it is a measure of the soul's power and superiority that it can destroy the body: 'It is the sinful soul that makes the flesh corruptible.'[90] When body and soul are rightly ordered, on the other hand, the mind will not work to the detriment of the body, nor be tainted by it, but will remain pure.[91] Thus in the next life, when grace has completely regenerated the soul, the body will also be restored to its original strength.[92]

---

[80] Trin 15.13.   [81] Ench 17.   [82] CD 11.2.   [83] Ench 17.   [84] PMer 2.26.   [85] GChr 2.13.
[86] Conf 12.25.   [87] VRel 34.64.   [88] CD 14.4; cf. CRud 11.11.
[89] Cf. NBon 35 and 37 and VRel 20.38.   [90] CD 14.3.   [91] Sol 1.12.   [92] VRel 23.44.

The sanctification that brings increase in knowledge of God comes at a price, and for all Augustine's stress on grace, he also insists that human beings have work to do if they are to know God, the content of which work is largely purification: 'If [the Incarnation] is difficult to understand, then you must purify your mind with faith, by abstaining more and more from sin, and by doing good, and by praying with the sighs of holy desire that God will help you to make progress in understanding and loving.'[93] Because corruption is pervasive, purification is necessary if we are to know God, and indeed, the higher and more specifically theological reaches of the mind are available *only* to the purified, for wisdom is the sweet light of a purified mind.[94] Purification not only impels us towards wisdom, however; without it, we would be shrouded in the darkness, carnal and weak.[95] Purification in fact seems to rehabilitate reason, a faculty of which Augustine remains suspect to the end of this life, so that he is willing to say that no authority may be set above the reason of a purified soul.[96]

In the late works, Augustine places no less emphasis on purification, but is more concerned to point to Christ as the antidote to vice, rather than human striving alone. It is Christ who purifies us,[97] and it is the mind especially that is purified by the Incarnation: God is truth taking on human nature without abandoning the divine.[98] In the late works, Augustine gives a more central role to Christ's work as mediator. After pointing to the disastrous effects of the Fall upon the mind, he continues: 'So the mind had to be trained and purified by faith; and in order to give man's mind greater confidence in its journey towards truth along the way of faith, God the Son of God, who is himself the truth, took humanity upon himself without abandoning divinity, and thus established and founded this faith, so that we might have a path to humanity's God through the human being who was God – for this is the mediator'.[99] Here the intellectual dimension of Christ's mediatorial role is only hinted at; in the *Confessions*, it is unmistakable: 'when the Word took human flesh, he must also have taken a human soul and a human mind.... [Christ did not have] only a human body, or a human body and a sensitive soul without reasoning, but was a complete human person'.[100] Augustine thus goes beyond mere denial of Apollinarianism; the significance of the Incarnation lies not simply in Christ's having a complete human nature, but also in the direct and continuing effect of the hypostatic union on the human intellect. Sanctification affects, not a soul

---

[93] Trin 4.31. [94] LArb 2.16.43; cf. Cred 16.34. [95] CD 10.24. [96] VRel 25.47.
[97] CD 10.24; cf 27. [98] CD 11.2. [99] CD 11.2. [100] Conf 6.19.

considered in such vague fashion as temporarily to bracket the intellect, but the mind itself, and thus implies intellectual regeneration. Purification, moreover, seems to confer endurance: 'the mind should be cleansed so that it can see the light and cling to it once it is seen'.[101] Holding to the path of virtue in turn cleanses the mind: faith, hope and charity are the remedies for a diseased mind[102] and it is only a healthy mind that can see God.[103] There is accordingly a reciprocal action of mind and virtue, each working purity on the other, a pattern which is well expressed in *On the Freedom of the Will*: 'The rational nature grasps the precept [praecepti], obedience to which brings wisdom.'[104] Perfect virtue and perfect wisdom are inseparable, for virtue is reason achieving its end.[105] That end is, quite literally, heavenly; the body we will have in heaven will be suited to its eternal home, purged of all earthly weakness and corruption and converted into celestial purity.[106] Not only will we ourselves be purified, moreover, but purity will enable us to find our fulfillment in encounter with God: 'When the mind has been imbued with the first elements of that faith which works by love, it strives by purity of life to attain to sight, where the pure and perfect in heart know that unspeakable beauty, the full vision of which is supreme happiness.'[107]

This quest for right order within the human person is none other than the battle with cupidity which surfaces throughout Augustine's work, and it explains the position he reaches regarding the relation of body and mind in his last works, in virtue of which the mind functions as a quasi-sense organ. It is cupidity that constantly threatens to overwhelm the human person, snatching power and exercising it tyrannically,[108] when it is mind that by rights ought to rule.[109] If cupidity represents the epitome of the wrong relation of body and mind, the converse is represented by sacrifice. The sacrifices of the covenant with Israel prefigure in the bodies of the animals the purity of flesh that will be ours in the Age to Come.[110] In the New Covenant, bodily sacrifice continues, in a sense, for as Paul enjoins us, we are to offer our own bodies as a living sacrifice to God. The effect of this sacrifice, however, is reformation of mind [reformemur in novitate mentis]:[111] it seems that even if the mind is intended to rule the body, the body nevertheless exerts a certain power over the mind. Augustine's description of this state of affairs as one of 'turbulence' [passionibus turbulentis][112] indicates the extent to which he views this

---

[101] Doct 1.10. [102] Sol 1.13. [103] Sol 1.12. [104] 3.24.72. [105] Sol 1.13. [106] FSym 6.13.
[107] Ench 5. [108] LArb 1.11.22. [109] CD 1.16 and 9.6. [110] CD 20.26. [111] CD 10.6.
[112] CD 9.6.

battle between cupidity and reason as disruptive of the smooth functioning of our lives; thus he equates the happy life with intelligence.[113] God, in contrast, suffers no such 'storms' [turbulentus affectus].[114]

If Augustine's meteorological imagery is avowedly borrowed from Platonists such as Apuleius[115] and the Stoics,[116] he nevertheless distances himself from the notion that all emotion is bad (and even quarrels with the Stoic who would say 'disadvantageous'[117]). Zealous indignation at the sinner, when prompted by concern for her correction, for instance, or fear for the endangered that leads to preventing her death – these are acceptable emotions.[118] The desideratum is, again, right ordering: 'Scripture subjects the mind to God for his direction and assistance and subjects the passions to the mind for their restraint and control, so that they may be turned into instruments of justice.'[119] When the rise of emotion leads to the exercise of Christian virtue, such as just compassion,[120] then emotion may be deemed the servant of reason, and is entirely proper – indeed, the text implies, necessary. Emotion may in fact provide a spur to right concern for others – and especially for their salvation – and accordingly, we should make good use of the emotions of the mind.[121] Above all, Augustine warns against driving out undesirable emotions in such a way that they are merely replaced with other, different and undesirable emotions; there is, he says, a large difference between smothering cupidity with despair and driving it out with the exercise of calm reason.[122]

The emotions are thus not to be exiled from rational life, but to be ruled by the mind,[123] just like the body. This rule is, however, not entirely tyrannical, for Augustine freely predicates desire of the mind; as we shall see shortly, he still considers that the mind ought to rule desire, as it should any emotion. Yet even as he concedes the human mind's proclivity to abdicate responsibility to govern, he retains some sense of the mind's monarchy, for as he reminds us, it is through the mind's own choosing that it becomes mired in cupidity[124] and this formulation suggests that the mind, far from being overpowered by the lesser faculties, remains in control, in some sense, in its very choosing of them.

Purification brings not only virtue in its obvious sense, but also apatheia, the condition in which all movement is rightly governed by the mind, a state to which Augustine accords a guarded approval. He inherits

---

[113] Sol 2.1. [114] CD 9.5. [115] CD 9.6. [116] CD 9.4. [117] CD 9.4. [118] CD 9.5.
[119] CD 9.5. [120] CD 9.5. [121] CRud 15.14. [122] Sol 1.19.
[123] LArb 1.8.18. [124] LArb 1.10.21.

and modifies the Greek philosophical tradition on this point; one of the reasons that the Greeks regarded apatheia as a virtue is that it seemed to them the human equivalent of divine impassibility.[125] To be 'apathetic' (in this sense) meant that the mind was not moved by lower functions, that it was impassible. Augustine quarrels with this vision of the good, and refuses to countenance the notion that the extreme form of this state is virtuous. He writes: 'If apatheia is the name of the state in which the mind cannot be touched by any emotion whatsoever, who would not judge this insensitivity to be the worst of all moral defects?'[126] If the mind is, in humanity's perfect state, meant to be directing the person as a whole, it is also meant to be actively engaged with the person's other constituents, and is even affected by them on occasion.

The mind is intended as a chastened ruler, therefore, one whose power is exercised within strict limits and constrained as appropriate. Or, to put it another way, humility is an intellectual, and not only a moral, virtue, and one which Augustine never tires of extolling. At times his exhortation to humility is rather general, as at the beginning of the *City of God*, where he praises humility for its power and excellence, which enable it to soar over the earth's heights and whose supremacy is granted by divine grace, in contrast to human arrogance.[127] More specifically, however, humility is a state of the soul that profoundly influences the mind. The demons, for example, have knowledge, but their arrogance precludes their having charity. The polar opposite of the demons is Christ, the paragon of humility. When human beings lack humility, they end up in the worst situation of all: their pride renders them unlike Christ, yet they lack the knowledge the demons have. For human persons to attain to the salvific knowledge which is Christ's own, we must imitate the humility of Christ.[128] Only through such humility, it appears, can we attain to knowledge that is worth anything.

This hint of a connection between humility and knowledge in Book 9 is confirmed in Book 14, when Augustine comments: 'Devout humility makes the mind subject to what is superior. Nothing is superior to God; and that is why humility exalts the mind by making it subject to God.'[129] This is the paradox in which Augustine revels: 'there is something in

---

[125] Augustine in fact makes an equivalent point, directing the reader of *On True Religion* (ostensibly one Romanianus) to transcend himself, if he should find his nature to be mutable (29.72). While it is not clear how exactly Romanianus would accomplish this, the text does show Augustine's identification of human nature with divine attributes, even those he regards as distinctively divine.
[126] CD 14.9.   [127] CD 1.pref.   [128] CD 9.20.   [129] CD 14.13.

humility to exalt the mind and something in exaltation to abase it'.¹³⁰ To be humble, moreover, is specifically to be identified with Christ, for Augustine attributes his own initial bridling at the doctrine of the Incarnation to his lack of humility: 'I was not humble enough to conceive of the humble Jesus Christ as my God, nor had I learnt what lesson his human weakness was meant to teach.'¹³¹

The need for humility does not contravene the prevailing pattern of the mind's rule over the emotions. In Augustine's survey of a variety of pagan thinkers on the subject, he finds little to reject. He cites Apuleius, for example, for evidence that it is the mind that is agitated by the tempests of passion [procellosis quodam modo perturbationibus agitari¹³²], not any lower faculty. The Stoics essentially acknowledge the same point.¹³³ The only point at which Augustine feels obliged to differ concerns a small group of commendable passions: being indignant with the sinner out of desire that she amend her ways; to feel sorrow for the afflicted and afraid for those in danger; and compassion.¹³⁴ Augustine is willing to admit such passions for two reasons, presumably. The first is that compassion and zeal for righteousness are deeply imbedded in the ethic of both the Old and New Testaments. If the bishop is virtually constrained by scripture to reach this conclusion, he nevertheless also supplies a reason for the conviction that is in him: truth and virtue, and *only* these, offer a centre of resistance against turbulent and degraded passions.¹³⁵ When emotion is reason's handmaid, when one shows compassion without detriment to justice,¹³⁶ then it is not only admissible, but necessary and good, from a Christian perspective.

The guiding principle of Augustine's thought on these issues is, once again, the sovereignty of mind. He would not banish emotion, but regards it as virtuous only when rightly governed. While the Stoic view (at least as Augustine himself presents matters) seems almost to deny the mind's power, in its refusal to countenance the validity of *any* emotion, Augustine once again seeks right order, and will admit emotion that is ruled by reason, a point he makes explicitly in Book 19 of the *City of God*:

The peace of the body is a tempering of the component parts in duly ordered proportion; the peace of the irrational soul is a duly ordered repose of the appetites; the peace of the rational soul is the duly ordered agreement of cognition and action. The peace of the body and soul is a duly ordered life and health of the living creature; peace between mortal human beings and God is an

---

¹³⁰ CD 14.13. ¹³¹ Conf 7.18; cf. 20. ¹³² CD 9.3. ¹³³ CD 9.4. ¹³⁴ CD 9.5. ¹³⁵ CD 9.3.
¹³⁶ CD 9.5.

ordered obedience... peace in human society is an ordered agreement of mind with mind; the peace of a home is the ordered agreement among those who live together about giving and obeying orders; the peace of the Heavenly City is a perfectly ordered and perfectly harmonious fellowship in the enjoyment of God, and a mutual fellowship in God; the peace of the whole universe is the tranquility of order, and order is the arrangement of things equal and unequal in a pattern that assigns to each its proper position.[137]

Further on in the same passage, Augustine connects the tranquillity of order and the state in which there is no disturbance of mind. The principle of order, then, so central to Augustine's aesthetics and theology generally, is itself governed by the principle of the sovereignty of mind, and this point alone is sufficient to indicate the importance of the intellect in Augustine's thought.

While the mind and what we can for the moment call the moral faculties are interdependent, and will continue to be so in any desirable state, the will ought always to be subordinate to the mind in this sense, that emotion never holds sway over reason. Augustine's counsels of apatheia thus differ from those of the Desert Fathers, to take one example, for whom the mind is not as important an agent of the Christian life. Nevertheless, Augustine does not seem merely to have imported the notion that apatheia is desirable from earlier ascetical theology, for what he has to say on this subject is consistent with the broader pattern of his thought: first, inasmuch as he views passion as a disturbance of the mind and not some other faculty, and second, inasmuch as he considers the human person may never rightly be governed by something other than mind.

The battle with cupidity represents one kind of qualification to the prevailing role of the mind's ascendancy: the ruler may sometimes abdicate its responsibility to rule. Now we must acknowledge a further qualification of a different kind. For all its importance in Augustine's thought, the mind of which he writes is conceived in rather broader fashion than it would be today. The less than purely intellectual quality of mind in his vision emerges most clearly in the texts in which he links the intellect and the will.

One example of both the linkage of mind and will in his theology and the complexity of his notion of the intellect is the labelling of failure to use the mind rightly as a sin. Failure to adhere to God is thus esteemed a perversion of the rational nature, and not purely of the will alone, as one

---

[137] CD 19.13.

might expect.[138] Habit can carry the mind away and hold it against its will[139] and on occasion the mind does not even succeed in commanding itself,[140] so much so that a divided will may be understood as the product of a diseased mind.[141] For this reason, along with the visible sacrifice of prayer and praise, we are to offer the invisible sacrifice of *both* a pure mind and a good will.[142]

The connection of mind and will can also work to the opposite effect, for right use of the mind inspires love[143] and will inspires us to seek wisdom.[144] The wise do not simply seek intelligible things, they love them[145] and no love is more rewarding than this love of truth.[146] To grasp the Augustinian notion of the knowledge of God, we must therefore look to what he says not only specifically of knowledge, but also of love, and of the relation between knowing and loving.[147]

Such assertions are scattered throughout the corpus, but it is in a mature work, *On the Trinity*, that Augustine most fully works out the relation of mind and will, of knowledge and love. In this treatise, he grounds the unity of both faculties in several distinct ways. The most important of these derives from the doctrine of the Trinity. Appropriating intellect, knowledge and wisdom to the second Person, and will and love to the Third, Augustine can claim that intellect and will may never function in isolation from one another: if these take their truest form in the divine Persons and those Persons are inseparably united, then so must intellect and will be inseparable. An alternative route to the same conclusion is via divine simplicity: if divine nature is one, then the attributes we erroneously think of as distinct are in reality one, which means love and knowledge are one in God. These principles derived from the doctrine of God create a context in which Augustine examines the unity of mind and will, turning it over and over in his mind and drawing from this principle multiple conclusions. To understand how Augustine gets from the doctrine of the Trinity to a claim regarding the nature of the mind's engagement with God, we need to begin with his understanding of the Trinity, the trinitarian structure of humanity's knowledge of God and the relation of knowledge and will in *On the Trinity*. Because

---

[138] CD 12.1. [139] Conf 8.5. [140] Conf 8.9. [141] Conf 8.9 [142] CD 10.19. [143] Sol 1.7.
[144] LArb 1.12.25; cf. SpLt 5. [145] VRel 31.58. [146] Conf 2.6.
[147] The reading presented here resembles in some respects that of Bourassa (1977, 1978). Bourassa also insists on the dual focus in the treatise on love and knowledge, and gives brief attention to transformation, contemplation and beatitude. Bourassa, however, sees these elements of Augustine's theology communicated primarily through the vestigia, rather than through the mutuality of the Trinity and the unity of substance. He also is not concerned to press his reading as implying an epistemology, or a statement about the relation between theology and spirituality.

the paradigmatic relation of mind and will is drawn chiefly from the doctrine of the Trinity, it is inherently personal: 'it is not one thing for God to be and another to be a person, but altogether the same [non enim aliud est deo esse, aliud personam esse sed omnino idem]'.[148] He then proceeds from this assumption of God as personal to identify the divine persons with knowledge and love, explaining the relations among them as having a specifically trinitarian structure. In so doing, he employs two distinct insights of trinitarian theology.

On the one hand, he freely makes use of a strategy of appropriation to identify knowledge, word and wisdom with the second person of the Trinity, and charity with the third.[149] Thus, the terms in which the Son and the Spirit are chiefly conceived are as knowledge and love, activities that are associated pre-eminently with those beings of whom one may predicate consciousness, that is, persons.[150] On the other hand, with a nod to the notion of perichoresis, Augustine insists that the divine persons are inseparable: 'just as Father and Son and Holy Spirit are inseparable, so do they work inseparably'.[151] This unity comes from not simply a unity of operation, but a coinherence: 'these three are together God because of their inexpressible mutuality [ineffabilem coniunctionem]'.[152] Thus, Augustine does not, as he is sometimes charged, locate the unity of the Trinity solely in the unity of substance, but also in the inseparability of persons.[153] If we put the insights from the side of perichoresis together with those from the side of appropriation, we find that as the Word and Spirit are inseparable in the unity of the Trinity so, we may surmise, must knowledge be inseparable from love of God.

Unity of substance, while by no means more important than personal mutuality, provides a second theological basis for the unity of knowledge and love. The converse of the appropriations strategy is that whatever is predicated of one person is rightly predicated of all Three.[154] The inseparability of charity and truth is grounded not only in the relations of the divine Persons, but also in simplicity: 'in that supremely simple nature substance is not one thing and charity another, but substance is charity and charity is substance'.[155] As the Trinity exists, so ought we, so that 'just as Father and Son are one not only by equality of substance but also by identity of will, so these men, for whom the Son is mediator with God, might be one not only by being of the same nature, but also by being

---

[148] Trin 7.11.   [149] Trin 15.29, 30 and 37.
[150] I do not, therefore, think Lonergan is quite right in maintaining that for Augustine 'person' simply denotes what there are three of in God (1974, 25).
[151] Trin 1.7; cf. 4.30.   [152] Trin 7.8; cf. 15.43.   [153] Trin 6.9.   [154] Trin 5.9.   [155] Trin 15.29.

bound in the fellowship of the same love'.[156] The same must hold true of truth or any other divine attribute. Thus, whatever one thinks of the doctrine of simplicity (and some these days do not think much of it[157]), what Augustine has done here is by contemporary standards extraordinary: he has not only drawn from a recondite doctrine a moral principle of human relations, but has also traced the preliminary outline of a distinctively Christian doctrine of the mind, in terms of which the mind, when rightly engaged, burns always with the fire of love.

What drives the epistemology of *On the Trinity* is this (by contemporary standards) peculiar conception of the mind, implying as it does that immediacy of contact with a person brings about increase of mental capacity:

> Our knowledge is therefore Christ, and our wisdom is the same Christ. It is he who plants faith in us about temporal things, he who presents us with the truth about eternal things. Through him we go straight toward him [per ipsum pergimus ad ipsum], through knowledge toward wisdom, without ever turning aside from one and the same Christ, in whom are hidden all the treasures of wisdom and knowledge (Col 2:3).[158]

To know God certainly entails mastery of information, but it also entails personal contact. Knowledge of God is personal knowledge in the fullest sense, in that it encompasses both knowledge-about and acquaintance-with, that is, both mastery of information related to the person and immediate personal contact with the same.[159] This sensibility also informs an earlier treatise, where he writes: '[the Spirit] is called the gift of God, because no one enjoys what she knows unless she loves it. To enjoy the wisdom of God is nothing else than to cleave to him in love; and no one has an abiding grasp of anything unless he loves it [frui autem sapientia Dei, nihil est aliud quam ei dilectione cohaerere].'[160] It is in the first instance because Augustine locates knowledge in the realm of the personal, identifying knowledge, wisdom and truth with divine persons in perfect communion, that he refuses to separate knowledge and love.

A third way in which Augustine grounds the unity of knowledge and love is the vestigia Trinitatis, triform structures in the human person that

---

[156] Trin 4.12; cf. VRel 46.86.
[157] For an example of a recent critique of simplicity, see Wolterstorff (1991).
[158] Trin 13.24.
[159] These terms are not used by Hoitenga (1998), but his description of the elements of knowledge in Augustine's thought resembles the analysis given here. Merton is also thinking in similar terms (1962, 13 and 254–55).
[160] FSym 19.

parallel the divine Trinity, such as memory, understanding and will; or the mind, its knowledge and love; or image, likeness and equality – there are two dozen or more of these. One of Augustine's purposes in tracing these trinities is to show the unity of knowledge and love. This reading of Augustine's theological method differs from one standard interpretation of *On the Trinity*, which assumes that its second half functions as a venture in natural theology. On this reading, Augustine examines the vestigia in order to establish that God is triune because those made in his image are so, at least in some sense, hence the treatise's epistemological claim is that because we are like God, we can come to knowledge of God by looking at ourselves. There are several factors counting against this reading, however.

One immediate reason to reject this interpretation of the vestigia's function is that Augustine explicitly denies one can extrapolate from natural world to God. To begin with, he is wary of the possible misuse of reason in theology. The purpose of his treatise, Augustine tells us in its opening pages, is to refute the sophistry of those deceived by a misguided use of reason.[161] Second, he is aware of the difficulties inherent in extrapolation from creation to God, because of the profound difference between the Uncreated and the created. If he is doubtful about the possibility of reasoning from creation to God, he is overtly contemptuous of the value of meditation upon ourselves as a theological end:

This trinity of mind is not really the image of God because the mind remembers and understands and loves itself, but because it is also able to remember and understand and love him by whom it was made.... If it does not do [this], then even though it remembers and understands and loves itself, it is foolish.[162]

Even more than the explicit statements questioning the possibility of natural knowledge of God, the structure of *On the Trinity* argues against reading it as a natural theology, since one can only deem it such by privileging its second half. The first half, comprising Books 1–8, treats the divine Trinity exclusively. As Augustine reminds us in his own summary, he begins by demonstrating the unity and equality of the Trinity from the scriptures.[163] The nature of the divine Trinity having been established,

---

[161] Trin 1.1.   [162] Trin 14.15; cf. 15.51.   [163] Trin 15.5.

and elaborated at some length, he then moves in Books 9–15 to seek analogies that might aid understanding:

> Let us believe that Father and Son and Holy Spirit are one God, maker and ruler of all creation... that they are a trinity of persons related to each other, and a unity of equal being. But let us seek to understand this, begging the help of him whom we wish to understand; and as far as it is granted us let us seek to explain what we understand.[164]

This impulse is similar to those we have seen in other parts of his work, which insist on humanity's need for grace in the quest for God. In this treatise, grace's end is that we might know God and the *vestigia* serve as a tool for penetrating belief and grasping it yet more fully, not a means for establishing the content of faith independently of, or prior to, scripture.

The *vestigia* also extend Augustine's anthropology beyond a conventional statement of the *imago Dei*, inasmuch as many of his triads point simultaneously to the intellectual and the volitional dimensions of the person. They function to show the particularly Christian character of the mind's engagement with God. Some focus entirely on the activities of the will: the lover, being loved and love in *On the Trinity* 7.14 and 9.2; the lover, what is loved and love in 15.10. Others encompass movements of both the mind and the will: memory, understanding and will in 4.30, 10.17–19, 14.8, and 10; the mind, love and knowledge in 9.4, 6, 7, 8, 15 and 18; and memory, understanding and love in 14.13 and 15.42 and 43. The implication of these dually-based triads is that humanity resembles God not simply in possessing the faculties of intellect and will, but in that these operate conjointly and harmoniously in the human person, just as they do in the divine Trinity.

The import of the treatise's structure, if we acknowledge the distinctive features of each half and trace the connections between them, is that of a theological epistemology, but a rather different one from the generic conclusions of a natural theology. If the *vestigia* are read together with the doctrine of God elaborated in Books 1–8, *On the Trinity* yields a specifically Christian understanding of the knowledge of God, according to which the relation of Trinitarian persons to one another, and the relation of God and humanity, are relations constituted by knowledge and love. Knowledge, like love, is a unitive force (to borrow a Dionysian phrase), thus knower is bound to known, lover to the beloved, and knowledge and love are united to one another. This Augustinian epistemology proposes three kinds of unity: of the divine Persons, of human persons and God, and of knowledge and love themselves as constituent principles of these

[164] Trin 9.prol.

personal relations. As the divine Persons are united through knowledge and love, so ought human persons to be united to God.¹⁶⁵ Because the 'shape' of divine nature is ineradicably stamped on human nature, the mind in the Augustinian schema can in practice never function in isolation from the will. The relationship of intellect and will in *On the Trinity* is nevertheless complex, both in the sense that Augustine finds it difficult to specify one logic of relation, but also in the sense that he grounds their ordering in several different ways, and if we are to understand what the intellect is in Augustine's thought, we must attend to the nature of their intertwining.

One of the ways in which he grounds the order of intellect and will is to compare the logic of divine relations with that of the vestigia. In so doing, Augustine hopes to show that as knowledge and love exist inseparably in God, so must they exist inseparably in humanity. Rather than viewing the vestigia as a means of reasoning from humanity to God, we can take Augustine to be offering a model of the relation of intellect and will which, because it is true of the divine Trinity, is also true of human persons. In this model, there can be no naked knowledge but only knowledge garbed in love. This unity is evident in the chief among the human triads he presents in *On the Trinity*, that of memory, understanding and will:

When I name my memory, understanding and will, each name refers to a single thing, and yet each of these single names is the product of all three; there is not one of these three names which my memory and understanding and will have not produced together. So too the trinity together produced both the Father's voice and the Son's flesh and the Holy Spirit's dove, though each of these single things has reference to a single person [cum ad personas singulas haec singula referantur].¹⁶⁶

Augustine's concern here is not to stress that each human being in some way reflects the Trinity (though he clearly thinks this is the case) but to claim that the distinct activities of remembering, understanding and loving are as inseparable as the Father, Son and Spirit.¹⁶⁷ His point is not

---

¹⁶⁵ Cf. Cooper (1984, 95). Similarly, Nash suggests that throughout his writings, Augustine insists that knowledge is not to be sought for its own sake, but so that through it we may attain happiness (1969, 3). Likewise, O'Connell suggests that in *On the Trinity*, Augustine reiterates his conviction that the primary task of inquiry is to discover how we are to become happy (1972, 47).
¹⁶⁶ Trin 4.30; cf. CD 5.11.
¹⁶⁷ Clark insists that intellect and memory are functions of the one soul, but does not address the necessity of love in Augustine's schema (1998, 108). Thus, to be a perfect image, one needs to integrate sapientia and scientia (109), but she makes no mention of love. While R. Williams acknowledges the dual focus of knowledge and love, he reads Augustine as claiming these are both necessary to the mind to know itself (1998, 122). This emphasis on self-knowledge characterises his

so much that human beings resemble God, but that what is inseparable in God must also be inseparable in us.

A second way of asserting the unity of knowledge and love is to point to the unity of human nature itself: 'These three then, memory, understanding and will, are not three lives but one life, not three minds, but one mind. So it follows of course they are not three substances but one substance.'[168] The inseparability of the three faculties consists in their being of one life and one mind, so that memory and understanding pertain to life and not only to mind, and will pertains to mind and not only life. Although these three elements of the human person are conceptually distinct, and perhaps actually distinct, they cannot function in isolation from one another.

However Augustine does not insist upon the arguments from anthropology or even from theology with the vehemence he accords the argument from the strictly logical relation of knowledge and love. To the question of the ordering of these two he returns again and again in Books 7–10 of *On the Trinity*. His musings on this subject indicate a great deal about the primacy of mind in his thought, for while he insists upon the inseparability of intellect and will, the intellect has a certain priority.[169] His primary argument for this priority, a qualified one as we shall see, is that we cannot love what we do not know. This principle determines also that thought precedes belief, since the latter implies assent to what the mind has first conceived.[170] Despite his small caveats, he stresses this point firmly and often. He asks: 'Who can love what he does not know?'[171] and: 'could [we] love the thing we believe and do not yet know from its likeness to what we do know? But of course this is simply not so',[172] and: 'How can [the mind] love what it does not know?'[173] As the text progresses, the rhetorical questions yield to flat statements: 'It is quite certain nothing can be loved unless it is known.'[174] A few chapters later, the claim has become an axiom upon which he bases another argument: 'But what is [the mind] loving? If itself, how, since it does not yet know itself and no one can love what he does not know?'[175]

---

essay as a whole. Similarly, Worthen claims that the ascent in which we are engaged in reading *On the Trinity* is a focusing ever more inwardly on the functioning of our own mind (1998, 519).

[168] Trin 10.18.

[169] In an earlier work, he insists on the unity of knowing and loving without according knowledge any primacy (though it still appears to have a logical priority, see VRel 31.58), as it has in the later *Enchiridion* (7 and 8, referring to the relation of faith, hope and charity). However, even faith requires the movement of the will (32) and charity remains the end of all the theological virtues (121).

[170] Prae 5.   [171] Trin 8.6.   [172] Trin 8.8.   [173] Trin 9.3.   [174] Trin 10.2.   [175] Trin 10.15.

Augustine does make one small qualification to this claim of the logical precedence of knowledge over love, a qualification necessary in virtue of the particular object of the knowledge and love which he is considering. He takes pains to deny that we can only love that which we know completely, since such perfect knowledge of God certainly does not belong to this life, and he makes a pastoral allowance for growth in faith. Thus, he states, we can indeed love the God in whom we believe, even though we have not yet seen him,[176] even though we must believe before we can understand.[177]

While the knowledge that precedes love need not be complete, Augustine hastens to qualify even this qualification, lest he be taken as undermining the necessity of knowledge: '"He loves to know the unknown" is not the same as saying "He loves the unknown".'[178] The unknown element of our relationship with God does not mean that relationship can be real when there is no knowledge whatsoever; he continues: 'it can happen that a man loves to know the unknown, but that he should love the unknown is impossible'.[179] To arrive at this conclusion Augustine does not rely solely on his axiom stipulating the necessary relation between love and knowledge. Rather, he investigates the nature of knowing to discover in precisely what sense one can be said to love the unknown:

'To know' is not put groundlessly in that first sentence ['He loves to know the unknown'] because the man who loves to know the unknown loves not the unknown but the actual knowing. And unless he had known what this was, he would not be able to say with confidence either that he knew something or that he did not know something.[180]

Even as Augustine concedes that the kind of knowledge of God which precedes love need not be complete, he rejects yet more thoroughly the devaluation of knowledge by claiming that we *love* to know. Conversely, elsewhere he maintains that we should delight in an intelligent understanding of charity.[181]

This configuration of knowledge and love in Augustine's theology bears immediate consequences for the Christian life; as Augustine notes: 'It is when the mind remembers and understands and *loves* its Maker that it becomes wise.'[182] Wisdom is distinct from love, but without love there can be no wisdom: 'Who will say that there is any wisdom where there is

---

[176] Trin 8.8.
[177] Trin 8.8. The manner of loving God seems to be particular, also; God is to be loved not after the fashion of anything whatsoever, but as one loves truth and charity (CRud 27.55).
[178] Trin 10.3.   [179] Trin 10.3.   [180] Trin 10.3.   [181] CRud 10.15.   [182] Trin 14.15.

no love?'¹⁸³ Love spurs many kinds of knowledge in the treatise. It teaches love of neighbour, as Augustine makes clear, flinging an impatient response at those who make of love a difficulty:

> Let no one say, 'I don't know what to love'. Let him love his brother, and love that love; after all, he knows the love he loves with better than the brother he loves. There now, he can already have God better known to him than his brother, certainly better known because more present, better known because more inward to him, better known because more sure.¹⁸⁴

Finally, mind and love are inseparable because love binds those within the community of faith to those outside it, indicating the principles that govern intellectual discourse with them:

> People ask us these questions [regarding the Trinity] to the point of weariness.... if we confess to our questioners that these matters live permanently in our thoughts because we are carried away by a love of tracking down the truth, then they can demand us by right of charity that we should show them what conclusions we have been able to reach on the subject.¹⁸⁵

Love here both impels the Christian to pursue the truth assiduously, and requires that she engage those who reject her beliefs. Far from being the refuge of the intellect, then, charity is its goad.¹⁸⁶

While Augustine generally seeks to link love and knowledge, there is nevertheless one respect in which he values charity because it works not with knowledge, but against it. If charity perfects the intellect, it is in part because it checks the pride that Augustine fears will often accompany knowledge.¹⁸⁷ Thus while there can be faith without charity, this kind of faith is of no use.¹⁸⁸

If Augustine's notion of the intellect differs from modern notions, so too does his view of love. If intellect and heart are not in conflict in his thought, it is because of the particular way in which he conceives them. As our examination of knowledge indicated the difficulty of separating knowledge and love in Augustine's thought, so his very definition of love will show the same: 'in this question we are occupied with, concerning

---

[183] Trin 15.12. This point is overlooked by commentators with surprising regularity. For example, contra Harnack, Cushman asserts Augustine is clear about the relation of faith and knowledge, but both Cushman and Harnack neglect to consider love (1955, 250). Likewise, Collinge claims *On the Trinity* represents a movement from faith to understanding (1987, 128) but does not mention the essential role of love in this process, an omission of which the usually scrupulous Hill is also guilty (1984).
[184] Trin 8.12.   [185] Trin 1.8; cf. 1.4.
[186] Contrast van Bavel, who gives three reasons that we must speak, in Augustine's view, none of which pertain to charity (in Lienhard 1998, 83).
[187] Trin 12.21.   [188] Trin 15.32.

the Trinity and about knowing God, the only thing we really have to see is what true love is, well in fact, simply what love is.... True love is that we should live justly by cleaving to the truth [haec est autem vera dilectatio ut inhaerentes veritati juste vivamus].'[189] Because Augustine's view of the mind is rather broader than the contemporary one, he is able not only to view the mind as joined to love, but as itself capable of love and desire: 'the more the thing is known without being fully known, the more does the intelligence desire to know what remains',[190] and in the *Confessions*, that great chronicle of desires, Augustine also speaks of the mind's loving.[191] Love, moreover, is what impels the mind to its true home with God, where it will attain to the heights of its capacity and of happiness.[192] Augustine's view of love is not far from the Dionysian maxim so important to Aquinas, 'love is a unitive force',[193] and in this respect bears a strong resemblance to knowledge: while love joins the lover to the beloved, knowledge is the offspring of the union of knower and the known.

The desiring mind, the mind that seeks to complete itself by finding God,[194] belongs to this life; to the next belongs the intellect's rest in consummation: 'There we shall see the truth without any difficulty, and enjoy it in all its clarity and certitude. There, there will be nothing for us to seek with the reasonings of the mind [mente ratiocinante], but we will perceive by direct contemplation [contemplante] why the Holy Spirit is not a son, though he proceeds from the Father.'[195] Two points are notable here. First, to understand Augustine's notion of the intellect, one must take into account his understanding of contemplation, because while contemplation is portrayed as distinct from 'the reasonings of the mind', it is also akin to them as their more perfect form. Second, Augustine's conception of paradise provides a sharp corrective to modern notions of spirituality, inasmuch as eternity will apparently be spent in the intellectual consideration of issues today deemed purely technical.

Augustine's strong awareness of the divine coupling of mind and will accounts in part for his readiness, despite his generally high estimation of the intellect, to see the possibility that an inherently good faculty might suffer misuse. Hence, he is suspicious of the purely secular dimensions of intellectual activity. This suspicion accounts for the opening of *On the Trinity* which issues a stern warning against 'an unseasonable and

---

[189] Trin. 8.10; cf. MEcc 12.20.   [190] Trin 10.2.
[191] Conf 2.2. This point is noted also by R. Williams (1988, 122).   [192] MEcc 12.21.
[193] Cf. Trin 8.12.   [194] Trin 10.6.   [195] Trin 15.45.

misguided love of reason'.[196] His quarrel is always with wrongful *use* of reason, rather than with the mind itself.

His distinction between knowledge [scientia] and wisdom [sapientia] springs from a similar ambivalence: 'action by which we make good use of temporal things differs from contemplation of eternal things, and this is ascribed to wisdom, the former to knowledge'.[197] While knowledge, as wisdom's precursor, is necessary and good,[198] Augustine evidently worries about the worldly associations of 'knowledge',[199] which is why he prefers to use 'wisdom' in connection with knowledge of God.[200] Augustine signals the distinctiveness of Christian knowledge in other ways, as well. In *On Christian Teaching*, for example, he portrays the Christian life as a series of steps in which knowledge occurs *after* piety and fear (timoris atque pietatis;[201]). If, however, the soul neglects to exert itself through study and piety, it will fall below even its natural level of ignorance, to the extent that we can apparently be demoted on the hierarchy of being to the level of the lower animals.[202] In the *Soliloquies*, Augustine outlines a variety of patterns for the attainment of wisdom, all of which integrate the strictly intellectual into a broader scheme of Christian life. Some are able to reach it without going through an ordered progression through the stages of wisdom, but these are few, since such progress requires unbelievable good fortune; most learn gradually. All, however, must grow strong in faith, hope and charity in order to arrive at true love of wisdom.[203]

A particular model of the human intellect is implied in this distinction, in virtue of which knowing God and knowing in God mean something quite different from either knowing other things or merely knowing about God in some quasi-technical manner. Wishing to uphold this distinction, Augustine might have posited two separate faculties, or at least a somehow divided faculty. Yet he does not. His distinction between wisdom and knowledge serves not to the end of a multiplication of

---

[196] Trin 1.1. [197] Trin 12.22; cf. 12.25. [198] Trin 15.10; cf. 14.3. [199] Trin 12.21.
[200] I thus reluctantly differ from Louth. He reads Augustine to be saying in Book 12 that one must relinquish scientia in order to embrace sapientia (1986, 143). It seems to me that Augustine rather maintains that the rational and practical part of the mind, which deals with worldly things and produces scientia, is 'drawn off' from the part of the mind that contemplates, but is thereby precisely *not* divorced or separated from the mind as a whole, or the mind that contemplates eternal things (12.3.4). If the two parts of the mind are not separated, it does not seem that their products would be, either.
[201] 2.7.10. [202] LArb 3.22.64.
[203] 1.23. In the *Retractions*, Augustine reproaches himself for this passage. His objection is rather fussy, however, for his regret concerns only the potential misunderstanding that might arise, whereby the reader might think there is a way to get to God besides Christ (1.4.3). He does not alter the essential point of the original passage, though, that the acquisition of wisdom is via the theological virtues.

faculties, but to the assertion of the relation of God and humanity, in virtue of which all knowledge worthy of the name is personal knowledge. The negative side of this claim is that the human intellect is not self-sufficient. The positive side of it, however, is that the mind is the locus of a divine–human encounter that may be described as either theology or prayer.

This close linkage of the mind with the body, the will and the emotions emerges also in Augustine's notion of the spiritual senses, which parallels that of Origen, but from whom his scheme does not seem to derive. The starting point for our examination of the spiritual senses must be the sharp lines Augustine draws in his epistemology between knowledge derived from the senses and knowledge derived from the mind. As we have seen, the senses are incapable of operating alone; the mind always works to filter what they report. The mind, in contrast, can and does operate alone when we perceive intelligible things. Here, too, the hierarchy exerts its influence, for the excellence of knowledge is determined by its object. For Augustine, the qualitative distinction between varieties of intelligibles is grounded in scripture, for it is there we learn the difference between what the mind can know and what the flesh can perceive.[204] Chief among those things that cannot be known by the senses is God[205] and since God is the most excellent of all that can be known, again it follows that knowledge derived from sense perception is clearly inferior, a view unsurprising in a Platonist of any stripe.

The influence of Paul, however, is clearly discernible when Augustine glosses 'sensible' and 'intelligible' as 'carnal' and 'spiritual', at least as far as Christian authors are concerned.[206] These categories are clearly value-laden, and imply that when the mind works independently of the senses, its goal is from a specifically Christian perspective higher and its operation more laudable. Augustine suggests as much in one of his earliest works: 'when we have to do with things which we behold with the mind... we speak of things which we look upon directly in the inner light of truth which illumines the inner man and is inwardly enjoyed'.[207] He later makes the point more explicitly, when he identifies the error of his youth as his attempt to find God through the senses of the flesh, rather than through the mind.[208] This dictum requires careful interpretation. The problem he identifies in the *Confessions* is not simply knowledge derived from the body, for in the *Enchiridion* he allows that

---

[204] Conf 13.18. [205] Sol 1.8; VRel 36.67; MEcc 12.20. [206] Mag 12.39; cf. SpLt 6.
[207] Mag 12.40. [208] Conf 3.6.

faith may be defended by reason, whose starting point lies either in the understanding of the mind (intelligentia mentis) or the bodily senses.[209] The latter do not necessarily constitute an obstacle, but one must apparently exert oneself if right use is to be made of either source.[210]

Augustine also believes that the senses belong to the soul[211] and are not far from reason and truth,[212] though, unlike intelligence, they do not belong to the soul alone. Far from being a concession to an Aristotelian (or quasi-scientific) worldview, however, this affirmation serves partially to explain the nature of our deception: there is no falsity in things themselves, but only in our senses.[213]

In view of these emphatically expressed priorities, Augustine's readiness to describe the mind's and soul's activity in sensual imagery must take us a little by surprise – although Origen took an even dimmer view of the flesh and he, too, makes use of this language. We need not go so far as to explain the recourse to sensual imagery as a somehow necessary compensation for the body's subordinate status in the system. The conjunction may be simply explained as the theologian's attempt to express the intangible in the tangible terms natural to the embodied.

A second reason for using the imagery of the senses is that Augustine views the mind as the interpreter of sensory images, speaking of the intellect as an 'interior sense' (sensum interiorem) that judges the bodily senses.[214] He adamantly privileges this sense: 'We have another sense, far more important than any bodily sense, the sense of the inner person, by which we apprehend what is just and what unjust, the just by means of the idea which is presented to the intellect, the unjust by the absence of it.'[215] It is because of mental 'seeing' that we are able to judge beauty, even the physical variety of which can only be perceived with the mind (conspectu mentis intelligi[216]). This role of the mind's explains in part its relation to beauty: even if we need the corporal senses to perceive many of the things that are beautiful (though not God and not mathematics), it is only the mind that can deem them so and appreciate them.[217] Augustine summarises this conception of the intellectual senses when he writes: 'We apprehend [material things] by our bodily senses, but it is not by our bodily senses that we form a judgement on them. For we have another sense, far more important than any bodily sense, the sense of the inner

---

[209] Ench 4.
[210] VRel 54.106. Qui vero bene utitur vel ipsis quinque sensibus corporis ad credenda praedicanda opera Dei ... intrat in gaudium Domini sui.
[211] Sol 2.3.3.   [212] VRel 30.54.   [213] Sol 2.3.3; cf. Ench 21.   [214] LArb 2.5.12; cf. VRel 29.53.
[215] CD 11.27; cf. 11.21.   [216] CD 8.6.   [217] VRel 30.56; cf. 33.62.

man, by which we apprehend what is just and what is unjust, the just by means of the "idea" which is presented to the intellect, the unjust by the absence of it.'[218]

In both early and late works, furthermore, he uses the imagery of particular senses to specify the nature of the mind's functioning. He is particularly fond of visual imagery, a surprising amount of which is not concerned with the *visio Dei*, but with other forms of looking and seeing, a set of images apparently of Augustine's own invention.[219] In the *City of God* he makes use of both aural and optical imagery, maintaining that we can hear God with mind,[220] and see the likeness of objects with the mind's eye.[221] The fool, on the other hand, is the one who is unable to see wisdom with her eyes.[222]

The purification necessary to the process of sanctification applies also to this 'sensory' perception of God. When the mind is purged from the desire for mortal things through faith, hope and charity, it may look, and in seeing, will attain to a vision that is equated with virtue 'for virtue is right and perfect reason'.[223] Indeed, this kind of knowledge may be considered mystical, for Augustine regards it as a form of union of God and humanity: 'This [perfect and ultimate] vision is knowledge compounded of the knower and the known.'[224] Because Augustine equates the *visio Dei* with knowledge of God,[225] it is true to say that knowledge of God in this life, in the most ordinary sense, is the anticipation of heaven, indeed, the beginning of heaven.[226]

The richness of Augustine's understanding of how the mind perceives, operates and judges explains in part its centrality in his thought. Certainly, it is the sensibility that accounts for his willingness to say in *On the Freedom of the Will*: 'what is intelligence but to live more intensely and more perfectly in the very light of the mind?'[227] Our relation to God lies both in our nature's innate, if partial, resemblance to God, and in our participation in the activities that characterise the Trinity: knowing and loving. Augustine's doctrine of the imago Dei and the vestigia Trinitatis in human nature constitutes a claim he makes principally, not about natural knowledge of God, but about the uniqueness of knowledge of

---

[218] CD 11.27.
[219] Sol. 1.12 and 13; CD 8.5; GChr 1.16; VRel 3.4; PMer 2.5; in *On the Trinity*, optical imagery abounds. For references to contemplation, see the section below; as examples of gazing, see 1.2 and 1.4; beholding, 15.5 and 39. References to sight and seeing abound; cf. 11.1–5, 9–10, 14–19.
[220] CD 11.2. [221] CD 8.5.
[222] Cred 13.28. For a more general reference to seeing the truth in this treatise, see 16.34 and cf. VRel 37.68.
[223] Sol. 1.13. [224] Sol. 1.13. [225] Sol. 1.14; cf. also Ench 5 and 121. [226] CD 10.32. [227] 1.7.17.

God and two kinds of unity in human engagement with God: the bonding of human intellect and will to the divine persons, and the unity of knowledge and love in God and in us. What Augustine's theology consistently suggests – its doctrine of God and its anthropology alike – is a doctrine of sanctification and a blueprint for understanding the intellect and knowledge of God as pertaining to both theology and spirituality, in virtue of an epistemology in which knowledge of God is distinct among forms of knowing, one in which the intellect cannot function without the will.

Augustine embeds some significant qualifications into his conception of the intellect; nevertheless, the role played by the mind in human sanctification and consummation indicates decisively that whatever reservations he had, they did not shake his fundamental conviction that the mind is the nexus of God and humanity, and accordingly, the conduit of grace. So important is the mind in this scheme that it is literally the beginning and means of furthering the Christian life and, as Augustine describes our end, it will have a decidedly intellectual character. The stages of spiritual growth described in *On True Religion*, for example, show an overall pattern of growth towards more excellent knowledge of that which is itself most excellent.[228] As the goal of the Christian life, intellectual activity determines the shape of both this life and the next: 'To understand the Trinity soberly and piously occupies all the wonderful care of Christians, and that is the goal of every advance.'[229] This notion follows from one of the most important principles of Augustinian theology, which we have already noted, that reason is known by reason.[230]

One of the ways in which mind meets mind is through prayer, which in the context of this theology of the intellect takes on a theological significance that it often lacks in modern theology. We will consider the connection between the intellect and prayer more fully when we examine the role of contemplation in Augustine's thought; for the moment, let us note that Augustine interprets the command to pray alone in one's room as an injunction to pray in one's inmost mind [in clausis cubiculis oremus, quo nomine significantur mentis penetrata].[231] Not only spiritual activities can have this overtly discursive quality, such as many forms of prayer; even the Eucharist takes on an intellectual character: 'By coming down among us [Christ] did not abandon the angels, remaining at the same time one with them and one with us, he nourishes them inwardly by his divinity, and outwardly by his humanity he admonishes us and fits us

---

[228] 36.49.   [229] LArb 3.21.60.   [230] LArb 2.19.51.   [231] Mag 1.2.

by faith to be nourished sacramentally like the angels. The rational creature feeds upon the Word as its own best food. But the human soul is rational.'[232] Even the Eucharist, the starkest sign of God's blessing on human flesh, is susceptible to interpretation as a matter of the intellect.

The mind is also the receptor of grace in a more general way and in this sense, also, may be deemed the locus of sanctification in human beings. If knowledge is salvific for Augustine, it is for this reason: 'When we learn to know God', he writes in the *Confessions*, 'we are made new in the image of the creator',[233] and in *On the Trinity* pleads for the increase of memory, understanding and will, that he may be entirely refashioned.[234] The life of faith, too, is in its entirety a matter of seeking God: Reason's promise is that it will allow us to see God. Indeed, Augustine predicates not only knowledge of God but what we would call spiritual progress upon the advances of the mind: '[The Word] is precisely sent to anyone when he is known and perceived by him, as far as he can be perceived and known according to the capacity of the rational soul either making progress toward God or already made perfect in God.'[235] Acquaintance-with, the intimate contact of one person with another, inevitably fosters knowledge-about, a grasp of facts concerning the person. Because Augustine conceives of the mind's growth in this way, he can enter into the act of speculative contemplation that is his formal theological reflection. Thus in *On the Trinity* he writes:

> The God himself we are looking for will help us, I confidently hope, to get some fruit from our labours and to understand the text in the holy psalm 'Let the heart of those who seek the Lord rejoice; seek the Lord and be strengthened; seek his face always' (Ps 105:3)[236]

Looking for God thus entails intimate contact with what we seek.[237]

Augustine's notion of the intellect's receptivity to holiness includes growth in virtues, however, and this, too, is portrayed as a product of the intellect. Through clinging to God with a spiritual embrace, the intellectual soul is filled with virtue.[238] Specific virtues, such as patience, are also located specifically in the intellect.[239] Conversely, heeding God's will – normally to be equated with moral and ascetical obedience – enriches the mind.[240] Up to a point, then, Augustine's view is substantially that of the pagan philosophers who preceded him: the pagans regarded

---

[232] LArb 3.10.30. [233] Conf 13.22. [234] Trin 15.51. [235] Trin 4.28. [236] Trin 15.2.
[237] Cf. Daniels: 'Augustine's doctrine of knowledge runs parallel to his doctrine of grace' (1977, 50).
[238] CD 10.3. [239] Pat 8. [240] CD 1.10.

perfection and happiness as created by a light shed on them from without and apprehended by the intellect,[241] and understood the soul's relation to this light as one of participation, a favoured notion among Neo-Platonists to describe the culmination of mystical experience.[242] Augustine however adds to the pagan portrayal of growth in virtues the specifically Christian trio of theological virtues derived from the New Testament, with particular emphasis on love, as well as the notions of personal reciprocity (the image) and the sanctifying effects of growth in personal knowledge.

The rubric under which Augustine above all understands the mind's transformative engagement with God is contemplation [contemplatio]. As we have seen with other writers, contemplation is a much more broadly significant item in Augustine's thought than it is in post-medieval Western theology. Like theoria in Greek, contemplatio implies both a sensuous activity (physical seeing) and an intellectual one ('seeing' the truth of an idea, for example). Its intellectual sense, furthermore, straddles both intellectual inquiry as we would think of it today and the kind of empirical research into divine nature that would today be called prayer.[243] The term should not, therefore, be taken as designating only an advanced form of mental prayer, nor understood as a primarily affective or volitional activity. Contemplation is for Augustine always a mental act, hence the need to consider it if we are to grasp his view of the intellect.[244]

In both its primary senses, of theology and of prayer, what contemplation does designate is a form of wondering and receptive knowledge of God. At one level, this contemplation seems close to a kind of exercise in natural theology: God speaks from the great book of nature 'so that we might see all things clearly in the wonder of contemplation

---

[241] CD 10.2. 'Obiecto quodam lumine intelligibili, quod Deus est illis et aliud est quam illi, a quo illustratur ut clareant atque eias participatione perfecti beatique subsistant.'
[242] CD 10.2.
[243] The contemporary writer who has treated contemplation most thoroughly is Merton, whose view of it bears a strong resemblance to that of the Fathers. While he clearly conceives contemplation as a form of prayer that transcends theological reflection (1962, 1–2, 4–5), he also includes within its scope the kind of unity of knowledge-about God and acquaintance-with that Augustine advocates (ibid., 13 and 253–55). Merton also acknowledges the need to communicate the fruits of contemplation, and while he is probably thinking in terms of ascetical theology, his understanding of this communication of fruits could easily include theology in general (ibid., 268–69; see also 1969, 98–99, 104, 144). Merton, however, is not generally considered a theologian, though he has been included in *A New Handbook of Theologians* (Musser and Price, 1996). The notion of prayer as a form of research comes from P. T. Forsyth (1916, 78); I am grateful to Professor Trevor Hart for tracing the reference for me.
[244] Pace Butler, who considers contemplation in Augustine under the rubric of mysticism (1924, passim). On the other hand, Burnaby insists upon Augustine's view of contemplation as the task of all Christians, not only those who have reached extraordinary heights in prayer (1938, 61 and 64).

[ut discernamus omnia contemplatione mirabili]'.[245] The perfection of the universe moreover forms a sort of framework in which all things may be contemplated,[246] all things in this case clearly including both fixtures of nature, such as the stars, and such abstractions as the spiritual or moral states of souls. Not only what one sees in the present, but also the images stored in the memory, serve as the objects of this intellectual activity.[247]

Making use of the distinction we have already examined between wisdom and knowledge, Augustine allies contemplation with the former: 'contemplation of eternal things... is ascribed to wisdom.... wisdom belongs to contemplation'.[248] Since what he calls wisdom corresponds to what we would more naturally call knowledge of God, he has here effectively equated that knowledge with contemplation. The first point to note, whose significance will become clearer as we go along, is that while in modern terms contemplation is a mental activity, and knowledge the product of such activity, the status of contemplation in Augustine's thought is ambiguous, seeming to belong exclusively neither to activity nor to product.

No more does contemplation belong exclusively either to the intellect or to the will. The engagement of the human person with God requires, in this context as in most others in the bishop's thought, the application of both: 'What does knowing God mean but beholding him and firmly grasping him with the mind? [et quid est deum scire nisi eum mente conspicere firmeque percipere?]',[249] Augustine writes, implying by 'beholding' both the regard of devotion and understanding, and by 'grasping' both comprehension and the reach of desire. His general rubric for this grasping and beholding is contemplation, and, as such, it is clearly not construed as a form of wordless prayer practised by the spiritually adept, as is the tendency in modern usage, but as a binding of the mind to God.[250]

The mind, however, encounters God in this way not only because of intellectual, but also spiritual, preparation: 'it is difficult to contemplate and have full knowledge of God's substance.... That is why it is necessary for our minds to be purified';[251] and: 'the rational mind is meant, once purified, to contemplate eternal things'.[252] Augustine's reason for insisting on purification is both spiritual and theological, pointing on the one hand to humanity's sin and need for grace, and on the other to

---

[245] Conf 13.18.   [246] LArb 3.9.25.   [247] Mag 12.39.   [248] Trin 12.22.   [249] Trin 8.6.
[250] Indeed, Nash defines reason in Augustine's thought as contemplation of the truth (1969, 64).
[251] Trin 1.3.   [252] Trin 4.24; cf. 13.24.

the ontological disparity between God and humanity and the salvific effect of the Incarnation. Yet he integrates these concerns seamlessly, assuming the alliance of spiritual and intellectual faculties inasmuch as both are directed to the same object: 'to contemplate God, which by nature we are not, we would have to be cleansed by him who became what by nature we are and what by sin we are not'.[253] Because of the modern associations of contemplation with advanced forms of prayer, the significance of this claim is easily missed; but if we bear in mind that Augustine equates contemplation with wisdom and that he uses wisdom to denote what we would call knowledge of God, we begin to see the far-reaching implications of his doctrine of contemplation. The Incarnation, along with its salvific and sanctifying effects, brings humanity to this end: 'grasping and holding' God with the mind. It is no exaggeration to say that contemplation is for Augustine the means and the end of the Christian life.

Augustine stresses this moral dimension of contemplation in an earlier work, when he lists three meanings of sin: neglect to receive the precept, or to obey it, or to hold fast to the contemplation of wisdom.[254] Here it seems that failure to contemplate is itself sinful – although it is not clear whether it is so per se, or because contemplative laxity brings sin in its wake. Contemplation may also yield self-knowledge of a generic variety, less specifically concerned with sin.[255] Contemplation, indeed, is central to the Christian life in any form. On this point, Augustine seems simply to repeat the conventional wisdom of classical antiquity, concerning the superiority of the philosophical life. Yet the bishop does give this life a distinctively Christian cast. He writes: 'no one should be so leisured as to take no thought for the interest of his neighbour, nor so active as to feel no need for the contemplation of God' [nec sic actuosus, ut contemplationem non requirat Dei].[256] The Christian life is one in which contemplation is not a retreat from engagement with the world (as it generally was for the neo-Platonist) and in which contemplation is the obligation of all, not just the leisured, well-educated wealthy (as was likewise the case with neo-Platonists). Those who are so fortunate as to be able to enjoy a life of sanctified leisure ought to apply themselves to the search for truth and contemplation, but out of compulsion of love.[257] The centrality of charity in this picture, and charity operative at several

---

[253] Trin 4.4.
[254] LArb 3.24.72. Peccatum autem malum est in negligentia vel ad capiendum praeceptum, vel ad observandum, vel ad custodiendam contemplationem sapientiae.
[255] LArb 3.25.76.   [256] CD 19.19.   [257] CD 19.19.

different levels, gives Augustine's version of the good life a characteristically Christian impetus.

A Christian interpretation of contemplation is also evident in the personal dimension which Augustine accords it, as is clear when he identifies it with the purpose of the incarnation. In *On the Trinity*, Augustine does not expatiate on the significance of the Word's enfleshment; nor is he concerned with the Second Person as the one whose role is the explication of the divine. Rather, the Word aids human knowledge of God as the object of vision: '[Christ] took a created form in which to appear to human eyes, thereby to purify our minds for contemplating him by faith.'[258] Here he stresses the visual dimension of contemplation and portrays the act of beholding God as a preparation of the mind for faith; again, acquaintance-with and knowing-about are firmly welded together. Christ also serves, however, to point the human eye away from his incarnate form and towards the immanent Trinity: 'he turns our attention to the godhead and points the minds of men upward, since to raise them up was the reason why he himself has come down'.[259] Indeed, Book 1 of *On the Trinity* locates the purpose of the Incarnation in aiding contemplation, to the extent that this facilitation becomes the heart of Christ's mediatorial role:

> The fact is that the 'man Christ Jesus, mediator of God and men' (1 Tim 2:5) ... is going to bring them to direct sight of God, to the 'face to face' vision, as the apostle calls it (1 Cor 13:12), that is what is meant by 'When he hands the kingdom over to God and the Father', as though to say, 'When he brings believers to a direct contemplation of God and the Father.'[260]

The Mediator, moreover, also brings knowledge of himself through contemplation: 'When he brings the believers to the contemplation of God and the Father, he will assuredly bring them to contemplation of himself.'[261] Once again, contemplation implies not only possession of theological information, but apprehension of the divine Persons. Part of the mystery of the Trinity, indeed, derives from the mysterious irreducibility of persons, although in this case there is the added element of mystery due to their distinction in unity. The mystery of personal unity in the divine Trinity inspires the most ardent contemplation, as Augustine notes in *On the Catechizing of the Uninstructed*: 'these mysteries of equality of the Father, the Son and the Holy Spirit, and the unity of this

---

[258] Trin 1.27. Hoitenga also takes vision as Augustine's characteristic term for knowledge by acquaintance and experience, although he concurs with John Burnaby that it is inadequate (1998, 295).
[259] Trin 1.27.   [260] Trin 1.16.   [261] Trin 1.18.

Trinity... will not always need to be spoken of in words of faith and uttered syllables, but will be imbibed in the purest and most burning contemplation in that silence'.[262]

Contemplation's Christian identity is evident also in the transformative power that Augustine accords it, as well as the goal he posits for it. It is through contemplation that the mind is made into light and becomes created wisdom.[263] While this wisdom is a far cry from the wisdom that itself creates, the two are equally clearly connected and it is contemplation that forges and sustains the link between them.[264] Contemplation brings joy, too, a joy that seems to begin in this life as an anticipation of that of the next: 'Let our light shine out in the world and from the humble crop of good deeds let us pass on to that more sublime harvest, the joy of contemplation so that we may come to possess the Word of life and shine in the world like stars set in the firmament of your scripture.'[265] This contemplation is further distinguished from its pagan varieties in virtue of its being the gift of grace: 'let us leave the contemplation of the beauty of things to those who have the divine gift of seeing'.[266]

The personal element of Augustine's doctrine of contemplation also underlies his view of contemplation's end. From the passages already examined, it is clear enough that we contemplate in this life; the fullness of contemplation, however, awaits the world to come: '[in heaven] we will perceive by direct contemplation'.[267] Indeed, contemplation forms the very substance of paradise: 'eternal life consists in that contemplation by which God is seen not to one's undoing but to everlasting joy [qua non ad poenam videtur deus sed ad gaudium sempiternum]';[268] for in that contemplation, 'God will be all in all (1 Cor 15:28), because nothing further will be desired of him; to be illumined and rejoiced by him will be enough'.[269] Contemplation even brings joy to the angels.[270] In its perfect form, contemplation will bring communion with the divine persons, a communion that brings illumination and joy. It is because paradisal joy forms the core of contemplation that it can also transform the saints in *this* life: 'it is the contemplation of [what is unchangeable and

---

[262] 25.47.
[263] Conf 12.15. Non invenimus ... illa Sapientia tibi, Deus noster ... sed profecto sapientia, quae creata est, intellectualis natura scilicet, quae contemplatione luminis lumen est.
[264] Conf 12.15.
[265] Conf 13.18. Erumpat temporanea lux nostra, et de ista inferiore fruge actionis in delicias contemplationis verbum vitae superius obtinentes appareamus sicut luminaria in mundo cohaerentes firmamento scripturae tuae.
[266] LArb 3.13.36.   [267] Trin 15.45.   [268] Trin 1.31.   [269] Trin 1.20.   [270] VRel 4.110.

everlasting] that makes us happy or blessed',[271] makes us happy, that is, *in via*.[272]

Because contemplation connects the knowledge of this life and that of the next, it is centrally concerned with truth. Certainly, a perfect and immediate grasp of the truth properly characterises the next life: 'There we shall see the truth without any difficulty, and enjoy it in all its clarity and certitude. There, there will be nothing for us to seek with the reasonings of the mind, but we will perceive by direct contemplation.'[273] Because contemplation is a vision of the truth, enjoyed perfectly in the next life and sought in this with the 'reasonings of the mind', it differs radically from the subjective and emotional varieties of spirituality that abound in our day.[274] Contemplation links the search for truth with all forms of seeking God, because truth can come only from God: 'the reason why it was not God the Father, not the Holy Spirit, not the trinity itself, but only the Son who is the Word of God that became flesh (although it was the trinity that accomplished this), is that we might live rightly by our word following and imitating his example; that is, by our having no falsehood either in the contemplation or in the operation of our word'.[275]

Augustine acknowledges the dangers of precisely the kind of speculation he undertakes: 'I am fully aware how many fancies the human heart can breed – what is my own heart, after all, but a human heart?'[276] If he

---

[271] Trin 13.2.
[272] Thus I would dispute LaCugna's claim that Augustine's contemplative approach to the Trinity led to a split between *oikonomia* and *theologia* (1991, 7–8). It is precisely the contemplative element in his thought that permits the drawing of a close, unbreakable bond between the inner life of the Trinity and human salvation. Cf. Gilson's notion that for Augustine wisdom is always identified with happiness (3) and that contemplation is the *sine qua non* of happiness (8), Cooper's claim that in the final chapter of *On the Trinity* Augustine deliberately connects his theological view of salvation with the philosophic quest for wisdom (1984, 104), and Burnaby's idea that knowing and loving God constitutes a kind of 'possession' of God (1938, 252).
[273] Trin 15.45.
[274] Cf. Butler: 'Truth for Augustine means not subjective or logical truth... but objective and ontological truth... [which] he ultimately identifies with Divine Being' (1924, 53–54). Cf. also Cavadini, who claims for Augustine our contemplative regard is pushed outward (1992, 109) and Rist: our own remembering, knowing and loving point beyond ourselves to God (1955, 90). Pace Lloyd, who denies that Augustine says the nature of a human person is an analogy of the Trinity (1972, 191) and in consequence claims: 'the love, the understanding, the knowledge that chiefly interest Augustine are each man's self-love, self-understanding, and self-knowledge' (204).
[275] Trin 15.20. Maschke notes two contrasting emphases in Augustine's writings on prayer: contemplative meditation and discursive communication, implying these activities are distinct. The reading suggested here is that these two elements are united both in the contemplation that is prayer and the contemplation that is theology (1998, 431).
[276] Trin 4.1. Cf. Daniels, who maintains that the argument of *On the Trinity* moves the believer-reader's attention from topics of faith concerning the Trinity [information-about] to a place of understanding (1977, 53). Muller points out that for Augustine the success of the 'project' of *On the Trinity* pivots on the ability of the Christian to mount to the sort of contemplative ascent that

continues despite these dangers, it is because he trusts the One he seeks to preserve him from error:

> But what I pray for to the 'God of my heart' (Ps 73:26) is that no such fancies should spill over into these pages masquerading as solidly true, but that the only things to appear on them should be what has come to me wafted by the fresh air of his truth.... I breathe in his truth the more deeply, the more clearly I perceive there is nothing changeable about it... like the wandering fancies of our spirits, not only in time and not even in imagined space, like some of the reasonings of our minds. For God's essence, by which he is, has absolutely nothing changeable about its eternity or its truth or its will; there truth is eternal and love is eternal; there love is true and eternity true; there eternity is lovely and truth is lovely too [et cara ibi est aeternitas, cara ueritas].[277]

The culmination of this life of contemplation is a paradise of contemplation *in patria*. Contemplation now may therefore be seen as a kind of preparation, even a spiritual exercise, for that activity with which we will be chiefly occupied in the Age to Come. That life is an enjoyment of the eternal truth in contemplation[278] and contemplation connects this life and the next: 'it is given to the rational and intellectual soul to enjoy the contemplation of God's eternity, so that, being armed and equipped with it, the soul may obtain eternal life'.[279] In that life, the body will be transformed, so as to present no obstacle to contemplation[280] in a life of vision of God that is eternal union.[281]

We have already glimpsed the extent to which continuity between this life and the next is an important theme in Augustine's theology. This principle is evident in the texts where he treats happiness, for Augustine virtually identifies truth and knowledge with the state of happiness. In the *Confessions*, for example, knowledge of God is not only what makes one happy, but is the *sole* means to happiness.[282] In *On the Freedom of the Will*, he states it more strongly still: 'No one is happy except by the possession of the chief good which is beheld and possessed in the truth which we call wisdom.'[283] The philosophers of classical antiquity would have agreed on this point, but Augustine makes it explicitly Christian, noting that the beatifying wisdom comes not simply from keeping

---

governs the latter half of the work (1998, 135). Muller's view of the kind of unity to which the treatise points – of the individual, of marriage, and of the community – nevertheless differs considerably from the kind of unity stressed here. Cf. also Worthen: Augustine and Anselm are similarly concerned to create texts that not only transfer knowledge but engage their readers in the process of coming to know, that will not only inform, but, rather, reform the careful reader (1998, 517).

[277] Trin 4.1. [278] LArb 3.21.60. [279] VRel 3.3. [280] CD 10.29.
[281] CD 10.32. Huius viae rectitudinem usque ad Deum videndum eique in aeternum cohaerendum.
[282] 5.4. [283] 2.9.26.

precepts, but from wisdom's eternal light.[284] His latest works confirm the thought, for in the *City of God* he speaks of God as the only good that can ever satisfy an intellectual creature.[285] In the life which seeks wisdom and truth, then, God will be present, yet Augustine is insistent that this presence bears in this life only a faint resemblance to its true form in the Age to Come. The mind is not in this life directed to its most fitting goal, which is God, because its prudence and right action are now directed to myriad other concerns.[286] Moreover, the search for truth in this life is impaired by one of our more innocuous frailties, namely fatigue, which will not hinder us in the next life.[287]

In the next life, in contrast, we will enjoy truth with no admixture of falsehood and this pure truth will be a blessing to us.[288] It is in this state that we will see God with our minds.[289] The extent to which this perception is intellectual or corporeal is a complex question. As noted, Augustine rejects the idea that the intelligible can be seen by the mind alone, on the grounds that this would entail God's not knowing the material beings he himself created. From this premise, Augustine concludes that our physical bodies will have some role in our sight in the next life, and to the yet odder conclusion that we will be able to observe each other's thoughts[290] – presumably in this state we will have nothing to hide. These claims do not, however, undermine the centrality of intellect in the schema as a whole, since the 'spiritual' eyes of our bodies will see God because they have an intellectual quality.[291] To be sure, the intellectual faculty in question is not the bare intellect that we might take it to be, for Augustine never abandons the notion, articulated in the early *Soliloquies*, that in the next life we will see by charity.[292] Nevertheless, Augustine's doctrine of God keeps his notions of salvation and sanctification alike firmly intellectual. In Book 11 of the *City of God*, he drives this point home with particular force. God speaks through the direct effect of the truth on the mind and is able to speak to us in this fashion because our highest faculty is second only to the divine mind. Faith purifies the mind of the weaknesses it contracts through sin and the Incarnate Truth provides a path from humanity to God. It is in this context of the Incarnation of Truth that Augustine speaks of Christ as Mediator.[293] In the journey to Truth, we walk along the road of Christ's humanity, pressing towards the goal that is his divinity.[294] The linking factor between

---

[284] LArb 3.24.72.
[285] CD 12.1. Non est creaturae rationalis vel intellectualis bonum, quo beata sit, nisi Deus.
[286] CD 19.20.   [287] CRud 25.47.   [288] Sol 2.36.   [289] CD 22.29.   [290] CD 22.29.
[291] CD 22.29.   [292] 1.14.   [293] 11.2.   [294] CD 11.2.

this life and the next, therefore, is precisely an intellectual function and the mind provides the mechanism whereby we are united to God.

Through knowledge and love, *On the Trinity* suggests, we are united to God as the divine Persons are to one another. Augustine's treatise therefore instantiates a mystical theology, that is, one that reflects on the conditions of the possibility of humanity's union with God. The core of the Christian conception of the next life is that we will be united with God, and such is also Augustine's view. Yet he does not limit union to the next life, and the fact that he does not creates an additional connection between Christian existence in via and in patria. In the unity of this life and the next, of God and humanity, the intellect plays a prominent role.

Many of Augustine's references to union do not use any form of the term 'coniunctio' and one must therefore be open to a variety of ways in which he expresses the same essential idea. *The Freedom of the Will*, for example, concludes with the notion of indwelling: 'The environment of the mind may be said to include the unchangeable Trinity', even though the Trinity of course far transcends the human mind.[295] While he hastens to mention divine transcendence, the essential point remains: doing the good and contemplating wisdom amount to a union of the human mind and the divine. The last paragraph of the treatise makes the same point: 'Such is the beauty of justice, such the pleasure of the eternal light, that is, of unchangeable truth and wisdom, that, even if we could not abide in it more than the space of a single day, for that day alone innumerable years of this life full of delights and abundance of temporal goods would be rightly and deservedly despised.'[296] Likewise, in a later treatise he speaks of 'abiding' [inhaerere] in faith in both this life and the next, that suggests a kind of intellectual indwelling [quod autem intellectu capitur, intus apud animum est].[297] This mental indwelling appears to be rather routine in Augustine's eyes, for previously in the same treatise he writes: 'So great is the power of sympathetic disposition of mind that, as they are affected while they are learning, we have our dwelling with each other' [habitemus in invicem].[298] The context here is catechising, nevertheless, and ordinary though he may find such intellectual indwelling, he does not assert it outside a Christian context.[299] Union designates also the state of peaceful

---

[295] 3.25.75. Intentioni animi subjacet, excepta incommutabilitate Trinitatis, quae quidem non subjacet, sed eminet potius.
[296] 3.25.77.   [297] CRud 25.47; cf. Cred 13.28.   [298] CRud 12.17.
[299] He *appears* to broaden the applicability of the principle, when in *On Faith and the Creed* he maintains that in speaking we produce a token of ourselves in the mind of another, but even here, the reference is to speaking the truth (3, 4).

harmony in this life that prefigures the next. In the third stage of spiritual development described in *On True Religion*, for example, the proficient 'marries' [mariantem] carnal appetite to reason, and rejoices at the sweetness of their union [in quadam dulcedine conjugali].[300] At other times, Augustine uses the imagery that so many of the mystics have reached for, of union as fire: 'by sharing in that unchanging light the rational soul is in a sense inflamed and becomes itself a created and reflected luminary, just as John was a burning and shining light'.[301]

As with all human goods, the joining of minds through the catechetical process is a local phenomenon that manifests a broader truth of divine–human engagement. Thus Augustine writes: 'The wise man is so closely united [conjunctus] with God in his mind that nothing can come between to separate them. God is truth and no one is wise who does not have truth in her mind [Deus enim veritas; nec ullo pacto sapiens quisquam est, si non veritatem mente contingat].'[302] This indeed is what religion is: that which binds us to God, mind touching mind without intermediary.[303] It is this intellectual union that is presupposed throughout Augustine's writings and which is in his view the end of human existence.

We began the analysis of Augustine with a consideration of order, and saw that intellect is one of the constituent ordering principles of the hierarchy. It determines to a great extent the rank of beings in the hierarchy, and even lies silently behind other ordering principles (such as immutability) that seem quite independent of it. It is the faculty in virtue of which we know God, and since knowledge precedes both assent and love, the theological virtues of faith and charity are fundamentally dependent on the intellect also. The particularities of his epistemology and the teleological drive of the system also indicate the intellect's significance for sanctification and consummation: it is the condition of the possibility of the reception of grace and the nexus through which we are ultimately joined to God in eternity.

Above all, the intellect is a central attribute of both God and humanity. While every Christian theologian either explicitly predicates or implicitly assumes mind in God, the Augustinian version of that assertion locates intellect not only in a divine nature rather statically conceived, but in the dynamism of intra-Trinitarian relations. This theological foundation in turn specifies the system as a whole in two quite different ways: first, the intellect is located in the context of personal encounter, and second, it is

[300] 26.49.   [301] SpLt 11.   [302] Cred 15.33.   [303] VRel 4.113.

defined in relation to love. Both factors exert an enormous influence on the shape of the theology as a whole and on its portrayal of the intellect.

These two constituent factors are inextricably intertwined: together they suggest the inseparability of intellect and love, and that personal relations are constituted by the conjoint operation of these two faculties. Because the mind is one of the mechanisms by which persons are united in relation to one another, it is suited also to function as one of the media by which God and humanity are united. In virtue of the unity-in-diversity of intellect and the loving will, however, the divine–human union must also be effected through love. It is by grounding his vision in the Trinity, where intellect and will are distinct, yet not opposed, that Augustine is also to insist that humanity need not, and indeed, cannot choose between knowledge and love, or between charity and truth. Because of the importance of love, Augustine does not seem embarrassed when he writes of the theological virtues – they fit naturally into the overall pattern because he has for the most part successfully balanced knowing and loving, and faith and charity therefore find natural employment.

We find less balance in his treatment of the body. Here we see both a sizeable suspicion and a determination to affirm the body as God's idea, and therefore good. His conviction of the body's subordinate status in relation to the soul may be taken today as evidence of an early Christian asceticism that turns out to be sub-Christian – as it seems often to be taken today – or it may simply reflect a conviction of the need for responsible governance. The fact that Augustine believes the mind is the faculty suited to ruling the body, and intended by God to do so, may be taken either as demeaning the body or as exalting the mind. The suggestion of this reading is that the interpretation most consonant with the texts is the latter.

His belief in the mind's priority is tempered by two factors, however. First, his use of sensuous imagery indicates simultaneously a desire to accord the corporal senses a higher status by suggesting the intellect works analogously to them, and also an acknowledgement of the body's centrality to human existence. Even when we are not actually perceiving by means of the body, it seems, we cannot help but think as if we were. Just as the Christian doctrine of the resurrection collides with the Platonist's view of salvation by refusing to exclude the body from consummation, so for Augustine, in our most exalted operation, the mental apprehension of Pure Mind, we continue to function as embodied beings and our language reflects this happy necessity. Second, because of the centrality of love in Augustine's system, it never becomes intellectualised to the point that felicity is only for the leisured and the bright, or that human life looks curiously one-sided, remote from the love and affection that obviously number among our chief preoccupations.

This must be the chief significance of Augustine's conception of the intellect: the degree of cohesion and integration he achieves – of intellect and will, of body and soul, of this life and the next, of human persons and God – all are bound in a cohesive and yet dynamic relation and grounded in the doctrine of the Trinity. For all its similarities to other Christian accounts of the intellect, Augustine's is at once 'merely' Christian and very much his own.

CHAPTER 5

Monastic writings

The authors surveyed thus far have all spanned what is from a modern perspective the gulf between 'school' theology and spirituality: their concerns fall in both areas and they move easily between the mood and rhetoric of academic, even combative, discourse and that of spiritual exhortation and contemplation. While some of them lived in a quasi-monastic style, at least for a time (Augustine and Gregory Nazianzen, for example), or simply practised some form of asceticism (Tertullian and Origen), none was either a cenobite or a solitary in the proper sense. In the earlier part of the period, of course, monasticism proper did not yet exist; if it had, conceivably Origen would have lived as a monk. Even in the later part of the period, the boundaries between the monastic and the non-monastic life seem to have been fine, with vowed religious leading lives of renunciation while living in the city and worshipping in ordinary parish churches.[1] By about the middle of the fourth century, however, the deserts of Egypt had become home to enough serious renouncers that we can speak of a form of monasticism (as yet not sharply distinguished between the eremitic and the cenobitic), and along with this development, a body of texts belonging to a recognisable genre, albeit one by no means definitively distinguished from other Christian writings of the period. These works are not incipient systematic theologies, like *On First Principles* or Nyssen's *Great Catechetical Oration*, nor dogmatic, speculative or controversialist writings, like those of Irenaeus, Nazianzen or Augustine; their purpose is much more specifically that of delineating the content and challenges of a dedicated spiritual life, a description they nonetheless ground in a firmly theological base.[2] That theological base proves much more important to these writings than commentators suggest. Owen Chadwick, for example, divides the literature into four

---
[1] Brakke (1995), 9.
[2] Bouyer concurs with Irénée Hausherr in regarding Evagrius' work on prayer as more than just coherent; it is the 'first complete system of Christian spirituality' (1960, 381).

groups: sayings, biographies, travellers' reports and 'ethical divinity', which he later glosses as 'moral theology'.³ A strong moral/ascetical strand undeniably runs through these writings, but it never reduces sheerly to moral exhortation, instead always maintaining a doxological element pointing implicitly, and often explicitly, to theological concerns.

Nevertheless, more than perhaps any other group of writings covered in this study, the notion of reading these systematically might invite quarrel. Their systematic quality does not reside in the organisation of the text (which is one sense in which theology may count as systematic), but in the way the theology coheres. Chadwick's analyses of books of the *Conferences*, for example, reveal their lack of linearity, of clear lines of development of thought,⁴ which he later explains by claiming they are collections of sayings, or the result of interpolations; they are 'confused'.⁵ Their structure is, perhaps, but not their thought, which although showing the complexities of the issues involved, reveals equally a coherent theology, with most of the standard loci of a systematic theology being either treated explicitly or readily inferable from what is stated explicitly. Therefore although we can also class the monastic writings as a subgenre of theological literature in this period on the basis of their more insistent focus on ascetical concerns, they evince the same level of interest in the mind and issues attending to it as do the non-monastic texts.⁶

One might however expect that in turning to these, we would encounter a heightened suspicion of the body, or at least of the flesh, concerned as those committed to celibacy must be with rigorous self-discipline. It is true that these writers warn of the spiritual effects of indulging the body's appetites, but overall they are not much more exercised on this account than the other writers surveyed. The theological basis for concern about the body – both with respect to its care and the temptation to indulge it – is articulated by Evagrius: the pure in heart

---

³ O. Chadwick 1968, 1 and 8.   ⁴ See, e.g., O. Chadwick 1968, 43 and 47.
⁵ O. Chadwick 1968, 47.
⁶ The theological consonance of the monastic writings with others examined in this volume in its own way calls into question the harsh polemic lobbed against monasticism and asceticism by some historians (notoriously, Gibbon and Harnack). If early Christian monasticism in fact represented the radical departure from Biblical ideals and the denial of the goodness of ordinary human existence, as some of its detractors claim, then one would have to explain why its theology is so consistently consonant with that of writers who have not been accused of comparable harshness. For examples of the more bitter appraisals of early monasticism, see the Introduction to Burton-Christie (1993). Likewise, if the gnostic influence on Egyptian Christianity ran as deep as some commentators claim (see Burton-Christie 1993, 37), it is hard to account for the overall theological consonance of these writings with those of different times and different locations.

know the Creator's grace by means of the body,[7] so the indisputable goodness of the body is affirmed, at the same time as a gentle rebuke is issued to those who might suppose that greater holiness lies in despising it; the truly spiritual know better. Just so, the conjunction of the body and soul, being of divine doing, can only be undone by the Creator. Cassian likewise affirms the unity of body and soul as a divine work, and is even willing to ascribe this wonder to fleshly being (although he does not thereby approve fleshly desires),[8] so there can be no question of attempting to drive a wedge between the two, either as a matter of principle or of practice.

Discipline is another issue entirely. In this regard, Evagrius makes a subtle distinction: to separate the body from the soul is the privilege of the one who joined them together, but to separate the soul from the body also lies within the power of the virtuous.[9] While the distinction at first seems puzzling, Evagrius must mean that the rupture of the psychosomatic unity which is physical death belongs to God to bring about, but that separation which is a matter of freeing the soul from being overpowered by the body belongs to those of right will, the virtuous. In a way the *Apophthegmata* provide the most theologically satisfying formulation: the body is to be disciplined because it is for the one who made it.[10] This, according to Theodora, is the Christian response to the Manichee, and the fact we find this notion voiced by a woman, who presumably would have had little access to formal theological or philosophical instruction, indicates that theological astuteness does not necessarily correlate with academic education, and we should accordingly beware assuming theological rawness of the desert monastics simply because they were supposedly unlettered.

The dominant sensibility running through all the monastic writings is the need for bodily discipline, a conviction grounded in the correct order of body and soul. This relation is expressed in rather negative terms by Athanasius, who lauds Antony for keeping the body under subjection [endoulagōgei],[11] and on occasion, the relation is conceived in terms that

---

[7] Prak 53.   [8] Cnfr 12.13.   [9] Prak 52.
[10] Theodora.4/PG65.204. All quotations from the *Sayings* are from the Greek alphabetical collection. This collection has been preferred over the Latin thematic one because of the broad contemporary agreement that the sayings were originally written down in Greek and because this is the most complete collection. Burton-Christie (1993) provides a convenient account of the various editions and their relation to each other (see ch. 3).
[11] LA 7.4. Brakke (1995) notes that the ascetic discipline of virgins not only preserved purity of the body, in Athanasius' view, but also focused the mind so that one might devote oneself to Christ in an undistracted manner. He is citing the Letter to Virgins (Brakke 1995, 34-35). For the dispute

are decidedly antithetical, as when Abba Daniel maintains that the body flourishes as the soul is weakened, and vice versa.[12] Elsewhere in the literature, however, the account is more indulgent, as when Cassian calls the body a beast of burden,[13] the servant of the mind.[14] Evagrius focuses the issue on the practice of prayer, merely claiming that one ought not to think of the body while praying: during prayer, one should take nothing from the flesh, as it only clouds one's vision;[15] Indeed, one should pay no attention to the needs of the body while praying.[16] Such advice could seem to suppose a complete location of the spiritual in some disembodied realm where one can worship truly because one has shed the encumbrance, but it is more likely grounded in conventional advice on dealing with distraction during prayer: the Fathers of the Church knew that the fidgeter who finds one excuse not to remain still will, once this itch has been scratched, soon feel another and yet another. The only route to mental stillness is bodily stillness and the only route to the latter is simply to ignore the child's perpetual sleeve-tugging, its endless complaints about itches, aching joints, heavy eyelids, and so on. The stories of monks who ignored vipers while they were praying[17] are thus not promoting some arcane practice of snake-handling, for no claim of immunity from snake bite is made, even if it seems that none of these athletes of prayer suffers as the result of his own insouciance.

Likewise, when Cassian claims that the body of sin is constructed out of the many members of the vices,[18] the problem lies not with the body itself, but with flesh in the Pauline sense, which is more a matter of imagination and desire than the press of sheerly bodily needs. While flesh stands in the way of discovering perfection,[19] and has a certain wantonness about it that must be combatted,[20] asceticism is not an end in itself. Indeed, even if bodily needs are to be ignored in prayer, Evagrius cites Macarius' view that one must treat the body as if one would live for many years to come.[21] This approach foreshadows the moderation evident in Benedict's Rule, although it stands somewhat in tension with the

---

over whether the *Life of Antony* is authentically Athanasian, see Brakke (1995) 15, n. 31. Brakke also notes that Athanasius' letters to the desert fathers, as well as the writings to the virgins, 'stress the reorientation of the body-mind relationship', as well as the 'direction of ascetic practices towards this goal' (140). Brakke comments that there is little evidence of actual contact between Athanasius and Antony and therefore takes the *Life* to be an idealised account (202); for our purposes, it makes no difference, and where in this chapter I refer to Antony, citing the *Life*, it should be understood that it is the character whom the bishop portrays who is in question, whose correspondence to an historical figure remains uncertain.

[12] Daniel 4/PG 65.156. [13] Cnfr 11.15. [14] Cnfr 21.21. [15] Pray 128. [16] Pray 105.
[17] E.g., Pray 107–09. [18] Cnfr 12.2. [19] Cnfr 23.16. [20] Inst 5.14.2. [21] Prak 29.

single-mindedness of the founder of Christian monasticism, Antony, in whose view one should devote all one's time to the soul rather than the body, although even he was willing to concede a little time to the body, sheerly out of necessity.[22]

Benedict's predecessor, Cassian, stands between Antony and the author of the Rule. His works show an abiding concern with the ever-present danger of bodily temptation: the struggle between flesh and the soul is nothing less than a war[23] consisting of daily battles between the desires of the flesh and the spirit.[24] If the flesh is recalcitrant, however, it is also frail,[25] and so the advantage remains on the side of the Spirit. Less dramatically, he characterises the impulses of the flesh in various images of heaviness: the mind uses its intellectual faculties better when free of fleshly heaviness;[26] and when it is not dulled by the coarseness of the flesh.[27] Mind does not always succeed in prevailing over matter, and for this reason there can be no uniform rule regarding fasting: the virtue of temperance in food cannot be achieved by mental rigour alone, as can other virtues.[28]

The last point indicates the overarching rubric of the monks' attitudes towards the body: it is an ever-present factor in their lives, but the root problem does not lie in the body itself, nor even in the flesh and its chaotic impulses, but ultimately in the will's, and therefore the mind's, failure to exercise due control. The Antony of the *Apophthegmata* – a rather kinder, gentler character than Athanasius' – points out that the body does not act of its own accord, but needs the consent of the soul[29] and afflicting it only manifests a lack of discernment [diakrisis].[30] Athanasius recognises as much when he notes that Antony urged all the monks who came to him to guard against the pleasures of the flesh[31] – the problem is not what the flesh itself does, but how the soul indulges itself by means of the flesh. Antony's own soul was free from confusion, his outer senses undisturbed,[32] reflecting the state the soul should have, of being overcome by desire for divine realities.[33] Desire, then, is no more inherently a problem than the body is: some desires are good, some unhelpful, and the latter may be conquered as effectively by being counterbalanced by the former as by extirpation. Hence for Evagrius, desire for God enables the monastic to control the body, and he claims

---

[22] LA 45.5. [23] Inst 5.11.2. [24] Cnfr 4.11. [25] Inst 5.16.2. [26] Cnfr 1.14.8.
[27] Cnfr 3.7; cf. Basil, who speaks of the soul's being dragged down to passionate desires [empatheis epithumias] AD1.FC 207/PG 31.869.
[28] Inst 5.5.1. [29] Antony 22/PG 65.84. [30] Antony 8/PG 65.77. [31] LA 52.2.
[32] LA 67.6. [33] LA 35.5.

that bodily intemperance can be calmed by singing psalms.[34] Just so, Macarius maintains that the fear of God burns up the body as well as purifying the mind [nous].[35] Certainly, the mind is affected by bodily states (integrity of mind is connected to an empty stomach, for example[36]) and it does not have complete control over the body. Cassian's curious preoccupation with nocturnal emissions reflects this recurrently expressed frustration (though he is by no means alone among the Fathers in his hand-wringing over this issue): no matter how vigilant the monk is during the day, the relaxation of the mind and will during sleep becomes the occasion for what we would now call the subconscious to go to work.[37] Christ's perfection is linked to the fact that he had no experience of the prickings of lust[38] and incorruption of the flesh consists in integrity of heart [integritate cordis], rather than bodily purity alone.[39] Indeed, there can be no bodily purity without the full participation of the soul: fasting, for example, means fasting with the soul and not just abstaining from visible food.[40] The fact that real bodily continence entails more than sheerly bodily discipline means that Cassian presumes the right relation of body and soul is not only natural but graced: the spiritually experienced are not warrior ascetics who grit their teeth and try harder, but those who know they cannot achieve the desired end on their own, because of the resistance of the flesh, and who therefore flee to the grace of God.[41] Consequently, eunuchs face an unexpected spiritual peril: thinking themselves to be free of danger in virtue of their physical condition, they become negligent in the pursuit of virtue.[42] For the less complacent, help is at hand, for although the Spirit will not dwell in a body subject to sin, even if the character of this sin is spiritual rather than corporeal (such as deception[43]), the body is also the subject of divine gracious activity: the Trinity is able to flow into it.[44] The eucharist accordingly purifies both body and soul (this is the rationale for communicating those possessed by demons daily: the sacrament both protects and purifies[45]).

Because the soul's calling is to cooperate with grace so as to order the whole person rightly, the soul and not the body is fundamentally to

---

[34] Pray 83.   [35] Macarius 12/PG 65.268.   [36] Cassian, Inst 5.9.
[37] As one example, see Cnfr 12.16. Stewart's treatment of the issue reflects less bafflement than my own (see 1998, 63–64, and 81–83).
[38] Cnfr 5.5.
[39] Inst 6.19. Cassian is citing Basil, who stated that although he had not known a woman, he was not a virgin. O. Chadwick (1968) notes this saying is not found elsewhere in Basil's works, but claims this absence does not mean much (61).
[40] Inst 5.21.1.   [41] Cnfr 23.10.   [42] Cnfr 12.5.   [43] Cnfr 14.2, quoting Wis 1:5, 4.
[44] Cnfr 7.13.   [45] Cnfr 7.30.

blame for undisciplined behaviour. On this point, the monks concur with all the writers surveyed: their commitment to asceticism does not overturn the fundamental anthropology operative throughout this period. The soul's goal can only be attained through diligence and perseverance,[46] yet the faculty by which the soul is able to persevere, the will, Cassian characterises as occupying a somewhat blameworthy middle position, neither enjoying vice nor welcoming the rigours of virtue.[47] This view contrasts with the generally high estimation of will in the work of other writers: there is no sense in this passage that possession of a will makes us akin to God, or enables us to imitate divine creativity or to love.[48]

Both Cassian and Evagrius however see the possibility of virtue's lodging in any part of the soul. For Evagrius, the concupiscible part of the soul desires virtue, the irascible part fights to obtain it, while the rational part applies itself to the contemplation of created things.[49] The various parts of the soul host different virtues: seated in the rational part are prudence, understanding [synesis] and wisdom; in the concupiscible part, temperance, charity and continence; in the irascible part, courage and patience or perseverance [hypomonē]; while justice is spread throughout the whole soul.[50] Cassian takes a more limited view, holding that the more precious part of the human person, that in which the imago Dei subsists, consists in the power of reasoning, the structure of which implies that mind will eventually shed its fleshly heaviness (rather than the body itself) and recover the full use of its faculties. Such casting off of the flesh betokens not only the healing of the Fall's debilities, but spiritual advancement well beyond healing: in spiritual ecstasy we forget we dwell in the flesh, yet we do not, it seems, forget the body, for the mystic smells odours sweeter than any fragrance made by human hands.[51] If virtues like chastity involve mental discipline, though, Cassian makes sure to point out that one still has to discipline the flesh as well, and to exercise bodily self-control.[52] Nevertheless it seems that for Cassian, the resistance of the flesh is not the main reason we go astray: the demons, who are sheerly spiritual substances, still make evil choices, though they have not even the figleaf of fleshly temptation as an excuse.[53]

The deep conviction of the need for discipline manifests itself in the monks' writings in the manner in which they treat the senses, for although this shares some characteristics with other writers examined, it

---

[46] Cnfr 1.4.   [47] Cnfr 4.12.
[48] In the history of Christian dogmatic theology, Cassian has chiefly been read for his non-Augustinian doctrine of grace, but his view of the will scarcely exalts its capacities.
[49] Prak 86.   [50] Prak 89.   [51] Cnfr 4.5.   [52] Cnfr 4.12.   [53] Cnfr 4.14.

also bears some distinctive marks. The Origenistic theme of the spiritual senses appears only fleetingly in the writings of the Desert Fathers, and there mostly takes up the imagery of vision. Thus Antony counsels that monks must have God always before their eyes.[54] Antony himself is the object of reverent regard: one of the abbas went to see him regularly, remaining silent, without asking for any counsel; when asked why, the monk replied 'It is enough for me to see you',[55] foreshadowing perhaps the later notion of a 'living rule', monks or nuns who so perfectly embody the order's Rule that it is said a novice might learn it just by observing their behaviour. Vision may be privileged by the early monastic tradition because in the desert, in the absence of human clamour, the fragrances of flowers, fine cuisine or luxurious surfaces, sight was the only sense with much potential for gratification. However the *Apophthegmata* also record the beginning of the equally venerable monastic tradition of the custody of the eyes, so a more likely explanation for the privileging of vision lies in its connection to heaven; thus Bessarion: 'The monk should be as the cherubim and seraphim, all eye.'[56] Not surprisingly, Evagrius follows the tradition, claiming sight is the most worthy of the senses.[57] Of the Eastern Fathers, Basil alone expresses reserve, pointing out that it is possible to commit adultery with the eye and to be defiled [molunthēnai] by hearing.[58] Basil's concern here is not so much any evil inherent in the senses themselves, but rather the possibility of sinning by the assent of the will, even in the absence of any outwardly sinful act. Adultery of the eye means sinning in the imagination, and ultimately the mind, and by insisting that even this most corporeal of faults has a mental origin and can indeed be culpable even when confined to the mind, he is of course following Christ's teaching; although he shifts the latter's centre of attention on the sinner's heart to the senses, the focus on intention and inward assent to sin remains the same.

Cassian's view falls within the broad tradition established before him, privileging sight above all the other senses. 'Gazing' denotes particularly that fixity of the heart's intention necessary to the pursuit of any end: the adepts at any art must set their eye on a goal,[59] and those intent on the kingdom of God must fix their gaze on that.[60] This gaze is identified not only with a future goal, but with the mind's unwavering union with God in contemplation, its freedom from distraction.[61] Sight is also attributed to God and is especially associated with divine omniscience, so that God's

---

[54] Antony 3/PG 65.76. [55] Antony 27/PG 65.84. [56] Bessarion 11/PG 65.142.
[57] Pray 150. [58] AD 1.FC208/PG 31.871. [59] Cnfr 1.2. [60] Cnfr 1.4. [61] Cnfr 1.13.

is the eye from which the secrets of the heart cannot be hidden.[62] This scrutinising role is linked to the human eye as well, which sheds light on one's thoughts and actions and discerns what is to be done.[63] The association of vision with discernment can also have negative implications, however: one can cover over the heart's eye with a thick veil of vice and so fail to see the truth about oneself, one form of which is failing to grieve, or discovering one is distracted from contemplation.[64] The holy, in contrast, are not subject to the darkened sight of lesser mortals, and condemn shortcomings in themselves that the rest of us fail to notice.[65] Anger especially shadows the mind, keeping us from acquiring discretion and a contemplative perspective [contemplationis intuitum].[66] The greater the progress one makes in contemplation, therefore, the more one presses onward to a lofty vision; the more purified one's mind, the greater the impurity and baseness one sees in oneself.[67]

Although sight predominates as an image of the human person's stretching towards God, then, it is linked at once to beatific vision and moral blindness. Smell, in contrast, figures far less frequently, yet with overwhelmingly positive associations. Moses gave off a sweet odour, Cassian claims, because of his practical and contemplative virtue.[68] Significantly, Cassian seems to place little emphasis on hearing, an absence notable in its contrast with the most broadly influential Christian monastic text, Benedict's Rule. The Rule contains very little of any bearing on our themes, except in prescribing the reading aloud of Cassian's *Conferences* (in chs 42 and 73). Its well-known opening words, 'Listen carefully, my child, to the master's instructions', inaugurate the theme of listening that recurs in the text, and is taken by writers of the Benedictine tradition to be linked to obedience, the Latin for 'listen' (audire) being the etymological root of the verb for obeying (oboedire).

In insisting upon the mind's governance of the body (and therefore, the mind's responsibility for sin), the monastic writers necessarily broach the issue of the role of will and appetite. While some rely on Aristotelian categories for their treatment of the virtues (the grouping of the intellectual virtues, for example), they rarely rely on the Aristotelian definition of the will as a rational appetite. Only Cassian and Evagrius concern themselves with the appetite to any significant degree (although in the *Apophthegmata* Biare identifies the road to salvation as lying in reduction of the appetite combined with little manual work and staying in one's

[62] Cnfr 1.15. [63] Cnfr 2.2. [64] Cnfr 23.6. [65] Cnfr 23.6. [66] Inst 8.1.1.
[67] Cnfr 23.19. [68] Cnfr 1.1.

cell[69]). Evagrius' ethic lays an emphasis on the inner movement of the will, foreshadowing Abelard's later focus on intention, for he warns against even giving mental consent to forbidden pleasure and firmly defines avarice as not the possession of money, but desire for it.[70] Cassian concurs; although one cannot help the mind's being troubled by thoughts, one is free to accept or reject them,[71] and not even the devil can deceive us unless our will assents.[72] We can even will ourselves into virtue in his view, for patience comes of humility and forbearance, and these depend on our will [arbitrio].[73] If it has seemed to some that Cassian has a severely deficient doctrine of grace, at least by a post-Augustinian Western standard, we must bear in mind his insistence that grace and freedom only seem opposed; in fact they are in accord with each other.[74] Exactly how they work together without conflict lies beyond the grasp of human reason, he frankly acknowledges,[75] but a hint of a solution to the conundrum may lie in the source of our freedom [liberum arbitrium], which is in itself a divine gift.[76]

That gift is in a sense a double one, for to will rightly, we must have the capacity to reflect upon the good, must – in other words – have minds, which are themselves a divine gift. In the writings of the Desert Fathers, concern with mind largely takes the form of worry about distraction during prayer.[77] In the *Life of Antony* the analysis goes a bit deeper, with the mind portrayed as not merely the victim of a swarm of distractions: the unity of the desert community results from the monks' being all of one mind [phronēma],[78] and Antony's own mind [nous] was not only unshaken and free from distraction[79] but more, joyous.[80] Basil takes up the concerns of the earlier tradition, alerting monks to the dangers of a wandering mind, which affects not only prayer but one's ability to love God and neighbour, and thence the whole of the Christian life.[81] His moral concern manifests itself also in his warning that the mind can become perverted by sin.[82] Moreover he doubts even the uncorrupted mind's ability to attain to the highest truth: even if all minds [dianoiai]

---

[69] Biare [unnumbered]/PG 65.146.   [70] Prak 75 and Gnos 30.   [71] Cnfr 1.17.
[72] Cnfr 7.8.   [73] Inst 4.42.   [74] Cnfr 13.11.   [75] Cnfr 13.18.   [76] Inst 12.18.
[77] Antony 34/PG 65.87. For example, the impetus to expand the monastic settlement as more and more are drawn to the desert is driven by the need for the right degree of physical separation, allowing contrast yet not fostering mental distraction.
[78] LA 44.4.
[79] LA 51.5. Brakke (1995) notes that Athanasius regarded the virgins' bearing of 'rationalities' [logismoi] as mirroring the Virgin Mary, who bore rationality [logos] itself (73, citing the First Letter to Virgins).
[80] LA 67.8. Mind here is *dianoia*.   [81] LR Q5, FC 241/PG 31.920.   [82] LR Q2 FC235/PG 31.911.

combined their researches, there would be no worthy result;[83] the mind simply cannot grasp the greatness of God.[84]

Evagrius, less the dogmatic theologian and controversialist than Basil was, concerns himself less with the mind's limitations. As the treatise addressed to monks draws to its close, he leaves his reader with the picture of knowledge raising the mind [nous] and presenting before it the very Trinity.[85] This exalted view of the mind's capacity does not blind him to its pedestrian infirmities, for he exhibits the same preoccupation as the earlier monastic writers with distraction during prayer, although strongly inclining to attribute much mental turbulence to demons: these suggest to the mind that there are pressing concerns needing attention and collude with the human memory, stirring it up so that the mind begins to search it;[86] endlessly inventive, they attack from all sides. One demon even stimulates a specific site in the brain, agitating the cerebral circulation (an undesirable state of affairs, apparently).[87] The precise status of these demons is somewhat unclear in Evagrius' writing; sometimes it seems they should be taken quite literally. However, at other times, it seems that Evagrius may simply be personifying destructive forces arising within, which are portrayed as hypostasised as a way of designating the perennial mystery of the maelstrom of desires within the human person: why is it that, genuinely wishing to be holy, we nevertheless fantasise about wrongdoing? Answering 'It's the demons' may be less primitively credulous than modern readers imagine, for sometimes the vices themselves are virtually personified: vanity is the source of the mind's illusions, although its effect is not to aggrandise the self, but to accord a form to divine nature, thus circumscribing it.[88] Likewise, avarice suggests to the mind a lengthy old age.[89] An author ready to personify virtues and vices may write with greater colour and fancy than a modern academic minimalist, and there is no real way of telling how much of the talk of demons denotes entities believed to exist and how much is vivid evocation of torments originating from within the psyche. On occasion, moreover, the source of distraction is objectified and portrayed as somehow distinct from the mind, although it is not demonised or in any way personified: the mind is hard to control in the presence of sinful fantasies.[90] If the

---

[83] CFth FC 63/PG 31.684.   [84] CFth FC 60/PG 31.681.
[85] Monc 136. The knowledge in question is of incorporeals [gnōsis asōmatōn].   [86] Pray 10.
[87] Pray 72.
[88] Pray 116. Bamberger takes a similar view, noting that some modern writers, such as Robert Bly, ascribe common psychological problems to demons (1992, 193).
[89] Prak 9.   [90] Prak 48.

desert seems more thickly populated by demons than by simple daydreams, the reason lies in the limited range of temptations it affords: those busy in the world of affairs feel tempted to misdeeds by their environment, but since the desert affords few opportunities for such misdoings, the demons strive against monastics chiefly through the medium of their thoughts.[91]

Intellectual peril knows more forms than just distractions and temptations. When enslaved to passion, the mind cannot see the place of spiritual prayer[92] and false opinion can tempt it, opinions regarding the ontological status of things, for example, their existence or non-existence.[93] These dangers are serious, given that they affect not only one's attentiveness in the moment, but one's ultimate destiny, for the term of the intellect's purification is spiritual knowledge [pneumatikēn gnōsin][94] and the rightness of one's thought significantly regulates one's capacity for relation with God.

Cassian's works exhibit the deepest and most persistent concern with mind of all the monastic writers, a concern manifesting itself both in the gravity with which he views its propensity to go astray and in its centrality to the spiritual life. He worries, naturally, about distraction, distraction which can spring from either mental or physical sources. Something as banal as a recent imperfectly digested meal can prevent the mind from functioning during prayer.[95] More vaguely, he wishes that the mind not be sullied by contact with fleshly coarseness.[96] His concern here may be his oft-expressed worry about nocturnal emissions (though he usually expresses himself unambiguously about these), since he attributes bodily impurity to mental negligence or weariness.[97] If integrity of mind comes with an empty stomach, however,[98] the mind has its own distinct ways of mimicking the body's worst excesses: not only wine inebriates it, for example; surfeit of any kind can have the same effect[99] so the mind should not only be virtuous, but abstinent. Whatever the merits of fasting, moreover, Cassian cites Chaeremon's opinion that monastics should not deprive themselves of food and sleep, for if they did, the body's torpor would cause their minds to lose their vigour.[100] Cassian himself seems to take a sterner view, even maintaining that excessive intake of water should be curbed, so that the law of the body would conform to that of the mind.[101]

---

[91] Prak 48. [92] Pray 71. [93] Gnos 42. [94] Gnos 47. [95] Cnfr 2.26. [96] Cnfr 3.7.
[97] Cnfr 12.2 and 12.16. [98] Inst 5.9. [99] Inst 5.6. [100] Cnfr 12.16. [101] Cnfr 12.11.

Most often, though, the mind's ailments arise from more purely spiritual causes: Cassian calls envy 'the food of the mind', and anger the 'food of the soul'.[102] Troubled by anxiety [anxietate animi],[103] the mind is shackled by its own ignorance [mens jugiter praepedita],[104] although he takes pains to stipulate that illiteracy excludes no one from perfection, as long as the mind keeps its attention steadily fixed on God.[105] Maintaining this fixity of attention is not easy, given the mind's innate flightiness. It tends to slip away, captivated by trivial distractions,[106] and cannot by any means remain in a single state.[107] The 'by any means' in this last statement seems curiously to allow for instability of mind even in heaven, a point on which Cassian is generally unclear. Although nous is, by definition, that which is always changeable and manifoldly unchangeable,[108] he claims that the soul's wanderings are not our fault, but nature's,[109] and that the mind [anima], of its very nature, can never stand idle,[110] all of which seems to imply that mental fluctuation belongs intrinsically to human nature, along with other forms of mutability and passibility, and not to the deleterious effects of the Fall. Cassian however has no doubts about the possibility of the mind's corruption. Evil both darkens the body and obscures the mind[111] and the individual mind seems capable of falling [conruat] after the general Fall.[112] Such movement seems however determined not by the primordial actions of the First Parents, but the weight of individual *habitus*: once the mind has accumulated the filth of vice, it will turn in a carnal direction.[113] The mind, subject to a plethora of afflictions, may be sickly [aegra],[114] as well as flighty, undisciplined and distracted. It may suffer confusion, enveloping it in a foul mist.[115] If hardened by passion, it degenerates day by day.[116] At worst, it may even suffer from vice.[117] Less drastically, it can simply be afflicted with the malady of sadness.[118]

Fortunately the mind, like the body, can be also strengthened through exercise: the monk's mind must be practised in endurance and moderation,[119] making an intellectual rather than appetitive determination of what is sufficient, and becomes stronger through a succession of victories over the passions.[120] The soul's goal and the mind's intention can therefore only be attained by perseverance.[121] This ability of the mind to

---

[102] Inst 5.21.2. [103] Cnfr 10.10. [104] Cnfr 10.8.
[105] Cnfr 10.14. [106] Cnfr 7.3. [107] Cnfr 6.14.
[108] Cnfr 7.4. 'Aekinetos kai polukinetos', Cassian cites in Greek, glossing as *semper mobilis et multum mobilis*.
[109] Cnfr 7.3. [110] Cnfr 7.4. [111] Cnfr 2.2. [112] Cnfr 1.17. [113] Cnfr 1.17. [114] Inst 6.3.
[115] Inst 10.2.3. [116] Inst 12.27.1. [117] Inst 5.11.2. [118] Cnfr 23.7. [119] Cnfr 5.11.
[120] Cnfr 5.14. [121] Cnfr 1.4.

return to its true nature is indicated by the very structure of reasoning [hoc ratio ipsius ordo contineat],[122] as long as it is able to forget its fleshly heaviness. In a state of ecstasy one may even lose awareness that the mind dwells in the flesh at all.[123] Renewal of the mind is nevertheless not a once-for-all attainment; it brings with it the responsibility to make progress every day,[124] although if polished by constant practice, the mind will eventually attain to perfect holiness.[125] The road to such sanctity is not easy, and while Cassian considers that the effects of sin are not such as to leave the mind bereft and helpless, he frequently uses images of bondage. The devil can fetter the mind through our desire for possessions,[126] but nothing is too hard for the one who takes up Christ's yoke with his whole mind [tota mente];[127] moreover, reading occupies the mind so that it cannot be taken captive by harmful thoughts.[128] Renewed by the study of scripture and enlarged by patience,[129] it may be possible for the mind to remain humble, tranquil and pure.[130]

Perhaps because of their stress on love, perhaps because of their keen awareness of how communal life can be destroyed by dissension, the monks express reserve about certain uses of the mind, declining in particular to place much value in dispute. Nonetheless, the monastic writings do not evidence the suspicion of intellectual endeavour one might expect to find in those bent on fleeing the world and its vanities. Matoes warns against arguing, or even harbouring a fondness for argument [philoneikian],[131] and Basil likewise warns against rash and dangerous dispute,[132] as well as fruitless or contentious discussion;[133] the picture emerging from Athanasius' and Cassian's works, however, is more nuanced.

Although in the *Apophthegmata* Antony is recorded as having heard a voice saying there are some things one should not even ask about, as these pertain to divine judgement,[134] the injunction does not foreclose intellectual inquiry in general. In Athanasius' *Life*, Antony figures as the trouncer of philosophers, who beats them at their own game: seeking to make him look foolish, they construct syllogisms concerning the cross, but the hermit refutes them by showing their reasoning implies the surds that God is mutable and irrational.[135] Seeing how the demons fear him, they retreat in amazement.[136] On other occasions, Antony's response

---

[122] Cnfr 1.14. [123] Cnfr 4.5. [124] Cnfr 6.14.
[125] Cnfr 12.5. [126] Cnfr 24.24. [127] Cnfr 24.23.
[128] Cnfr 14.10. [129] Cnfr 16.27. [130] Cnfr 11.9 and 9.2. [131] Matoes 11 and 12/PG 65.293.
[132] LR Q. 47 FC325/PG 31.1056. [133] Mors Rule 25 FC 105/PG 31.744. [134] Antony 2/PG 65.76.
[135] LA 74. [136] LA 72.5.

seems to represent a more fundamental refusal of philosophical methods of inquiry. How is God known, he asks, which is prior, proofs or faith? Where faith is active, logical demonstration is unnecessary, perhaps even useless,[137] and syllogisms do not convert people to Christianity. Antony's point here is quite limited: he passes no judgement on the value of philosophy or reasoning in general, only on its powerlessness to accomplish certain ends, and given what he understands by Christianity, with its vigorous commitment to virtue and prayer, it would be difficult to imagine any radical conversion of morals would result from bandying about a few major and minor propositions. Antony's response to the request for syllogistic reasoning is therefore a reasoned one, in the sense that it replies to the very demand for a reasonable faith by showing formal logic to be an unsuitable tool in this particular context. Antony declares that Christians persuade by faith that precedes argumentation, implying not the superfluousness of the latter, but that its true motivation is faith.[138] Significantly, Athanasius records that the philosopher marvelled at Antony's intelligence [synesis].[139] Antony himself, on Evagrius' report, told a philosopher that his book was the nature of created things [physis tōn gegonotōn], in which he read the words of God.[140] If this repudiation could be taken as a rejection of philosophy *tout court*, it could equally be taken as an incipient natural theology. The book of nature and of life stands beside the Book of Books; in another story from the desert, Evagrius recounts how one of the desert fathers sold his copy of the gospels, giving the proceeds to the poor and saying 'I have sold the book that says "Sell your possessions."'[141] The refusal here is not of reading itself, and certainly not of the Bible, but rather, of reading as a substitute

---

[137] LA 77.5.
[138] Brakke interprets chs. 72–80 of LA, those dealing with dispute with philosophers, as proof of Athanasius' lack of interest in Antony as a 'simple, illiterate Copt' and of the bishop's desire to create a portrait of an ascetic that would suit his political purposes, contrasting the Christianity of Athanasius' episcopate with the 'Christianity of the schoolroom' (257). The text itself discloses a portrait of Antony, but does not announce its author's motive; Brakke may be correct, but his opinion remains a speculation. He clearly extends beyond the text in contrasting what the philosophers represent and what Antony stands for; the notion that one requires faith to know God does not mean, as Brakke claims, that one knows God 'intuitively' (257), nor does faith exclude knowledge that comes through reading or reflection. Athanasius' Antony certainly advocates living the Christian faith, but he does not claim that this lived faith and other forms of knowledge are mutually exclusive, as Brakke suggests, but merely that the latter is by itself inadequate. The fact that the philosophers supposedly marvel at Antony's wisdom indicates that the standard they represent has not been rejected or mitigated, but that Athanasius is showing that a holy Christian can be as clever as a secular philosopher and more. Certainly, such claims tell us little of the historical Antony, but they testify eloquently to the theology of Athanasius.
[139] LA 80.1.   [140] Prak 92.   [141] Prak 97.

for practice, and the subtle temptation to indulge avarice on the occasion of holy things. If so, Antony's words need not be taken as preferring the book of nature and life over revelation, but as the testament of one who has thoroughly assimilated the Bible's teaching.

Cassian's position is more ambiguous, differing only in having a perhaps slightly more negative cast. He describes Antony as unmoved by human teaching,[142] although he also notes Abba Daniel was said to be devoted to Christian philosophy, apparently no bad thing in Cassian's view.[143] Philosophy (of whatever variety) seems licit, therefore, at least up to a point. In trying to grasp the conundrum of divine and human agency, however, Cassian suggests sheer reasoning must be rejected when it leads to the conclusion that God would remove freedom he himself once granted. One way of reading this dictum is to see it as dismissing the value of reason in Christian hard cases. Another equally plausible option is to view it as a metarule for interpreting conflicting claims, both of which are reasonable: the logic of the divine gift of freedom overrides conclusions derived from other axioms or data. Either way, Cassian does not deride reasoning altogether, but exalts it, even as he acknowledges it sometimes raises questions as much as answering them. His admonition might be viewed as Anselm *avant la lettre*: we do not acquire faith from understanding [ex intellectu] but understanding from faith.[144]

It is therefore not surprising that he considers true knowledge belongs only to true worshippers of God, not to those merely possessed of disputational skills and elaborate rhetoric. The dangers of the latter were apparently real, since professed monks had been deceived by philosophical teachings.[145] Nevertheless, the deeper problem seems to be not the inherent wrongness of their views, but their lack of interior purity of mind, a particular form of chastity [animi castitatem] demanded of the monk.[146] Again, the gap between conviction and practice, which constitutes a kind of toying with truth while failing actually to apprehend it, seems to be the real problem. Thus Cassian portrays God as saying to the soul 'Remove your evil thoughts from my sight.... Come, dispute [arguite] with me.'[147] This engagement with God, as opposed to the construction of elaborate proofs about him, is crucial. Thus, while Evagrius seems to have benefitted from the usual training in logic, he concurs with Antony in denying the power of this kind of knowledge to

---

[142] Cnfr 3.4. [143] Cnfr 4.1.1. [144] Cnfr 13.18. [145] Cnfr 1.20. [146] Cnfr 13.5. [147] Cnfr 20.8.

reach to the reality of God.¹⁴⁸ In each case, what matters are the realities of the Trinity, of life *coram Deo*, rather than the postponement of discipline and adoration while one displaces one's attention elsewhere.

For the monks, pointed dwelling on *ta theia* occurred above all on the occasion of the sacred page. The monastics' attitude to book-learning follows from their commitment to scripture, on the one hand, and on the other, their awareness that living contemplation cannot be equated with acquired knowledge. So Abba Arsenius contrasts the virtue of peasants, which is real, with the emptiness of the monks' education.¹⁴⁹ In a similar vein, the seeker who asks advice of Eutrepius marvels at his teaching, whose soundness exceeds anything to be found in the many books he had read (the astonishing piece of wisdom offered by Eutrepius is that one should not speak before being spoken to).¹⁵⁰ Elsewhere in the *Apophthegmata*, cautions apply only to ownership (it is best to possess nothing, not even books, maintains Theodore¹⁵¹), or the kind of reading material one chooses: do not allow a woman to enter your cell, Sopratus advises, and do not read apocryphal literature.¹⁵² Some of the Desert Fathers esteem books and book-learning. Epiphanius differs from Theodore on the matter of ownership. In his view, Christian books are essential for those able to read them; indeed, the mere sight of them reduces the impulse to sin,¹⁵³ as does actually reading them.¹⁵⁴ Ignorance of the Law

---

[148] Gnos 4. What exactly constitutes this knowledge he admittedly leaves rather vague: it is the *exōthen gnōsis*, which we know *dia tōn logōn*.

[149] Arsenius 5 and 6/PG 65.88–90.   [150] Eutrepius 7/PG 65.172.

[151] Theodore of Pherme 1/PG 65.188. Obviously, a caution against owning books cannot be equated with a disdain for their content; it may be less obvious that cautions against reading cannot be equated with disdain for content, either. As Burton-Christie (1993) points out, the ambivalent attitudes toward scripture in the *Apophthegmata* may be understood in light of the shift that was occurring from an emphasis on oral to written discourse (108). Burton-Christie, referring to the story of the brother who sold his book of the Gospels saying 'I have sold the book which told me "Sell your possessions and give to the poor"', oddly speaks of a 'biting irony characteristic of the desert' (115). This saying does not strike me as either biting or ironic, but rather bespeaks the simplicity and radicality of one taking the gospel more seriously than most Christians have the courage to do. As O. Chadwick notes, the ethical suspicion of books derived from the fact that they were possessions, property; yet, as he remarks, 'books were kept, and books were written' (1968, 24).

[152] Sopratus [no number]/PG 65.414.   [153] Epiphanius 8/PG 65.165.

[154] Epiphanius 9/PG 65.165. Again, here I differ from Burton-Christie (1993): 'There was a clear sense among the educated ones who came to the desert that learning would have to start over in this place. In the desert, a clear distinction was made between the kind of knowledge that could be acquired through "worldly education" and what could be gained through the hard work of the simple desert monks' (58). The alternatives are not so stark, and while it is true the monastic writers have little use for purely secular learning, this does not mean they all reject all forms of book learning. Cp. Leclerq's summary of the attitude expressed in Benedict's Rule: in order to meditate, one must read, and in order to read, possess books; in the monastery, therefore, it is necessary to learn how to read, if one does not already know (1982, 13), and ownership of books is

and of scripture, far from constituting bliss in his view, imperils one's salvation.[155] The pattern of light scepticism of the value of secular education but a high estimation of scripture prevails in the *Life of Antony*. The Greeks sail abroad to get an education, but Christians who seek virtue need not cross the sea:[156] the scriptures suffice for instruction,[157] and Antony absorbed the whole of it.[158]

Basil, too, extols scripture, though he passes over the value of secular education without comment – prudently, given that he himself obviously profited from it. Scripture contains a store of knowledge whose reach is limited only by the capacity of its readers to grasp it.[159] The Word of the Lord ought to be received with complete assent[160] and every word and deed should be ratified [pistousthai] by scripture:[161] although other sorts of knowledge exist (such as medicine), their origin lies also in God.[162] Scripture also restrains human judgement and what it does not condemn, neither should we.[163] Although his silence in the ascetical works regarding secular learning could be taken as evidence of disdain, the hint that all real truth comes from God, is bestowed by the Holy Spirit[164] and is thus not remote from spiritual gifts, suggests otherwise.

Evagrius shows little of even the mild ambivalence evident in the writings of the Desert Fathers, or perhaps discernible in Basil's reticence. Knowledge is one of humankind's great possessions, the 'fellow-worker' [synergos] with prayer,[165] and prayer is the prelude to knowledge.[166] It makes sense, therefore, to pray to be delivered from ignorance, as one must first pray to be purified from the passions.[167] The connection between prayer and knowledge is particularly close for Evagrius because much of what he understands by the latter is contemplative. The kingdom of God is knowledge of the Trinity,[168] and 'theology' names the goal of contemplative knowledge, as the goal of the ascetic life is charity.[169] Progress in contemplation brings the diminution of ignorance,[170] but also has immediate practical effects: having attained contemplative knowledge

---

licit. By Benedict's time, it was assumed that monks are not illiterate; only a few are judged unable to read and to study (14). If we accept Leclerq's claims regarding the linkage of later generations of monks to the earlier (90), there would be important implications for the earliest monastics' attitudes towards learning and books.

[155] Epiphanius 10 and 11/PG 65.165.　[156] LA 20.4.　[157] LA 16.1.　[158] LA 3.7.
[159] CFth FC 62/PG 31.684.　[160] Mors Rule 12, FC 89/PG 31.721.
[161] Mors Rule 26, FC 106/PG 31.744.　[162] LR Q 55, FC 331/PG31.1044.
[163] Mors Rule 54, FC 134/PG 31.780.　[164] CFth FC 64–65/PG 31.685.　[165] Pray 86.
[166] Pray 85. His enthusiasm for learning is remarked by several commentators. Stewart describes the oeuvre as a 'research theology', intended to engage philosophically-educated readers (2001, 175), and Dempf remarks upon his use of Aristotelian logic and epistemology (1970, 301).
[167] Pray 37.　[168] Prak 3.　[169] Prak 84.　[170] Prak 87.

one no longer gives in to vanity.[171] More fundamentally, Evagrius distinguishes between knowledge from external sources, known by the mediation of words and concepts (the opposite of which is error), and knowledge given directly by grace, which needs no intermediaries (the opposite of which are anger and irascibility).[172] Only this knowledge enables us to unite with holy powers,[173] and the soul approaching it ceases to sense its irrational part, for knowledge carries the soul away, separating it from sensible things.[174] This knowledge is not, however, meant for the personal comfort of the adept: the gnostic should not be remote from others or difficult to approach, for such aloofness indicates one does not know 'the reasons of beings' [tous logous tōn ginomenōn] and who does not desire the salvation of all.[175] Here we see the characteristic link in monastic writings between knowledge and love of neighbour, the refusal to separate theology and contemplation from ascesis and morality.

Cassian makes a similar connection, though his attitude towards scripture reveals some unexpected ambivalences, surprisingly, given that he stands as the immediate predecessor of the Benedictine tradition with its emphasis on lectio divina. On the one hand, he commends continual reading of and meditating upon the Bible,[176] yet when he wishes to reflect on the nature of the soul, he concedes he must set scripture aside,[177] as he does when, with apparent approval, he cites Theodore's response to someone claiming scriptural authority for the notion that God created evil: at times scripture descends into catachresis, calling mere misfortunes 'evils', he warns.[178] Parts of the Bible can moreover only be made into spiritually nourishing food through allegorical interpretation.[179] Cassian's worry about the dangers inherent in allowing people to reason for themselves from the plain word of the Bible emerges from an anecdote he relates of a bishop fulminating against the heresy of anthropomorphism: Cassian reports that the desert monks thought he should be abominated [decerneret detestandum], since his view seemed contrary to scripture.[180]

---

[171] Prak 32.
[172] Gnos 4. The opposition of error to words and concepts [logous] is an interpolation found in a thirteenth-century manuscript, to which the SC editor gives little credence, though the suggestion seems more obvious than this opposition of graced knowledge and anger, whose authenticity is not in doubt.
[173] Prak 56.   [174] Prak 66.   [175] Gnos 22.   [176] Cnfr 1.2.   [177] Cnfr 1.14.
[178] Cnfr 6.6. Pace Burton-Christie (1993), who reads Cassian as viewing secular learning as an impediment to absorbing scripture (58).
[179] Cnfr 8.3.4.
[180] Cnfr 10.2. Cassian tends to portray the desert monks as theological simpletons, but as O. Chadwick notes: 'Greeks perhaps exaggerated the simplicity of anyone who could not write or speak Greek' (1968, 24).

Such considerations no doubt lie behind his commending both the authority of scripture and the tradition of the Fathers,[181] as a guard against perverse [prava] interpretations attaching themselves to the pure gold of the Bible.[182] Correct understanding of the Bible thus entails the humility to allow one's own judgement to be corrected by the authority of the community and of tradition. Whatever benefit one obtains from reading can moreover be cancelled out by the loss one incurs through contempt for a brother[183] and the vice of vanity seeks out weak spots, attacking the soul from every side and inflicting wounds in such vital activities as speech, prayer, reading and knowledge.[184]

These caveats by no means ultimately devalue reading and meditating upon scripture, in Cassian's view. In the first place, adhering to diligence in reading accompanies advancement in practical ethics,[185] and the monk accordingly never omits meditation on scripture, whether during the daily prayers or while doing menial work.[186] This meditation is a form of chewing [ruminatione] on heavenly food,[187] an image which reverberated down the Christian centuries as a metaphor for reflective reading of scripture. As fasting and vigils refine the mind, so do reading and compunction.[188] Reading and the hard work of scrubbing away sin stand in a reciprocal relation: despite his worries about the possibilities of misunderstanding scripture, Cassian cites Theodora's advice against spending time reading commentaries if one wishes to attain to a knowledge of scripture; much better, in his opinion, to work on cleansing oneself of carnal vice, for in that way, the eyes of the heart will naturally contemplate the mysteries of scripture.[189] True knowledge is not increased by acquiring more of its second-hand variety derived from what others have discovered, but from the enlightenment that comes of moral and spiritual purification.

For the monastics, then, 'knowledge' comes in many forms, of which not all are equal. For Abba Poemen, self-knowledge [heautōi prosechein] is one of the guides of the soul,[190] while for Antony the most luminous knowledge of God [theognōsia] is that which shines forth from the life and teaching of Christ.[191] Basil shares this high view of knowledge of God, a knowledge that surpasses all other,[192] but depreciates the value of knowledge available in this life, scanty and indistinct as it is.[193] Cassian's view, in contrast, seems wholly positive. Although he distinguishes

---

[181] Cnfr 3.6.   [182] Cnfr 1.20.   [183] Cnfr 1.7.   [184] Inst 11.3.   [185] Cnfr 14.9.
[186] Inst 3.2.   [187] Cnfr 11.15.   [188] Inst 5.14.1.   [189] Inst 5.34.   [190] Poemen 35/PG 65.331.
[191] LA 79.4–5.   [192] Judg FC49/PG 31.669.   [193] CFth FC 61/PG 31.631.

between true knowledge and worldly learning, the latter being stained with vice, the former able to flourish even in virtual illiterates,[194] he links spiritual knowledge to virtue (it cannot exist independently from chastity, for example).[195] It is impossible for the impure mind to receive spiritual knowledge and true knowledge accordingly belongs solely to those who worship truly.[196] Not only one's conduct, but one's motives must be pure, for if one reads simply to attract the admiration of others, one does not merit true knowledge, which comes as a gift.[197] The worthy receptacle of knowledge is therefore the ark one prepares in one's own heart by cleansing it from vice and worldly preoccupations.[198] Not all knowledge need be acquired with labour, however, for Cassian holds that complete knowledge of the law has been poured into every human being as a natural endowment; the law was only promulgated because it was not observed.[199] Here Cassian parts company with the school of thought which holds that to know the good is to do it, although he does not go so far as to say we fail to do the good because a damaged will leaves us incapable of doing so.

A few excel in knowledge, and of these Cassian especially extols the desert monks: Paphnutius, whose knowledge was resplendent and covered all virtues,[200] as well as ability to see the future (though this foreknowledge was a gift of grace[201]); Daniel, who is lauded for his grasp of Christian philosophy;[202] and Theodore for knowledge generally, linked with holiness; his knowledge, though it includes familiarity with scripture, was not obtained by zealous reading or worldly learning but solely by purity of heart.[203] The fact that Cassian's exemplars are all desert monks in itself signals a conception of knowledge which joins the intellectual and the spiritual. Fortunately, knowledge does not lie beyond reach of those on the lower levels of sanctity; lesser lights have to work, but the vigilant monk, by devoting little time to leisure and much to meditation, progresses swiftly and enjoys as the fruit of both his manual labour and his meditation a 'luminous' knowledge.[204] Characteristically, Cassian balances this paean to toil with a later attribution of enlightenment and knowledge to direct divine instruction.[205] The moral delicacy of the matter lies in the conundrum that while one must be virtuous to

---

[194] Cnfr 14.16.   [195] Inst 6.18.
[196] Cnfr 14.10 and 14.16. Cp. Stewart's claim that for the Alexandrian tradition (Clement, Origen and their heirs, Cassian and Evagrius), contemplation is closely tied to *gnōsis* (1998, 48). This knowledge is not, however, for Cassian at least esoteric, but 'the ability to see more deeply into the Biblical material that constitutes a monk's daily prayer' (51).
[197] Cnfr 14.10.   [198] Cnfr 14.10.   [199] Cnfr 8.23.   [200] Cnfr 3.1.   [201] Cnfr 4.1.   [202] Cnfr 4.1.
[203] Inst 5.33.   [204] Inst 2.14.   [205] Inst 12.17.6.

know rightly, great knowledge brings with it the possibility of temptation to vanity, although spiritual prowess (such as excellence in observing vigils) bears the same risk, so intellectual attainments are by no means singled out as spiritually hazardous.[206]

Cassian nevertheless seems to approve those who dedicate themselves to the pursuit of knowledge,[207] and if he does so, despite his misgivings, it may be because he strongly connects knowledge to God. God's knowledge, vast as it is, prompts human wonder[208] and knowledge of God elicits similar marvelling. The riches of salvation are identified with the wisdom and knowledge of God,[209] and as one ascends to the manifold knowledge of God [multiformem scientiam dei],[210] and finally to the vision of God, one attains to a state in which one feeds on nothing more than the beauty and knowledge of God.[211] It is perhaps Evagrius who best sums up the monastics' holistic attitude towards knowledge. In his treatise addressed to monks he writes: 'Faith is the beginning of love; its end is the knowledge of God.'[212]

The same thread, stretching from the quotidian morality of how one treats one's neighbour to the highest reaches of the mind's encounter with God, runs through the Evagrian writings. Evagrius' conception of knowledge (generally gnōsis) is one of the most subtle and broadly conceived in the monastic literature. Here we see a psychologically astute man's grasp of the mind's internal conflict, for he warns that memories (specifically the memory of injury) can chase away this knowledge.[213] Other emotional or spiritual afflictions also interfere with knowledge, such as irascibility [thumos].[214] External circumstances, like wealth, can equally inhibit the acquisition of knowledge, though God can overcome such obstacles.[215] Like Cassian, Evagrius equates knowledge and spiritual development, so ignorance is allied to evil and knowledge with holiness.[216] The difference between true and false knowledge even appears to bear salvific significance: true knowledge is the feast of God [heortē theou], while false knowledge ends shamefully [aischrōs].[217] When he maintains, therefore, that knowledge is the ornament of the heart [kosmos kardias],[218] he does not designate it as a superfluous frippery, but an essential element of the beauty of holiness.

For all the dangers presented by knowledge, lacking it seems worse than the alternative: knowledge keeps guard over a monk's condition of

---

[206] Inst 11.6. [207] Cnfr 1.10. [208] Cnfr 1.15. [209] Cnfr 11.13, quoting Is 33.6. [210] Cnfr 10.11.
[211] Cnfr 1.8. [212] Monc 3. [213] Monc 13. [214] Monc 35. [215] Monc 17. [216] Monc 24.
[217] Monc 43. [218] Monc 27.

life [politeia] and is associated with gentleness,[219] while descending into ignorance leads to falling in with thieves.[220] Evagrius links knowledge to the highest on his scale of virtues, apatheia and love, apatheia preceding love and love preceding knowledge.[221] Likewise, although he does not equate the two, gnōsis and wisdom [sophia] are closely associated,[222] as are gnōsis and contemplation.[223] However, knowledge is not a static possession for Evagrius, nor does it recede simply as the result of forgetfulness. Vile speech wards off knowledge,[224] so one must watch what one expresses outwardly, but keeping watch over one's heart is of equal importance.[225]

This concern to guard the heart finds frequent expression in the monks' attitudes towards thoughts. The monks, though no less preoccupied with intellectual activity than other writers, manifest this interest in areas consistent with their particular preoccupations, not surprisingly, reaching a focusing on the role of thought in prayer. The fact that many of these thoughts turn out to be distractions does not indicate a negative attitude towards the activity of the mind so much as a pragmatic recognition of its importance. Thus Theodora commends perpetual prayer, but points out that as soon as one resolves to practise it and live at peace, along come various disturbances, including evil thoughts [logismois] – since these ills afflict both mind [psychē] and body, though, there is no sense that the mind itself constitutes any special sort of hindrance.[226]

If the monastics are worried by this issue, it is because of its potential dire consequence: evil thoughts cause separation from God.[227] Here is the reason for the stress on 'manifestation of thoughts' to the elders, a form of confession and spiritual direction: the Enemy rejoices over those who buck at the idea of doing this,[228] presumably because of the likelihood that those who will not face the reality of their thoughts in the presence of an elder will not confront them on their own, either. The most seriously committed can be trusted to examine their consciences rigorously, hence Eulogius' being instructed by one of the elders in the discernment of thoughts and self-control.[229] The *Life of Antony* manifests a similar concern: evil thoughts are held to be stumbling blocks [skandala][230] and

---

[219] Monc 99.   [220] Monc 63.   [221] Monc 67.   [222] Monc 68.   [223] Monc 110.
[224] Monc 71.   [225] Monc 94.   [226] Theodora 3/PG 65.301.
[227] Olympius 1/PG 65.313.   [228] Poemen 101/PG 65.345.
[229] Eulogius 1/PG 65.172. Eulogius is literally to control what is human [panta ta anthrōpina] in himself.
[230] LA 23.1.

so Antony advises recording both acts and every movement of the soul [kinēmata tēs psychēs] as if reporting them to someone else, as a means of keeping impure thoughts at bay.[231] Antony dispensed more than exhortation, it seems, for in addition to advice, he provided those who came to see him with a calming presence that actually enabled them to control their thoughts.[232]

These themes are elaborated at much greater length in the spiritual manuals that are the writings of Evagrius and Cassian. Basil's Long Rules, in contrast, is terse: one cannot gain proficiency in prayer when plagued by distractions,[233] but even outside the set times of prayer, one should strive to avoid losing the thought of God.[234] Evagrius goes into much greater detail. His method of dealing with distracting thoughts is the classic one: just ignore them.[235] More specifically, one must free oneself from every thought coloured by passion; this leads, not simply to apatheia, but the vision of the One beyond thought [ennoia] and perception, and the person who maintains such control is accordingly compared to Moses removing his shoes at the burning bush.[236] Control of disturbing thoughts constitutes a preliminary step, a clearing away of obstruction, but Evagrius sees the problem as more complex than a momentary loss of focus. With great psychological acumen, he describes how the quiet of prayer opens a space for smouldering anger to burst into flame; a picture of the offending person flashes before one's eyes and, in addition to the angry thoughts, come bodily weakness, pallor and the illusion that one is under some sort of animal attack (as indeed, in a sense, an angry person is).[237] Less spectacularly, angry thoughts often take the form of an internal quarrel with the object of one's anger[238] and because of this connection between thoughts and emotions, Evagrius maintains that thoughts agitate the heart of those who are not careful.[239] If some prompters of thought (like emotions) arise from within, some are at least nominally external, such as the demons. These roam in the realm of thought, enabling one to diagnose which tempters have arrived according to the thoughts passing through the mind. Accurate diagnosis permits one to deal with them effectively, before they disturb one's mental equilibrium.[240] Evagrius cannot be taken as advocating a flight into some intellectually denuded realm of the spiritual; there is no such realm, on his terms, for the spiritual includes within it intellectual activity.

---

[231] LA 55.9. [232] LA 87.6. [233] LR Q 6, FC246/PG 31.925.. [234] LR Q5 FC243/PG 31.921.
[235] Pray 9. [236] Pray 4. [237] Prak 11. [238] Prak 23. [239] Monc 37. [240] Prak 43.

This overarching framework must be borne in mind when interpreting some of his sterner advice, for in addition to warning against passionate thoughts, he sometimes seems to rule out thought altogether. He advises against immediately turning to prayer when tempted, on the grounds that one cannot pray purely when under the influence of 'various thoughts' [tina rhēmata].[241] Since these arise in the context of temptations, however, they must arise from the passions, as do all the thoughts occasioning negative comments in his work. Sadness, for example, comes from thoughts springing from memories of one's parents and former home, tempting the monk to rue or even abandon his vocation.[242] The demons understand the power of insidious thoughts and hope that they will ultimately keep us from praying, so 'snatching' away our intelligence [ho daimōn ho synarpazōn ton noun].[243] Since dispelling bad thoughts is a complex matter, however, Evagrius warns against the too-ready assumption that one has freed oneself from evil thoughts.[244] While thoughts, like passions, seem to arise suddenly, in fact the context of one's life and character has a great deal to do with one's success in managing thoughts, and even whether or not they arise in the first place. The soul of good habits, such as charity and continence, does not experience such disturbances, whether related to the senses or the passions.[245]

Although Evagrius' position is complex, it leans in a slightly more positive direction than Cassian's; nevertheless, Cassian's view of thoughts retains the emphasis on their centrality in Christian life. The problems remain: the mind cannot avoid being troubled by thoughts, although one always has the option of accepting or rejecting them.[246] The pestering by unwanted thoughts is a feature of this life, however, and one which may be kept in check by meditation on scripture and the beatitude which awaits us in the next life.[247] Cassian's analysis of the kind of thoughts which afflict is less nuanced than Evagrius': earthly ones seem to afflict even holy people,[248] although the latter do not allow entry to carnal thoughts, which separate the mind from true light.[249]

A great deal of the difficulty with thoughts lies not in what they evoke in the mind's eye, or in any inherently bad content, but their sheer abundance[250] and plasticity: they fluctuate and rove about unstably[251] and hence one must maintain a continual watch for the heads of the serpent, which are their beginning.[252] Even though thoughts have been the downfall of some (as for Lucifer, the one who foolishly believed in his

---

[241] Prak 42. [242] Prak 10. [243] Prak 46. [244] Pray 133. [245] Prak 38. [246] Cnfr 1.17.
[247] Cnfr 1.18. [248] Cnfr 23.10. [249] Cnfr 23.8. [250] Cnfr 10.11. [251] Inst 2.14. [252] Inst 4.37.

own self-sufficiency[253]), stability of thought can be attained through the visitation of the Spirit,[254] and continuous meditation and reading means that we cannot become captive to harmful thoughts.[255] Some thoughts moreover constitute more than passing temptation, slipping into the realm of outright trespass and even holy people cannot help but fall into such sins of thought.[256] The ease with which distraction turns to transgression indicates why Cassian tirelessly counsels self-examination and discretion: the content of our minds is subject to divine scrutiny.[257] This process of self-examination is not necessarily grim or terrifying, however, for its criterion is love: all thoughts are to be adapted or rejected in accordance with it and our mind must revolve around the love of God alone, the still centre.[258]

Consistent self-scrutiny, watch over the heart and fixing the mind's eye on God require discipline, and discipline constitutes what Ignatius Loyola would later term the remote preparation for prayer, hence the exhortations to control the tongue and the stomach.[259] Asceticism by itself is accorded little value, however; as Antony also notes, some have afflicted their body, but lack discernment.[260] Similarly, Agathon likens the human person to a tree, with asceticism as the leaves, and vigilance, the fruit.[261] However desirable, indeed necessary, bodily discipline may be, it is subordinated to the mind, to mental acts of judgement, but also to obedience. It would seem that the characteristic monastic emphasis on obedience constitutes a vote against reason, the abandonment of one's own better judgement in favour of blind subservience to a superior or a Rule. Overtones of such an approach may be detected here and there in Cassian's writings, where he advocates unquestioning obedience [indubitatem fidem et indiscussam oboedientiam] to institutes and rules[262] and links one's degree of zealousness in pursuit of obedience to purity of heart, spiritual progress and knowledge of divine things [divinarum rerum scientiam].[263] Likewise, Basil extols obedience above continence [engkrateian][264] and Syncletica values it above asceticism, at least for those living the monastic life.[265] The deeper purpose of obedience, however, seems to be twofold: first, to counteract pride, the chief enemy of virtue and a particular danger for those engaged in the ascetical

---

[253] Inst 12.4.3. [254] Cnfr 10.10. [255] Cnfr 14.10.
[256] Cnfr 11.9. [257] Cnfr 7.13. [258] Cnfr 24.6. [259] Antony 6/PG 65.78.
[260] Antony 8/PG 65.77. [261] Agathon 8/PG 65.112.
[262] Inst 1.2.4. The immediate context concerns monastic dress, but the principle is couched broadly.
[263] Inst 1.11.1. [264] AD 2.FC219/PG 31.884. [265] Syncletica 16/PG 65.426–28.

life, and second, to ensure that the inexperienced do not become the victims of their own untutored judgement.

Despite the expected stress on obedience to rules and superiors, the monastic writers also repeatedly insist on the importance of discernment, as we have already seen. This emphasis is not surprising, given that the spiritual life could never reduce simply to formal or general principles; these would always need to be applied to particular cases, a process requiring deliberation and judgement. No matter what role the monks might be inclined to accord the mind in the life of prayer, therefore, they would necessarily also need to allow for it in the direction of souls and this consideration in itself would keep the monastic writings from the most blatant forms of anti-intellectualism.

Discernment does not become the province of a wise few charged with spiritual direction or monastic oversight, moreover; as Poemen notes, vigilance [to phulassein], self-knowledge [heautōi prosechein] and discernment [diakrisis] are the guides of the soul.[266] The implication here is that the monk directs himself, hardly surprising given the largely eremitic character of the desert sketes. The *Apophthegmata* abound in tales of consultation and its fruit in sage or pointed counsel, but the frequent stress on staying within one's cell must have meant that the monk spent much time alone, at the mercy of the welter of thoughts, fancies and emotions that bubble up during prolonged silence. Still, given that Poemen himself was much admired for his discernment,[267] it is clear that direction of others was also practised. In Athanasius' account of Antony's life, the father of monasticism seems more sought out by philosophers who wish to trap him in disputation than by monks needing guidance (the *Apophthegmata* gives a different impression), but discernment remains important: the visitations to the solitary by various apparitions are often ambiguous, necessitating discrimination between the presence of good and evil; this is possible, in Antony's view, when God so grants it;[268] God evidently did grant it to Antony himself, for he is renowned for his gift in discerning spirits.[269]

Cassian concurs that discretion is a gift of grace,[270] which is why he can contrast the discretion by which the Spirit guides the elders with their own 'rigidly obstinate mind';[271] it is not that discretion is not also seated in the mind but that the latter perceives and operates quite differently depending on whether it judges with the aid of grace. Hence also,

---

[266] Poemen 35/PG 35.332. [267] Poemen 170/PG 65.364. [268] LA 35.4. [269] LA 44.1.
[270] Cnfr 2.1. [271] Cnfr 17.23.

discretion is described as a light, albeit one that vanishes in the face of anger.[272] The fact that discretion comes as a divine gift does not mean human effort plays no role in its acquisition, for it comes with humility.[273] Here Cassian sets up an inferential closed circle, for discretion is itself the root of all virtues,[274] although most particularly the intellectual ones of wisdom, knowledge [intellectus] and understanding [sensus], without which no spiritual growth seems possible.[275] Although Cassian may well be simply contradicting himself at this point, an equally plausible interpretation is that he is underlining the holistic character of the spiritual life, for if discretion should examine all thoughts,[276] exercising an intellectual governing role, it can equally suffer utter defeat by the body; a full stomach breeds lasciviousness and weighs down the mind so that not even discretion can govern it. It is impossible to be advanced in one virtue while lacking the others, and although Cassian does not make the point, it would follow from the simple nature of divine holiness, which ours, if authentic, must resemble.

A significant element of holiness is negative: restraint or extirpation of the passions; yet although one might expect the monastic writers above all to be concerned with the control of the passions, ascetics as they all were to some degree, the interest displayed in these works is not noticeably greater or more intense than in other patristic writings.[277] The Desert Fathers hold the expected views, at times associating passions with the flesh,[278] yet the body's temptations and besetting sins prove to be of surprisingly little interest to them. Pityrion, for instance, is content to associate the passions with the demons,[279] yet does not claim the passions arise at the demons' instigation, but rather that demons can only be driven out if the passions are first subdued. The passions can be controlled by the saints, though not, it appears, altogether eradicated,[280] and it is a sign of a spiritual master that one can conquer them, as when

---

[272] Inst 8.22.   [273] Cnfr 2.16.   [274] Cnfr 2.9.   [275] Cnfr 2.4.   [276] Cnfr 1.20.
[277] Acknowledging this point has important consequences. Chadwick claims that the idea 'cut away the passions and grace will flow' is found either explicitly or implicitly in all the sources of the Egyptian desert (1968, 110; he cites as evidence the work of W. Völker and A. Hoch). Chadwick subsequently modifies the claim, without quite explaining whether he finally intended to stand by the views of the latter scholars, as he seems to in the passage cited, or to accept the view only in a radically altered form. I see little evidence for the claim in its stronger form: the writings of the Desert Fathers are simply not concerned with the issue of the relation of freedom and grace; the view that failure to stipulate the priority of grace represents a prioritising of human will simply supplies a default answer to a question that is not being debated in these texts.
[278] John the Dwarf 3/PG 65.205. He speaks of the passions of the flesh [ta pathē tēs sarkos], which probably implies there are other sorts of passions as well.
[279] Pityrion 1/PG 65.376.   [280] Abraham 1/PG 65.132.

Joseph exults, 'I am king today, for I reign over the passions'[281] – notably, he makes no claims about tomorrow. There is no middle ground, it appears: apatheia means enslaving the flesh,[282] and allowing the passions free rein means being enslaved to them. When the passions stop pouring out of one altogether, it is a sign one has 'conceived' the Holy Spirit.[283] The problem of the passions, then, is spiritual rather than corporeal, which is why Poemen advises that one should kill them and not the body[284] and why both Agathon and Hyperechius stress above all control of the tongue.[285]

Basil perhaps comes closer to the heart of the problem when he speaks, not of conquest or control, but of quietening the passions; the object of the effort is not to expel one form of turmoil with another, but to lull what is unruly into a seemly docility. When one attains to this impassibility, one resembles the Creator.[286] Cassian, in contrast, not only stands closer to the spirit of the Desert Fathers; he outdoes them, speaking of extinguishing the passions and subjugating thought to the rule of reason.[287] The mind's domination is crucial, in his view: one cannot expel the passion of sadness, for example, until the mind is occupied constantly with meditation.[288] Conversely, the passions squeeze out knowledge if allowed to flourish: no one in whom they dominate (and especially, who gives rein to fornication) will possess spiritual knowledge.[289]

Of all the monastic writers surveyed here, Evagrius worries the most about the passions, and particularly about anger. Anger clouds the eye of the mind [ton noeron ophthalmon][290] and above all seizes the mind at prayer, flashing the object of one's ire before the imagination's eye. The effects of this imaginary intrusion Evagrius describes in terms both dramatic and psychologically astute, as we have noted: the body becomes weak and pale and one feels as if under animal attack.[291] Like other writers, Evagrius speaks of the mind's being agitated [ektarassonta] by passion,[292] not so much fatally infected as momentarily unable to see, yet this veiling forbids entry to contemplative knowledge. When he maintains, therefore, that the passions are set in motion by the senses,[293] it would seem that he must take 'senses' in the broad Origenistic sense, not only the physical senses, but what can be perceived by the mind functioning as a sensory organ via imagination and memory. The passions can therefore be either the intellect's slaves or its master, but the point at which they threaten to

---

[281] Joseph of Panephysis 10/PG 65.251.   [282] Monc 6.   [283] Longinus 5/PG 65.257.
[284] Poemen 184/PG 65.368.   [285] Agathon 1/PG 65.109; Hyperechius 3/PG 65.429.
[286] AD1, FC 207/PG 31.872.   [287] Cnfr 7.5.   [288] Inst 9.13.   [289] Cnfr 14.16.
[290] Pray 27.   [291] Prak 11.   [292] Prak 99.   [293] Prak 38.

engulf us differs in the various stages of our life: for the young, it is the belly that breeds temptation; for the old, the danger lies rather in the heart.[294] Pride remains the most persistent and pernicious lure, for it leads the monk to deny God's assistance.[295] Fortunately, the force of passion diminishes in one making progress in the ascetical life.[296]

Evagrius nevertheless does not advocate the total extirpation of the passions. We fight against demons by turning their own weapons against them: anger enables us to rebuff them.[297] Furthermore the parts of our nature which give rise to the passions can be used for good: the concupiscible part of the soul desires virtue, while the irascible part fights to obtain it.[298] Thus, while the spoken word, along with bodily movement, may be a sign of passion,[299] one can rise up against afflictions [ton thlibonta] by denouncing them angrily;[300] the psyche will 'flare up' against passionate thoughts (as well as against the demons' evil smell[301]).

Because of this two-edged quality of the passions, as Evagrius sees them, discernment is vital, so it is no surprise that he links apatheia to the intellectual virtue of prudence [phronēsis].[302] Prayer itself however he defines as habitual apatheia,[303] although a chicken-and-egg relation between the two seems to obtain, since one must pray to be purified of the passions.[304] What is fatal is not renouncing them; this Evagrius equates with resisting virtue and truth,[305] while freeing oneself of the passions seems virtually identical with holiness: Moses' removing his shoes at the burning bush symbolises the act of freeing oneself of the passions; only then can one see the One who is beyond thought and perception.[306]

Perfect governance of the passions by the mind is of course apatheia, the human equivalent of divine impassibility. That the monastic writings should stress the need for dispassion is not surprising; if anything, their

---

[294] Gnos 31. What I render as 'heart' [thumos] could also mean irascibility, the translation preferred in the SC edition.
[295] Prak 14.   [296] Prak 87.   [297] Prak 24.
[298] Prak 86. Bouyer claims that for Evagrius apatheia is simply the domination of the passions in us that are opposed to charity (1960, 386).
[299] Prak 47.
[300] Prak 42. *Thlibonta* is ambiguous and could denote demons (who are the subject of the surrounding chapters), but since Evagrius does not in this chapter specify them as such, and given the close association he habitually makes between the demons and passions, the word may just as well denote passions.
[301] Prak 39.   [302] Monc 105.   [303] Pray 52. Katastasis esti proseuchēs hexis apathēs.   [304] Pray 37.
[305] Pray 141.
[306] Pray 4. Because of the complexity of his view of the passions, allowing for them, as well as commending apatheia, I would question O'Driscoll's contention that for Evagrius, a monk must be passionless to enter into knowledge (1990, 337).

interest in the theme is comparatively mild, and appeal to it occurs overwhelmingly in the Evagrian writings. A saying from the *Apophthegmata* summarises the thrust of the rest of the work. Evagrius (attributing the advice to an unnamed other), advises moderation in eating; this moderation will lead to the threshold of apatheia – if it is joined to charity.[307] Two points stand out here: first, self control only opens the way to dispassion, rather than being equated with it; second, and more importantly, one cannot reach even that threshold through restraint alone, for the negative movement of reining in appetite must be coupled with the positive outflowing of love. Here again, the holistic nature of the truly spiritual life emerges, as it does from the claim in the introductory letter to the *Praktikos* that the virtues give birth to apatheia. Apatheia seems both precondition and fruit, but most importantly, Evagrius continues, it has a child called agapē. The latter, in turn, keeps the door to knowledge of created things [gnōseōs physikēs] and then, ultimately, theology and beatitude.[308] Here, in miniature, is almost a whole theology: consummation expressed as knowledge of God, based on the contemplation of this life which is theology, grounded in ordinary knowledge of the world available to us as rational beings endowed with senses, but all of these made possible because of bodily and spiritual discipline and charity. The pattern is important enough to be elaborated again in the same work.[309] What is missing from the pattern is grace, but Evagrius had previously stipulated this: we are brought to apatheia by the mercy of Christ.[310] As for Cassian, however, grace is not portrayed as replacing the effort of self-discipline; both are needed, but discipline is for Evagrius very much a matter of mind, and not simply will. The dispassionate soul is the one not only unperturbed by outward events, but unmovable even in the face of memory,[311] and in the perfect ascetic passion is absent not only from daytime thoughts but from dreams as well,[312] an indication that Evagrius is not advocating anything so straightforward as repression. The attainment of apatheia is thus a delicate business, yet a crucial one, for Evagrius identifies it with the very kingdom of heaven.[313]

---

[307] Evagrius 6/PG 65.176. The text actually says that dryness [xērotera] and irregular way of life [anōmalos diaita] will do the trick, but the note on the text in PG indicates other mss. insert *kai mē*, negating 'irregular'.
[308] Prak prol [8].   [309] Prak 78–81.   [310] Prak 33.   [311] Prak 67.   [312] Prak 56.
[313] Prak 2. The relational dimension of Evagrius' theology is well expressed by Bunge: 'Gnosis ist ein Vergang zwischen Personen, dessen Initiative im letzten bei Gott liegt' (1988, 59). Bouyer claims that Cassian's prudence kept him from mentioning apatheia, because it had been compromised by the anti-Origenists and Pelagians (1960, 508), a claim that seems to be borne out by the absence of citations of Cassian (as opposed to Evagrius) in relation to the issue in Stewart (1998).

While Evagrius' determined linkage of apatheia and love is not matched by other writers, the monastic corpus insists on the centrality of love in the spiritual life.[314] According to Athanasius, Antony unfailingly taught the same message: to have faith in the Lord and to love him; these he places first in his list of counsels, even before the exhortations to self-discipline.[315] For Basil, love is the end of all monastic striving, whether in virtue or in prayer: one loves by keeping God constantly before the mind, never losing the thought of him [ennoia].[316] Love, for Basil, is the content of monastic life, a point which Evagrius makes in a slightly different way: on the one hand, charity restrains vices (such as anger[317]), yet is itself the fruit of apatheia. Love is thus presupposed to virtue, yet charity is equally the goal of the ascetic life.[318] Cassian, in contrast, tends overwhelmingly to portray love as the pinnacle of Christian life. Nothing exceeds the sublimity of love, he maintains,[319] and early on in the *Conferences*, he exhorts his readers to ascend to the perfection of love by the disciplines of fasting, reading, solitude and control of the passions;[320] even fasting only becomes acceptable to God when crowned with the fruits of charity.[321] Love and knowledge are closely related in Cassian's thought, as they are for Augustine, albeit in a slightly different manner. Worldly knowledge is stained by fleshly vice and so differs fundamentally from spiritual knowledge;[322] accordingly true knowledge of scripture only comes through humility and love.[323] Love for Cassian pertains to both the practical and the theoretical/contemplative: the Apostle calls practical knowledge 'love' yet the whole of beatitude also consists in love.[324]

If love resides in the soul of one whose heart is pure, it follows that constancy of the soul, its rootedness in God, is the key to the Christian life. Prayer for the monastics is the name of this state of mind, heart and soul, and not exclusively of particular mental or vocal acts. While it is scarcely surprising to find monastic writers concerned with prayer, the writings of the earliest Christian cenobites and solitaries are marked by the connection they make between prayer and both salvation and the intellect. The sayings of Antony contained in the *Apophthegmata* connect

---

[314] Cf. Burton-Christie (1993): 'Love was at the heart of the desert fathers' world' (261). He devotes a whole chapter (9) to the significance of the love commandment in the *Apophthegmata*.
[315] LA 55.2.   [316] LR FC 243/PG 31.921.   [317] Prak 38.   [318] Prak 84.
[319] Cnfr 11.12.   [320] Cnfr 1.7.
[321] Inst 5.35. Cp. Stewart's contention that for Cassian the equation of purity of heart with love is part of a deliberate strategy to forestall misunderstanding about the place of ascetical discipline (1998, 44). Purity of heart, furthermore, is not an end in itself; rather, its point is to see God, an endeavour that begins in contemplation (47).
[322] Cnfr 14.16.   [323] Cnfr 14.10.   [324] Cnfr 15.2.

prayer to salvation, either identifying the two outright[325] or joining prayer with work as the dual way to being saved.[326] In light of later Western theological developments, this connection risks being interpreted solely through the lens of the Pelagian controversy; the issue then becomes whether the linkage of prayer and salvation does not make the latter into a human work, attainable by human effort without grace. Simply to say we are saved by prayer does not in itself imply we save ourselves, however, for prayer can never on the Christian account be solipsistic. Framing the matter as one of the relation of human works to salvation is moreover to import into it a question that the monks do not pose. The issue is not whether prayer enables us to save ourselves without grace; the monks arguably do not stipulate the need for grace because they assume it. They equally assume that God is not coercive, however, and that grace is therefore resistible. Our efforts do not procure God's work within us, but they can prevent its being blocked. The concern to identify the agent of salvation, meanwhile, can obscure the more remarkable point in the link between prayer and salvation: that it implies that the salvific force acts upon the mind, and not just on the unruly will.

Arsenius' approach illustrates this principle. For him, prayer, along with flight and silence, is the root of sinlessness (or so a voice tells him) and sinlessness would presumably lead to salvation.[327] If we were to doubt that prayer in itself could lead to sinlessness, we would have to question even more flight and silence; the only way these could lead to salvation is by creating a space for divine power to work; just so prayer. Other desert maxims seem to belie this pattern, as when Theodore of Enaton maintains that carelessness in psalmody results in exclusion from salvation.[328] The root problem here may be grasped by juxtaposing this warning with one of Evagrius': praying without distraction is good, attentiveness in chanting [psallein] is even better.[329] In other words, if what one means by prayer is merely rattling off words, then prayer will do the rattler little good. It is when the mind remains fixed on God that, through it, the whole person may be renewed and lifted up. The preoccupation with distraction seems natural enough on the part of those whose every waking moment, literally, was devoted to prayer. This never-ending struggle against the contemplative's great adversary may explain Agathon's

---

[325] Antony 19/PG 65.81. He begins by suggesting to those who ask how to be saved that they follow various gospel commands, such as turning the other cheek. It is when the brethren say they are unable to follow them that Antony says 'what you need is prayers'.

[326] Antony 1/PG 65.76

[327] Arsenius 2/PG 65.88.   [328] Theodore of Enaton 3/PG 65.198.   [329] Evagrius 3/PG 65.173.

characterisation of prayer as 'struggle [agōnos] to the last breath'.³³⁰ If distraction gnaws away the fabric of true prayer, however, prayer combined with fasting militates against evil thoughts.³³¹ Why fasting? Because traditionally, it reminds one of one's frailty and dependence on God, so throwing one back upon the object of one's attention in prayer.

The battle with distraction thus constitutes a form of the mind's engagement with itself, a deliberate confronting of one's internal conflicts, yet it is not a purely mental exercise and could not be, given the fact of human embodiment, of which the monastics were always aware. If you want to pray without distraction, says Nilus, sell your possessions and deny yourself;³³² no one's prayer is so sheerly cerebral as not potentially to suffer from the effects of self-indulgence. Although the battle for mindfulness seems largely fought against interior adversaries, the sheer presence of other people tends to divert one's gaze from God. At times, the anonymous compilers of the *Apophthegmata* exhibit a flash of humour, as in the story of John the Dwarf, whose absorption in divine thoughts was so great that when a courier came to pick up some goods from him, and John went to fetch them, he returned to his absorbed state on entering his cell and entirely forgot the waiting driver; the latter's forbearance with eccentric holy men must have been great, for it took three reminders before John managed to complete the errand.³³³ To the worldly eye, this is absent-mindedness; to the contemplative, it is supreme mindfulness, the mind's being full of its highest object, God, even in the face of an intrusion from the outside world. On other occasions, John cannot maintain this steady gaze: the harvest (a time when one is with others) and visits interrupt his prayer to the point that he can reproach one caller with having driven God away.³³⁴ If frustration with disruption sometimes elicits a seemingly uncharitable response, the solitary is nevertheless not cordoned off from society; ill feelings towards others, such as revenge, will yield unwanted fruit,³³⁵ while conversely, all love of wisdom [philosophēseis] will bear fruit in prayer;³³⁶ hence it is the wise man who practises perpetual prayer.³³⁷

Evagrius, true to form, follows the basic pattern evident in the thought of the earlier writers, but draws out the connection between prayer and the intellect more strongly. His estimation of prayer emerges unmistakably from the maxim for which he is most often cited: if you are a

---

[330] Agathon 9/PG 65.112.   [331] Syncletica 3/PG 65.422.
[332] Nilus 4/PG 65.306.   [333] John the Dwarf 31/PG 65.214.
[334] John the Dwarf 32 and 35/PG 65.214–15.   [335] Nilus 1/PG 65.306.
[336] Nilus 5/PG 65.306.   [337] Theodora 3/PG 65.201.

theologian [theologos], you pray truly and if you truly pray, you are a theologian.[338] Stewart goes so far as to coin a maxim: 'Tell me how you think that you think and I can tell you how you pray'; Evagrius did not actually write this, Stewart notes, but he might well have.[339] Like the desert monks, Evagrius is acutely aware of the battle with distraction (literally, the invasions of the demons), his solution also being simply to ignore them.[340] The challenge of doing so is however increased because he, too, takes the command to pray without ceasing in earnest; we have an obligation to pray incessantly[341] and prayer, he says, is no less than conversation [homilia] with God that is constant and unwavering [ametastrophōs],[342] the ascent of the spirit to God.[343] Prayer for Evagrius therefore has a decidedly intellectual bent: perfect prayer means bringing forth one's best thoughts for God[344] and whatever difficulties one endures for the sake of wisdom [philosophēseis] will bear fruit in prayer.[345] Knowledge [gnōsis], likewise, is to be sought in prayer and results from prayer,[346] and since it is also a co-worker with prayer, he can maintain that thoughtfulness consists, not in endless churning under one's own power, but in turning to God in prayer when the mind is in need of enlightenment[347] and thus prayer nourishes the mind [it is 'tou nou... trophē'].[348]

Although the spiritual exertion Evagrius advocates concerns not only one's inner state but one's outward behaviour – the one who desires to pray must not sadden others, for example[349] – fundamentally, prayer remains for Evagrius an intellectual act, indeed the intellect's highest act, at least when it is undistracted,[350] and the content of prayer matters as much as the avoidance of extraneous thoughts, for prayer is appropriate to the dignity of the mind [nou].[351] One must not imagine God resembles oneself;[352] rather, one must free oneself of all material associations and awareness of sensible experience.[353] One might be tempted to imagine that Evagrius' concern here is the avoidance of grossly distorted notions of God, as in the story told by Cassian, for example, of Serapion, one of the more literalist monks, who got so confused during prayer when he realised his anthropomorphic image of divine nature had vanished from his heart that he burst into tears, no longer knowing whom to address or adore.[354] Evagrius does not however allude to this story (a workhorse

---

[338] Pray 60. [339] 2001, 186. [340] Pray 91. [341] Prak 49. [342] Pray 3. [343] Pray 35.
[344] Pray 126. [345] Pray 19. [346] Pray 38 and 85. [347] Pray 94. [348] Pray 101. [349] Pray 20.
[350] Pray 34. The explicit statement of this point is found in a sentence added in the Philokalia text; the same point is however strongly implied in Migne.
[351] Pray 84. [352] Pray 66. [353] Pray 119 and 120. [354] Cnfr 10.3.

among desert anecdotes) when he commends sheer contemplation, so we may assume his hesitation about material conceptions was rooted in something deeper than simply concern to avoid the worst intellectual crudities. One must avoid all forms and images during prayer;[355] the goal is perfect formlessness [teleian amorphian].[356] Not only material thoughts are problematic, for Cassian urges that the Spirit withdraw from flesh during prayer, as from every variety of thought.[357] When not in complete retreat from memory, one must at least keep it under close guard.[358] The purpose of prayer, then, is a single-pointedness, an absolute Godward orientation of the whole person, a state of maximum receptivity to the divine. Evagrius does not merely extol such prayer, but arguably writes to provoke it.[359]

Perhaps because of his very high view of prayer, Evagrius manifests an idiosyncratic tendency to see angels involved in the process. He claims, based on an allegorical reading of Revelation 8.3, that an angel infuses knowledge of true prayer[360] and during prayer, one can expect enlightenment from angels about created things [tōn ginomenōn][361] – ironically, since these would presumably be largely material entities and therefore fundamentally different from the angels. Hyperbolically, perhaps, Evagrius makes the claim that by true prayer the monk becomes the equal of the angel,[362] although in prayer, the human spirit is prepared for the work of exercising its own powers [energeian].[363]

Cassian's understanding of prayer knows neither the depth nor the exuberant forays into angelology that characterise Evagrius'. Where the earlier writers stress undistracted prayer, Cassian's more modest suggestion is for diligence and perseverance.[364] More positively, he can simply advocate prayer with an attentive mind [intento animo],[365] which seems to imply effort in the direction of mindfulness, rather than the actual attainment of perfect contemplative focus. Indeed, he almost reverses the emphasis of the other authors, for rather than holding that the mind must be free of distraction in order to pray, he claims the wandering mind [vagam mentem] may achieve stability through meditation and prayer.[366]

---

[355] Pray 114.
[356] Pray 117. The authenticity of this chapter has been disputed, but the sentiment it expresses is perfectly congruent with other sayings in the treatise.
[357] Pray 61.   [358] Pray 44.
[359] Cp. O'Driscoll's contention that Monc was designed to provoke meditation (1990, 361). Evagrius, on this account, is working within the tradition of giving a word for meditation to one's disciples (362), so that following the writer's train of thought, the reader arrives at the very knowledge of God (376).
[360] Pray 75.   [361] Pray 80.   [362] Pray 113.   [363] Pray 83.   [364] Cnfr 1.17. and 9.2.
[365] Cnfr 9.34.   [366] Cnfr 10.14.

Perhaps because he is most consciously writing when institutionalisation has begun to set into monasticism and is accordingly aware that some of his audience may not be the great athletes of the spiritual life that the original inhabitants of the desert supposedly were, Cassian explicitly makes room for the more pedestrian forms of prayer. In the *Conferences*, we find one of the earliest instances of a typology of prayer later to become standard: prayer is supplication [obsecratione], intercession [postulatione] and thanksgiving [gratiarum][367] (later lists would add confession and adoration). What Cassian classifies as prayer is thus verbal prayer, to be regarded by later writers as constituting the foothills of the spiritual life, largely fit for dimmer souls or rank beginners. Cassian shows no such disdain. Wordless prayer is experienced by only a few and this kind of prayer seems moreover sheerly a gift, not something one can attain by striving, for it comes as the illumination by heavenly light.[368] If it seems that the minds of all are capable of arriving at 'incorruptible' [incorruptionem] prayer in this life,[369] the quality of our prayer reflects the quality of our life (what Ignatius of Loyola would later term the 'remote preparation' for prayer).[370] Ecstasy, accordingly, lies only within reach of the very holy, like Antony.[371] Characteristically, however, Cassian seems equally impressed by Chaeremon, whose back was so bent by both age and constant prayer that he went about with his hands touching the ground:[372] the monk who looks downward in humility provides as worthy an example as the one gazing ecstatically up to heaven.

However flighty and wandering it is prone to be, the mind is supposed to be attached to God.[373] Not to be mindful of God is the state only of those who sin and of the departed, the oblivious in soul and body. The mind's capacity for memory means that its present state is determined by its previous state, and that the content of its thought before the time of prayer shapes its content during prayer,[374] hence the importance of constant striving in virtue. What happens in prayer depends in part upon what the monastic does in those particular moments, but equally upon

---

[367] Cnfr 9.9, citing 1 Tim 2.1. The list is actually fourfold, including prayer itself [oratione] in addition to the three elements cited above.
[368] Cnfr 9.25.
[369] Cnfr 10.11. In Stewart's view, prayer and spiritual knowledge converge in Cassian's method of unceasing prayer, rooted in continual meditation on a phrase from the psalms (1998, 85). The latter, it would seem, lies within the reach of almost all. Prayer is moreover anchored on this verse, though in the context of the chanting of the whole psalter, the reading of lessons from Scripture and the broader practice of meditation on the Bible (112).
[370] Cnfr 9.3.3.   [371] Cnfr 9.31.   [372] Cnfr 11.4.   [373] Cnfr 1.8.   [374] Cnfr 9.3.

the habits of thought cultivated – or allowed to flourish – at other times. One needs contrition, therefore, a turning away from sin, if one is to attain to stability of mind.[375] The mind hardened by stubbornness refuses to heed the advice of the more spiritually experienced,[376] but the mind may equally be dissolved by charity [in illius dilectionem resoluta], that is, flung headlong into the pool of divine love.[377]

Whatever its propensity for distraction, it does ultimately have the ability to reject the plethora of thoughts tumbling about like a storm of uninvited gnats, by repeating the mantra 'Lord, come to my aid',[378] so that the whole life of the person of prayer becomes one continuous prayer.[379] Eventually, if we persist, the mind will arrive at incorruptible prayer [orationis incorruptionem],[380] having been brought to its higher levels via a series of stages of intercession.[381] The incorruptibility of this prayer signifies both its stability and its purity: to lack in extraneous matter, such as sinful or trivial thoughts, equals abiding in the thought of God. Wordless prayer represents for Cassian not simply a supreme contemplative feat, but the replacement of human discourse with that of the Spirit, yet ironically Cassian characterises the heights of contemplation – gazing on the most sublime mysteries – using animal imagery: the monk conforms to the rational stag [rationabilis cervi] and grazes upon apostolic mountains.[382] Then, with the mind stripped of earthly things,[383] the monk may forget to eat regularly, so Cassian commands a system of carefully apportioned food, in order that those who attain to 'ecstasy of mind' may keep track of what they need to eat.[384] In its most exalted state, it seems that the mind's innate restlessness may attain to purposeful movement, turning around the love of God alone as a fixed centre.[385]

The concerns with prayer and distraction, so evident throughout the monastic literature, are paralleled by an interest in contemplation, although the latter proves less constant throughout the period. In the earlier writings, contemplation figures only fleetingly. Theonas more prosaically attributes captivity to the carnal passions to the failure to maintain contemplation.[386] In Athanasius' depiction, Antony seems to have been yet more dedicated, rejoicing in the contemplation of divine realities [tōn theiōn].[387] Basil also associates contemplation with joy: it is

---

[375] Cnfr 7.6.   [376] Cnfr 2.24.   [377] Cnfr 9.18.   [378] Cnfr 10.11.
[379] Cnfr 10.7.   [380] Cnfr 10.11.   [381] Cnfr 9.16.
[382] Cnfr 10.11.   [383] Cnfr 19.8.   [384] Cnfr 19.4.   [385] Cnfr 24.6.   [386] Theonas 1/PG 65.197.
[387] LA 84.2. The *Life of Antony* does not seem therefore to bear out Brakke's contention that Athanasius 'removed intellectual contemplation from the center of his spirituality and instead

because of the saints' insatiable eagerness to enjoy the vision of divine Beauty that they prayed their contemplation would last eternally.[388]

Evagrius shows an awareness of this breadth of meaning of 'contemplation' in the earlier tradition. He points out that the mind may devote itself to the contemplation of things [pragmata] and even if these are real, they still lead away from God;[389] or if it does fix on something non-corporeal, it might be something intelligible that is still less than God.[390] Nevertheless, the sheer labelling of these activities as contemplation suggests their positive value, an impression further confirmed by Evagrius' linking of the blood of Christ with the contemplation of created things: by both means one becomes wise.[391] Likewise, contemplation can 'colour' other activities: the demons become infuriated with those who practise active virtue in an increasingly contemplative manner [gnōstikōteron].[392] As always, however, virtue also paves the way for prayer: no demon can impede contemplation unless he can first stir up passion.[393] Conversely, spiritual contemplation can be bestowed by angels.[394]

Most essentially, however, contemplation represents for Evagrius something of a higher order than the struggle against the passions and for virtue. Keeping the commandments does not suffice to heal the powers of the soul; the latter requires contemplative exercise as well.[395] The rational part of the soul applies itself to the contemplation of created things

---

defined the Christian life in ascetic terms as control of the body's passions and cultivation of virtue' (1995, 144). These are not only incidentally compatible ends, but in LA, as in other early Christian writings, the last two are conditions of the former. So there can be no question of contrasting them in the way Brakke does; one could conceivably leave contemplation out of the picture altogether, of course, but Athanasius does not do so. If, as Brakke contends, the character of his theology is more ethical and less intellectual than that of earlier Alexandrians (145), it could not be because his emphasis on the distinction of Creator and created made him question any optimistic assessment of humanity's likeness to God' (146). First, it is far from clear that Origen goes so far as to blur the Uncreated–created distinction, as Brakke implies Origen does, but second, adhesion to it by no means entails the denial of likeness. Likeness precludes identity: we do not say two things are similar when they are identical.

[388] LR Q. 2, FC235/PG 31.912.. [389] Pray 56.
[390] Pray 57. It is because he is willing to designate these activities as theoria that I am not sure that O. Chadwick is right to identify the latter exclusively with wordless prayer (1968, 90-91). Evagrius does indeed claim prayer entails rejecting concepts, but that does not necessarily entail the mind's losing all consciousness, as Chadwick claims. The Greek text of the treatise does not contain, as far as I know, any exhortation to 'Make your intelligence dumb', which Chadwick cites from Hausherr's edition of the Syriac and Arabic versions.
[391] Monc 119.
[392] Prak 50. Gnōstikōteron could mean simply 'knowledgably', or 'in a theoretical way', but Bamberger translates it as 'contemplative', and in this instance he seems justified in doing so (though his translation in general appeals to theoria perhaps too freely).
[393] Prak 51. [394] Prak 76. [395] Prak 79.

[tōn gegonotōn],³⁹⁶ and the goal of this contemplative knowledge is theology.³⁹⁷ Thus Evagrius identifies Christianity with the 'dogma of Christ' and divides it into *praktikē*, the contemplation of the physical world, and *theologia*, contemplation of God.³⁹⁸ In fact, the two go together, for the man [here anēr] versed in *praktikē* will know the reasons of providence [logoi pronoias] and the contemplations of judgement [kriseōs theōriai].³⁹⁹

In Cassian's thought, the pre-eminence of contemplation as the form in which humanity encounters God achieves something like a codified form. Christ himself considered the chief good to reside in contemplation, as is evident in his reading of the story of Mary and Martha,⁴⁰⁰ although the later use of this story to ground the distinction between the active and contemplative forms of the religious life and to assert the intrinsic superiority of the latter does not match Cassian's. He assumes contemplation is the more exalted way, but holds that everyone will graduate to it.⁴⁰¹ The difference between Cassian's position and what became the received view in the West lies in part in his conviction that one can actively cultivate contemplation; there is no hint in his thought of the later distinction between acquired and infused contemplation, hence his emphasis on laying the ground for it: even in its highest forms, one can prepare to contemplate. Diligence in keeping vigils, fasting and prayer prepare the mind for the contemplation of *ta theia*,⁴⁰² and training in virtue must accordingly parallel intellectual discipline.⁴⁰³ Solitude, however, is also requisite and here Cassian evidently feels torn. On the one hand, contemplation requires silence and this is more easily maintained in solitude. The rush of would-be ascetics to the desert caused the fire of contemplation to chill,⁴⁰⁴ and even receiving letters dilutes the quality of attentiveness [intentionem].⁴⁰⁵ However Cassian recognises that there are other legitimate claims on even the ascetic's attention. The

---

³⁹⁶ Prak 86.
³⁹⁷ Prak 84. Here again, I follow Bamberger's translational decision in specifying the knowledge as contemplative, because of Evagrius' identification in this sentence of *gnōsis* with *physikē theōria*. Cp. Bamberger: 'the culminating stage of contemplative activity is theology, a mystical knowledge of God himself' (1992, 191).
³⁹⁸ Prak 1.
³⁹⁹ Monc 132. Bunge notes that for Evagrius, spirituality is nothing else than interiorised theology (1988, 70).
⁴⁰⁰ Cnfr 1.8.
⁴⁰¹ Cnfr 1.10. Cassian's notion of contemplation is therefore rather broad; as O. Chadwick comments, in places he seems to identify it with meditation on scripture (1968, 101). Chadwick seems to find this identification curious, but as we have seen, it is in keeping with most of the authors surveyed here.
⁴⁰² Cnfr 1.17.   ⁴⁰³ Cnfr 9.3.   ⁴⁰⁴ Cnfr 19.5.   ⁴⁰⁵ Inst 5.32.

exigencies of work or hospitality, for example, will rouse the most dedicated monk from silence; true, Cassian attributes this perennial fact of the solitary's life to existence in the body, but he still does not condemn this corporeal existence.[406] Similarly, a gift for practical matters causes one to be torn between remaining in theoria and attending to earthly work, and although Cassian clearly regards the former as a better thing, he does not imply that labour to a different and more practical end is misguided[407] – he could scarcely do so, given his chosen example of one who divided his energy between labour and contemplation was the Apostle Paul. Contemplation itself is nevertheless not concerned with earthly things – in this respect his usage differs from Evagrius' – and one progresses in purity to the extent that the mind withdraws from them.[408] Intensity of focus matters above all; when the mind inclines to wander away from theoria, we must bind it by attentiveness of heart, even though it slips away as quickly as an eel.[409]

Straying from spiritual contemplation is an ever-present possibility,[410] one avoidable only by giving the mind some sort of object for its attention; fortunately it can be trained by fairly simple means, for even reflection on a verse of scripture will lead to theoria.[411] Conversely, it seems that contemplation can compensate for serious ills: if something appears wicked, one should judge it by its intention or inner devotion of the heart [intimam cordis inspiciens pietatem] if done for contemplation,[412] for the dignity of theoria exceeds even that of virtue.[413] This great dignity is the reason it is vital never to be deluded by vain thoughts and never to waver in contemplation, which is the only true good.[414] The dedicated contemplatives who know this to be true do not allow disruptive thoughts to interrupt their prayer even briefly, or if this does happen, they regard the transgression as a form of sacrilege,[415] for Christ is the only person up to Cassian's own day who was so able to still the vagaries of his own mind as to remain in constant contemplation of God.[416] If extraneous thoughts may distract from theoria, however, the latter may also defeat the former: only by keeping the mind fixed in contemplation of virtue will one have the strength to spurn the pleasures of the table, for example.[417] Sadness can cut off the vision of divine contemplation,[418] but theoria itself brings constant tranquillity.[419] Indeed,

---

[406] Cnfr 1.12. [407] Cnfr 23.5. [408] Cnfr 10.6. [409] Cnfr 7.3. [410] Cnfr 10.8.
[411] Cnfr 10.10. [412] Cnfr 17.17. [413] Cnfr 23.3. [414] Cnfr 23.5. [415] Cnfr 23.8.
[416] Cnfr 23.8. [417] Inst 5.14.3. [418] Inst 9.1. [419] Cnfr 23.13.

all sorrows can be routed by contemplating beatitude[420] and the contemplation of death deals a lethal blow to all vice.[421]

Contemplation, then, is fundamental to the spiritual life in its entirety, but also to what today is called theology: although one may arrive at contemplation in numerous ways, God is known only through wondering at his incomprehensible substance;[422] here is an essay at an answer to the perpetual puzzle of how our only happiness can lie in the Trinity, whose greatness is unfathomable. The monks' treatment of contemplation is brief, surprisingly so, given the later development of the concept in Western spirituality, but this brevity perhaps reflects the subject of the discourse. One can prepare, create the conditions conducive to the flourishing of theoria, but ultimately one can only beckon and wait. Detailed instructions for the summoning of vision are as superfluous as the 'content' of theoria is indescribable.

Burton-Christie points to the differences among monastic texts, stressing particularly the disparity between the simple, pithy sayings of the *Apophthegmata* and the lengthier, more highly intellectualised discourse recorded in the writings of Cassian.[423] While there are differences of detail among all the monastic texts surveyed here, no pattern emerges which could allow us to label one text or group of texts 'intellectual' or 'academic' and one 'monkish' – or more starkly, one 'sophisticated' and the other 'simpleton'. The sayings of the Desert Fathers may not have been uttered in any systematic form, but it was not long before they were marshalled into the thematic Latin version; the sheer fact that it occurred to the Latin translators to do so indicates a certain degree of systematic coherence latent in them.

The monastic emphasis on constant contemplation, combined with the strongly intellectual character of prayer and contemplation, manifest even in the sayings of the supposedly anti-intellectual semi-literates of the desert, means that their vision of the spiritual life is of absorption in the things of God, what we would today call theology. To reflect on divine nature and divine works, holding these constantly in mind, is not so much the central task of monastics, but their whole life. In a real sense, they are as dedicated to the life of the mind as any of the dogmatic or speculative theologians of the early church – or, for that matter, the philosophers of pagan antiquity or modern academics.

---

[420] Inst 12.12. [421] Inst 12.33.2. [422] Cnfr 1.15. [423] 1993, 94.

Epilogue

The journey through the preceding centuries has shown the diversity of ways in which the intellect functions in early Christian theology. For all this variety, however, one prominent characteristic of the texts we have examined is the adhesive power of the assertion of mind: it functions as a kind of glue within the system, binding discrete components together. In light of that role, one might expect that the doctrine of God would loom larger than it has in the preceding pages, and that divine intellect would figure more prominently within it.

One question arising out of this study, then, is why the Fathers do not make more of intellect in God. Certainly, we find references throughout the period to divine wisdom, or the Logos, but lists of divine attributes, much less extended treatment of them, are neither abundant, nor does intellect invariably figure in them. Against the paucity of direct references to divine mind we must set the fact that much of what is explicitly asserted (such as divine governance or judgement) presupposes intellect. The assumption that one need not stipulate mind does not set patristic theology apart from its successors or reflect an omission attributable to the non-systematic form of its texts, moreover; in the opening questions of that most systematic of systems, the *Summa theologiae*, for example, Aquinas treats a series of key divine attributes and faculties, including will, but devotes not one article explicitly to divine mind. It is tempting to see the omission as reflecting no more than the absurdity of envisioning a mindless God, but, from a Christian perspective, a divine nature lacking will or goodness would be equally unfathomable and Aquinas stipulates these, as the Fathers also insist upon them. A more plausible explanation might be the subtle force of Aristotelianism; for Aristotle, divine substance was intellect, and someone thinking along Aristotelian lines might therefore regard the stipulation of mind as a tautology. The immediate objection to this explanation would be that however apt it might be for an overt, card-carrying Aristotelian like Aquinas, it would scarcely do for the Fathers of the church. As noted in the introduction, the content of patristic theology bears some marked similarities to Aristotle, despite the usual assumption of a pervasive Platonism, similarities attributable to acquaintance with Middle Platonism, were one anxious to find a genetic lineage and reluctant to credit the Fathers with a first-hand knowledge of Aristotle. The fundamental objection to explanations from supposed influence would still apply, though: a tradition which freely rejected key elements of the Aristotelian picture of God (such as its remotion and lack of ability to love) could just as easily have questioned its assertion of divine nature as intellectual substance. I see no straightforward answer to the question of why the Fathers assume mind in God but seldom bother to stipulate it, although a hint of a possible explanation emerges from the writings of Augustine, in whose work we find the most extensive treatment of the divine intellect, namely in *On the Trinity*.

We shall return to Augustine and his treatise on the Trinity, but for the moment, we might seek where the weight of interest in patristic theologies does lie, as far as the assertion of mind is concerned. Answering this question presents no difficulties: despite the prevailing theocentrism of patristic theology, the human mind looms much larger than the divine as a theological theme. Although it must be equally obvious to assert mind of human beings as of God – one could scarcely write theology or read it without an intellect – early Christian theologies take pains to insist not only that we have minds, but that our capacity to think, reflect, reason and know is constitutive of our identity as human beings. That identity consists in part in our similarity to other creatures (to the angels and the demons in having minds, to the 'beasts' in having bodies), but above all, in our likeness to God in virtue of the imago Dei. Here, too, we encounter a curious aporia, for this human identity subsists in part in our having souls endowed with both mind and will and in part in embodiment. We resemble God and the angels with respect to the first two and the other animals with respect to the latter. What locates us uniquely in relation to God is the fact that we are made in the divine image, the 'content' of which the Fathers consistently identify with either mind, or mind and will together. That way of parsing the image however raises the question of why the angels are not also said to possess the image, since they are as fully intellectual and volitional as human beings are. The Fathers do not as far as I know address this question, but that omission – perplexing as it is – does not weaken the clear link between the image and human nature as intellectual. No more is the significance of the intellect in this theology called into question by the absence of arguments to establish that there *is* intellect in God and humanity. Assumptions may not be acknowledged as such or expressed, but they are not thereby silent. The fact that an author chooses not to argue on their behalf may signify their value in that author's eyes. The absence of arguments to ground divine and human nature as intellectual indicates not that patristic theologians thought it insufficiently important to mount a defence, but that they accorded it the status of an axiom within their systems. Intellect does not function as a locus, even in the context of anthropology, because it is virtually a meta-principle, whose function is in significant part connective.

The essential relationality assumed as a consequence of asserting the imago Dei is a given of the Biblical and Christian tradition, but in patristic theology, the imago was pressed into more extensive service. The nature of the mind's relation to other constituents of human nature, notably the body and the will, signifies its role as a capstone: without a body and a will, we could not on the Christian account be considered human, but both the body and the will are secondary to the mind, in the sense that the mind directs both. The mind therefore functions as a connector, the medium by which we relate to God, the ordering principle of our relation to the complex that is our selves, and the director of external relations, inasmuch as our moral existence stands at its command; our relation to self and world can be no better than is indicated by our powers of discernment and judgement. The human mind locates us in relation to every other creature, as well as the Creator, and relates every other human faculty and organ to the whole that is the human person. Part of its significance lies in its role as governor – it is meant to direct the will and the body and hence all our acts and dispositions – and part lies in its role as synthesiser and harmoniser. Its role as ruling agent is obvious, this second relational function much less so, yet it is the latter which suggests a way of accounting for the pattern observed in the doctrine of God. If one systematic function of asserting the intellect is expressing relationality, then it becomes clearer why comparatively little would be made of intellect in the context of doctrine of God, for there, divine simplicity (sometimes asserted by the Fathers though as often merely implied) precludes any possibility of relationality: intellect does not stand in relation to other divine attributes or faculties, for divine nature just *is* all of these, *simpliciter*. If so, and if intellect must be assumed of God (as asserting will, wisdom, and providence require), then intellect simply *is* divine substance, as Aristotle held, though one can conclude so departing neither from Aristotelian presuppositions nor in deference to the Philosopher's authority.

The 'level' at which relationality may be predicated of God is in the context of trinitarian doctrine, and this is precisely where we find the most extended treatment of divine mind in the texts surveyed, in Augustine's treatise devoted to the Trinity. One way in which we may, for all our limitations, gain some dim grasp of the radically intertwined relation of intellect and will, knowledge and love, in the simple nature so utterly unlike our own is to view these through the lens of the dynamic relations of Father, Son and Spirit, who are the subject of the appropriations. What Augustine's treatise does, via the vestigia, is to draw a parallel between the relations of the divine persons *ad intra* and the relation of God and humanity, and in doing so, points again to the relational function of mind in the theology as a whole.[1] Right relatedness within oneself – the will acting in accord with right thinking – is the condition of right relatedness to God, not because we can determine that relation from the human side, but because grace acts on the faculties God has given us: the imago is given, both that we may resemble God as we are created, but also that we may grow into greater likeness to him. Acquiring the likeness to God that is the image's restoration and perfecting therefore entails rightly relating the constituent faculties of intellect and will, as well as their 'products', knowledge and love; entails, that is, a love that desires ardently to know the Beloved and a knowledge that bursts forth in praise. Right willing (will acting in accord with reason and faith in God) expresses an ordering within the human soul that reflects the relation of the divine Persons to each other, and so establishes and expresses the right ordering of the human persons to the Trinity.

Does Augustine then represent a culmination, the very existence of which implies a deficiency in earlier authors? The evidence suggests otherwise. Already in the work of Irenaeus, for example, knowledge of God has relational and existential implications: these indicate both the sanctifying power of right understanding of self, other creatures and that ultimately the Other who is God, but also right understanding of oneself as an intellectual, moral and spiritual agent. Seeing oneself and others in this way is in itself transformative, but also bears important consequences for the understanding of theology, for it means that knowledge of God has moral and spiritual import and that theology itself therefore has such

---

[1] Cp. Bouyer, who points to the impressive unity of Augustinian spirituality, which he claims imposed itself on the Latin Middle Ages as a 'quasi-definitive Summa' (1960, 491).

import. To think of God has consequences for how one prays and to think of God is the beginning of prayer; all theology must therefore be taken as spiritual theology, just as all prayer rests on dogmatic assumptions and bears dogmatic implications and is in some measure a form of theological reflection. The content of our identity as creatures made in the image of God is necessarily relational and the systematic quality of theology, in itself necessarily relational, reflects this identity: the systematic quality of this theology instantiates the ontological relationality it articulates.

The summary account just given raises a number of questions, especially in light of the questions raised in the introduction. The first concerns the relation of early Christian theology to the Greek philosophical past and the neo-Platonism that is contemporary to it. This survey of patristic literature should indicate that whatever resemblance early Christian theology may bear to ancient philosophy, it proceeds from axioms, many of which are Biblical and definitively Christian, and argues within a systematic framework that is equally distinctive. One may be able to explain isolated similarities by recourse to theories of influence, but the complex as a whole suggests that the advent of Christian theology represents a striking caesura in Western thought. One can dismiss the notion that there *is* a complex as a whole, claiming the idea of systematisation enters the tradition only with the rise of scholasticism and is therefore anachronistically applied to patristic theology. The latter move, however, falters in light of Greek philosophy's own appeal to the notions of rational, structured arguments whose internal coherence betokens their correspondence to the order of divine nature and the world God created, an appeal present even in the earliest fragments of the Western philosophical tradition. If we acknowledge a similarity between these philosophical principles and those underlying patristic theology, then we would also have to acknowledge that Christian theology could only adopt specific tenets of other philosophical systems to the degree that these were compatible with a specifically Christian framework, one which included Biblical givens and the church's sacramental and liturgical practice. In light of the latter, there could be no question of a wholesale, or even uncritical, adoption of philosophical ideas. The question of influence can only be considered in light of the systems implicit in this theology, and, once considered in that light, assertions of influence must become much more tentative. Christian theology may have developed the notion of systematic discourse from Greek philosophical antecedents, but the very concept of system means that once specifically Christian premises are introduced into it, it would either have to part company with its philosophical presuppositions or cease to be a system, in virtue of its incoherence. Its recourse to philosophy is therefore self-undermining, the recourse to precisely that principle that ensures the theology will not assimilate itself uncritically to that which it consults.[2]

Another question raised by this study is what exactly accounts for the change in Christian theology from texts in which philosophical, dogmatic and spiritual concerns mingle easily, to texts in which these are polarised, and when this shift occurred. The Fathers, as we have seen, are for the most part fairly casual in explicitly stipulating mind in God, so they do not differ from later theology in this respect, nor does later theology do other than assume human beings are rational, as the Fathers did. The difference appears more at the level of the intellect's role in prayer, in the regulation of the passions and as the fulcrum of human resemblance to God, and more generally, in the systematic work that is being done by the notion of intellect. The absence of sustained consideration of prayer and the passions in later academic theology, for example, may perhaps be attributed to the rise of ascetical theology as a distinct area of concern. In the Middle Ages, we certainly observe a difference between school theology and the writings of the mystics, whether the latter in the sense of accounts of mystical experience or manuals of the spiritual life. Nevertheless, the school theologies also treat ascetical matters and the mystics are frequently good theologians, including those such as Julian of Norwich and Hildegard of Bingen, whose sex would have limited their access to formal theological education. While the beginnings of a rift between school and ascetical theology are visible by the late Middle Ages (there is little of a common sensibility to be found in the works of Occam and Margery Kempe, for instance), there are also examples of a more unified approach closely resembling the Fathers', as in the work of Ruusbroec, for example. More decisive signs of a fracture are evident in the thought of the Reformation and the Enlightenment, mounting in the nineteenth and twentieth centuries as theology becomes increasingly preoccupied with countering secularisation. Ascribing reasons for historical shifts over long periods is necessarily a speculative and risky affair, but we may note that the decrease in attention to mind and the estrangement of theology from

---

[2] The comparison to Nussbaum's study of Stoicism is instructive in this regard. She asks whether it is possible to accept Stoic views of anger while rejecting their attack on passions such as love, fear and grief, and admits that in large measure she failed in her attempt to do so (1994, 507–10). One way of accounting for the difficulty of making any such adjustment is the systematisation of Stoic philosophy: its level of internal coherence is such as to make it 'tamper-resistant'.

spirituality seems to correlate with the exile of the notion of contemplation to the realm of spirituality. Modern theology simply does not possess a category that covers both academic theology and prayer, as the notions of theoria and *contemplatio* served to do for the Fathers.[3]

The conception of the intellect in early Christian theology differs from modern secular conceptions of mind (and it is far from clear that modern theology has been concerned to question these to the extent it might have), in that one of its definitive functions is to locate us *coram Deo*, both in virtue of what we are and in virtue of what we do, that is, both in virtue of the mind's role as the seat of the imago Dei and in virtue of the mind's definitive task of contemplating God. In neither respect is it remote from the ordinary activities of reasoning, or even arguing, though its tasks and identity extend far beyond these. The absence of definitions of terminology pertaining to mind and intellect in patristic texts suggests that it was not the content of these notions that interested their writers – that in fact, such content was assumed – but their intrinsic systematic potency. The concept of mind can have such connective potential only if one assumes its capacity to operate in contexts as various as the doctrine of God and the life of prayer. To appreciate the role of mind in this period is not to opt for a theology remote or abstracted from the world, the Bible and the church, but precisely the opposite. It is not the early Christian account of mind that risks seeming sterile, but the secular one, and to the extent that modern theological appraisals draw on secular notions, they too risk sterility. Observing this difference in the 'quality' of mind then and now raises the question of whether the function of mind in this theology does not point to a distinctively Christian conception of the intellect corresponding, for example, to Origen's 'divine sense', one which modern theology might be enriched by rediscovering.

The systematic impetus in the corpus as a whole must also lead us to ask whether there is not a distinctively Christian conception of the relation of the intellect to matter and to sensuality. This relation springs from a doctrine of God which insists both that the sheerly intellectual and intelligible God is immaterial and that this God intentionally created a material world and called it good. This divine base of the doctrine of

---

[3] Leclerq insists upon the continuity between patristic theology and medieval monastic culture, as upon the persistence of the notion of contemplation in the Middle Ages (1961, 106 and 100), although in confining the scope of his defence of medieval thought to monastic culture, he allows for a split between the latter and school theology that would support the notion that patristic thought really is rather different. He himself alludes to the latter possibility (212), although he insists that the traditional meaning of the word 'theology' as 'praise of God' persisted to the time of Abelard (225).

creation dictates that Christian theology could neither disdain the body nor distance it from the mind; mind and body cannot be taken as inimical to one another (although one could, as early Christianity did, maintain they subsist in an hierarchical relation, the disruption of which leads to irrational behaviour and some forms of sin). The divine mind creates matter which the human mind is meant to govern, this latter activity requiring a sustained attentiveness to matter that by definition admits of no abstraction from it. These considerations, too, shade the Christian conception of mind, giving it quite a different cast from the dominant impression yielded by Platonism in its many varieties.

The systematisation of theology as a formal principle correlates to the role of the intellect as a material one; what we may say of God reflects the intellectual character of divine nature and the way God has created us to be, as those with the capacity to know ourselves and the one who made us in his image. The relational dimension of intellect therefore concerns not only the relation of God and humanity, or of theology and spirituality, but of the very nature of Christian theology and its relation to other systems of thought. The force of implicit system explains why we find no large disparity between the monastic writings and the other patristic literature: whether a writer had a fair acquaintance with philosophy or not, whether a writer was more generally sympathetic to philosophical searching or not, the overall theological framework shows a remarkably stable set of concerns, many of which devolve upon the systematic force of the assertion of intellect and the supple way in which the intellect is being conceived.

The stability of the core concerns of patristic thought itself underwrites the possibility of speaking of systems in relation to theology that is generally deemed to be un- or pre-systematic. To be unsystematic would in effect mean no less than being irrational, and Christian theology can no more be so by intention than human beings can be mindless (as opposed to irrationally behaved), or the ultimate subject of theological discourse be something other than divine nature, which is intellectual. The names for the human mind's assiduous desire to seek and know the divine are 'theology' and 'contemplation' and the significance of the intellect in patristic theology therefore suggests both the contemplative nature of Christian theology and the deep significance of system for it – though fully to explore the latter would require another book.

Bibliography

Full bibliographic information is given only for works outside standard numbered series; for works falling within such series, only the series abbreviation and volume number are given.

PRIMARY TEXTS AND TRANSLATIONS
Apostolic fathers

Texts: in the Loeb Classical Library 24–25; most are also available in SC: Ignatius letters, 10; Polycarp, letters and martyrdom, 10; Clement's Epistle to the Corinthians, 167; the Shepherd of Hermas, 53; the Epistle to Diognetus, 33; the Epistle to Barnabas, 172; the Didache, 248.

Translations: ANF 1. There are numerous others, but notable for its accuracy and ready availability is: *Early Christian Writings: the Apostolic Fathers*, tr. Maxwell Staniforth. Rev. tr. Andrew Louth. London: Penguin, 1968, rev. ed. 1987.

Apophthegmata (Sayings of the Desert Fathers)

Texts: The Alphabetical Collection. PG 65, cols. 71–440.

Translation: *The Desert Christian: the Sayings of the Desert Fathers*, tr. Benedicta Ward. New York: Macmillan, 1965. (There are many others.)

Justin Martyr

Texts: *Apologies*, ed. André Wartelle. Paris: Editions Augustiniennes, 1987.

Dialogus cum Tryphone, ed. Miroslav Marcovich. Berlin: Walter de Gruyter, 1977. *Cohortatio ad Graecos, De Monarchia, Oratio ad Graecos*, ed. Miroslav Marcovich. Berlin: Walter de Gruyter, 1990; G. J. Goodspeed, ed. *Die ältesten Apologeten*. Göttingen: Vandenhoeck & Ruprecht, 1914, rpt. 1984.

Translations: ANF 1, FC 6 and ACW 56.

Irenaeus

Texts : SC 264, 294, 211, 100 and 153.
Translations: portions of *Adversus haereses* are in ANF 1.

Tertullian

Texts: CC, Series Latina, 1 and 2.
Translations: ANF 3–4 and of some of the apologetic works in FC 10.

Clement of Alexandria

Texts: of *The Teacher*, SC 70, 108, and 158; of the *Protreptikos* in SC 2; and of the *Stromateis* 1 in SC 30; 2 in 38; and 5 in 278 and 279. The complete corpus may be found in GCS 12, 15 and 17.
Translations: ANF 2.

Origen

Texts: The Greek and Latin texts of *On First Principles* may be found in SC 252, 253, 268, 269 and 312 and of *Contra Celsum* in SC 132, 136, 147, 150, and 227. The Greek of *On Prayer* may be found in *Die griechischen christlichen Schriftsteller der ersten drei Jahrhunderte*, ed. Paul Koetschau. vol 2: Origenes. Leipzig: J. C. Hinrichs'sche Buchhandlung, 1899.
Translations: ANF 4; of the *Contra Celsum, Origen: Contra Celsum*, tr. Henry Chadwick. Cambridge: Cambridge University Press, 1965 (corrected edition); of *On First Principles*, in *Origen: On First Principles*, ed. G.W. Butterworth, London: SPCK, 1936 (being a translation of the Koetschau edition). Various works, including *On Prayer*, may be found in *Origen: Selected Works*, tr. Rowan A. Greer. (Classics of Western Spirituality). New York: Paulist, 1979.

Gregory Nazianzen

Texts: SC Orations 1–3 in SC 247; 4–5 in SC 309; 6–12 in SC 405. 20–23 in SC 270; 24–26 in SC 284; 27–31 in SC 250; 32–37 in SC 318; 38–41 in SC 358; 42–43 in SC 384. Texts of the other orations may be found in PG 35–36.
Translations: of a large number of the orations may be found in NPNF 7. There are a number of translations of the 'Theological Orations' (orations 27–32), the most readily available of which is that of Edward Rochie Hardy in *Christology of the Later Fathers* (LCC). Philadelphia: Westminster, 1954.

Gregory Nyssen

The Greek texts may for the most part be found in the Jaeger edition:
1 (1960): *Contra Eunomium Bk 1* and *Against Eunomius' Second Book*

2 (1960): *Contra Eunomium Bks 2–12.*
3.1 (1958): *Ad Eustathium, Ad Ablabium, Ad Simplicium, Adversus Macedonianos*
3.2 (1987): *On Infants' Early Deaths*
4.1 (1996): *Great Catechetical Oration*
7.1 (1964): *Life of Moses*
7.2 (1992): *On the Lord's Prayer, On the Beatitudes*
8.1 (1963): *On the Christian Mode of Life, On What It Means to Be a Christian, On Perfection, On Virginity.*

The Greek of *On the Making of the Human Person* may be found in *Sancti Patris Nostri Gregorii Nysseni*, ed. G. H. Forbes, vol. 1. Bruntisland: Pitsligo, 1855; the text of *On the Soul and Resurrection* may be found in *S. Gregorii episcopi Nysseni De anima et resurrectione cum sorore Macrina dialogus*, ed. J. G. Krabinger. Leipzig: In Libraria Gustavi Wuttigii, 1837.

Translations: of many of Gregory's works in NPNF 5; other translations which may be profitably consulted are: *Great Catechetical Oration* in Hardy, *Christology of the Later Fathers* (see details under Nazianzen); *The Soul and Resurrection*, tr. Catherine P. Roth. Crestwood, NY: St Vladimir's, 1993; *The Lord's Prayer and The Beatitudes* ACW 18.

The Life of Moses, tr. Abraham J. Malherbe and Everett Ferguson. (CWS). New York: Paulist, 1978; *What It Means to Call Oneself a Christian, On Perfection* and *On the Christian Mode of Life*: in *Saint Gregory of Nyssa's Ascetical Works* FC 58.

Augustine

Texts of many of the works cited herein may be found in the *Opere di Sant' Agostino*. (Nuova biblioteca agostiniana). Rome: Città Nuovo, 1967–, as well as in:

The City of God: CC 47 and 48.

Confessions: CC 27 and in J. J. O'Donnell. *Confessions*. V. 1: Introduction and Text. Oxford: Clarendon, 1992.

On the Usefulness of Believing: CSEL 25.
On the Catechizing of the Uninstructed: CC 46.
On Christian Teaching: CC 32.
Enchiridion: CC 46.
On Faith and the Creed: CSEL 41.
On the Grace of Christ: CSEL 42.
On the Freedom of the Will: CC 29.
On the Morals of the Catholic Church: CSEL 90.
On Patience: CSEL 41.
De Pec Mer: CSEL 60.
On Predestination: PL 44
Soliloquies: CSEL 89.
On the Trinity: CC 50.
On True Religion: CC 32.

Bibliography

Translations of Augustine's works abound. Most of those cited here can be found in NPNF; a modern series that is working its way towards comprehensiveness is the New City Press series.

Athanasius

Text: in SC 40.
Translation in: *The Life of Antony and the Letter to Marcellinus.* Tr. Robert C. Gregg. (CWS). New York: Paulist, 1980.

Basil of Caesarea

Texts: PG 31.
Translation: of works cited herein, in FC 9.

Cassian

Texts: of *Conferences* in SC 42, 54 and 64; of *Institutes*: text in SC 109.
Translations in ACW 57 and 58.

Evagrius Ponticus

Texts: of *Praktikos* in SC 170–71; of *Gnostikos* in SC 356; of *Ad Monachos* (text and translation) in ACW 59.
Translations: in *The Praktikos. Chapters on Prayer.* Tr. John Eudes Bamberger. (Cistercian Studies Series; 4). Kalamazoo, MI: Cistercian Publications, 1981.

SECONDARY SOURCES

Ackrill, J. L. 1981. *Aristotle the Philosopher.* Oxford: Clarendon.
Armstrong, A. H. 1967. *The Cambridge History of Later Greek and Early Medieval Philosophy.* Cambridge: Cambridge University Press.
　　1979. *Plotinian and Christian Studies.* London: Variorum. (Reprints of essays dated 1936–77.)
　　3rd ed. 1977. *An Introduction to Ancient Philosophy.* London: Methuen. [s.l.]: Littlefield, Adams (rpt.).
Ayers, Robert H. 1979. *Language and Reason in the Church Fathers.* (Altertumswissenschaftliche Texte und Studien; 6). Hildesheim: Georg Olms.
Balthasar, Hans Urs von. 1988. *Presence and Thought: an Essay on the Religious Thought of Gregory of Nyssa.* Tr. Mark Sebanc. San Francisco: Ignatius, 1995. French original: *Présence et pensée: Essai sur la philosophie religieuse de Grégoire de Nysse.* Paris: Beauchesne.

Bamberger, John Eudes. 1992. '*Desert Calm* Evagrius Ponticus [*sic*]: the Theologian as Spiritual Guide'. *Cistercian Studies* 27: 185–98.
Barnard, L. W. 1967. *Justin Martyr: His Life and Thought*. Cambridge: Cambridge University Press.
Barnes, Timothy David. 1971. *Tertullian: A Historical and Literary Study*. Oxford: Clarendon.
Battenhouse, Roy W. ed., 1955. *A Companion to the Study of St. Augustine*. New York: Oxford University Press.
Bavel, T. J. van. 1998. 'God in between Affirmation and Negation According to Augustine', in Leinhard 1998, 73–97.
Bebis, George S. 1966–67. 'Gregory of Nyssa's "De Vita Moysis": a Philosophical and Theological Analysis'. *Greek Orthodox Theological Review* 12: 369–93.
Behr, John. 2000. *Asceticism and Anthropology in Irenaeus and Clement*. Oxford: Oxford University Press.
Berchman, Robert. 1992. 'Origen on *The Categories*: A Study in Later Platonic First Principles', in Daly 1992, 231–52.
Bergman, Sigurd. 1995. *Geist, der Natur befreit: die trinitarische kosmologie Gregors von Nazianz im Horizont einer ökologischen Theologie der Befreiung*. Mainz: Matthias-Grünewald.
Bertrand, Dominique. 1999. 'L'Implication du *nous* dans la prière chez Origène et Évagre le Pontique'. In Bienert 1999, 355–64.
Bienert, W. A. and U. Kühneweg eds. 1999. *Origeniana Septima: Origenes in den Auseinandersetzungen des 4. Jahrhunderts*. (Bibliotheca ephemeridium theologorum lovaniensum; 137). Leuven: Leuven University Press.
Böhm, Thomas. 1996. *Theoria, Unendlichkeit, Aufstieg: Philosophische Implikationen zu* De vita Moysis *von Gregor von Nyssa*. (Supplements to Vigiliae Christianae; 35). Leiden: Brill.
Bourassa F. 1977. 'Théologie trinitaire chez Saint Augustin'. *Gregorianum* [Part I] 58: 675–725.
———. 1978. 'Théologie trinitaire chez Saint Augustin'. *Gregorianum* [Part II] 59: 375–412.
Bouyer, Louis. 1960. *The Spirituality of the New Testament and the Fathers*, tr. Mary P. Ryan. (History of Christian Spirituality; 1). London: Burns & Oates. (French ed.: *La Spiritualité du Nouveau Testament et des Pères*. Paris: Editions Montaigne.)
Brakke, David. 1995. *Athanasius and Asceticism*. Baltimore: Johns Hopkins University Press. (Rpt of *Athanasius and the Politics of Asceticism*. New York: Oxford University Press.)
Bunge, Gabriel. 1988. *Geistliche Vaterschaft: Christliche Gnosis bei Evagrios Pontikos*. (Studia Patristica et liturgica; 23). Regensburg: Friedrich Pustet.
Burnaby, John. 1938. *Amor Dei: A Study of the Religion of St. Augustine*. London: Hodder and Stoughton.
Burton-Christie, Douglas. 1993. *The Word in the Desert: Scripture and the Quest for Holiness in Early Christian Monasticism*. New York: Oxford University Press.

Butler, Dom Cuthbert. 1924. *Western Mysticism: The Teaching of SS. Augustine, Gregory and Bernard on the Contemplative Life*. New York: Dutton.

Cavadini, John. 1992. 'The Structure and Intention of Augustine's *De Trinitate*'. *Augustinian Studies* 23: 103–23.

Cavarnos, John. 1955. 'Gregory of Nyssa on the Nature of the Soul'. *Greek Orthodox Theological Review* 1: 133–41.

— 1976. 'The Relation of Body and Soul in the Thought of Gregory of Nyssa', in Dörrie, 61–78.

Chadwick, Henry. 1966. *Early Christian Thought and the Classical Tradition: Studies in Justin, Clement, and Origen*. Oxford: Oxford University Press.

Chadwick, Owen. 1968. *John Cassian*. Cambridge: Cambridge University Press. 2nd ed.

Clark, Mary T. 1998. 'Augustine on Person: Divine and Human', in Leinhard 1998, 99–120.

Collinge, William J. 1987. '*De Trinitate* and the Understanding of Religious Language'. *Augustinian Studies* 18: 126–50.

Cooper, John C. 1984. 'The Basic Philosophical and Theological Notions of Saint Augustine'. *Augustinian Studies* 15: 93–113.

Cox, Patricia. 1985. 'Origen and the Bestial Imagination', in Hansen 1985, 65–69.

Crouzel, Henri. 1985. 'La Personnalité d'Origène', in Hansen 1985, 9–25.

— 1987. 'L'Apocatastase chez Origène', in Lies 1987, 282–90.

— 'Seminar III: Origène et Plotin', in Lies 1987, 430–35.

— 1989. *Origen*. tr. A. S. Worrall. Edinburgh: T. & T. Clark. (French ed: *Origène*. Paris: Editions Lethielleux, 1985.)

— 1995. 'Le Contexte spirituel de l'exégèse dite spirituelle', in Dorival 1995, 333–42.

Cushman, Robert E. 1955. 'Faith and Reason', in Battenhouse 1955, 287–314.

Daly, Robert ed. 1992. *Origeniana Quinta*. (Bibliotheca ephemeridium theologorum lovaniensum; 105). Leuven: Leuven University Press.

Daniélou, Jean. 1970. *L'Être et le temps chez Grégoire de Nysse*. Leiden: Brill.

— 1955. *Origen*. Tr. Walter Mitchell. London: Sheed & Ward. (French ed: *Origène*. Paris: La Table Ronde, 1948.)

— 1953. *Platonisme et théologie mystique: Doctrine spirituelle de Saint Grégoire de Nysse*. 2nd ed. (Théologie; 2). Aubier: Editions Montaigne.

Daniels, Donald E. 1977. 'The Argument of the *De Trinitate* and Augustine's Theory of Signs'. *Augustinian Studies* 8: 33–54.

De Mello, Anthony. 1984. *Sadhana: a Way to God*. Garden City, NY: Image/Doubleday. (Originally published Poona, [s.n.], 1978).

Dempf, Alois. 1970. 'Evagrios Ponticos als Metaphysiker und Mystiker'. *Philosophisches Jahrbuch im Auftrag der Görres-Gesellschaft* 77: 297–319.

Dillon, John. 'Origen's Doctrine of the Trinity and Some Later Neoplatonic Theories', in O'Meara 1982, 19–23.

Dorival, Gilles. 1987. 'Origène et la Résurrection de la Chair', in Lies 1987, 291–321.

— and Alain LeBolluec eds. 1995. *Origeniana Sexta: Origène et la Bible*. (Bibliotheca ephemeridium theologirum lovaniensum; 118). Leuven: Leuven University Press.

Dörrie, Heinrich, Margarete Altenburger and Uta Schramm, eds. 1976. *Gregor von Nyssa und die Philosophie*. (2nd International Colloquium on Gregory of Nyssa). Leiden: Brill.

Ellverson, Anna-Stina. 1981. *The Dual Nature of Man: a Study in the Theological Anthropology of Gregory of Nazianzus*. (Acta Universitatis Uppsaliensis; Studia Doctrinae Christianae Upsaliensia; 21). Uppsala: [s.n.].

Festugière, A. J. 1936. *Contemplation et vie contemplative selon Platon*. (Bibliothèque de philosophie; 2). Paris: Vrin.

Forsyth, P. T. *The Soul of Prayer*. London: C. H. Kelly, 1916.

Gilson, Étienne. 1960. *The Christian Philosophy of Saint Augustine*, tr. L. E. M. Lynch. New York: Random House.

Goodenough, Erwin R. 1923. *The Theology of Justin Martyr*. Jena: Fromansche Buchhandlung.

Hansen, R. P. C. and Henri Crouzel, eds. [1985.] *Origeniana Tertia*. [s.l.]: Edizioni dell'Ateneo.

Harrison, Verna E. F. 1989. 'Receptacle Imagery in St. Gregory of Nyssa's Anthropology'. *Studia Patristica* 22: 23–27.

— 1992. *Grace and Human Freedom According to St. Gregory of Nyssa*. (Studies in the Bible and Early Christianity; 30). Lewiston, NY: Edwin Mellen.

Heine, Ronald E. 1975. *Perfection in the Virtuous Life: a Study in the Relationship between Edification and Polemical Theology in Gregory of Nyssa's Life of Moses*. (Patristic Monograph Series; 2). Cambridge, MA: Philadelphia Patristic Foundation.

Hill, Edmund. 1971. 'Karl Rahner's Remarks on the Dogmatic Treatise *De Trinitate* and St. Augustine'. *Augustinian Studies* 2: 67–80.

— 1984. 'Unless You Believe, You Shall Not Understand: Augustine's Perception of Faith'. *Augustinian Studies* 25: 51–63.

Hoitenga, Dewey. 1998. 'Faith Seeks Understanding: Augustine's Alternative to Natural Theology', in Leinhard, 1998, 295–304.

Hussey, Edward. 1972. *The Presocratics*. (Classical Life and Letters). London: Duckworth.

Jaeger, Werner. 1961. *Early Christianity and Greek Paideia*. Cambridge, MA: Belknap/Harvard University Press.

Kobusch, Theo. 1987. 'Das Christentum als die wahre Philosophie', in Lies 1987, 442–46.

LaCugna, Catherine Mowry, 1991. *God for Us: The Trinity and Christian Life*. San Francisco: Harper.

Lear, Jonathan. 1988. *Aristotle: the Desire to Understand*. Cambridge: Cambridge University Press.

Leclerq, Jean. 1961. *The Love of Learning and the Desire for God: a Study of Monastic Culture*, tr. Catherine Misrahi. New York: Fordham. (French ed.: Paris: Cerf, 1957.)

Lefeber, P. S. A. 1999. 'The Same View on Prayer in Origen's Sermons and His Treatise on Prayer', in Bienert 1999, 33–38.

Leinhard, Joseph C., Earl C. Muller and Ronald J. Teske, eds. 1993. *Augustine: Presbyter Factus Sum*, (Collectanea Augustiniana.) New York: Peter Lang.
Leys, Roger. 1951. *L'Image de Dieu chez Saint Grégoire de Nysse: Esquisse d'une doctrine.* (Museum Lessianum; Section Théologique, no. 49). Brussels: L'Edition Universelle.
Lies, Lothar ed. 1987. *Origeniana Quarta.* (Innsbrucker theologische Studien; 19). Innsbruck: Tyrolia-Verlag.
Lloyd, A. C., 1972. 'On Augustine's Concept of a Person', in Markus 1972, 191–205.
Lonergan, Bernard. 1974. 'The Depersonalization of Dogma', in *A Second Collection*, eds. William F. Ryan and Bernard J. Tyrrell. Philadelphia: Westminster.
Louth, Andrew. 1987. Introduction to *Early Christian Writings* (see Apostolic Fathers, under Primary Texts).
　1986. 'Augustine' in *The Study of Spirituality*, eds. Cheslyn Jones, Geoffrey Wainwright and Edward Yarnold. New York: Oxford University Press, 134–45.
　1981. *The Origins of the Christian Mystical Tradition: From Plato to Denys.* Oxford: Clarendon.
Ludlow, Morwenna. 2000. *Universal Salvation; Eschatology in the Thought of Gregory of Nyssa and Karl Rahner.* (Oxford Theological Monographs). Oxford: Oxford University Press.
Markus, R. A., ed. 1972. *Augustine: A Collection of Critical Essays.* (Modern Studies in Philosophy). Garden City, NY: Anchor.
Maschke, Timothy. 1998. 'Augustine's Theology of Prayer: Gracious Conformation', in Leinhard, 1998, 431–46.
McGuckin, John A. 2001. *St. Gregory of Nazianzus: an Intellectual Biography.* Crestwood, NY: St. Vladimir's.
McLelland, Joseph C. 1976. *God the Anonymous: a Study in Alexandrian Philosophical Theology.* (Patristic Monograph Series; 4). Cambridge, MA: Philadelphia Patristic Foundation.
Meredith, A. 1989. 'The Concept of Mind in Gregory of Nyssa and the Neoplatonists'. *Studia Patristica* 22: 35–51.
Merton, Thomas. 1962. *New Seeds of Contemplation.* New York: New Directions. 1961.
　1973. *Contemplative Prayer.* London: Orton, Longman and Todd.
Mueller, Earl C. 1998. 'The Priesthood of Christ in Book IV of the *De Trinitate*', in Leinhard 1998, 135–49.
Mühlenberg, Ekkehard. 1966. *Die Unendlichkeit Gottes bei Gregor von Nyssa: Gregors Kritik am Gottesbegriff der klassischen Metaphysik.* (Forschungen zur Kirchen- und Dogmengeschichte; 16). Göttingen: Vandenhoeck & Ruprecht.
Musser, Donald W. and Joseph L. Price, eds. 1996. *A New Handbook of Theologians.* Nashville: Abington.
Nash, Ronald A. 1969. *The Light of the Mind: St. Augustine's Theory of Knowledge.* Lexington, KY: University Press of Kentucky.
Noel, Virginia L. 1992. 'Nourishment in Origen's *On Prayer*'. In Daly 1992, 481–87.

Norris, Richard A. 1965. *God and the World in Early Christian Theology: A Study in Justin Martyr, Irenaeus, Tertullian and Origen*. (Studies in Patristic Thought). London: Adam and Charles Black.
Nussbaum, Martha. 1994. *The Therapy of Desire: Theory and Practice of Hellenistic Ethics*. (Martin Classical Lectures; n.s. 2). Princeton, NJ: Princeton University Press.
O'Cleirigh, Padraigh. 1987. 'Knowledge of the Word in Origen', in Lies 1987, 349–51.
O'Connell, Patrick F. 1983. 'The Double Journey of Saint Gregory of Nyssa: The *Life of Moses*'. *Greek Orthodox Theological Review* 28: 301–24.
O'Connell, Robert J. 1972. 'Action and Contemplation', in Markus, 1972, 38–58.
O'Driscoll, Jeremy. 1990. 'A Key for Reading the *Ad Monachos* of Evagrius Ponticus'. *Augustinianum* 30: 361–92.
O'Hagan, Angelo. 1968. *Material Re-Creation in the Apostolic Fathers*. (Texte und Untersuchungen zur Geschichte der Altchristlichen Literatur; 100). Berlin: Akademie Verlag.
O'Meara, Dominic J., ed. 1982. *Neoplatonism and Christian Thought*. (Studies in Neoplatonism; 3). Albany, NY: State University of New York Press.
Osborn, Eric. 1987. 'Causality in Plato and Origen', in Lies 1987, 362–69.
 1992. 'Origen: the Twentieth Century Quarrel and Its Recovery', in Daly 1992, 26–39.
 1997. *Tertullian, First Theologian of the West*. Cambridge: Cambridge University Press.
 2001. *Irenaeus of Lyons*. Cambridge: Cambridge University Press.
Patterson, L. G. 1967. *God and History in Early Christian Thought: A Study of Themes from Justin Martyr to Gregory the Great*. (Studies in Patristic Thought). London: Adam and Charles Black.
Pépin, Jean. 1971. *Idées grecques sur l'homme et sur Dieu*. Paris: Les Belles Lettres.
 1982. 'The Platonic and the Christian Ulysses', in O'Meara 1982, 3–18.
Plagnieux, Jean. 1951. *Saint Grégoire de Nazianze théologien*. (Études de science religieuse; 7). Paris: Editions Franciscaines. [n.d.; imprimatur 1951].
Quasten, Johannes. 1950. *Patrology*. Vol 1: The Beginnings of Patristic Literature. Westminster, MD: Christian Classics. (Rpt).
Rist, John. 1994. *Augustine: Ancient Thought Baptized*. Cambridge: Cambridge University Press.
Roberts, Robert E. 1924. *The Theology of Tertullian*. London: Epworth.
Roukema, Riemer. 1999. 'Nicht die Philosophie, sondern die Hoffnung und die Liebe haben bei Origenes das letzte Wort: "Dei Liebe komme nie zu Fall" (1 Kor 13,8A) als Argument des Origenes gegen einem neuen Abfall der Seelen von Gott', in Bienert 1999, 15–24.
Rowe, J. N. 1985. 'The Eventual Reconciling of Human Beings to the Father by Christ, and His Consequent Subjugation to the Father', in Hansen 1985, 139–50.
Ruether, Rosemary Radford. 1969. *Gregory of Nazianzus: Rhetor and Philosopher*. Oxford; Clarendon.

Somos, Róbert. 1999. 'Origen, Evagrios Ponticos and the Ideal of Impassibility', in Bienert 1999, 365–74.
Špidlík, Thomas. 1971. *Grégoire de Nazianze: introduction à l'étude de sa doctrine spirituelle*. (Orientalia Christiana Analecta; 189). Rome: Pont. Institutum Studiorum Orientalium.
Stead, Christopher. 1982. 'The Concept of Mind and the Concept of God in the Christian Fathers', in *The Philosophical Frontiers of Theology: Essays Presented to D. M. MacKinnon*, eds. Brian Hebblethwaite and Stewart Sutherland. Cambridge: Cambridge University Press, pp. 39–54.
Stewart, Columba. 2001. 'Imageless Prayer and the Theological Vision of Evagrius Ponticus'. *Journal of Early Christian Studies* 9: 173–204.
——— 1998. *Cassian the Monk*. (Oxford Studies in Historical Theology). New York: Oxford University Press.
Stritzky, Maria-Barbara. 1973. *Zum Problem der Erkenntnis bei Gregor von Nyssa*. (Münsterische Beiträge zur Theologie; 37). Münster: Aschendorff.
Torjesen, Karen J. 1987. 'Pedagogical Soteriology from Clement to Origen', in Lies 1987, 370–78.
Trigg, Joseph. 1992. 'Origen, Man of the Church', in Daly 1992, 51–56.
Völker, Walther. 1955. *Gregor von Nyssa als Mystiker*. Wiesbaden: Franz Steiner.
Wainwright, Geoffrey. 1980. *Doxology: the Praise of God in Worship, Doctrine and Life*. New York: Oxford University Press.
Wallis, R. T. 1972. *Neoplatonism*. London: Duckworth. (2nd ed. 1995).
Widdicombe, Peter. 1994. *The Fatherhood of God from Origen to Athanasius*. Oxford: Clarendon.
Wilken, Robert Louis. 2003. *The Spirit of Early Christian Thought: Seeking the Face of God*. New Haven, CT: Yale University Press.
Williams, Rowan. 1985. 'Origen on the Soul of Jesus', in Hansen 1985, 131–37.
——— 1998. 'The Paradoxes of Self-Knowledge in the *De Trinitate*', in Leinhard 1998, 121–34.
Wingren, Gustaf. 1947. *Man and the Incarnation: A Study in the Biblical Theology of Irenaeus*, tr. Ross Mackenzie. Edinburgh: Oliver and Boyd, 1959. (Swedish ed: Lund: Gleerup, 1947.)
Winslow, Donald F. 1979. *The Dynamics of Salvation; a Study in Gregory of Nazianzus*. (Patristic Monograph Series; 7). Cambridge, MA: Philadelphia Patristic Foundation.
Wolterstorff, Nicholas. 1991. 'Divine Simplicity', in *Philosophical Perspectives, 5: Philosophy of Religion*, ed. James E. Tomberlin. Atascadero, CA: Ridgeview, 531–52.
Worthen, J. F. 1998. 'Augustine's *De Trinitate* and Anselm's *Proslogion*: "Exercere Lectorem"', in Leinhard 1998, 517–29.
Young, Robin Darling. 1997. '*Theologia* in the Early Church'. *Communio* 24: 681–90.

Index

adoption *see* participation
analogy 131, 132
ancient philosophy 9, 18, 64, 87, 89, 99
angels 91, 145, 176–77, 182, 225, 228
anger 1, 112, 202, 208, 213, 217–19, 221
animals, irrational, *see* 'beasts'
anthropology (*see also* body, imago Dei, soul, will) 3, 39, 50–51, 57, 60, 82, 93–95, 98–99, 102, 114, 140, 144, 149, 166, 168, 176, 196
anthropomorphism 45, 150, 208, 224
apatheia 30, 95, 109, 144, 158–59, 161, 212–13, 218–21
Apollinarianism 47, 86, 156
Apophaticism 4, 22, 66, 85, 87, 89–90, 132–33
appetites 2
argumentation/proof/demonstration 17, 64–67, 74–78, 129, 131, 203, 204
Aristotle/Aristotelianism 8, 14–15, 16, 17–18, 28, 38, 70, 77, 91, 116, 122–23, 128, 131, 174, 198
ascesis / ascetical discipline / asceticism / ascetical theology 1–2, 6–8, 16, 41–43, 84, 109, 112–14, 128, 142, 161, 177–78, 190, 208, 215, 219
attributes of God, *see* God

baptism (*see also* sacramental practice/theology) 72, 149
'beasts'/irrational animals 54, 91–92, 100, 109, 138, 145
beatitude 34, 93, 125, 220–21, 231
beauty 49–50, 52, 70, 89, 93–95, 99, 102–4, 111, 116, 119, 132, 134, 139, 143, 146–47, 157, 162, 174, 182, 186, 147, 150, 211, 228
Bible/scripture 40, 44, 46, 60, 64–65, 67–68, 74, 78, 81, 87, 104–6, 120, 124, 126, 130–32, 138, 141, 145, 158, 165–66, 182, 203–8, 209, 210, 214, 221, 229–30
body and flesh / embodiment 3, 6, 6, 25–26, 28, 30, 35, 40–41, 41–42, 47, 49, 51–52, 54–56, 59, 63, 70–73, 76–77, 82–85, 86, 90, 92–93, 97, 101, 102, 109–12, 114, 116–17, 120, 127, 134, 137, 142, 143, 149, 151–52, 155–58, 160, 167, 173–74, 177, 183, 188–89, 191, 195–96, 198, 201–3, 212, 215, 217–18, 223, 225–26, 228, 230

Christ/Christology 14, 22, 25, 27–28, 30, 36, 44, 46–50, 62, 64, 67–68, 70, 72–73, 77, 79, 84, 86, 90, 93, 97–101, 103–4, 106, 108, 112–14, 116, 119, 121–22, 125, 129, 137, 139, 148–49, 152, 156, 159–60, 164, 172, 176, 181, 185, 192, 195, 197, 203, 209, 220, 228–30
communicatio idiomatum 47, 99–100
comprehensibility/incomprehensibility 134
concupiscence/cupidity/concupiscible 37, 38, 103, 157–58, 161
consummation 43, 54, 82, 87, 171, 176
contemplation / contemplative dimenstion of theology 2, 7, 12, 15, 16, 42, 49, 55, 59, 61–62, 69–71, 80, 84, 84, 89, 92–93, 97, 101, 107, 122, 126, 136, 140–42, 142, 143, 162, 171, 177, 184, 190, 197–98, 206–8, 210, 212, 220–21, 225, 227, 231
creation/Cosmos 3–4, 60, 71, 75, 80, 89, 92–93, 95, 100, 104–5, 109, 118, 122, 124, 134, 143–47, 152, 165
Creed/Rule of Faith 44

demons/devil 36, 52, 60, 91, 145, 159, 195–96, 199–200, 201, 203, 213–14, 217, 219, 224, 228
discernment 198, 215–16, 219
discipline 74, 84, 138, 192, 195–96, 206, 215, 220–21, 229
distraction 42, 199–201, 202, 212–13, 222–25, 227
doctrine 23, 83, 88, 93, 109, 120, 126, 127, 133, 140
dogmatic theology 1–2, 196

education 57–58, 68, 71, 73, 79, 199, 206–7
emotions 38, 70, 111, 158, 161, 213
epistemology 4, 33–34, 38, 89, 124–25, 137, 162, 166, 173, 176, 187

Index

eucharist (*see also* sacramental practice/theology) 72, 195
Eunomianism 28, 29, 86

faith 76, 156–57, 164, 166, 168–70, 172–73, 175, 177, 181, 185–86, 188, 204–5, 211, 221
Fall 39, 44, 55, 58–59, 69, 95, 145, 149, 156, 196, 202
fasting 1, 42, 194–95, 201, 209, 221, 223, 229
Father (first person of the Trinity) 23, 32, 41, 47–51, 65, 74, 84, 90, 106, 114, 119, 163, 166–67, 171, 181, 183, 187
flesh, *see* body
foreknowledge 30, 32, 39–40
forms (Plato's) 10, 81
freedom 25, 34, 40, 60–62, 93, 96–97

geometry 17
God / doctrine of God / divine attributes (*see also* particular attributes) 3, 33, 35–36, 40, 36, 45, 48, 50, 53, 58, 66, 74, 87–88, 90, 92, 94–95, 97, 112, 134, 144–45, 162, 166, 176
goodness 62
grace / divine gift 29, 29, 39–40, 52, 62–63, 67, 71–73, 76, 78, 80, 82, 93, 102, 105–7, 110–11, 117, 121, 123, 131, 138, 149, 151, 154–56, 159, 164, 166, 176–77, 179, 182, 187, 192, 195–96, 199, 205, 207–8, 210, 216–17, 220, 222
Greek philosophy (*see also* ancient philosophy) 159

hegemonikon 8
humility 159, 160, 199, 217, 221, 226

idolatry 23, 40, 45, 87, 118, 185
imago Dei / image of God 5–7, 14, 6, 25, 28, 30, 34–35, 40, 42, 47, 50, 52, 54, 84, 91–95, 99, 111, 136, 147, 149–51, 154, 165–66, 196
illumination 34, 72, 74, 78, 89, 106–8, 114, 143, 145, 148–50, 182, 226
imagination 53, 56, 104, 218
immortality 34
incomprehensibility 35, 124
infinity 86–87, 103, 119, 134–35, 136
irrationality 23, 25, 36–37, 39, 45, 49, 65, 69, 71–72, 94, 102, 109, 120, 128, 146

justice 36, 196

knowledge 22–24, 32–33, 39–40, 43, 44–45, 47, 49, 51, 53, 62, 66–67, 69–76, 78–79, 83, 89, 91–92, 101–6, 108–9, 113–14, 116–18, 120, 123, 125–26, 134, 138, 145–48, 150, 152–53, 155–56, 159, 162–64, 170–71, 172, 173, 175–81, 184, 186–88, 200–1, 204–9, 212, 215, 217–21, 224–26, 229

liturgy / liturgical practice 1, 85
logic 5, 64, 66, 75, 104, 128–31, 149, 154, 167, 204–5
logos, *see* Christ
love/charity 69–70, 72, 75, 80, 151, 157, 162–64, 170–2, 175–76, 180, 184–89, 196, 199, 203, 207–8, 211–12, 214–15, 220–21, 223, 227

Manichaeism 47
memory 151, 165–67, 177, 179, 168, 200, 218, 220, 225
method (Theological) 45, 64–66, 69
monastic theology/texts 1, 7
morals/morality/moralism 22–24, 53, 61, 65, 75, 79–80, 159, 204, 208–9, 211

natural theology 66, 140, 155, 165–66, 178, 204
Neo-Platonism (*see also* Platonism) 8, 11–15, 11, 80, 128, 178, 180

obedience 22, 78, 157, 161, 177, 198, 215, 216
order 143–44, 160–61, 187, 217

participation in God 24, 34, 51–53, 59, 76, 79, 113, 151
passibility/impassibility 49–50, 218–19
passions 9, 29, 30, 40, 49, 65, 69–70, 77, 92, 94–95, 102, 109–13, 115, 117, 119, 160, 201–2, 207, 214, 217, 220, 221, 228
perception 35, 101–3, 213, 219
perfection 34–37, 99–100, 115, 179, 202, 221
philosophy (*see also* ancient philosophy) 29, 31, 65–69, 112, 114, 122–23, 126–27, 129, 131, 140, 142, 129, 205
Plato/Platonism (*see also* Neo-Platonism) 6, 8–9, 11, 27–28, 30, 38, 40, 54, 63, 68, 76, 78, 80–81, 89–90, 93, 102–4, 116, 126–28, 158, 188
prayer 1, 6, 7, 42, 73–74, 85, 112, 136, 138–40, 142, 162, 173, 176, 178–80, 183, 190, 193, 199–201, 204, 207, 209–10, 212–16, 218–19, 221, 227–31, 193, 227
presocratics 16–18, 17
purgatory / Purgatorial state 41, 64, 80

rational beings 47, 51–52, 54–57, 59–60, 69, 75, 78, 82, 84, 88, 97, 146, 220

ratio/rationality/rationalism 3, 4, 16, 23–24, 28, 36–38, 40, 43, 45, 49–50, 52, 54, 56–57, 60, 64–66, 69, 72, 87–88, 100, 106, 111, 127, 131, 146, 149, 154, 199
reason/reasoning 32, 36, 51, 53–54, 60–61, 64–67, 73, 77, 79, 88–91, 96, 98, 100, 110–13, 117–22, 124–25, 129–32, 135, 153, 156–58, 160–61, 165, 174–76, 179, 183–84, 187, 199, 203, 205, 215, 218
revelation 39

sacramental practice/theology 1, 14, 15, 23, 25, 28, 30, 43, 100, 108, 112
sanctification 2, 30, 43, 54, 61, 71–73, 79, 82, 87, 100, 144–45, 156, 175–77, 185, 187
scholastic theology 1, 3, 103
scripture 5, 40, 85, 160
senses / sense perception / spiritual senses 38, 42, 46–47, 65, 73–74, 76, 81, 84, 89, 91, 93, 101, 104, 105, 107, 126, 138, 150, 152, 154, 173, 175, 197–98, 214, 218, 220
sensible/intelligible distinction 10, 57, 104, 105, 152–53, 173
sight (*see also* vision) 198
simplicity 32, 45, 50, 88–89, 150, 162–64, 206, 208
sin 23, 49, 59, 61, 64, 69–72, 93–94, 119, 149, 151, 154–56, 161, 179–80, 185, 193, 195, 197–99, 203, 206, 209, 215, 226–27
soul 9, 26, 28, 30, 35, 39, 41–42, 47, 48, 49–50, 52–56, 59–62, 69–73, 77–84, 86, 90–97, 101, 102, 104, 106–12, 114–15, 117, 119–20, 128–29, 136, 138–40, 148–49, 151–53, 155–56, 160, 174, 177–79, 184, 187–89, 192, 202, 205, 208–9, 213–14, 216, 219–21, 226, 228, 196
Spirit, Holy 52, 60, 72–74, 79–80, 84, 102, 105–6, 108–9, 114–16, 118, 122, 125, 131, 139, 143, 156, 163–64, 166–67, 171, 181, 183, 195, 207, 215, 218
spirituality 1, 2, 7–8, 19, 42, 46, 141, 171, 176, 183, 227, 229, 231
stoics/Stoicism 8, 28, 160
syllogism / syllogistic reasoning 65–66, 129, 131, 130, 203–4, 227
synergy 62–3

system / systematic theology 2–4, 5, 6, 16, 18, 21, 42, 44, 44, 84, 86, 109, 174, 187, 189, 190–91, 227, 231, 191

terminology 5
theoria, *see* contemplation
thought 39, 84, 86–87, 89, 97, 102, 120, 125–26, 135, 168, 201, 212, 218–19, 225, 227, 230, 215
tradition 57, 209
Trinity/trinitarian 22–23, 27, 36, 39, 42, 46, 53, 55–56, 75, 78–79, 87, 90, 92, 107–9, 126–27, 139–40, 143–44, 162–63, 165–67, 170, 175–76, 181, 183, 186, 188–89, 195, 200, 206–7, 231
truth 36, 64–68, 71–72, 78, 88, 97, 102, 106–8, 118, 120–21, 123, 126, 130, 141, 143–44, 146–48, 150, 154–55, 160, 162–64, 170–71, 173–75, 179–80, 183–87, 198–99, 205, 219

understanding 166, 170, 174, 183, 168, 196, 209, 217

vestigia trinitatis 164, 175, 168
virtue/virtues 50, 53, 55, 60–63, 70–73, 76, 79, 93, 95–96, 107, 112–15, 122–23, 139, 143, 151, 157–60, 168, 172, 175, 177–78, 187–88, 194, 196, 198, 200, 207, 210, 212, 215, 217, 219, 221, 226, 228–30
vision /sight / Vision of God / beatific vision 31, 34, 84, 107, 157, 175, 183–84, 198, 211, 213, 228, 231

will 6, 40, 46, 52, 60–61, 79, 86, 93, 96, 111–14, 116, 120–21, 126, 142, 143, 154–55, 161–62, 176, 179, 184, 188–89, 168, 194, 196–99, 210, 217, 220, 222
wisdom 35–36, 43, 45, 47, 49–51, 57, 62–63, 67–68, 73, 77–78, 80, 84, 50, 79, 89–90, 96, 103, 113, 115–16, 119–21, 126, 131, 123, 143, 147, 149, 151, 154, 156–57, 162, 164, 169, 172, 175, 179–80, 182–86, 148, 173, 179, 196, 204, 211, 217, 223–24
word (of God) (*see also* Christ) 72, 77–78, 83, 86, 90–91, 98, 103, 116, 118, 120–22, 132, 134–35, 139, 156, 163, 177, 181, 183, 207